VICO IN THE TRADITION OF RHETORIC

GIAMBATTISTA VICO

From a portrait hanging in the Accademia dell'Arcadia in
Rome, copy of a lost painting by Francesco Solimena.
Photograph kindly furnished by the Arcadia.

Vico IN THE
TRADITION OF RHETORIC

MICHAEL MOONEY

PRINCETON UNIVERSITY PRESS
PRINCETON, NEW JERSEY

All Rights Reserved
Library of Congress Cataloging in Publication Data will be found on
the last printed page of this book

ISBN 0-691-05431-2

Publication of this book has been aided by a grant from the
Publications Program of the National Endowment for the Humanities

Permission to quote the following materials has been graciously given by
their publishers:

An Essay on Human Understanding by John Locke. Copyright © 1894 by
Oxford University Press.
The New Science of Giambattista Vico, translated from the Third Edition
by Thomas Goddard Bergin and Max Harold Fisch. Copyright © 1968 by
Cornell University, copyright © 1961 by Thomas Goddard Bergin and Max
Harold Fisch, copyright © 1948 by Cornell University. Published by
Cornell University Press.
On the Study Methods of Our Time by Giambattista Vico, translated by
Elio Gianturco. Copyright © 1965 by The Bobbs-Merrill Company, Inc.,
New York/Indianapolis.
On the Heroic Mind by Giambattista Vico, translated by Elizabeth Sewell
and Anthony C. Sirignano, *Social Research*, vol. 43. Copyright © 1976 by
New School for Social Research.

This book has been composed in Linotron Sabon

Designed by Jan Lilly

Clothbound editions of Princeton University Press books are printed on
acid-free paper, and binding materials are chosen for strength and
durability

Printed in the United States of America
by Princeton University Press, Princeton, New Jersey

With the most agreeable tie of speech, reason bound together men who had hitherto been solitary.

Cicero, *De republica*

Humanity is the affection of one man helping another. This is done most effectively through speech—by counseling, warning, exhorting, consoling, reproving—and this is the reason I think that studies of languages are called "humanities" [*studia humanitatis*], the more so since it is through languages that humanity is most strongly bound together.

Vico, *De constantia jurisprudentis*

CONTENTS

PREFACE

If among the many truths of Vico's *New Science* there is one that is deepest, it is the truth that language, mind, and society are but three modes of a common reality. That reality, in Vico's term, is the *mondo civile*, the world of man. It is a world of many guises, many faces, and if we were to hold to those faces a mirror, we would find as the image reflected therein the full array of contemporary arts and sciences, all the disciplines of learning and technique by which, so Vico judged, humanity attains its perfection.

Humanity in its perfection, however, is so rare a moment, so delicate and subtle a state, that it is not ever to be found among the nations of the world—or is found in so fragile a form that it threatens always to crack and fall to the ground. When that happens, or to the extent that it happens, a society may be rescued only by the same forces by which its humanity, and thus its perfection, was first begun. It must find, or find again, through bursts of ingenuity, the connections between things that were previously absent, or overlooked, and so establish, or reestablish, the bonds of a common sense of things. Such bonds of common sense, at first merely felt, are inevitably cast into the language of gestures and action, which over time become both more conscious and more articulate. In whatever form or state, however—primitive or refined, dumb and mute or developed to the point of elaborate sciences— these marks of civility deserve, Vico thought, to be called "wisdom." Rendered as it must be in language (if not always in words), and borne, appropriated, and renewed by whatever eloquence a culture can muster, such wisdom may be said to speak. That is the subject of this work.

The unity of wisdom and eloquence is an ideal that fairly describes what has come to be called in the West the "Latin" or "Roman" tradition, in contrast to the "Greek." On the Greek view, the apogee of human culture is science and abstract thought; on the Roman, it is eloquence and the prudence of law. Asked to ponder the *Protagoras*, the Greek will linger in triumph on the words that tell of Prometheus's theft of fire from the gods, finding therein the promise of knowledge and power to the select of the race; the Roman, in contrast, will read further, nodding pensively at the news that Zeus, in a desperate effort to equip our kind for life in society, gave us in addition to fire a sense for justice, distributing it in equal measure to all. As a common, not a reserved gift, the sense for justice is concomitant with humanity itself, such that *our* history is *its* history. It may rely on knowledge and make use of techniques, but finally it is neither of these. It takes root in social urgencies, in the need to act when the facts are muddled or their meaning unclear, and the form it acquires, when finally it does, is given it in the song of bards, the words of poets, the eloquence of jurists. Over time it is built up and collected, some of it written, some of it not, and in that form takes on authority and a noble name. That name is *jurisprudence*.

Like other labels of its kind, the contrast of "Greeks" and "Romans" disguises as well as reveals, for there were "Greeks" among the Romans and "Romans" among the Greeks, and not a few Western thinkers would refuse the choice if put to them so baldly. Yet there is in the West a persistent line of thinking that has flourished from time to time, and never so brilliantly as among the ancient Romans, which holds that language is primary in culture, metaphor a necessity, and jurisprudence our highest achievement. This was the position of the ancient Sophists—of the more thoughtful ones, if not of those who so rightly exercised Socrates. It was the position of the "prudential" Aristotle, the Aristotle of the *Ethics* and *Politics*, of the *Topics*, the *Rhetoric*, and the *Poetics*. It was consummately the position of the "reformed" school of Roman orators, headed by Cicero, and of the "civic humanists" of the early Italian Renaissance, who in their writings and practice gave new meaning and dignity to the *vita activa*. And it was the position of Giambattista Vico, who not only received and cherished the tradition, but looked deeply into it, saw what its principles implied, and so made ready for the great social theorists of the nineteenth century and our own. That is the thesis of this work.

• • •

Arriving at this thesis, and with it the concept of this book, was not a tranquil or direct process. When I first read Vico a decade ago, I laid out a plan to follow in his writings the shifting conceptions of religion and law, with an end to showing the layers of meaning in the wonderful baroque phrase he came eventually to use for his work, "a rational civil theology of providence." Religion and law are notions that fairly dominate his text, above all during the formative years of his thought, and by taking them as my focus, I reasoned, I might resume contact with a solid tradition of late-nineteenth-century interpreters, notably Karl Werner and Carl Cantoni, whose work was forgotten in the triumph of Idealism, as well as with the writings of more recent authors, above all Antonio Corsano and Guido Fassò, who well understand the actual genesis of Vico's ideas.

Two developments in my work caused me to enlarge my agenda. The first was a reading of Vico's *Institutiones oratoriae* in the old edition of Pomodoro, which caused me to see clearly the classical cast of Vico's mind and the theoretical and affective links that exist between his pedagogical and scientific thought. The second was the need I increasingly felt to run clear of the Idealist framework with its epistemological orientation, which Benedetto Croce had imposed on Vico interpretation with his brilliant and beguiling *La filosofia di Giambattista Vico* (1911), and which continues to hold sway among many contemporary readers. The *verum/factum* principle in particular, I felt, had assumed (and continues to assume) a centrality in Vico criticism unwarranted by its actual importance in his thought, and perspective could be restored to it, as to other concepts stressed by Croce, only through a resolute, even tedious, effort to read Vico through the classical and humanist authors whose ideas and terms he consciously reformulates.

The outcome of this effort was perhaps inevitable: I came to see Vico as part of a very long tradition indeed, one that begins with pre-Socratic poets and orators and leads on after him, not to romanticism, but to the social theorists of Enlightenment and post-Enlightenment times, certainly to Paris of the 1830s, and possibly on to the Finland Station. At the center of this tradition is the concept of language as the bond of society and the instrument of its change; *eloquence* is the traditional word for the phenomenon, a word that Vico insisted on defining, after Cicero, as "wisdom speaking." Explicitly in Vico, then, *eloquence* became what it had always been potentially in the tradition: a description for social process itself, for the very course of civilization, a course with a definable logic—namely *rhetoric*—and a systematic account of its triumphs—namely *jurisprudence*, a term that Vico understood as the Roman jurisconsults themselves had, as "the knowledge of all things human and divine," most notably the institutions of religion and law. With this realization, I concluded that a study of religion and law in Vico, which I hope to accomplish next, needed first to have a broad and deep fundament that would establish his place within the tradition of eloquence and show what it became in his hands. That is the work I present here.

After an introductory chapter on Vico himself, in which his intellectual world and his movements within it are sketched, the work unfolds in three parts, which treat successively of rhetoric, pedagogy, and culture, each proceeding from a major Vichian text. In Chapter 2, the tradition of rhetoric in its manifold involvements with philosophy is first laid out, in order then to look closely at Vico's own *Principles of Oratory*. From its analysis Vico's classicism is discovered, as is his steadfast concern to see rhetoric, both in its substantive and linguistic aspects—as *res* and as *verba*—as a process of judicial reasoning, indeed as the logic of all social discourse. Plain from the beginning is his appreciation for metaphor as a necessity of communication and for ingenuity as the faculty of seeing connections and thus making and remaking social structures. These themes are deepened in Chapter 3, where Vico's correspondence and school writings, centering in *The Study Method of Our Time*, are used to show the nature of civil life and the sagacity needed to manage it. In the portrait of the sage as jurisconsult, as the "knower of human and divine institutions," as well as in Vico's early sketch of the history of Roman Law as the continual accommodation, through language, of fact to authority and authority to fact, the transformation of pedagogy into a theory of culture is seen to begin. Chapter 4 draws the leads together, using Vico's scientific writings, especially the final *New Science*, to show how, with philological discoveries in the poems of Homer and in ancient Roman Law, he fashioned a theory of the "poetic" beginnings of language, mind, and society; of their gradual maturation; and of the tension between their youth and maturity.

• • •

Of the many who have read and commented on Vico, there are some who will agree with the argument I make and some who will not. Even those who share my view, moreover, may find in what I write a challenge to their own ideas, for my work proceeds from several strong convictions.

The first is that the rhetoric about which Vico thought and wrote is not literary but judicial rhetoric—rhetoric as argumentation, a process of reasoning. In reaction to Croce, who thought Vico unaffected by the rhetoric he taught professionally, a growing number of critics have come forward, concerned to expose the rhetorical roots of Vico's thought. Marked at times by speculative boldness and at times by philological astuteness, their work is important and unfailingly interesting. Too frequently, however, they will ignore the pedagogical impulse of Vico's thought and its insistent context of Roman jurisprudence, and so lead Vico's work to the conclusion Croce found it to have—in a revolutionary aesthetics or linguistics, or in a fully new theory of mind or knowledge. I do not doubt there are these implications in Vico—and to ignore them is to deny him a part of his legacy—but they are entirely secondary to the cultural and sociological theories that are his consuming interest. The rhetoric that Vico taught and pondered was civil discourse, set always in the context of social life, and the use to which he eventually put it was as part of a general science of society.

A second conviction is implied by the first. If Vico was a scientist, as I believe him to have been, he was one in the Roman mode, in the tradition of philology and law. "A jurisprudence of humanity" is the title he once gave his work, betraying with that phrase the initial, and arguably the most trenchant, form in which he presented his science. Historians of ideas are only now coming to see the important links, of which Vico is a powerful one, between the tradition of Roman jurisprudence and the development of the social sciences. When that task has gotten further along, we will see more clearly than we do now the kind of science that Vico's is. Like every scientist, Vico wished to know truly the causes of things. What the nature of those causes is; how they are determined and presented; what their validity is and how it is tested; and what relation there is between Vico's theories and the practices of the society of which he was a part—these and similar questions fit within a tradition that began with the jurisconsults themselves and continued in efforts to derive first a universal law and eventually a science of society. To help clarify the context of this discussion, if not to uncover the evidence that will truly advance it, is part of the task I set myself in the present work. Correspondingly, the conclusions I come to draw about the nature and novelty of Vico's science, as valid and fundamental as I take them to be, do not exhaust so vast and complex a subject, nor could they. Many issues remain to be studied, several of which I hope eventually to pursue myself.

The last conviction I feel the need to state is the most fundamental of all: that ideas have histories and are not to be known apart from them. No stranger to the notion himself,

Vico states and restates it with increasing emphasis as his work proceeds. "The nature of institutions," he writes in the end, "is nothing but their coming into being at certain times and in certain guises." The certain and the true, the *certum* and the *verum*, as he puts it, are joined in human history, but are artificially separated by the disciplines that purport to study them, philology and philosophy. What is needed to study the history of the nations, he concludes, is a "new critical art" that steadfastly combines philology and philosophy, the "history of ideas and institutions" and their simultaneous "criticism." That is a method of study we are well advised to adopt in examining his own remarkable mind, for in it there was fused together in a totally mercurial fashion every bit of ancient, Renaissance, and contemporary wisdom that, in his judgment, might illuminate the marvelous course the nations follow as they rise from their brutish, feral beginnings to a state of refined humanity. Vico was, in the apt phrases of Arnaldo Momigliano, a greater genius than his colleagues in Naples, but a much poorer scholar. Nothing seems ever to fit in his writings, yet somehow it always does; and even when he botches his facts, his arguments seem always to come out right. To follow the unfolding of his mind is nearly as tortuous and uncertain a course as the one he traced for the nations of the world, and very nearly as awesome. To set one of his ideas in the context of another, and to put them in turn in the multiple contexts of thought and expression of which he was so constantly aware will not, it is true, solve every issue his writings bring to mind; but to fail to do so, I am convinced, is to forgo the chance to understand truly both what he was saying and how it was original.

ACKNOWLEDGMENTS

This book had its start, as so many of my ideas did, among friends and former colleagues in Halifax, Nova Scotia, especially Stanley Armstrong, Robert Bollini, Patrick Kerans, and Burkhardt Kiesekamp, in whose company I was introduced to Vico many years ago. During graduate studies at Columbia University, I again encountered Vico in lectures on theories of myth and religion by J. A. Martin, Jr., who urged me to formulate a study of Vico and to undertake it in the manner in which Vico thought "all doctrines should take their beginning"—"from that of the matters of which they treat." While reading Vico and his sources, I received the steady encouragement of Giorgio Tagliacozzo, who invited me to join him in organizing a conference on Vico in New York in 1976 and to bring the results of my study before it. I did both, and out of the effort came a volume of essays, published that year as the Autumn and Winter issues of *Social Research*, of which my own, "The Primacy of Language in Vico," formed the first, condensed statement of my thesis.

Turning that paper into a book brought new friendships and new support. Especially helpful were Jeffrey Barnouw, professor of comparative literature at the University of Michigan; Gustavo Costa, professor of Italian literature at the University of California at Berkeley; Max H. Fisch, professor emeritus of philosophy at the University of Illinois; Ernesto Grassi, professor emeritus of philosophy at the University of Munich; and most particularly Donald R. Kelley, professor of history at the University of Rochester—all of whose conceptions of Vico and his significance, shared generously with me in letters and conversations as well as in their writings, helped me immensely in refining my own. As a text emerged, it received a critical reading by various friends and teachers at Columbia, including Irene Bloom, Julian H. Franklin, James Gutmann, Gillian Lindt, Maristella Lorch, Wayne Proudfoot,

Robert E. Somerville, and Florian Stuber, as well as by Marie-Rose Logan of Rice University and Donald P. Verene of Emory. And as the text became a book, it was cared for well by the very able assistant director of Princeton University Press, Sanford G. Thatcher, who asked all the right questions and offered me flawless advice. Evelyn Ledyard typed the manuscript and Diane Grobman edited it, each bringing to her task an intelligence and wit that left the text more readable than she found it at the start. Luciana Ames worked tirelessly with me on the index. As easy as they are to recognize, intellectual debts of this kind are difficult to specify and impossible to repay. My work itself must be the coin of payment, and I hope with it to render my creditors a modest tribute.

Gratitude of an entirely different order is due my mentor and friend, Paul Oskar Kristeller, under whose direction I wrote this work as a doctoral dissertation. Justly praised for his scholarship, he is also a man of uncommon humanity, one for whom the Romans reserved their most revered epithet, *vir honestus*. He has been and continues to be for me what he has been and remains for numerous others, a devoted guide, unsparing in criticism, unstinting in kindness. He is not merely the most learned man I know; he is also the most honorable. I dedicate this work to him.

NOTE ON REFERENCES

References to Vico's writings, the chronology and editions of which are set forth in an appendix, are to the *Opere di G. B. Vico*, 8 vols. in 11 (Bari: Laterza, 1911–1941):

Volume 1: *Le orazioni inaugurali, il De Italorum sapientia e le polemiche* (1914; reprint, 1968)

Volume 2: *Il Diritto universale* (1936)
    Part 1: *"Sinopsi" e "De uno principio"*
    Part 2: *"De constantia jurisprudentis"*
    Part 3: *"Notae," "Dissertationes," nota bibliografica e indici*

Volume 3: *La Scienza nuova prima con la polemica contro gli "Atti degli eruditi" di Lipsia* (1931; reprint, 1968)

Volume 4: *La Scienza nuova seconda giusta l'edizione del 1744 con le varianti dell'edizione del 1730 e di due redazioni intermedie inedite* (1911–1916; 2d ed., 1928; 3d ed., 1942; 4th ed., rev., and enl. with the unpublished notes of a student of Vico, 1953)
    Part 1: *Libri 1–2*
    Part 2: *Libri 3–5 e appendice*

Volume 5: *L'autobiografia, il carteggio, e le poesie varie* (1911; 2d ed., rev. and enl., 1929)

Volume 6: *Scritti storici* (1939)

Volume 7: *Scritti vari e pagine sparse* (1940)

Volume 8: *Versi d'occasione e scritti di scuola con appendice e bibliografia generale delle opere* (1941)

With the exception of Volume 5, which was originally prepared by Benedetto Croce, and Volume 1, on which Giovanni Gentile collaborated, the edition is entirely the work of Fausto Nicolini. Volume 2 is in three parts, continuously paginated, and Volume 4 is in two, separately paginated but with continuous paragraph enumeration. References are given by volume and page numbers, except in the case of Volumes 3 and 4 where paragraph numbers are used. When not obvious from the text, the work of Vico being cited is also noted.

The titles and contents of Volumes 3 and 4 require explanation. Following its publication in 1725, the *Scienza nuova* underwent repeated manuscript revisions, leading to new editions in 1730 and 1744. So different were the versions of 1725 and 1730, in fact, that Vico himself chose to refer to them as *Scienza nuova prima* and *Scienza nuova seconda*, and suggested that when the latter was reissued, the former should be printed with it (*Opere* 5.72). Nicolini, as other editors before him, honored the suggestion, though not without changing the meaning of the title, *Scienza nuova seconda*. Since the 1744 edition was not nearly so different from that of 1730 as that of 1730 was from the initial edition in 1725, Nicolini chose to print the edition of 1744 as the *Scienza nuova seconda*, and to include in an appendix the variants in the edition of 1730 and intermediary versions. The paragraph enumeration that he supplied for the text of 1744 he continued for the variants in the appendix. Scholars have followed him in this usage, which has now become standard.

I retain the designations *Scienza nuova prima* and *Scienza nuova seconda* in my own work, routinely in the footnotes and also in the text whenever one or the other is being discussed in particular. When the *Scienza nuova* is spoken of without further specification, it refers usually to the edition of 1744, completed days before Vico's death, though on occasion it may describe collectively all the published manuscripts of that title which record the intellectual effort during the last two decades of Vico's life. All other works of Vico are cited by full title, with these exceptions:

Inaugural Orations   Six addresses of various titles delivered in Latin at the University of Naples to initiate the academic year

De studiorum ratione	*De nostri temporis studiorum ratione*
De Italorum sapientia	*De antiquissima Italorum sapientia ex linguae latinae originibus eruenda*
First *Risposta*	*Risposta del signor Giambattista Vico, nella quale si sciogliono tre opposizioni fatte da dotto signore contro il primo libro "De antiquissima Italorum sapientia"*
Second *Risposta*	*Risposta di Giambattista Vico all'articolo X del tomo VIII del "Giornale de' letterati d'Italia"*
De uno principio	*De universi juris uno principio et fine uno liber unus*
De constantia jurisprudentis	*De constantia jurisprudentis liber alter*
Notae in duos libros	*Notae in duos libros, alterum "De uno universi juris principio et fine uno," alterum "De constantia jurisprudentis"*
Autobiography	*Vita di Giambattista Vico scritta da se medesimo*
Vici vindiciae	*Vici vindiciae: Notae in "Acta eruditorum" lipsiensia mensis Augusti anni MDCCXXVII, ubi inter "Nova literaria" unum extat de eius libro, cui titulus "Principi di una scienza nuova dintorno alla natura delle nazioni"*
First *Ragionamento*	*Ragionamento d'intorno alla legge delle XII Tavole venuta da fuori in Roma,* a discourse appended to the 1731 version of the *Scienza*

	nuova, but omitted from the edition of 1744
Second *Ragionamento*	*Ragionamento secondo d'intorno alla legge regia di Triboniano*, a discourse appended to the 1731 version of the *Scienza nuova*, but omitted from the edition of 1744

Citations from Vico appear in English in the text, but are given in the original (with modern and standardized orthography) in the notes. For the *Vita di Giambattista Vico scritta da se medesimo* and the *Scienza nuova seconda*, the English of Max Harold Fisch and Thomas Goddard Bergin is used: *The Autobiography of Giambattista Vico* (Ithaca, N.Y.: Cornell University Press, 1944) and *The New Science of Giambattista Vico*, rev. trans. of 3d ed. (Ithaca, N.Y.: Cornell University Press, 1968). Passages from the *De nostri temporis studiorum ratione* follow generally the very graceful rendering of Elio Gianturco, *On the Study Methods of Our Time* (Indianapolis, Ind.: Bobbs-Merrill, 1965), but I occasionally supply a more literal version where the argument requires it. Unless otherwise noted, all other translations of Vico and other foreign-language sources are my own.

References to the classics in the text and notes make use of the following abbreviations:

Arist.	Aristotle
An. Post.	*Posterior Analytics*
An. Pr.	*Prior Analytics*
Cael.	*De caelo*
Eth. Nic.	*Nicomachean Ethics*
Poet.	*Poetics*
Rh.	*Rhetoric*
Soph. el.	*De sophisticis elenchis*
Top.	*Topics*
August.	Augustine
De civ. D.	*City of God*

Cic.	Cicero
Acad.	*Academicae quaestiones*
Brut.	*Brutus*
De opt. gen. orat.	*De optimo genere oratorum*
De or.	*De oratore*
Fin.	*De finibus*
Inv. Rhet.	*De inventione rhetorica*
Nat. D.	*De natura deorum*
Off.	*De officiis*
Orat.	*Orator*
Rep.	*De republica*
Top.	*Topica*
Tusc.	*Tusculanae disputationes*
Dig.	*Digest of Justinian*
Hom.	Homer
Od.	*Odyssey*
Hor.	Horace
Ars P.	*Ars poetica*
Sat.	*Satires*
Isid.	Isidorus
Etym.	*Etymologiae*
Lactant.	Lactantius
Div. Inst.	*Divinae institutiones*
[Longinus]	Pseudo-Longinus
Subl.	*De sublimitate*
Lucr.	Lucretius
De rer. nat.	*De rerum natura*
Pl.	Plato
Alc.	*Alcibiades*
Grg.	*Gorgias*
Leg.	*Laws*
Phdr.	*Phaedrus*
Resp.	*Republic*
Polyb.	Polybius
Hist.	*The Histories*

Quint.	Quintilian
Inst.	*Institutio oratoria*
Sen.	Seneca (the Younger)
Ep.	*Epistulae*
Ter.	Terence
Eun.	*Eunuch*

VICO IN THE TRADITION OF RHETORIC

CHAPTER 1

VICO: PEDAGOGY AND
CULTURE

> There is a continuous mingling of philosophical, jurid-
> ical, and philological matters, for Signor Vico has de-
> voted himself particularly to these three sciences and
> pondered them well.
>
> Jean Le Clerc, cited by Vico,
> Autobiography

"Whom are we to believe? Arnauld, who rejects, or Cicero,
who embraces, the *ars topica* as the most potent source of his
eloquence?"[1] Vico's rhetorical query, put some short way into
his celebrated discourse on the ancients and the moderns,
showed no particular boldness or courage. He was speaking
after all in Naples, not Paris, and of his twenty-eight colleagues
there assembled for the commencement of the academic year
1708–1709 fully twelve—and they the best paid and most
prestigious—were from the faculty of law; certainly they were
disposed to hear a rousing defense of the "copious" method
of traditional rhetoric, a virtual adjunct to their own discipline, against the sterile practices of the Cartesians, then so
fashionable in the north.[2] And surely the younger of Vico's

[1] "Utri credendum, Arnoldone, qui negat, an Ciceroni, qui se a topica
potissimum eloquentem factum affirmat et profitetur" (*De studiorum ratione,
Opere* 1.83).

[2] At the time of Vico's oration, there were twenty-nine chairs at the university, twenty-two of which were in "professional" studies—five each in
theology and medicine, in addition to the twelve in law. There was a single
tenured (*perpetua*) post in mathematics and one untenured (*quadriennale*) in
physical philosophy (see Nino Cortese, "L'età spagnuola," in *Storia della
università di Napoli*, ed. Francesco Torraca [Naples: Ricciardi, 1924], p.
304).

listeners, disproportionately law and prelaw students, were receptive to an apology for the kind of prudential flexibility and sharp-witted ingenuity basic to the sundry careers in civil life for which most of them were training. Descartes could have his hearing in the various academies and literary salons of the city, but here at the royal university, and in the society that it served, Cicero reigned supreme.

Vico's entry into the *querelle des anciens et modernes*, the most significant of his early initiatives, took the form of a protest against the curtailment of reason. Reasoning, he saw, belongs to the fabric of life. When men act publicly, or when they urge a course of action upon others, they must be ready with their reasons. Reasons are most readily given, adherence to one's views is most easily won, by compelling assent through demonstration, by showing through a line of unbroken argument that what one holds is implied in intuited truths. Such clarity, however, is rarely available in everyday life. "To introduce geometrical method into practical life," wrote Vico, "is 'like trying to go mad with the rules of reason' [Ter. *Eun.* 62–63], attempting to proceed by a straight line among the tortuosities of life, as though human affairs were not ruled by capriciousness, temerity, opportunity, and chance. Similarly, to arrange a political speech according to the precepts of geometrical method is equivalent to stripping it of any acute remarks and to uttering nothing but pedestrian lines of argument."[3]

Vico held these notions more than casually, for he expressed them similarly on various occasions.[4] Quite possibly they formed

[3] "Et vero, si methodum geometricam in vitam agendam importes, 'nihilo plus agas, quam si des operam ut cum ratione insanias': et tamquam in rebus humanis non regnarent libido, temeritas, occasio, fortuna, per amfractus vitae recta pergas. Methodo autem geometrica orationem civilem disponere, idem est ac nihil in orationem acutum admittere, nec nisi ante pedes posita commonstrare" (*De Italorum sapientia, Opere* 1.181). The quip from Terence was possibly suggested by Grotius (*De jure belli ac pacis*, prol. 4), who invoked the line to characterize his opponents' view that warfare and law are irreconcilable.

[4] See, for example, *Institutiones oratoriae, Opere* 8.161.

something of a personal topos, a line to which he appealed when pressed to justify the "copious" method of rhetoric. The sentiments, of course, are ancient in origin. It was Aristotle who noticed how intractable life is to the requirements of theoretical science (*epistēmē*). Certain activities, such as baking bread or cobbling shoes, might rely on "art" (*technē*)— practical knowledge culled from repeated experience. For the rest, however, mortals must depend on mere prudence (*phronēsis*)—a facility acquired through studied circumspection. Not all men, however, are prudent, he realized, and even those who are will disagree in deliberating courses of action. Besides being prudent, consequently, men must also argue, seeking to make plausible the actions they favor by relating them to commonly held assumptions. Such everyday discourse, not limited to specialists or to certain subjects of inquiry, Aristotle called *dialectic*. Enriched by charm and appeals to emotion and adapted to instances of formal oratory, dialectic in turn becomes *rhetoric*, that form of public reasoning "in such matters as we deliberate upon without arts or systems to guide us, in the hearing of persons who cannot take in at a glance a complicated argument."[5] If public life has no certainty, therefore, it should not on that count be mindless. To reason in the face of contingency, however, means finally to be prudent, honest, and eloquent.

SCIENCE AND RHETORIC

Westerners have generally been restless with this verdict, distrustful of a life abandoned to the rule of mere prudence. From science to philosophy to simple standards of decorum they have sought to elicit more reliable guidance in the affairs of everyday life. Cicero, for instance, in *De oratore* (1.41.185–42.191), noted the disarray in humane disciplines and proposed their reduction to "arts"; if the area of prudence could

[5] *Rh.* 1357a1–4; trans. W. Rhys Roberts, *The Works of Aristotle*, ed. W. D. Ross, 12 vols. (Oxford: At the Clarendon Press, 1908–1952), vol. 11.

not be narrowed, its instruments at least could be taught systematically. To the Renaissance, weary of the intricate ways of school disputation, the suggestion seemed inspired, and *redigere ad artem* became a routine phrase in humanist literature.[6] Others, however, found the proposal much too timid. If human affairs were so untidy, it was because we permitted such shabby thinking in the public forum. Our task should be to seize upon instances of clear human thinking, analyze their dynamics, and resolve never to allow other styles of argument.

Not surprisingly, the examples of clear thinking that have inspired such radical demands have typically been mathematical in form. Periods of methodological monism in the West can generally be paired with advances in mathematics and the mathematical sciences. The Platonic conception of perfect science, unitary in structure and univocal in application, was immediately indebted to plane geometry, known to us as Euclidean. Formalized by Aristotle in the *Posterior Analytics*, it was delivered to posterity as the method of "demonstration" (*apodeixis*)—of showing facts to be implied in principles (*archai*) intuitively assured.[7] Likewise in our own century, the symbolic logic of the Vienna Circle, conceived as an adequate measure of the meaningfulness of any proposition, grew directly from a concern with antinomies in modern mathematical theory.[8]

In terms of sheer intimidating force, however, neither of these instances could compare with the methodological totalitarianism that followed the success of Cartesian analytic geometry. In Plato's time the power of mathematics was not yet realized, its function largely propaedeutical; in our own, the mathematics of physical research is exceedingly rarified,

---

[6] The humanist notion of an "art" is not precisely that of Cicero, which in turn differs from that of Aristotle—a matter to be touched on in Chapter 3, below. In all three instances, however, "art" has the note of serving a useful function in everyday life.

[7] See *An. Post.* 71b8–72b4; 74b5–75a18. Cf. John Herman Randall, Jr., *Aristotle* (New York: Columbia University Press, 1960), pp. 32–51.

[8] See Victor Kraft, *Der Wiener Kreis: Der Ursprung des Neopositivismus*, 2d ed. (Vienna: Springer, 1968), pp. 12–21.

even beyond the ken of most educated men. But in the seventeenth century the effect of the "new math" was direct and incontrovertible. Seemingly overnight (though in fact after two hundred years of painstaking advance),[9] mathematics ceased to be a mere adjunct to a liberal education and became the very basis of natural philosophy, capable of clarifying so many perennial physical and philosophical issues. Suddenly the pattern of cosmic movements, the motion of bodies in ethers and fluids, the behavior of projectiles in various constraints, the question of infinite divisibility and of the priority of discrete or continuous quantity—these and similar problems, virtual conundrums in the past, acquired a new lucidity, admitting at least of fruitful discussion if not of final solutions. To Descartes, the lesson was clear: "Only those objects should engage our attention, to the sure and indubitable knowledge of which our mental powers seem to be adequate."[10] In a single gesture Descartes suppressed the realm of the merely probable, that arena in which, as the ancients knew, the affairs of men must largely be conducted. The true and the false were now polar opposites, between them nothing but an unbridgeable chasm. Gone, too, was that struggle for truth through public discourse whereby one man seeks to persuade another by fitting appropriate words to carefully chosen facts. "Those who have the strongest power of reasoning," wrote Descartes, "and who most skillfully arrange their thoughts in order to render them clear and intelligible, have the best power of persuasion even if they can but speak the language of Lower Brittany and have never learned Rhetoric."[11] For Descartes, the public weal would be best served if men only could be taught to think clearly

[9] See Ernst Cassirer, *Das Erkenntnisproblem in der Philosophie und Wissenschaft der neueren Zeit*, 3d ed. (Berlin: Bruno Cassirer, 1922), 1.41–54, 130–135, 257–271, 300–313, 347–352, 367–377, 388–396, 418–435; Anneliese Maier, *Die Mechanisierung des Weltbildes* (Leipzig: Meiner, 1938).

[10] *Regulae ad directionem ingenii*, Rule 2, *Oeuvres de Descartes*, ed. Charles Adam and Paul Tannery, 12 vols. (Paris: Cerf, 1897–1910), 10.362; trans. Elizabeth S. Haldane and G.R.T. Ross, *The Philosophical Works of Descartes*, 2 vols. (Cambridge: At the University Press, 1911), 1.3.

[11] *Discours de la méthode*, in *Oeuvres*, ed. Adam and Tannery, 6.7; trans. Haldane and Ross, *Works of Descartes*, 1.85.

and orderly. Deliberate thought, not effective speech, became the key to social advance.

If Descartes was the fount of his age's new wisdom, its most able purveyor was Antoine Arnauld. It was through his *Art de penser*, coauthored with Pierre Nicole, that Cartesian method achieved its widest influence.[12] The work had every virtue of a successful textbook, fitting the new logic into the familiar structure of Aristotle and expressing the new method more clearly and cogently than Descartes himself had done. Running into numerous editions in several languages, it became the dominant logic text in the West for over two hundred years. In Vico's lifetime alone it was printed twenty-one times in French and twelve times in Latin. Despite its Jansenist affinities, it managed by 1700 to gain acceptance even at the Sorbonne.[13] To a traditional mind such as Vico's, the implications of its success were so menacing that he railed against it in an annual lecture before his class, urging against a premature training in Arnauld's logic the fuller and more leisurely program of Ciceronian Topics.[14]

Vico was right to set Cicero against Arnauld. Cicero—*non hominis nomen, sed eloquentiae* (Quint. *Inst.* 10.1.112)—embodied an age in which to be educated meant to command the skills of eloquence. His *De oratore*, written in answer to Plato's *Gorgias*, presented the "finished orator" as a public servant whose ability with words is informed by a command

---

[12] Known more commonly as the Port Royal Logic, the work was first published as *La logique; ou, L'art de penser* (Paris: Charles Savreux, 1662). Whether because of his greater notoriety or because his role in the task was truly dominant, Arnauld is usually considered the principal—sometimes the sole—author.

[13] On the Port Royal Logic and its influence, see C. A. Saint-Beuve, *Port-Royal*, ed. René-Louis Doyon and Charles Marchesmé, 10 vols. (Paris: "La Connaissance," 1926–1932), 5:72–83; and the edition of the *Logique* by Pierre Clair and François Girbal (Paris: Presses universitaires de France, 1965), pp. 1–9.

[14] See the Autobiography, *Opere* 5.13–15. Vico's disgust with the new logic, however, did not keep him from reporting, on the same page and with obvious satisfaction, that a friendly critic had found his work, *Universal Law*, to be written *con metodo mattematico* (ibid., pp. 15, 47).

of the entire cycle of learning. The Sophists of fifth-century Athens had attempted a similar ideal, claiming an ability to teach political *aretē* and finding in oratory the natural center of the curriculum. But their apparent acceptance of moral relativism, which allowed rhetoric to degenerate into crass political partisanship, provoked the ridicule of Socrates, Plato's spokesman in the *Gorgias*. Like "cookery," said Socrates, rhetoric is a mere routine (*empeiria*), a knack for producing gratification. Both form parts of a kind of shrewdness well described as "flattery" (*kolakeia*). Just as cookery is the semblance of medicine—the proper art of the body—so rhetoric is the sham of justice—the proper art of politics. To redeem itself, rhetoric must take its start from philosophy, conceived as a fully independent enterprise, and helped by this normative knowledge, set about exposing inequities.[15] To Callicles, the inveterate defender of rough-and-tumble politics, such high-mindedness subverted civil life. Like a lisp, he noted, philosophy is a charming thing in youth, but one ought eventually to set it aside for training in public discourse. Not to do so rendered one vulnerable to the machinations of false accusers and could cost the philosopher his life. And what wisdom is there in an art, he asked, that left one worse off than at the start, "unable either to succor himself or to deliver himself or anyone else from the greatest dangers, but like to be stripped by his enemies of all his substance, and to live in his city as an absolute outcast?"[16]

Unlike Callicles, Cicero was not the foil of Socrates; thus, his reaction to the exchange could penetrate its root difficulty—the artificial separation of philosophy and rhetoric. Speaking through Crassus in *De oratore*, he writes:

Whereas the persons engaged in handling and pursuing and teaching the subjects that we are now investigating were designated by a single

[15] *Grg.* 462c–465c; 480a–d.
[16] *Grg.* 486b–c; trans. W.R.M. Lamb, Loeb ed. Cf. generally *Grg.* 434c–486d. On the Sophists, see Werner Jaeger, *Paideia: The Ideal of Greek Culture,* trans. Gilbert Highet, 2d ed. (New York: Oxford University Press, 1945), pp. 286–331, esp. 289–298, 321–331.

title (the whole study and practice of the liberal sciences being entitled philosophy), Socrates robbed them of this general designation, and in his discussions separated the science of wise thinking from that of elegant speaking. . . . This is the source from which has sprung the undoubtedly absurd and unprofitable and reprehensible severance between the tongue and the brain, leading to our having one set of professors to teach us to think and another to teach us to speak.[17]

Eloquence without knowledge is hollow and empty; but knowledge without eloquence is mute and powerless, incapable of effect in men's lives. "So," Cicero concludes dryly, referring to the followers of Epicurus, "let us dismiss these masters without comment, as they are excellent fellows satisfied in the belief in their own happiness; only let us warn them to keep to themselves as a holy secret, though it may be extremely true, their doctrine that it is not the business of a wise man to take part in politics—for if they convince us and all our best men of the truth of this, they themselves will not be able to live the life of leisure which is their ideal."[18]

RHETORIC AND PHILOLOGY

It was here, within the rhetorical tradition and its concern for the functioning of public life, that Vico began his way to the *New Science*. His earliest pronouncements on the origin of culture were thoroughly uninspired, mere repetitions of a

---

[17] "[Socrates] eis qui haec quae nos nunc quaerimus tractarent, agerent, docerent, cum nomine appellarentur uno quod omnis rerum optimarum cognitio atque in eis exercitatio philosophia nominaretur, hoc commune nomen eripuit, sapienterque sentiendi et ornate dicendi scientiam re cohaerentes disputationibus suis separavit; . . . Hinc discidium illud exstitit quasi linguae atque cordis, absurdum sane et inutile et reprehendendum, ut alii nos sapere, alii dicere docerent" (*De or.* 3.16.60–61; trans. E. W. Sutton and H. Rackham, Loeb ed.).

[18] "Quare istos sine ulla contumelia dimittamus, sunt enim et boni viri et, quoniam sibi ita videntur, beati, tantumque eos admoneamus ut illud, etiam si sit verissimum, tacitum tamen tanquam mysterium teneant, quod negant versari in republica esse sapientis: nam si hoc nobis atque optimo cuique persuaserint, non poterunt ipsi esse, id quod maxime cupiunt, otiosi" (ibid., 3.17.64; cf. also 1.4.17; 1.6.20; 1.11.48; 1.12.51).

pedestrian, intellectualistic bias. The role of fantasy in myth-making was recognized, but the poets who made myth were, as Bacon had said, merely casting high thoughts in attractive dress and embodying in gods the inventions most useful to mankind.[19] Civil law, too, rested on the imperturbable foundation of the Law of the Twelve Tables, which, however curiously "horrid and coarse" its language, had been drafted, as the ancients had said, on the basis of the recondite codes of the Athenian sage, Solon.[20] As late as 1712, in fact, Vico rejected as futile any attempt to study ancient Rome through her opaque rites and fragmentary laws, preferring instead the charted course of Latin etymologies.[21]

The rhetorician's sense that drew him to language and its construction, however, also led him to reflect on speech and its dynamics. His first insight into the nature of religion and law was not into their obscure, brutish beginnings, but into their actual functioning in contemporary civil and ecclesiastical oratory. Of what use is logic to the preacher, he mused, whose task is to move hardened sinners to remorse; or to the barrister, who must often defend a true, but apparently implausible, case; or to a senator, who must persuade to action minds that are set on a variety of equally defensible courses? "Whoever is not training in physics or mechanics," he wrote, "but intends a career in public life, whether in the courts, the senate, or the pulpit, should not waste much time in his youth on studies taught by [Cartesian] method. Let him cultivate an ingenious mind through the study of plane geometry; let him

---

[19] See the First Oration, *Opere* 1.9, 12; the Fifth Oration, *Opere* 1.53; and *De studiorum ratione, Opere* 1.98. Vico's perspective on myth at this time derives from his accepting the conventional notion of the poet as philosopher: "Nam poeta delectando docet, quae severe philosophus" (*De studiorum ratione, Opere* 1.97).

[20] See the Fifth Oration, *Opere* 1.52, and especially the Second *Risposta, Opere* 1.243. Significantly, Vico's recognition, in his *Institutiones oratoriae* of 1711 (*Opere* 8.172), of the plain language of the Law of the Twelve Tables was the first hint he had of its nonphilosophical nature; and by the time he recast this passage in 1737 (cf. *Opere* 8.201–202), he could refer the reader to his theory of the origin of language and literature in the *New Science*.

[21] Cf. the Second *Risposta, Opere* 1.242–248.

master the art of topics and defend both sides of a controversy, be it on nature, man, or politics, in a freer and brighter style of expression, so he can learn to draw on those arguments which are most probable and have the greatest degree of verisimilitude."[22] Public life is a blur of uncertain ways to which only the ingenious are equal. Vico's first conclusion, pedagogical in form, would become in time a central tenet in his science of civilization.

The transposition of the principle from pedagogy to culture occurred through a double agency—Vico's sense for "philological" inquiry and his passion for systematization. If the latter was a complex phenomenon, drawing inspiration and support from a variety of sources, the former coincided simply with the literary or scholarly dimension of Vico's task as a professional humanist.

That Vico was a humanist—in the most traditional sense— is incontestable.[23] Like rhetoricians from the Middle Ages to his day, he was a wordsmith of high society, furnishing "ap-

---

[22] "Qui neque in physicum, neque in mechanicum eruditur, sed ad rempublicam, vel foro, vel senatui, vel sacris concionibus instituitur, in hisce studiis, qua [sic] methodo traduntur, nec puer, nec diu immoretur; geometriam ad formas ad ingeniosam rationem addiscat; topicam excolat, et de natura, de homine, de republica libero ac nitidiori disserendi genere in utramque disputet partem; ut quod probabilius verisimiliusque in rebus sit, amplectatur" (De studiorum ratione, Opere 1.95–96). Here, as so often elsewhere, Vico adapts a dictum in Cicero (De or. 1.34.158): "Legendi etiam poetae, cognoscenda historia, omnium bonarum artium scriptores ac doctores et legendi, et pervolutandi, et exercitationis causa laudandi, interpretandi, corrigendi, vituperandi, refellendi; disputandumque de omni re in contrarias partes, et, quidquid erit in quaque re, quod probabile videri possit, eliciendum atque dicendum."

[23] On the origin and nature of Renaissance humanism, including notes on the rise of the term and a survey of humanist scholarly work and literary genres, see Paul Oskar Kristeller, "The Humanist Movement," *Renaissance Thought: The Classic, Scholastic, and Humanist Strains* (New York: Harper Torchbooks, 1961), pp. 3–23; idem, "Humanist Learning in the Italian Renaissance," *Renaissance Thought II: Papers on Humanism and the Arts* (New York: Harper Torchbooks, 1965), pp. 1–19. On the professional employment of humanists as teachers and public servants and on the medieval precedents of these activities, see Kristeller, "Humanism and Scholasticism," *Renaissance Thought*, pp. 92–119. See also Hanna H. Gray, "Renaissance Humanism: The Pursuit of Eloquence," *Journal of the History of Ideas* 24 (1963):497–514.

propriate" language for solemn occasions. He delivered nuptial poems and funeral orations; gave commemorations, allocutions, and elegies; and prepared inscriptions of all kinds. When Charles of Bourbon entered Naples as its new king in 1734, it was Vico who greeted him in the name of the university, just as, some thirty years before, he had paid tribute to Charles's father, Philip V of Spain, on his visit to the city as king.[24] During Philip's reign he was defeated in a competition for city clerk (*segretario della città*)—a usual humanist occupation—but under Charles was appointed historiographer royal—likewise a humanist position. He also wrote a commissioned biography and, for his own pleasure, reams of Latin and Italian poetry, much of it of high quality.[25]

Clearly, all these activities required considerable literary skill. An even greater and more purely scholarly competence, however, was expected of Vico in his principal occupation as professor of rhetoric, a position that he won in 1699 with a discourse on some lines in Quintilian and that he held until 1741. The study of letters at the University of Naples had originated in the reign of Ferdinand I (1423–1494), who took advice, it seems, from no less distinguished a humanist than Giovanni Pontano. Throughout the sixteenth and seventeenth centuries two "literary" chairs had survived, one in *umanità* and another in Greek language and literature, though the former lay vacant from 1581 and the latter was suppressed between 1627 and 1681. With the reforms of the Conde de Lemos in 1614–1616, the vacant chair in humanities was replaced by a chair in rhetoric, and it was to this post that Vico succeeded at the turn of the century.[26] Despite the additional position in Greek—the only one lower in stature than

---

[24] Cf. *Opere* 7.119–132, 179–180.

[25] Vico's commissioned works as professional rhetorician, of which he speaks in the Autobiography (*Opere* 5.20, 23–24, 38, 56–61), appear in Volumes 6 and 7 of the *Opere*. The commissioned verse is ranged chronologically with the rest of his poetry in Volumes 5 and 8.

[26] See Riccardo Filangieri di Candida, "L'età aragonese," in *Storia della università di Napoli*, ed. Torraca, pp. 151–199, esp. 186–191; and Nino Cortese, "L'età spagnuola," pp. 201–431, esp. 255–271, 301–304, 335–336, 354–357.

Vico's—and a separate chair in ethics and political philosophy, it is clear that Vico's agenda coincided largely with the range of studies identified by his chair's earlier title—the traditional *studia humanitatis*, which embraced not only grammar and rhetoric, but also poetry, history, and "moral philosophy."[27] So broad, indeed, was the scope of Vico's concerns that, were it not for the fact that his task was the more modest one of preparing young students for "higher" studies in philosophy, theology, medicine, and law, his chair might properly have been considered a distinct *facoltà letteraria o filologica*.[28]

To Vico, however, as to every humanist of Ciceronian mind, there was no conflict between rhetorical propaedeutics and philological scholarship. "He never discussed matters pertaining to eloquence apart from wisdom," he wrote in the Autobiography, "but would say that eloquence is nothing but wisdom speaking; that his chair was the one that should give direction to minds and make them universal." Accordingly, he "lectured every day with as much elegance and profundity in various branches of scholarship as if famous men of letters had come from abroad to attend his classes and to hear him."[29]

Vico's philological activities were considerable, and they contributed variously to the growth of his ideas. Some, such as his lifelong study of the *Iliad* and the *Odyssey*, were decisive in the development of his mature theory of culture, while others, such as his annotations of Horace's *Art of Poetry* and his commentary on the *Annals* of Tacitus, were routine hu-

---

[27] For an account of moral philosophy as a humanist enterprise and a survey of its representative forms, see Kristeller, "The Moral Thought of Renaissance Humanism," *Renaissance Thought II*, pp. 20–68, esp. 26–32.

[28] See Michelangelo Schipa, "Il secolo decimottavo," in *Storia della università di Napoli*, ed. Torraca, pp. 433–466, esp. 437–438.

[29] "Non ragionò mai delle cose dell'eloquenza se non in seguito della sapienza, dicendo che l'eloquenza altro non è che la sapienza che parla, e perciò la sua cattedra esser quella che doveva indirizzare gl'ingegni e fargli universali; ... Talché ogni giorno ragionava con tal splendore e profondità di varia erudizione e dottrina, come se si fussero portati nella sua scuola chiari letterati stranieri ad udirlo" (*Opere* 5.77–78). That Vico's students shared the judgments in this self-assessment seems clear from evidence adduced in Croce's note, *Opere* 5.127–128.

manist endeavors. Of whatever significance, however, all such activities had an impact on the shape of the *New Science*. As a work that accounted for the rise and fall of all nations, past and present, the *New Science* had—on principle—to attend to every datum of philological discovery. No item of information was too modest to be ignored; it had all somehow to fit. Thus, for instance, a bit of commissioned work on a commemorative tablet for a medieval monastery in Campania yielded, in later versions of the *Scienza nuova*, an example of "natural asylums" in the period of "second barbarism." Indeed, the parallel Vico saw between "extended" monastic life in the early Middle Ages and the clustering of frightened, god-fearing men at the dawn of civilization enabled him to consolidate his theory of cultural *ricorso*.[30]

This same example illustrates a further aspect of Vico's philology. His theory of *ricorso* was apparently inspired by the time-honored analogy of medieval fiefs with ancient Roman *clientelae*. To develop the analogy into a theory of "recurrence," Vico found for each analogue a prior "divine age"— the corresponding "natural asylums"—then "confirmed" the parallel with a series of etymologies—*opera* and *servitium; vades* and *vassalli; nexi* and *legati*.[31] Always we find the confirming etymologies! Perhaps no one since Valla was more enamored of language than Vico. Incessantly, almost compulsively, he garnered "evidence" for his claims from the origins of Greek and Latin terms and from their parallels in later vernaculars. His first effort to recover the wisdom of the ancient Latins—an abysmal failure—relied completely on an etymological method. Even later in his career, however, when he drew support from broader inquiries into poetry, myth, and law, his writings remained studded with etymological "confirmations"; then, as before, the results were generally the same—some derivations borrowed and routine; others imaginative and plausible; but most far-fetched and embar-

[30] Cf. *Opere* 6.417–418; *Opere* 4, §1056.
[31] See *Opere* 4, §§1057–1066.

rassing.[32] At least on one occasion, however, the issue of such effort was unreservedly pleasing. Competing for the chair of rhetoric as a young man of thirty, he lectured on the opening lines of Quintilian's chapter, *De statibus causarum* (Quint. *Inst.* 3.6), "limiting himself to the etymology of the term *status* and the distinction of its meanings. The lecture was full of Greek and Latin erudition and criticism, and won him the chair by an ample number of votes."[33]

That Vico chose to analyze the phrase *status causarum* is indicative of his truest philological interests. *Causa* in classical rhetoric has generally a forensic meaning; it is a "case" from the standpoint of the judge, a "cause" from that of the opposing attorneys. A *causa* is a matter that can be litigated, debated, and settled; it is thus the paradigmatic form of the *questiones finitae*—those particular, concrete questions with which all oratory is concerned. From the agonistic character of a *causa*—the squaring off of rival orators—emerge the various *status*, the "issues" deriving from competing claims. Thus *status*, too, is prototypically a legal concept.[34] Of Vico's many curiosities, none was more insistent than that for jurisprudence; and of all his scholarly interests, none was more sustained, or yielded quite such important results, as that for Roman Law.

Vico's formal training in law consisted of two months of lectures on the minutiae of court practice. Finding the lessons

[32] An intriguing attempt to defend the "fanciful, surprising, mythopoetic" etymology of Vico in contrast to the more "rational and careful" approach of Voss is offered by Andrea Battistini, "Vico e l'etimologia mitopoietica," *Lingua e Stile* 9 (1974): 31–66.

[33] "Così il Vico vi concorse . . . , contenendosi dentro l'etimologia e la distinzion dello 'stato,' ripiena di greca e latina erudizione e critica; per la quale meritò ottenerla con un numero abbondante di voti" (Autobiography, *Opere* 5.24). In fact, Croce notes, he squeaked through twelve to ten (cf. *Opere* 5.112).

[34] Cf. Heinrich Lausberg, *Handbuch der literarischen Rhetorik*, 2 vols. (Munich: Hueber, 1960), §81: "Der *status* ist die Art der Frage, die sich für den Richter aus der ersten Konfrontierung der den Kern der *causa* betreffenden widersprüchlichen Aussagen beider Parteien ergibt." See generally §§73–83. The rhetorical and judicial aspects of *causa* are treated at length by Ennio Cortese, *La norma giuridica: Spunti teorici nel diritto comune classico*, 2 vols. in 1 (Milan: Giuffrè, 1962–1964), esp. 1.97–296.

tedious and disorganized, he continued his study with private readings in civil and canon law, guided by the manuals of Vulteius and Canisius, and achieved in this way sufficiently rigorous legal knowledge to take a degree *utriusque juris*. He defended at least two cases in court and, but for the pull of his wide literary interests, might have passed his life as a barrister—the usual occupation for a gifted youth in his day. Even after winning the chair in rhetoric, he aspired to a "more worthy" university position, meaning a lectureship in civil law. Largely to improve his chances for such a post, Vico wrote the three books of his *Diritto universale* (1720–1722), ranging widely—and often diffusely—over issues grand and small in the history of Roman Law. In 1723, at the age of fifty-five, he did in fact compete for a position vacated in the higher faculty, lecturing again on the opening lines of a text— this one Papinian's *De praescriptis verbis* in the *Digestum vetus*. Losing the competition, he abandoned hope for further professional advancement, but parlayed his legal erudition into the *Scienza nuova*, first published in 1725 and rewritten and refined over the next twenty years.

The *lezione di prova*, later committed to writing, has not survived, though Nicolini has attempted to reconstruct it from hints in the Autobiography.[35] The content, so far as we know it, is significant for what it tells us of Vico's sensitivities as a legal scholar. While he did defend, during part of his talk, the glosses of Accursius against the attacks of Antoine Fabre, it is plain that his sympathies lay with the school of sixteenth-century French humanist scholars, represented in the address by Jacques Cujas and François Hotman. Nicolini conjectures, in fact, that apart from the works of Cujas and Hotman, Vico prepared his lecture solely from standard manuals and the commentary of Dionysius Gothofredus.[36]

[35] See *Opere* 5.44–47; *Opere* 8.288–297. Vico's legal training and court experience are reported in the Autobiography, *Opere* 5.6–8, and in *Opere* 8.297.

[36] See *Opere* 8.295, where Nicolini also surmises that Vico's hasty and careless preparation led him into one of his typical confusions and may have cost him the competition.

His predilection for the philological-historical approach to law, manifest in the lost trial lecture, is strongly in evidence in the *Diritto universale*. Progressively in the three books of that work and throughout the versions of the *Scienza nuova*, Vico wrestles with touchstone issues in the history of Roman Law: the rise and development of *dominium, libertas*, and *tutela*; the codification of unwritten law and the relation of law to custom; the origin of the *jus quiritium* and the relation of public to private law; the nature and circumstances of the *lex regia* of Tribonian; the growth of legal procedures; and the changing relation of *jus* and *aequitas*. Notwithstanding their importance, however, these and similar inquiries are entirely overshadowed by Vico's constant fascination with the genesis of the Law of the Twelve Tables—the core of Roman Law and the mainstay of early Italian culture. For the development of his thought, it is comparable in significance only to his probings into the question of Homer. In the end, in fact, Vico could call ancient Roman Law "a serious poem" (*un serioso poema*) and establish the Homeric epics and the Law of the Twelve Tables as exact analogues; the generative function of the former for Greece is precisely that of the latter for Rome.[37]

Philology, then, in the broad sense of humanist usage, complemented Vico's interest in the logic of social discourse. In combining the philological with the propaedeutical, Vico continued the longstanding effort by purveyors of the *trivium* to expand their subjects into what we now call the "humanities." If in the days of Quintilian it was *grammatice* that had swelled, through sundry literary pursuits, "to the dimensions of a brimming river" (Quint. *Inst.* 2.1.4), by the time of Valla in the fifteenth century it was rhetoric that was known for philological curiosity. In neither age, however, and especially not in that of the humanists, was either grammar or rhetoric a purely formal art of correct or effective speech. Thus the *studia humanitatis*, though framed by grammar and rhetoric, con-

[37] See *Scienza nuova seconda, Opere* 4, §§904, 1037.

tained *in nuce* the full range of modern literary and historical studies. This fertility of the rhetorical tradition, older and more varied than the tradition of science, remains largely an untold story.[38] When it comes to be told in full, it is clear that Vico must occupy a significant chapter.

PHILOLOGY AND PHILOSOPHY

No degree of philological diligence, however, could have succeeded in turning pedagogical tenets into principles of culture apart from a second agent. From the beginning of his university career, said Vico, he had been turning over in his mind "a theme both grand and new, to unite in one principle all knowledge human and divine."[39] Grand the theme was, but hardly new. In part it, too, continued a claim of the rhetorical tradition. The "knowledge of all things human and divine" was the Stoic definition of *wisdom*, one revived and deepened by a significant school of Renaissance humanists.[40] And it was just such wisdom, encyclopedic in scope, that it was the orator's task to enliven. "Eloquence," wrote Cicero, "is so potent a force that it embraces the origin and operation and developments of all things, all the virtues and duties, all the natural principles governing the morals and minds and life of mankind, and also determines their customs and laws

[38] On this, see Donald R. Kelley, *Foundations of Modern Historical Scholarship: Language, Law, and History in the French Renaissance* (New York: Columbia University Press, 1970), which itself tells an important part of the story. See also his "Vera philosophia: The Philosophical Significance of Renaissance Jurisprudence," *Journal of the History of Philosophy* 14 (1976): 267–279, one of several articles in which Kelley is now tracing the foundations of modern sociology.

[39] "Un qualche argomento e nuovo e grande . . . , che in un principio unisse egli tutto il sapere umano e divino" (Autobiography, *Opere* 5.31).

[40] Thus Seneca, *Ep.* 89.5: "Sapientiam quidam ita finierunt, ut dicerent divinorum et humanorum scientiam. Quidam ita: sapientia est nosse divina et humana et horum causas." Cf. Cicero, *Off.* 2.2.5; *Tusc.* 4.26.57. For the humanists' development of the formula, see Eugene F. Rice, Jr., *The Renaissance Idea of Wisdom* (Cambridge, Mass.: Harvard University Press, 1958), chap. 4. Cf. generally Charles Trinkaus, *In Our Image and Likeness*, 2 vols. (Chicago: University of Chicago Press, 1970).

and rights, and controls the government of the state, and expresses everything that concerns whatever topic in a graceful and flowing style."[41] Thus Vico could claim of his work as a teacher that, "no matter what the subject, he showed in his lectures how by eloquence it was animated as if by a single spirit drawing life from all the sciences that had any bearing upon it."[42] To gather up the fragments of learning and bring them to life through speech—this ancient Ciceronian ideal Vico took for his professional task.

Vico's concern to organize learning, however, was also inspired by intellectual movements in his own day. On the one hand, it reflected his involvement with developments in jurisprudence that had been in process, particularly in northern Europe, over the two previous centuries. Already in the mid–sixteenth century, certain of the French legal humanists, whose philological and historical criticisms of Roman Law had led them to see the disarray of the *Corpus juris*, had mounted a sustained effort to reduce the Law "to system" (*redigere ad artem*). What began as an innocent attempt to bring order to the *Corpus*, however, led quickly—in François Baudoin, François Hotman, and especially Jean Bodin—to a rejection of the authority of Roman Law and the reorganization of jurisprudence on the basis of universal, comparative history. This latter effort, in turn, had important, if oblique, affinities with the quite separate tradition of jusnaturalism, then taking shape among the theologians of Spain and destined in the following century—in Grotius, Selden, and Pufendorf—to achieve a definite measure of historical circumspection. It is in the context

---

[41] "Illa vis autem eloquentiae tanta est ut omnium rerum, virtutum, officiorum omnisque naturae quae mores hominum, quae animos, quae vitam continet originem, vim mutationesque teneat, eadem mores, leges, jura describat, rempublicam regat, omniaque ad quamcumque rem pertineant ornate copioseque dicat" (*De or.* 3.20.76; trans. Sutton and Rackham).

[42] "D'ogni particolar materia dintorno al ben parlare discorreva talmente ch'ella fusse animata, come da uno spirito, da tutte quelle scienze ch'avevan con quella rapporto" (Autobiography, *Opere* 5.78; translation slightly amended).

of both these traditions—the humanist and the jusnaturalist—
that Vico's work of systematization is to be seen.[43]

On the other hand, Vico's passion for system has a simpler,
more immediate explanation. Since at least 1605, when Francis Bacon, lord chancellor of England, magnanimously surveyed the deficiencies of learning, until at least 1714, when
Leibniz wrote his *Monadology*, Europe was alive with a sense
of adventure. Finally, it was felt, the "rubble of ages"—as
Bacon so quaintly put it—could be swept away and knowledge
erected on "proper foundations." The building of surer foot-
ings was characteristically expressed as the formulation of new
"principles"—possibly the most fashionable term of the century. Not since that of Aristotle had an age been more preoc-
cupied with "principles" or more confident of its ability to
find them. Descartes capped his career in 1644 with the *Principia philosophiae*, claiming to have dealt with every phenomenon in nature, and Newton, some forty years later, made a
similar (and more plausible) claim in his *Principia mathe-
matica* (1687). Nor was the discovery of new principles limited
to the world of nature. We are told in the *De cive* (1642) by
Hobbes that he has finally uncovered that "idoneous principle
of tractation" which had eluded all previous political theorists; and in the *Ethica* (1677) of Spinoza the tenets of the
Moral Order are found to be coterminous with the principles
of Descartes's Nature. There is, consequently, already a touch

---

[43] Vico nonetheless related his concern for principles of universal law to
attempts by the humanists' distant opponents—the "Accursians" or Scholastic interpreters of the *Corpus*—to deduce, through exegesis of related legal
passages, series of *brocardica* or general maxims of justice, and credited the
humanists solely for their philological interests (cf. *De studiorum ratione,
Opere* 1.110; Autobiography, *Opere* 5.7–8). Yet those humanists who were
also jurists were as interested in a properly philosophical systematization of
the law as they were in criticizing the glossators for their lack of philological
rigor. This struggle between the Scholastic and the humanist interpreters, or
between the *mos Italicus* and the *mos Gallicus*—a theme to be resumed in
Chapter 4, below—is the subject of a large literature. See, for example, Guido
Kisch, *Erasmus und die Jurisprudenz seiner Zeit: Studien zum humanistischen
Rechtsdenken* (Basel: Helbing and Lichtenhahn, 1960); Julian H. Franklin,
*Jean Bodin and the Sixteenth-Century Revolution in the Methodology of Law
and History* (New York: Columbia University Press, 1963).

of triteness in the title Vico chose for his work of 1720, *De universi juris uno principio et fine uno*, and even in the titles of the various versions of the *Scienza nuova*, each of which contains the word "*principio*—though, significantly, always in plural form.

Less common, however, were the claims Vico made for the content of his works. In July 1720, having just finished the *De uno principio*, Vico wrote to Father Bernardo Maria Giacco:

> I have tried my best to work out a system of civilization, of republics, laws, poetry, history—in a word, of the whole of human culture, and thus a scientific [*ragionata*] philology. All the things that, from the time of the early Greeks, have been handed down to us as either vacuous or uncertain or absurd (such as the idea that there were times when men spoke with no thoughts in mind either because they were not understood or because they babbled about) I have shown to have reasons, such reasons indeed that, agreeing as they do with countless other principles, the mind is at ease.[44]

To have made sense of human history! To have shown the "reasons" in men's artifacts! To have reduced "philology," not merely to an "art," but to a science!—nothing less was the substance of Vico's claims. Human life in the making may be tortuous and uncertain; but one could, with the sharper vision of Minerva's owl, look back on history and find, not merely tracks, but clearly patterned movements, designs as marvelous as those in nature. The confidence with which Vico, in 1720, announced the finality of his system was soon eroded, but he never doubted that culture ran a regular course. Like Leibniz, his older contemporary, he was obsessed with system and his advance in study is marked by successive "visions of the whole." No less than nine times over the next quarter of

---

[44] "Io mi sono sforzato lavorare un sistema della civiltà, delle repubbliche, delle leggi, della poesia, della istoria e, in una parola, di tutta l'umanità, e in conseguenza di una filologia ragionata; e di tutto ciò che fin da' primi greci ci è pervenuto così o vano o incerto o assurdo (come vi fossero stati tempi che gli uomini o parlassero senza idee o per non esser intesi o per cianciare da senno) io ne rendo ragioni tali e sì fatte, che, con quelle altre innumerabili convenendo, vi riposa sopra sodisfatta la mente" (*Opere* 5:150).

a century, whenever his philological theories progressed, Vico recast his system, always in search of the perfect synthesis. Only in the dedicatory letter of the final *Scienza nuova*, written days before his death in January 1744, did he again permit himself the exuberance expressed in 1720. All previous tracts on the universal law of the peoples, he wrote to Cardinal Troiano d'Acquaviva, have been composed by "northerners" (*oltramontani*) who, however intelligent, were beyond the embrace of the Catholic religion; but now for the first time the principles of this law have sprung from an Italian mind and are fully consonant with the faith.[45] Exaggerated as it was, the letter served a purpose: Vico died in peace.

[45] *Scienza nuova seconda, Opere* 4, §§1488–1492.

CHAPTER 2

RHETORIC: *RES* AND *VERBA*

> No matter what the subject, he showed in his lectures
> how by eloquence it was animated as if by a single spirit
> drawing life from all the sciences that had any bearing
> upon it.
>
> Vico, Autobiography

Vico developed his theory of culture, then, by combining with
classical principles of oratory his growing insights into particular—principally Roman—forms of poetry, myth, religion,
and law. Surprising as his achievements were, however, his
beginnings were fully conventional. He took his start from a
simple concern for the vitality of civil life and for the integrity
of rhetoric as a form of public discourse. Faced with the confident claims of Cartesian science to universal competence, he
sought to exempt civil affairs from the constraints of the new
method and to regain for rhetoric a share in the task of reasoning.

This could be done, he knew, only by showing the dynamics
of social life and the logic of public discourse. Not an incon-
siderable portion of his published and especially his unpublished writings are taken up with this effort. It is a fairly
constant refrain in his correspondence, and it surfaces occasionally even in his poetry and commissioned addresses. It
figures obliquely in the *Pratica della Scienza nuova*, the curious
paragraphs prepared for inclusion (though eventually suppressed) in the third edition of his principal work in the hopes
of helping human prudence "toward delaying if not preventing

the ruin of nations in decay.''[1] Above all it is the theme of his early inaugural orations at the University of Naples, especially that entitled *De nostri temporis studiorum ratione*, given in 1708 and published the following year.

Though Vico's concern for society and the function of discourse within it was doubtless sincere, it was inspired in large measure by his professional employment as professor of rhetoric, and were he not so employed—it can be plausibly argued—he would not have advanced to his science of humanity. Notions that emerge in his early orations and that recur with new meanings in his mature thought—imagination and ingenuity, probability and plausibility, precedent and authority—were long familiar concepts in the rhetorical tradition. Similarly, arguments that give structure to the *New Science*, such as the origin of culture in the poverty of language and the priority of poetry over prose, were first formulated by Vico in his classroom lectures.

We are fortunate in having, though yet in uncritical form, versions of Vico's course manual, *Institutiones oratoriae*, from two critical points in his career. It was the custom in his day for students to prepare *quaderni* or "exercise books" from a professor's class notes, dictated progressively in the course of

---

[1] *Opere* 4, §1405. The full text fills §§1405–1411 and appears now in an English version by Thomas G. Bergin and Max H. Fisch entitled "Practice of the New Science," in *Giambattista Vico's Science of Humanity*, ed. Giorgio Tagliacozzo and Donald P. Verene (Baltimore: Johns Hopkins University Press, 1976), pp. 451–454. See also in the same symposium the articles by Angela Maria Jacobelli (pp. 409–421), Max H. Fisch (pp. 423–430), and Alain Pons (pp. 431–448), each of whom offers a view on the relation of theory and practice in Vico, and the paper by Pietro Piovani, "Apoliticality and Politicality in Vico" (pp. 395–408), which assesses the controversy surrounding the essay of Giuseppe Giarrizzo, "La politica di Vico," *Quaderni contemporanei*, no. 2, *Giambattista Vico nel terzo centenario della nascita*, ed. Fulvio Tessitore (Salerno: Istituto universitario di magistero, 1968), pp. 63–133. In that essay, Giarrizzo argues forcefully for the practical, even the political, concerns of Vico, and finds connections between political events in Naples and the development of Vico's ideas—a thesis that, even in its overstatement, manages well to document Vico's overwhelming practical sensitivity and to rebuff the romantic interpretations of his thought that have been so much in fashion.

a year during the first half-hour of each day's lesson, and through this practice we have a record of Vico's instruction for the years 1711 and 1738.[2] Over fifty years ago, Benvenuto Donati insisted on the importance of the *Institutiones* for interpreting Vico's published works.[3] Croce, however, had already read them and confessed to find in them nothing but "a dry rhetoric manual, prepared for school use, in which one looks in vain for a shadow of Vico's own ideas."[4] Accordingly, Nicolini merely summarized the two texts in his edition of Vico's works, noting that their many classical citations and Scholastic distinctions were so commonplace in rhetorical treatises that full reproduction was unnecessary.[5]

POETRY AND ORATORY

There is a reason for Croce's unfriendliness to rhetoric. Wishing to claim for Vico the anticipation, indeed the estab-

[2] Since both Vico and his son, Gennaro, who succeeded him in the chair of rhetoric, used the *Institutiones*, and since the latter's tenure lasted until after 1800, Nicolini conjectures that hundreds, if not thousands, of copies of the manual were made by students over the years. Yet only four seem to have survived—two identical copies of the 1711 version, one of the version of 1738, and another of uncertain date. Concerning the last, Benvenuto Donati, its discoverer, accepts the year in which it was copied—1741—as the date of its composition, while Nicolini, for excellent reasons, assigns its composition to a much earlier period. See Nicolini's notes in *Opere* 8.222–228. For Donati's argument, see "Le lezioni di 'Rhetorica' del Vico: A proposito di un manoscritto dell' 'Institutiones oratoriae,' " *Nuovi studi sulla filosofia civile di G. B. Vico* (Florence: Le Monnier, 1936), pp. 134–161, esp. 134–148.

[3] *Nuovi studi sulla filosofia civile di G. B. Vico*, pp. 148–150.

[4] *Estetica come scienza dell'espressione e linguistica generale: Teoria e storia*, 3d rev. ed. (Bari: Laterza, 1908), p. 260; trans. Douglas Ainslie, *Aesthetic as Science of Expression and General Linguistic*, 2d ed. (London: Macmillan, 1922), p. 230.

[5] Cf. *Opere* 8.228–229. The summaries appear in *Opere* 8.159–203. Subsequent references to the 1711 version of the *Institutiones* are to the text of Carlo Tipa included in Volume 8 of the *Opere di Giambattista Vico, versione italiana col testo latino a piè di pagina*, ed. Francesco Sa. Pomodoro, 8 vols. (Naples: Morano, 1858–1869), and are given by page number only. Additional indication is given, in the usual manner, for passages that appear also in Nicolini's summary.

lishment, of romantic aesthetic, Croce could only be embarrassed by Vico's link with the rhetorical tradition. For nothing is quite so foreign to romanticism as any thought of utility, and nothing is further from the spirit of oratory than the romantic idea of self-expression.[6] Both in preparing and delivering an oration, a rhetor must, before all else, bear in mind the presence of his audience. To wish only to express intuitions is to forgo the chance to persuade. Persuasiveness, or audience effectiveness, however, is the principal basis on which the ancients, and later the humanists, saw poetry and rhetoric as related. Both, they held, are "productive" arts of language with power to influence their auditors. In the case of poetry, to be sure, such influence is exerted indirectly, through the skillful imitation (*mimēsis*), in concentrated form, of human and nonhuman reality; but as in the case of the orator, success in moving or instructing an audience is the test of a poet's strength.[7]

This pragmatic end of poetry—its necessary relation to an audience—was classically expressed by Horace in a line that

[6] Cf. Meyer Howard Abrams, *The Mirror and the Lamp: Romantic Theory and the Critical Tradition* (New York: Oxford University Press, 1953), pp. 8–26.

[7] See Heinrich Lausberg, *Handbuch der literarischen Rhetorik*, 2 vols. (Munich: Hueber, 1960), §§10, 34–35. The link of poetry with oratory was established by the time of the Sophists and received a theoretical foundation through the juxtaposition of their corresponding arts in the corpus of Aristotle. Though never fully out of fashion, the association of the two arts was particularly prominent during the Renaissance, especially from around the middle of the sixteenth century, when Aristotle's *Poetics* and *Rhetoric* began to exercise increasing influence. Cf. Donald L. Clark, *Rhetoric and Poetry in the Renaissance* (New York: Columbia University Press, 1922), esp. pp. 5–42, 69–75, 103–138; Paul Oskar Kristeller, "The Modern System of the Arts," *Renaissance Thought II* (New York: Harper Torchbooks, 1961), pp. 163–227, esp. 166–179. Of the vast literature on the subject, three survey works by Charles Sears Baldwin are useful: *Ancient Rhetoric and Poetic* (New York: Macmillan, 1924); *Medieval Rhetoric and Poetic (To 1400): Interpreted from Representative Works* (New York: Macmillan, 1928); *Renaissance Literary Theory and Practice: Classicism in the Rhetoric and Poetic of Italy, France, and England, 1400–1600*, ed. Donald Lemen Clark (New York: Columbia University Press, 1939). Also helpful is Francesco Tateo, *"Rhetorica" e "Poetica" fra Medioevo e Rinascimento* (Bari: Adriatica editrice, 1960).

would be much debated in the history of aesthetics: "Poets aim either to benefit, or to amuse, or to utter words at once both pleasing and helpful to life."[8] Commenting on this passage late in his career, Vico recast the idea in terms of the *New Science*: "When it first arose, poetry had utility for an end, the utility by which the nations were founded. Utility gradually declined in importance until it was replaced by pleasure. No poetry is useful to a republic, however, unless, with pleasure as its means, it takes utility as its principal end." And to this he added some lines later: "First, or vulgar, wisdom was poetic in nature. Thus from poetic history are to be sought the origins of republics, laws, and all the arts and sciences that make civilization complete."[9]

These brief statements, representative of so many others, sufficiently indicate that "poetry" for Vico is not primarily an aesthetic concept, but a notion within his civil philosophy. Although poetry represents, as Croce saw, a form of knowledge that is imaginative and not intellectual, it does *not* mark, as he also held, the boundary between arts and sciences. Not only does Vico maintain, with Bacon his mentor, the traditional understanding of "arts," but he also assigns a "poetic" origin to the entire cycle of learning—sciences as well as arts. Poetry—or "poetic wisdom," as Vico more commonly called it—designated that earliest phase of human culture which was spontaneous, synthetic, and constructive, in contrast to a later phase, which was reflective, discursive, and critical. Vico had no interest, as Croce so vainly hoped, in "forms of the spirit" independent of the course of concrete history. He was totally absorbed in the question of how humanity arose and, once

[8] "Aut prodesse volunt aut delectare poetae / aut simul et jucunda et idonea dicere vitae" (Hor. *Ars P.* 333–334; trans. H. Rushton Fairclough, Loeb ed.).

[9] "Finis poeseos, quum primum orta est, fuit utilitas, qua gentes fundatae sunt, ut paullo inferius dicetur; deinde alter successit, delectatio. Sed poesis reipublicae utilis nulla, nisi quae, media delectatione, utilitatem sibi praecipuum finem proponat" (*Opere* 7.74). "Prima sapientia vulgaris fuit poetica. Quare ab historia poetica sunt repetendae origines rerumpublicarum, legum omniumque artium ac scientiarum, quae humanitatem perfecere" (*Opere* 7.76).

established, how it advanced from its crude beginnings to an age of critical intelligence. Within his theory of culture, poetry is the crucial reality. It is the clarion call of civilization, the first, clear sign of humanity's birth. More than its sign, however, it is also its cause. For poetry is not simply language; it is *effective* language, wisdom that establishes humanity. Myth, in Vico's account, is its principal form, but it has other forms as well—hieroglyphs, sign languages, coats of arms, medals, currencies, and the like. Whatever form it takes, however, its effect is one and the same: Through it, the *giganti* are transposed from aimlessly wandering individuals into rough, but nonetheless true, citizens. What Croce considered an excrescence, therefore, a "dark nook in a general blaze of light," occupies the center of Vico's position. Poetry, like eloquence, has intrinsically a civil end. It addresses creatures in their isolation, reverses the habit of independent action, and shapes them into a people. Poetry, in fact, *is* eloquence. It is the language that constitutes humanity.[10]

THE TRADITION OF RHETORIC

Poetic wisdom as effective language! Hidden in this simple phrase is a full history of concern for the triangular relation of rhetoric, poetic, and logic, and for the relation of these arts

[10] For Croce's argument, see his chapter on Vico in *Aesthetic*, trans. Ainslie, pp. 220–234, the last sentence of which reads, "To purge Aesthetic of the remains of ancient Rhetoric and Poetics as well as from some over-hasty schematisms imposed upon her by the author of her being: such is the field of labour, such the progress still to be achieved after the discovery of the autonomy of the aesthetic world due to the genius of Giambattista Vico." His antagonism to rhetoric is more fully presented in a later chapter, "Rhetoric; or, The Theory of Ornate Form," pp. 422–436. See also his *La filosofia di Giambattista Vico* (Bari: Laterza, 1911), chap. 4. On the matter of Croce's interpretation of Vico, see Hayden V. White, "What Is Living and What Is Dead in Croce's Criticism of Vico," in *Giambattista Vico: An International Symposium*, ed. Giorgio Tagliacozzo and Hayden V. White (Baltimore: Johns Hopkins University Press, 1969), pp. 379–389, and in the same symposium, the article by Tullio De Mauro, "Giambattista Vico: From Rhetoric to Linguistic Historicism," pp. 279–295: "Whereas Croce tries to dissolve language into poetry, Vico . . . dissolves poetry into language" (p. 293).

to the exigencies of civil life. The sources of the notion return to the formative phases of Greek and Roman culture and to the successive adaptations of classical learning in the West.[11]

Whether oratory arose, as one tradition holds, with the rise of cities (Cic. *Inv. Rhet.* 1.1.2), or, as another maintains, with the need of newly liberated citizens in Sicily to press their claims for restitution (Cic. *Brut.* 12.46), or whether it came about simply through the gradual perfecting of an innate talent—Quintilian's more pedestrian view (*Inst.* 3.2.2–4)—the man whose words are "crowned with beauty" has long been esteemed in the West, and there are few in our heritage who would not agree with Homer that the gift of eloquence, like beauty of form and strength of mind, is a human excellence resembling that of the gods (Hom. *Od.* 8.167–174). To Plato and his followers, the importance of language was that it should bear one's thought, or at least one's feelings, and that the two should be so conformed that the "inner" and the "outer" man are one (Pl. *Phdr.* 279b–c). For Aristotle and his followers, the glory of language was that it could shape reality and guide human action in those instances where no Truth prevails but prudence alone holds sway. And from both these emphases arose in time the Roman ideal of eloquence

---

[11] Of the copious literature on classical rhetoric, see the historical survey of Wilhelm Kroll, "Rhetorik," in Pauly-Wissowa, *Realencyclopädie des classischen Altertums*, Supplement, vol. 7 (Stuttgart: Metzler, 1940), cols. 1039–1138, and the systematic presentation of Lausberg, *Handbuch der literarischen Rhetorik*, cited in note 7, above. Though a comprehensive history of rhetoric has yet to be written, the works of Baldwin and Clark also mentioned in note 7 cover its principal chapters, as does the recent work of George A. Kennedy, *Classical Rhetoric and Its Christian and Secular Tradition from Ancient to Modern Times* (Chapel Hill: University of North Carolina Press, 1980). See also the essay of Paul Oskar Kristeller, "Philosophy and Rhetoric from Antiquity to the Renaissance," *Renaissance Thought and Its Sources* (New York: Columbia University Press, 1979), pp. 211–259, both for its luminous survey and its valuable bibliographical notes. A full-scale history of rhetoric is now emerging in the successive studies of George A. Kennedy: *The Art of Persuasion in Greece* (Princeton, N.J.: Princeton University Press, 1963); *The Art of Rhetoric in the Roman World, 300 B.C.–A.D. 300* (Princeton, N.J.: Princeton University Press, 1972); and *Greek Rhetoric Under Christian Emperors* (Princeton, N.J.: Princeton University Press, 1983).

as *ars bene dicendi*, where *bene* has at once an aesthetic, a political, and a moral meaning: The orator is to speak aptly and effectively so as to move men to action, but only the honest man should speak.[12]

Is rhetoric, then, a kind of poetic, or a kind of logic, or is it an adjunct to ethics and politics? In the Aristotelian corpus—which was to be so influential in the late Renaissance and down to Vico's time—it is both all and none of these things, carefully placed next to the *Poetics* yet filled with constant reference to both dialectics and politics.[13] Whether he was following the suggestions of Plato in the *Phaedrus*, it is plain that Aristotle, in the first two, and oldest, books of his *Rhetoric*, first developed a notion of oratory as a logic of persuasion or argumentation, as the kind of reasoning that goes on among nonspecialists in matters that are merely or mainly probable. In time he would enlarge this "logical" vision—a virtual addendum to the *Topics*—and would come to argue that persuasion depends on the oratorical act as a whole—not merely on the proofs, or *logoi*, in the speech itself, but also on the manner, or *ethos*, of the rhetor and on the emotional response, or *pathos*, evoked in the auditors (*Rh.* 1356a). Thereafter, in hundreds of treatises down to Vico's own, rhetoricians would say that the orator's task is threefold—*docere, delectare, commovere*. And scores of arguments would be mounted as to the importance and appropriateness of the three parts of persuasion: Can a rhetor stand on argument alone? Is it grossly ignoble or simply indispensable to appeal to emo-

[12] Cf. John Herman Randall, Jr., *Aristotle* (New York: Columbia University Press, 1960), p. 287: "It is hardly too much to trace back through Cicero to Aristotle the central conviction running through the whole tradition of literary humanism in medieval and modern times, which derives from Roman educational practice, that the study of good writing and good speaking must be indissolubly wedded to the study of good living, and that the pursuits of the arts of letters are *ipso facto* pursuits of humane wisdom."

[13] The development of Aristotle's rhetorical theory is closely argued by Friedrich Solmsen, *Die Entwicklung der aristotelischen Logik und Rhetorik*, Neue philologische Untersuchungen, no. 4 (Berlin: Weidmann, 1929). See also Kennedy, *The Art of Persuasion in Greece*, pp. 82–114.

tion? Is rhetoric pure charm and no substance or is it that mode of linguistic behavior most truly human?

Moreover, Aristotle came to add to his treatise, in what is now book 3 of the *Rhetoric*, a long discussion on composing and delivering the speech itself, and in so doing he developed a theory of prose composition akin to his *Poetics*. "It is not enough to know *what* we ought to say," he wrote. "We must also say it *as* we ought" (*Rh.* 1403b15). Under the general rubrics of "style" and "arrangement," he considered such themes as the parts of an oration, the tropes and figures of speech, and oratorical styles and prose rhythms. In due course, rhetoricians would also give advice on memorization and delivery, and by the time of the Hellenists the parts of the rhetorical treatise were set at five: finding the available means of persuasion (*inventio*); arranging them in an effective order (*dispositio*); choosing appropriate language (*elocutio*); memorizing the speech (*memoria*); and delivering it (*pronunciatio*).[14]

There were thus two focuses of classical rhetoric—that of *res*, cared for by the parts of the treatise that train one to identify and properly arrange the things to say (*inventio* and *dispositio*); and that of *verba*, cared for by the parts that train one to select the most appropriate language, memorize the speech, and deliver it most forcefully (*elocutio, memoria,* and *pronunciatio*).[15] In an extreme sense—well exploited by modern critics—every instance of human communication is shaped by *res* and *verba* and thus fits within the pale of rhetoric and its principles; but to the ancients three situations in civil life were paradigmatically oratorical: the court of law, in which two barristers (or a barrister and a judge) wrestle over the fate of an accused—and this they called forensic or *judicial* oratory; the political assembly, in which courses of state action

---

[14] See Lausberg, *Handbuch der literarischen Rhetorik*, §§225–259; Kroll, "Rhetorik," cols. 1096–1098. Cf. Cic. *De or.* 1.31.142; Quint. *Inst.* 3.3.14.

[15] Cic. *De or.* 3.5.19: "Nam cum omnis ex re atque verbis constet oratio, neque verba sedem habere possunt si rem subtraxeris neque res lumen si verba semoveris." Cf. Quint. *Inst.* 3.5.1; 8.pr.6.

are debated—*deliberative* oratory; and the public address, in which praise or blame is distributed or a view set forth on an issue of interest or controversy—demonstrative or *epideictic* oratory (most akin to poetry). To these oratorical forms, writers of the early Christian era would add the homily; during the Middle Ages the letter, church and state documents, and varieties of public speaking would also become subjects of formal arts.

Clearly, within such variety the links to traditional rhetoric were at times tenuous, and too often the mantle of Isocrates was made to cover pedantry and rank formalism. Yet no claimant to rhetorical art, however routine his duties or leaden his ways, could fail to pursue what is, in every account, the aim and end of all oratory: to so marshal *res* and *verba*, thoughts and words, ideas and language, as to say what is— at the moment—"called for," suited to the occasion, fitting and proper, appropriate and decorous, and so advance the cause of public life. A stock of phrases were used by the Latins to define this aim of the oration—*aptum, congruens, accommodatum, quid deceat, decorum*—all an effort to capture the gist of what the Greeks took to be the virtue of both a good speech and a good life—*prēpon*.[16] As usual, it was Plato who gave subtlety to the notion: Whether making a speech, crafting a boat, or building a life, one must not work randomly but toward a "certain form," compelling each element to "fit and harmonize with the other" until a "well-ordered and regulated whole" has been achieved (*Grg.* 503d–504a). Plato required of the rhetor and his words the same virtue he found among the spheres of the heavens, the same that he demanded of the parts of a man's soul and the classes of citizens in an ideal state (*Resp.* 441d; 444d): harmony, integrity, coherence, form, order. Language is not mere talk; it is the shape of things social, and thus a public responsibility. The grandeur of the

---

[16] Cic. *Orat.* 21.70: "Ut enim in vita sic in oratione nihil est difficilius quam quid deceat videre. *Prēpon* appellant hoc Graeci, nos dicamus sane decorum." See also Cic. *De or.* 3.10.37; Quint. *Inst.* 11.1.1–8. Cf. Lausberg, *Handbuch der literarischen Rhetorik*, §§54–57, 258, 1055–1062.

idea—soaring and philosophical in Plato, trenchant in Aristotle and Cicero—had within it the kernel of a social theorem; and the connection would not be lost on Vico.

CICERO AND THE ROMAN IDEAL

In its full extent, therefore, traditional rhetoric was both a theory of argumentation (or a logic of social discourse) and a theory of prose composition and elocution, and its subsequent history in the West may fairly be plotted by the varying emphasis given its logical and its literary dimensions. Modern philosophers of rhetoric, concerned with rhetoric as argumentation, lay stress on the gradual eclipse of the logical dimension;[17] for as it was received and developed in the Latin West, rhetoric came to be seen progressively less in terms of its power of persuasion and progressively more in terms of its literary products. In time, the written composition and the epideictic speech replaced judicial and deliberative oratory as the primary subject of analysis, and the part of the treatise concerned with style, always important, grew in stature and richness, while that on finding and arranging arguments stagnated and at times disappeared. Those concerned with Roman provenance for the development could look to Quintilian. "It is one thing to speak grammatically," he wrote, "another to speak as the Latins do,"[18] and from his time onward there was no lack of effort to expound the requirements of *Latinitas*.

If Quintilian, the great synthesizer of Roman ideals, found in style "the chief object of our study" (*Inst.* 8.pr.14) and held that the "art of persuasion" inadequately defined rhetoric—for "many things have the power of persuasion"

---

[17] See, for example, Chaïm Perelman and Lucie Olbrechts-Tyteca, *Rhétorique et philosophie: Pour une théorie de l'argumentation en philosophie* (Paris: Presses universitaires de France, 1952); idem, *La nouvelle rhétorique: Traité de l'argumentation*, 2 vols., continuously paginated (Paris: Presses universitaires de France, 1958).

[18] "Quare mihi non invenuste dici videtur, aliud esse Latine aliud grammatice loqui" (*Inst.* 1.6.27), paraphrased by Vico ("Aliud est grammatice, aliud latine loqui") in his *Institutiones oratoriae*, p. 74; *Opere* 8.170.

(2.15.6)—he could not claim at this point to be speaking for Cicero, the man whose name, he had said, was synonymous with eloquence.[19] To be sure, Cicero had once claimed that the use of language is the quality that most distinguishes the orator (*Orat.* 18.61), and during the years of the Atticist challenge had produced three works given entirely to this subject (*Brutus*, *De optimo genere oratorum*, and *Orator*, all dated to 46 B.C.). Yet in a youthful work, *De inventione*, and in two later studies, *De partitione oratoria* and the *Topica*, he gave nearly exclusive attention to the logical offices of rhetoric. It is, however, neither for his treatment of *res* nor for that of *verba* that Cicero is remembered, but for his sturdy insistence that the two are to be linked, even as the aim of a rhetorical training is a public servant both eloquent and wise. His first work on rhetoric, *De inventione*, opens with the solemn assertion that "wisdom without eloquence does too little for the good of states, but eloquence without wisdom is . . . never helpful"; and the *Orator*, one of his last, contains the confession that "whatever ability I possess as an orator comes not from the workshops of the rhetoricians, but from the spacious grounds of the Academy."[20]

Alain Michel argues forcefully, and correctly, that the focus of Cicero's efforts is not oratory as such, much less the oration or the rhetorical precepts that should guide it, but the orator himself, indicated well by the titles that Cicero gave his most important works on the subject: *Orator* and *De oratore*.[21]

[19] "Quare non immerito ab hominibus aetatis suae regnare in judiciis dictus est, apud posteros vero id consecutus, ut Cicero jam non hominis nomen, sed eloquentiae habeatur" (*Inst.* 10.1.112). Yet even Quintilian devotes three of the twelve books of his work to *inventio* (4–6), one to *dispositio* (7), and only two to *elocutio* or style (8–9).

[20] "Ac me quidem diu cogitantem ratio ipsa in hanc potissimum sententiam ducit, ut existimem sapientiam sine eloquentia parum prodesse civitatibus, eloquentiam vero sine sapientia . . . prodesse nunquam" (*Inv. Rhet.* 1.1.1); "Fateor me oratorem, si modo sim aut etiam quicumque sim, non ex rhetorum officinis, sed ex Academiae spatiis exstitisse" (*Orat.* 3.12).

[21] "Nous voyons dès maintenant l'intérêt de ces titres: *De oratore, Orator*. En les donnant à ses ouvrages, Cicéron ne dit pas: je vais traiter de rhétorique. Mais au contraire: je vais étudier dans l'éloquence ce qui est au-dessus de la

Particularly in the latter of these, as in the *De republica*, written at about the same time, we find set forth those social and
pedagogical ideals which marked the Republic and which were
later revived, to such happy effect, by Renaissance humanists.
It is the statesman, the man of public affairs, that Cicero means
by "orator," and not in the narrow sense of a public official,
but with the wider meaning of a practitioner of one of the
many arts required to sustain social and political life. Within
the strifes and complexities of Roman life the vocation was
not an obvious one, yet against the lure of the Hellenistic call
to retreat Cicero defended it as supreme: "There is no other
occupation in which human virtue approaches more closely
the august function of the gods than that of founding new
states or preserving those already in existence."[22]

The education of the statesman was correspondingly serious. Building a *copia rerum et verborum*—the task a rhetorical
training assigned itself—had to be more than a stockpiling of
commonplaces and clever phrases. The orator could not afford
to pander in facts or trifle in words; he had to be a man of
true wisdom and eloquence. For on his speech hung the fate
of an accused, the reputation of an opponent, indeed the tenor
of a society, the strength of its resolve, the focus of its worship,
the direction of its future. "In an orator," Cicero writes, "we
must demand the subtlety of the logician, the thoughts of the
philosopher, a diction almost poetic, a lawyer's memory, a
tragedian's voice, and the bearing almost of the consummate
actor. Accordingly, no rarer thing than a finished orator can
be discovered among the sons of men."[23]

---

rhétorique, qui lui donne tout son prix: l'orateur. Je vais étudier ce dernier
pour lui-même, c'est-à-dire pour ce qui le rend supérieur à son art. Nous
sommes tout à fait ici dans le contexte romain sur lequel nous avons tant
insisté. Il ne s'agit pas d'un *rētōr* mais de l'*orator*, un grand homme qui
consent à être habile" (*Rhétorique et philosophie chez Cicéron* [Paris: Presses
universitaires de France, 1960], pp. 40–46, at 42).

[22] "Neque enim est ulla res, in qua propius ad deorum numen virtus accedat
humana, quam civitatis aut condere novas aut conservare jam conditas" (*Rep.*
1.7.12).

[23] "In oratore autem acumen dialecticorum, sententiae philosophorum, verba

The wisdom required of the orator was not the theoretical science of nature or the subtle discipline of logic—the prized achievements of the Greeks—but the study of human life, of men and morals, what the ancients call prudence and the Stoics ethics or moral philosophy, including poetry, literature, and history, and culminating in the prudence of law, jurisprudence. These were intrinsically public sciences, disciplines of the forum, the court, the marketplace, taking root in the arena of the probable and the contingent, out of debate and argumentation, and achieving in time the status of wisdom, a kind of solid, confident, but unfinished knowledge. For such wisdom the orator must strive, seek out its company, learn its ways, its rhythms, its cadences, for it is nothing less than the soul of the society the orator is to lead, the heritage he is to take into trust, the tradition whose future is largely in his hands. Little wonder, then, that the perfect orator is presented, late in Cicero's career, as a never fully realized ideal in our mind, and as such comparable to a Platonic idea (*Orat.* 1.8–10).[24] Yet it was a serious ideal to which Cicero was sworn uncompromisingly:

I give full leave to anybody who wishes to apply the title of orator to a philosopher who imparts to us an abundant command of facts and of language, or alternatively I shall raise no obstacle if he prefers to designate as a philosopher the orator whom I on my side am now describing as possessing wisdom combined with eloquence, only provided it be agreed that neither the tongue-tied silence of the man who knows the facts but cannot explain them in language, nor the ignorance of the person who is deficient in facts but has no lack of

prope poetarum, memoria jurisconsultorum, vox tragoedorum, gestus paene summorum actorum est requirendus. Quam ob rem nihil in hominum genere rarius perfecto oratore inveniri potest" (*De or.* 1.28.128). Note that Cicero summarizes here the five offices of rhetoric in terms of their demands on the orator—another indication of the pedagogical focus of his interests.

[24] Kristeller, "Philosophy and Rhetoric from Antiquity to the Renaissance," p. 223, suggests that Cicero is here adapting to the orator the notion of the ideal sage that the Stoic philosopher Panaetius, a favorite author of Cicero, formulated in his ethics. Indeed, Cicero will say later in his treatise (*Orat.* 21.70) that life and oratory have a common challenge—*decorum* or *prepon*—this, too, a central idea in Panaetius.

words, is deserving of praise. And if one had to choose between them, for my part I should prefer wisdom lacking power of expression to talkative folly; but if on the contrary we are trying to find the one thing that stands top of the whole list, the prize must go to the orator who possesses learning.[25]

With this judgment, glossed by Quintilian's splendid chapters on the *vir bonus dicendi peritus* (*Inst.* 12.1–3), the Roman ideal was bequeathed to history.

DICTATORES AND HUMANISTS

The fate of rhetoric during the Middle Ages has been the subject of increasing debate.[26] At its start, clearly, it is dominated by the *De doctrina christiana* (397–426) of Augustine and the *De nuptiis Philologiae et Mercurii* (410–439) of Martianus Capella, two works of late antiquity that determined, respectively, the practice of sacred oratory and the shape of the secular curriculum in the early Middle Ages; and at its close stand the *Summulae logicales* (ca. 1245) of Peter of Spain, which introduced the new "terminist" or language-

[25] "Nunc sive qui volet, eum philosophum qui copiam nobis rerum orationisque tradat per me appellet oratorem licet, sive hunc oratorem quem ego dico sapientiam junctam habere eloquentiae philosophum appellare malit, non impediam: dummodo hoc constet, neque infantiam eius qui rem norit sed eam explicare dicendo non queat, neque inscientiam illius cui res non suppetat, verba non desint, esse laudandam. Quorum si alterum sit optandum, malim equidem indisertam prudentiam quam stultitiam loquacem; sin quaerimus quid unum excellat ex omnibus, docto oratori palma danda est" (*De or.* 3.35.142–43).

[26] Baldwin, *Medieval Rhetoric and Poetic (To 1400)*; Richard McKeon, "Rhetoric in the Middle Ages," *Speculum* 17 (1942): 1–32; Ernst Robert Curtius, *Europäische Literatur und lateinisches Mittelalter*, 2d ed. (Bern: Franke Verlag, 1954), trans. Willard R. Trask, *European Literature of the Latin Middle Ages* (New York: Pantheon Books, 1953); Tateo, *"Rhetorica" e "Poetica" fra Medioevo e Rinascimento*; James J. Murphy, *Medieval Rhetoric: A Select Bibliography* (Toronto: University of Toronto Press, 1971); idem, *Rhetoric in the Middle Ages* (Berkeley: University of California Press, 1974); Kristeller, "Philosophy and Rhetoric from Antiquity to the Renaissance," pp. 228–242; Kennedy, *Classical Rhetoric*, pp. 161–194. On the development of rhetoric in medieval Italy, see Alfredo Galletti, *L'eloquenza dalle origini al XVI secolo*, Storia dei generi letterari italiani (Milan: Villardi, 1904–1938), pp. 1–141, 413–486.

based logic, and the *Rhetorica novissima* (1235) of Boncompagno, which described a forensic oratory that had been all but forgotten since the end of antiquity. Between these markings run some eight hundred years of social and curricular development, to whose intricate and subtle ways the history of rhetoric is unmistakably bound.

In a classic article on the subject, Richard McKeon has defined three separate lines (in several phases) along which rhetoric developed in the Middle Ages. In the first instance, he finds, it developed as a part of logic, among those rhetoricians who sought to limit rhetoric, on the strength of Boethius's distinction between "thesis" and "hypothesis," to probable reasoning on specifically circumscribed questions. In a second tradition, one based on Augustine's distinction between sacred and profane eloquence, it developed as the prince of the arts and the servant of theology, leading in time to a rhetorically based pattern of scriptural exegesis and the *sententiae* program of theological discourse. And finally, it developed simply as an art of words, blissfully unconcerned with either logic or theology, with making arguments or unfolding the Word of God, but given over instead to the forms of writing, preaching, and verse making, and to devices for remembering and amplifying thoughts and constructing the figures and rhythms that would embody them most gracefully. If the three traditions shared anything, McKeon argues, it was their growing estrangement from that Ciceronian vision of rhetoric as "civil science" which had initially joined them. Though the dialectical and theological traditions never forgot the ethical and political bearings of the art, and though the artistic tradition was firm in its insistence on rhetoric's practical character, none of the three forms of rhetorical concern had about it that wide and consistent vision which could make of it, as in Roman times, the basis for an educational program.[27]

Though McKeon shows the least interest in it, it is the

[27] McKeon, "Rhetoric in the Middle Ages," *Speculum* 17 (1942): 1–32, esp. 11–15.

tradition of rhetoric as an art of words that must be seen, both for its literary output and for its influence on a subsequent age, as the dominant form of medieval rhetoric—a point that has been made, with great clarity and persistence, by Paul Oskar Kristeller.[28] Public oratory may largely have died with the Ciceronian age, but the need for correct form in the drafting and handling of documents persisted and even increased as societies grew more complex; thus the *ars notaria*, which could supply the essential literacy and rudimentary legal knowledge that the handling of documents required, thrived. The need for such counsel extended to the drafting of letters as well, first to official and business correspondence and eventually to even private forms of communication, and in time a full-fledged epistolography, or *ars dictaminis*, took form. Together with the cognate art of poetry (*ars poetica*) and an eventual *ars arengandi*—the art of secular oratory that, with the reappearance of public speaking in the Italian city-states of the late twelfth century, grew up to join an already flourishing art of sacred eloquence, the *ars praedicandi*—these formed the unmistakable core of medieval rhetoric.

The purveyors of these arts—*dictatores*, as they were commonly known—left in their wake literally thousands of treatises and collections of models; but for our purposes this is a less significant fact than that the *dictatores* in all this activity were the immediate ancestors of the humanists of the Italian Renaissance.[29] With the expansion of the city-states and con-

[28] Cf. "Philosophy and Rhetoric from Antiquity to the Renaissance," pp. 228–242, esp. pp. 232–239. Kristeller also finds (ibid., p. 232) that McKeon misstates the issue by saying that rhetoric, in the one tradition, was made subservient to logic. *Logic* is to be understood here, Kristeller argues, as a synonym for the *artes sermocinales* or the *trivium* of the liberal arts, a schema within which rhetoric was routinely grouped together with grammar and *dialectic*, the term then preferred for the art of reasoning.

[29] Cf. Kristeller, "Humanism and Scholasticism in the Italian Renaissance," *Renaissance Thought: The Classic, Scholastic, and Humanist Strains* (New York: Harper Torchbooks, 1961), pp. 92–119, esp. 100–108; and "Renaissance Philosophy and the Medieval Tradition," *Renaissance Concepts of Man and Other Essays* (New York: Harper Torchbooks, 1972), pp. 110–155, esp. 122–127. Both articles are now reprinted in *Renaissance Thought and*

sequent growth of secondary education, the need for the arts of speaking and writing became all the more critical, and masters of these skills enjoyed a new prestige not only as tutors and teachers of the liberal arts but also as chancellors and secretaries to princes and republics. The literature they produced—treatises, models, works on imitation, letters, orations, poetry, commissioned biographies and histories (genres that describe fully a third of Vico's extant writings)—was truly prodigious. Unlike that of their medieval predecessors, however, their writings were informed, both in substance and in spirit, by a novel interest and a new competence: classical Greek and Latin scholarship. This marriage of the arts of language with classical literature and philology led quickly to its formalization in a cycle of studies known as the *studia humanitatis*—grammar, rhetoric, poetry, history, and moral philosophy—a schema that consolidated the "humanities" as we know them and gave their masters a new name—"humanists"—but one that, fatefully, excluded logic and the mathematical sciences, subjects that had been part of the traditional *artes liberales*. Thus the Marriage of Philology and Mercury that Martianus had arranged some one thousand years before had in Renaissance humanism its delayed fulfillment, though by the time of this happy event the partners in marriage were scarcely the same.

Enjoying new social respectability and managing a curriculum that was coherent in theory and indispensable in practice, the Renaissance humanists could be expected to challenge, as they did so successfully, the hegemony of Scholasticism, not by offering a new, countervailing philosophy, which they did not agree upon and thus could not share, but by setting forth a fresh pedagogical ideal.[30] At the heart of this ideal was

---

Its Sources, pp. 85–133. See also Jerrold E. Seigel, "From the *Dictatores* to the Humanists," *Rhetoric and Philosophy in Renaissance Humanism: The Union of Eloquence and Wisdom, Petrarch to Valla* (Princeton, N.J.: Princeton University Press, 1968), pp. 200–225.

[30] William Harrison Woodward, *Studies in Education during the Age of the Renaissance, 1400–1600* (1906; reprint, New York: Teachers College

the ancient Ciceronian vision of the union of wisdom and eloquence. Though there was scarcely an agreement among humanists as to the nature and scope of such wisdom—whether it was merely human or also divine; whether it served active or contemplative ideals; whether, indeed, it was a type of knowledge or a form of virtue[31]—that it should be conjoined with a rhetorical training so as to form men who were both learned and effective was a conviction almost universally shared.

As with every successful reform movement, the established were useful foils. The current philosophic fashion, complained Petrarch (1304–1374) of the Scholastics, finds eloquence unworthy of a man of letters. "Thus only 'infantile inability to speak' and perplexed stammering, 'wisdom' trying hard to keep one eye open and 'yawning drowsily,' as Cicero [*De or.* 3.51.198; 2.33.144–145] calls it, is held in good repute nowadays. . . . From Aristotle's ways they swerve, taking eloquence to be an obstacle and a disgrace to philosophy, while he considered it a mighty adornment and tried to combine it with philosophy, 'prevailed upon,' it is asserted [*De or.* 3.35.141] 'by the fame of the orator Isocrates.' "[32] As Petrarch's words make clear, the intent of the early humanists, of whom he was the first and most famous, was not to subvert philosophy nor even to deny it precedence. The pursuit of eloquence, rather, was an effort to abandon the "merely intellectual" in favor of the "actively persuasive."[33] To combine philosophy with

---

Press, 1967); Eugenio Garin, *L'educazione umanistica in Italia: Testi scelti e illustrati* (Bari: Laterza, 1949); idem, *L'educazione in Europa (1400–1600): Problemi e programmi* (Bari: Laterza, 1957); Gregor Müller, *Bildung und Erziehung im Humanismus der italienischen Renaissance* (Wiesbaden: Steiner, 1969).

[31] Cf. Eugene F. Rice, Jr., *The Renaissance Idea of Wisdom* (Cambridge, Mass.: Harvard University Press, 1958).

[32] *De sui ipsius et multorum ignorantia, Opera omnia*, 3 vols. (1554; reprint, Ridgewood, N.J.: Gregg Press, 1965), 2.1143; trans. Hans Nachod, *The Renaissance Philosophy of Man*, ed. Ernst Cassirer, P. O. Kristeller, and J. H. Randall, Jr. (Chicago: Chicago University Press, 1948), pp. 53f.

[33] These are the apt phrases of Hanna H. Gray, "Renaissance Humanism: The Pursuit of Eloquence," *Journal of the History of Ideas* 24 (1963): 497–514, at 501.

rhetoric, it was argued, would not only ennoble its content; it would relieve it of its terrible isolation, give it power and application, and permit it to take effect in men's lives.[34] To the extent that Scholasticism withdrew from this purpose, ignored the training of the will, and left to chance the deciding of affairs that should engage the debate of intelligent men— to this extent it was the foe of Italian humanism and subject to its grating insult.

Equally a philosopher and an orator, Petrarch could sustain with little effort a moderate view. During the quattrocento, however, his balanced Ciceronianism gave way to a sharp debate, and by the sixteenth century—by which time the new science was in its infancy—a curious division between res and verba had set in. Coluccio Salutati (1331–1406), the most famous humanist in the generation after Petrarch, brought the matter into the fifteenth century with an extreme restatement of his forebear's position: "It is best for wisdom and eloquence to join together, so that the latter expounds what the former comprehends . . . The pursuit of eloquence is itself a function of wisdom. Eloquence is placed under wisdom, and contained in it as in the sum of all things that can be known, so that whoever pursues wisdom necessarily pursues eloquence with it."[35] That was a curious position to take for one who was trained solely in rhetoric, for it seemed to deliver his trade

[34] Cf. Galletti, L'eloquenza dalle origini al XVI secolo, pp. 538–594, esp. 543–544: "In fatto di arte letteraria il pensiero degli umanisti è in reciso contrasto colle teorie romantiche predominanti nella critica moderna. Per i romantici l'arte non può nulla, l'ispirazione è tutto: ogni opera letteraria deve essere poesia e dall'entusiasmo, dall'intimo ardore lirico nasce, adeguata e perfetta, l'espressione verbale. Se la coscienza riflessa e la volontà critica dello scrittore intervengono, infiacchiscono, non rafforzano il misterioso processo creativo. Gli umanisti tengono per verità fondamentale del loro insegnamento che i moti più spontanei dello spirito a nulla riescono senza la cosciente elaborazione artistica e ripetono la sentenza di Cicerone nel proemio del Paradossi: non esistere fatto o idea così triviale che non possa essere purificata e nobilitata dalla bellezza della forma; opinione pericolosa, che abusata dai mediocri, giustificò l'artificio fraudolento di coloro che con belle parole coprivano la meschinità del pensiero."

[35] Epistolario di Coluccio Salutati, ed. Francesco Novati, 4 vols. in 5 (Rome: Istituto storico italiano, 1891–1911), 3.602.

simply into the hands of the philosopher. What generosity it implied was quickly retracted by his younger disciples, Poggio Bracciolini (1380–1459) and Leonardo Bruni (1369–1444), the latter in particular gaining much of his fame by baiting the Scholastics in Florence. Bruni's tack was to remake Aristotle, his favored philosopher, into one of the orators' own. From a hint in Cicero, he insisted that Aristotle had been led during his career to add the art of eloquence to his curriculum and had filled his writings with figures and ornaments of speech. To bear out his point, he issued the works in a new translation, against which those of the Schoolmen seemed brittle and lifeless, and ended by regrouping Aristotle's interests into the familiar three fields—ethics, logic, and natural philosophy—before all of which he placed a fourth, rhetoric.[36] Dante's *il maestro di color che sanno* thus became the *qui honeste dicere et sciet et audebit* of Quintilian, and the wisdom of the ancients became fully the rhetor's ware.[37]

Who, then, commands the culture, the philosopher or the orator? Or are they somehow vassals of separate domains, in liege to a higher principle? These were the lines of the quat-

[36] Cf. his *Vita Aristotelis*, in Leonardo Bruni Aretino, *Humanistisch-Philosophische Schriften*, ed. Hans Baron (Leipzig and Berlin: Tuebner, 1928), pp. 43–49. Already Petrarch in his *De ignorantia* (*Opera omnia*, 2.1159), had invoked the authority of Cicero in praising the "sweet and elegant and ornate" character of Aristotle's original Greek, not realizing, as Bruni after him did not either, that Cicero's claim was made in behalf of Aristotle's lost popular writings, not his philosophical works. Cf. P. O. Kristeller, *Eight Philosophers of the Italian Renaissance* (Stanford, Calif.: Stanford University Press, 1964), p. 10.

[37] Since I have so shamelessly borrowed from Jerrold Seigel's chapter on Bruni, it is only right that its closing words be heard in full: "When Bruni died in 1444 he received an elaborate funeral, and was honored by a remarkable marble tomb in the Franciscan church of Santa Croce. According to the inscription, his passing from life caused history to grieve and eloquence to be silent, while none of the Latin or Greek muses could hold back their tears. This monument is testimony to the respect with which his contemporaries regarded Bruni, but it is noteworthy that philosophy was not listed among the mourners" (*Rhetoric and Philosophy in Renaissance Humanism*, p. 136). The significance of the epitaph was first noticed by P. O. Kristeller, "Humanism and Scholasticism," *Studies in Renaissance Thought and Letters* (Rome: Edizioni di storia e letteratura, 1956), p. 572, n. 58. See also Georg Voigt, *Die Wiederbelebung des classischen Altertums*, 2d ed., 2 vols. (Berlin: Reimer, 1880–1881), 1.309–315; 2.165–173.

trocentro debate and they were resumed late in the century in the course of a famous exchange.[38] A letter from Ermolao Barbaro (1454–1493) to Giovanni Pico della Mirandola (1470–1533), casually damning the Scholastics as "dull, rude, uncultured barbarians" whose works would go unremembered, touched the matter off. Having just given six of his young years to Scholastic studies, Pico may rightly have been expected to take offense, as indeed he did. Replying through a fictitious Scholastic in the most polished oratorical form (for which reason many, including Barbaro, have thought him facetious), he gave a ringing defense for the separation of philosophy and rhetoric: "So great is the conflict between the office of the orator and the philosopher that there can be no conflicting greater than theirs. For what else is the task of the rhetor than to lie, to entrap, to circumvent, to practice sleight of hand? . . . Will there be any affinity between this and the philosopher, whose entire endeavor is concerned with knowing the truth and demonstrating it to others?" Oratory "belongs to those whose business is not in the academy but rather in that commonwealth where things done and things said are weighed in a public scale under the eye of one to whom flowers weigh much more than fruits." Thus, "when you approach flutists and citharists, be all ears; when you approach philosophers, call yourself away from the senses, return to your own self in the innermost parts of the soul and the hiding-place of your mind." For "the barbarians have had the god of eloquence not on the tongue but in the heart"; "if eloquence they lacked they did not lack wisdom."[39]

[38] Cf. Quirinus Breen, "Giovanni Pico della Mirandola on the Conflict of Philosophy and Rhetoric," *Journal of the History of Ideas* 13 (1952): 384–426, where the texts of the exchange—both the correspondence between Pico and Barbaro (1485) and the later reply of Philipp Melanchthon (1558)—are translated in full, and Breen's *Christianity and Humanism* (Grand Rapids, Mich.: Eerdmans, 1969), pp. 1–67, where the translations are reprinted. The Latin texts of Pico and Barbaro are included in *Prosatori latini del Quattrocento*, ed. Eugenio Garin (Milan and Naples: Ricciardi, 1952), pp. 804–823, 844–863. Melanchthon's letter is in the *Corpus Reformatorum* 9 (1842), cols. 687–703.

[39] *Prosatori latini*, ed. Garin, pp. 808, 814, 808; Breen, "Pico della Mirandola," pp. 395, 396, 398, 395.

Barbaro's answer was terribly clever and terribly subtle, put in the mouth of a Paduan barbarian who, with the full armature of Scholastic method (and not a little humanistic learning), showed that Pico's defense of their cause would not survive logical scrutiny. He concludes, "Either they have a clear and compelling case for us, or they do not. If they have, let them bring it forth at once, and I will be satisfied; but I do not want the protection of an eloquent man." To which Barbaro adds in his own name: "What else is this desire to defend a barbarous and stupid method of philosophizing than ... attempting to make a grindstone grow, for you expect favor from fellows whom the divine Graces never knew? ... Wherefore I advise you, my Pico, being a land-lubber, do not put out to sea; ... and in making new friends, my good friend, do not forget your old ones."[40]

Earlier in his reply, Barbaro had compared philosophy to "divine beings who have no need of human treasures yet wish to be reverenced and given presents. That is why philosophy not only permits herself to be adorned but even loves it and labors at it."[41] If indeed this was his sense of the matter—and there is no reason to think otherwise—Barbaro thought of the orator's role as one of simple adornment. It was quite otherwise with Philipp Melanchthon (1497–1560), who joined the debate some seventy-five years later. A mark of refinement it may be, but oratory, he insisted, forms the living center of the human universe, not only of society but even of its learning: "There is no use for wisdom unless we can communicate to others the things we have with wisdom deliberated and thought upon ... I call a philosopher one who when he has learned and knows things good and useful for mankind, takes a theory out of academic obscurity and makes it practically useful in public affairs."[42] That was of course, nicely para-

[40] *Prosatori latini*, ed. Garin, p. 862; Breen, "Pico della Mirandola," p. 412.

[41] *Prosatori latini*, ed. Garin, p. 848; Breen, "Pico della Mirandola," p. 406.

[42] *Corpus Reformatorum* 9 (1842), cols. 689, 692; Breen, "Pico della Mirandola," pp. 414, 418.

phrased, Cicero's conception of the ideal orator, and there is some irony in its being set forth in the north just as the influence of humanism was on the wane and a menacing new view of wisdom was about to sweep the Continent.

HUMANISM AND RAMISM

If rhetoricians themselves could be men of wisdom, could not their art give guidance to logic, the philosophers' tool of trade? The reform of logic through rhetoric, a sustained humanist effort that filled much of the fifteenth and sixteenth centuries, was in very large part the polemic underside of the concern to unite wisdom and eloquence.[43] It was a work of many faces, from the *De inventione dialectica* of Rudolf Agricola (1442–1485), which sketched a rhetorical logic in the service of statesmen, to the *In pseudo-dialecticos* of Luis Vives (1492–1540), which set purity of language as a standard of clear thinking, to the *Antibarbarus philosophicus* of Marius Nizolius (1488–1567), which replaced the abstraction of universals with a terminist form of "comprehension." In its extremes, nonetheless, both chronologically and ideologically speaking, it was dominated by two towering figures of the Renaissance era—Lorenzo Valla (1406–1457) and Peter Ramus (1515–1572)—whose works took to task, respectively, the two traits of Scholastic method the humanists found so deadening—its barbarous language and its powerless syllogism.

Among works of an intemperate spirit, Valla's *Dialecticae disputationes contra Aristotelicos* (1439) must surely be accorded a place of privilege. Valla wrote the work to be contentious, and he succeeded admirably. From at least the time of Aristotle, it had been agreed that science could speak a private, even an abstruse, language, for it was largely a private business conducted quietly among experts, whereas oratory needed a colorful and concrete tongue, never straying far from

[43] Cf. Neal W. Gilbert, *Renaissance Concepts of Method* (New York: Columbia University Press, 1960), pp. 74–77; Cesare Vasoli, *La dialettica e la retorica dell'umanesimo* (Milan: Feltrinelli, 1968).

the idiom and common fund of knowledge of the masses. Valla would have none of this arrangement. There is no need for the philosopher to depart "from the paths and pavements frequented by the crowd"; "the people speak better than the philosopher, and the best authors agree with them."[44] *Entitas, quidditas, haecceitas*—Scholastic double talk, the lot of it, and ungrammatical at that; ban all *itas* words.[45] As for the Master himself, Aristotle spent his time in philosophy, not in politics, military affairs, law, medicine, history, poetry, and the other civil disciplines in which the most distinguished men devote themselves; thus he affords no model and deserves no honor.[46] In brief, "philosophy is like a soldier or a tribune under the command of oratory, the queen," and both its method and its language should take their standards from her practice.[47] If the work of Vico, as one great commentator argues plausibly, marked the parting of ways between the sciences and the humanities, that of Valla was the first clear statement of intent.[48]

The concern of Peter Ramus was quite different, and the effect of his work more serious and lasting.[49] He was, of

[44] "At philosophia ac dialectica non solent, ac ne debent quidem recedere ab usitatissima loquendi consuetudine, et quasi a via vulgo trita et silicibus strata" (*Disputationes dialecticae* 1.3; *Opera*, 2 vols. [1540; reprint, Turin: Bottega d'Erasmo, 1962], 1.651). "Melius igitur populus, quam philosophus loquitur: cum quo summi quiquam autores consentiunt" (*Disputationes dialecticae* 1.17; *Opera*, 1.685).

[45] Ibid., 1.4; *Opera*, 1.652–653.

[46] Ibid., preface; *Opera*, 1.644–645: "Non enim in his rebus operam dedit, unde praestantes viri maxime dignoscuntur: aut consiliis publicis, aut administrandis provinciis, aut exercitui ductando, aut caussis agendis, aut medicinae factitandae, aut juri dicundo, aut responsis consultorum aut scribundis historiis, aut poematibus componendis."

[47] "Siquidem philosophia velut miles est aut tribunus sub imperatrice oratione, et ut magnus quidam Tragicus appellat, regina" (*De voluptate, ac de vero bono*, 1.10; *Opera*, 1.907). See also the later version of this work, *De vero falsoque bono*, in the critical edition of Maristella De Panizza Lorch (Bari: Adriatica, 1970), p. 74.

[48] See Isaiah Berlin, "The Divorce between the Sciences and the Humanities," *Salmagundi*, no. 27 (Summer–Fall 1974), pp. 9–39.

[49] On Ramism and its sequels, see Wilbur S. Howell, *Logic and Rhetoric in England, 1500–1700* (Princeton, N.J.: Princeton University Press, 1956),

course, a Frenchman, and for most of his adult years a Huguenot. The context of his thought was not the rhetorically centered culture of Italian humanism—for which indeed he showed some contempt—but the dialectically centered culture of the north. There, at a time when cultural hegemony was slowly being regained for France, a distinctively modern mood was rising. Experimentalism had begun to take force, vernacular in the schools was now being pushed, and curricular change was again being argued. The need for new, more coherent textbooks was plain, and a new book-printing industry stood ready to lend a hand.

Like Agricola, his great Dutch forerunner, Ramus was disgusted with Scholastic logic and keen on its reform. It was a dry, pedantic, wasted form of reasoning, he thought, one that so rarely led to anything new. Instead of being the clean, efficient art of the natural workings of reason, dialectic had become overgrown with artifices and devices, and gave entirely too much attention to subjects beyond its scope. But such was the problem with the entire liberal arts curriculum, especially logic and rhetoric. These arts clung foolishly to Aristotle's claim for two modes of argumentation—one for science and another for opinion—and thus their instruction overlapped, duplicating one another's efforts. In fact, Ramus argued, the matter was quite plain: Dialectic is the art of disputing well, and thus should train in discovery (*inventio*) and arrangement (*dispositio*); rhetoric is the art of speaking well, and thus should train in style (*elocutio*) and delivery (*pronuntiatio*). Grammar, as the art of correct speech, would teach etymology and syntax.[50] To develop a coherent liberal

---

pp. 146–281; and the magisterial work of Walter J. Ong, *Ramus, Method, and the Decay of Dialogue* (Cambridge, Mass.: Harvard University Press, 1958).

[50] Cf. *P. Rami Scholarum rhetoricarum, seu Quaestionum Brutinarum in Oratorem Ciceronis, libri XX*, ed. Joan. Piscator (Frankfurt, 1593), pp. 13–14: "Duo vero sunt universa deorum munera hominibus tributa, unde alia fere omnia profecta sunt, ratio et oratio; rationis doctrina, Dialectica est: ideoque quicquid rationis ac mentis propriu[m] fuerit, quod sine ratione tractari et exerceri [non] possit, id proprie dialecticae arti attribuito. Rationis

arts curriculum one need only proceed from these definitions and through a largely dichotomous *methodus a generalibus ad specialia* work out their implications.

Together with an associate, Omer Talon, who worked on the rhetoric while he rewrote dialectic, Ramus did just that. His *Dialecticae institutiones* appeared in 1543, just before Talon's *Institutiones oratoriae* (1545), and these gave way in turn, after much rethinking and recasting, to two parallel works of 1555—the *Dialectique*, which Ramus cast into Latin as *Dialecticae libri duo* the following year, and the *Rhétorique française*, Foclin's French version of Talon's *Rhetorica* (5th edition, 1552), which Ramus brought out as *Rhetoricae libri duo* in 1562, the year of Talon's death. The *Dialectique* had a spectacular success, having 250 printings over the next hundred years. Separately and in French, the *Rhétorique* did far less well, but its several Latin versions, often combined with the *Dialecticae* to form a complete *Organum dialecticum et rhetoricum*, had a very wide currency indeed.[51]

The reform of learning had been Ramus's intent, but his sole achievement was a bit of curricular tidiness, and even this was purchased at a great price. His attempt to enliven logical invention through a systematization of the ancient *to-*

---

due partes sunt, Inventio consiliorum et argumentorum: eorumque judicium in dispositione enuntiati, syllogismi, et methodi: dispositionis umbra quaedam est memoria: quoniam ista omnia in hominibus mutis et omni orationis facultate carentibus insunt. Nam et res cogitant et judicant et meminerunt; et omnes omnino homines haec aliquando tacendo melius quam dicendo faciunt. Tres itaque partes illae, Inve[n]tio inquam, Dispositio, Memoria, dialecticae artis sunto. Orationis laudes ad istam regulam metiamur; et Gramaticae primum suas partes assignemus. Puritas autem sermonis est et elegantia: quae perspicitur in singulis verbis ex etymologia, in conjunctis ex syntaxi. Hic Gramaticae fundus totus et proprius esto: Dialectica hic, neque Rhetorica quicquam suum ducito. Quid ergo? quid rhetoricae relinquetur? non elocutio solum in tropis et figuris (quam tamen solam his putas oratoris esse propriam) sed actio."

[51] The same is true of the *Petri Rami Scholae in tres primas liberales artes*, a composite of his *Scholae grammaticae*, his *Quaestiones Brutinae in Oratorem Ciceronis*, and his *Animadversiones in Organum Aristotelis*. The complicated history of the texts of Ramus and Talon is traced with great skill by Walter J. Ong, *Ramus and Talon Inventory* (Cambridge, Mass.: Harvard University Press, 1958).

pica may have had some bearing, in the manner of Francis Bacon, on the climate of experimentation, but his concept of method, to which he devoted so many lines, was nowhere near the mathematical procedure that would soon define the new science. In transferring to logic the rhetorical offices of discovery and arrangement, on the other hand, he deprived rhetoric of its remaining claim to be a logic of public discourse. Without the task of finding and judging its own arguments, without the need to examine a rhetorical situation, sifting its elements to find the most telling and effective, oratory became a purely literary enterprise, and its art a matter of gestures and words. Once an art of argumentation, rhetoric was now to be a theory of ornate form. "In this economy," writes Ong of the sequels of Ramism,

> where everything having to do with speech tends to be in one way or another metamorphosed in terms of structure and vision, the rhetorical approach to life—the way of Isocrates and Cicero and Quintilian and Erasmus, and of the Old and New Testaments—is sealed off into a cul-de-sac. The attitude toward speech has changed. Speech is no longer a medium in which the human mind and sensibility lives. It is resented, rather, as an accretion to thought, hereupon imagined as ranging noiseless concepts or "ideas" in a silent field of mental space. Here the perfect rhetoric would be to have no rhetoric at all. Thought becomes a private, or even an anti-social enterprise.[52]

RAMUS AND THE CARTESIANS

In dismembering rhetoric, Ramus had offered a consolation: Invention and disposition, though disjoined from rhetoric, would be set more ambitious tasks, reforming the logic of the Schools and participating in the search for a new method. The rise of Galilean science, formalized by Descartes into a novel theory of mathematical method, utterly destroyed this comfort. No less than Ramus did Descartes (1596–1650) believe in a single method for the whole of science and learning,

[52] *Ramus, Method, and the Decay of Dialogue*, p. 291.

but in place of the cumbersome offerings of the topical categories he insisted on the purer data of clear and distinct ideas, conceived on a mathematical model. Science consists not in reducing phenomena to their contrary qualities, but in showing, deductively, that what is as yet sought or unknown (*quaesitum*) is necessarily contained in simpler knowns (*data*) and finally in fundamental mathematical relationships, intuitively assured. In the *Regulae* (1628) of Descartes, as in its more generalized statement in the *Discours de la méthode* (1637), the effort of centuries to replace a logic of classification with a logic of functional analysis achieved its final success, and science was set on a new course.[53]

The work that interpreted Descartes to the world and showed the implications of his ideas in logic and rhetoric was the *Art de penser* (1662) of Antoine Arnauld (1612–1694), a book better known as the Port Royal Logic.[54] If ever a thinker knew his own mind, it was Arnauld. Introducing the work's second edition (1664), Arnauld defended the claim that his Logic was in fact a complete art of thinking, a guide to all activities of mind, and insisted that the work combined with the precepts of logic everything that was useful from the other sciences:

Take rhetoric, for example, a subject that we felt contributed little toward thought, expression, or embellishment. The mind furnishes sufficient thought; custom suggests expressions; and as for figures and ornaments, these are all too abundant anyhow. Rhetoric's only practical use is as an aid in avoiding certain unfortunate manners of writing and speaking, especially in avoiding a certain artificial style replete with false and exaggerated thoughts and with forced metaphors—the worst of all styles.[55]

---

[53] The *Discours de la méthode* and the *Regulae ad directionem ingenii* are contained in volumes 6 and 10, respectively, of the *Oeuvres de Descartes*, ed. Charles Adam and Paul Tannery, 12 vols. (Paris: Cerf, 1897–1910). On the gradual development of the logic of science, see Ernst Cassirer, *Das Erkenntnisproblem in der Philosophie und Wissenschaft der neueren Zeit*, 3d ed. (Berlin: Bruno Cassirer, 1922), 1.399–418, 463–464.

[54] *La logique; ou, L'art de penser*, ed. Pierre Clair and François Girbal (Paris: Presses universitaires de France, 1965).

[55] *L'art de penser*, p. 29; trans. James Dickoff and Patricia James, *The Art of Thinking* (Indianapolis, Ind.: Bobbs-Merrill, 1964), p. 22.

What then of the Categories of Aristotle and the Topics of Cicero? Have they no role, as Ramus so desperately argued, in finding ideas and developing lines of argument? "To speak the truth, [Categories] are in themselves of very little use," and may even hinder judgment, for they "are regarded as being established by reason and by truth, rather than as entirely arbitrary," and their study "accustoms men to be satisfied with mere words."[56] As for the Topics, "the very limited use which the world has made of this method is a clear proof of the method's otioseness. . . . We must realize that this abundance of thought sought after by the method of the Topics has very little advantage. Most men do not suffer from too few thoughts but rather from too many; their discourses are all too cluttered."[57] One imagines Arnauld, *ex impossibili*, leafing through the *New Science*.

The Ramists protested, of course, as did the Jesuits. Père Pomey's Latin manual, *Novus candidatus rhetoricae* (1659), held its own in the schools, teaching class after class the fineries of ornate speaking, while in the vernacular, Pomey's confreres presented elegant cases for rhetoric as part of the *belles-lettres*—the fashionable new term for what were, in the main, the *studia humanitatis* of old. Doubtless, in reply to that most famous of all Port Royalists, Pascal (1623–1662), whose *L'esprit géometrique* (1655) had told of two avenues by which opinions are received into the soul—the understanding and the will (the latter being "base, ignoble, and irrelevant" except in matters of divine truth)—René Rapin (1621–1687) argued in his *Discours sur la comparaison de l'éloquence de Démosthène et de Cicéron* (1670) that there are indeed two rhetorics, one of the mind and understanding, best represented by Demosthenes, the other of the heart and will, of which Cicero was the master, the former having perhaps a more lasting effect, but the latter being more immediately moving. Unlike

[56] *L'art de penser*, p. 51; *Art of Thinking*, pp. 43–44.
[57] *L'art de penser*, pp. 235–236; *Art of Thinking*, p. 239.

Fénelon (and Vico!), he preferred Cicero.[58] His colleague
Dominique Bouhours (1628–1702) later wrote a "thornless
logic ... and a short and easy rhetoric," a series of four
dialogues entitled *La manière de bien penser dans les ouvrages
de l'esprit* (1687), which held that thoughts, besides being
true, needed also sublimity, delicacy, and agreeableness, while
one's style should be plain, clear, and intelligible. But it was
the non-Jesuit classicist and one-time rector of the University
of Paris, Charles Rollin (1661–1741)—whose many volumes
on the histories of ancient civilizations bear so many formal
resemblances to Vico's own *New Science*—who showed the
endurance of the belles-lettres tradition of rhetoric with his
immensely popular *De la manière d'enseigner et d'étudier les
belles lettres, par rapport à l'esprit et au coeur* (4 volumes,
1726–1728), a full volume of which is given to rhetorical
precepts, composition, and study of the great authors.[59]

Even so, it was not these writings but the starker works of

---

[58] This discussion in France prompted the biting comments of Vico in the
De Italorum sapientia, Opere 1.181, a passage that just follows his quip on
the use of the geometrical method in civil discourse, which I cited toward
the beginning of Chapter 1. Vico favors Demosthenes, not because of his
spare, geometric method (*At hercule!*), but because he embodies, for Vico,
the supremely sagacious orator who will make now this point, now that,
seemingly unrelated, only to draw them all together in the end and bring
down, like a thunderbolt, the compelling force of his argument. See also the
Vici vindiciae, Opere 3.307, and the "De chriis," *Opere di Giambattista
Vico*, ed. Fausto Nicolini (Milan: Ricciardi, 1953), p. 958.

[59] A comparative study of Vico (1668–1744) and Rollin (1661–1741),·
whose pedagogical and philological interests were so similar, has not to my
knowledge been undertaken. Rollin, of course, had the more orderly mind
and was more a historian than a philosopher, as seen in the thirteen volumes
of his *Histoire ancienne des Egyptiens, des Carthaginois, des Assyriens, des
Babyloniens, des Medes et des Perses, des Macédoniens et des Grecs* (Paris,
1731–1738) and the nine volumes of his *Histoire romaine* (Paris, 1738–
1741). Yet anyone doubting Vico's originality may compare the premises
Rollin set forth in the preface to his *Histoire ancienne* with the *degnità* stated
at the beginning of the *New Science*. I know of no evidence of Rollin having
known that work, whose editions of 1725 and 1730 were not widely circulated. The copy of the 1730 edition that Costa has shown to be available
to French intellectuals through the library of Falconet did not arrive in Paris
until 1732–1733, by which time Rollin's first volume was already in print
(see Gustavo Costa, "Vico, Camille Falconet e gli Enciclopedisti," *Bollettino
del Centro di Studi vichiani* 3 [1973]: 147–162).

Fénelon and Lamy that survived their age. Though in essence a Ramist work, the *De l'art de parler* (1675) of Bernard Lamy (1640–1715) breathed the spirit of Port Royal; even its title suggests Arnauld, and Lamy, an Oratorian, seems not to have discouraged the association. Its four parts focus wholly on language: grammar and usage, the tropes and figures, speaking and reciting, and style. Though a discrete appendix on the five Ciceronian arts is added, it contains one of the sharpest attacks of the day on the use of the "places" in argument; doubtless fecund, their fecundity is nonetheless inconvenient, for if the orator understands his subject he can resolve any difficulty without the topics, and if he does not, he will use them only to make his talk tedious and long-winded. The *Dialogues sur l'éloquence* of François de Salignac Fénelon (1651–1715), written late in the century but not published until 1718, were of much the same mind, but their subject of special concern—pulpit oratory—gave them a particular urgency. In the spirit of Plato and Augustine, Fénelon held that the subject of an oration should be truths the orator did not need to find—"nonartistic," in the technical phrase—and should be cast in a simple structure delivered in a plain style; only if one's words moved men to see the hidden truths of their being could the orator be called eloquent. For an age with its back to disputation, looking to pure reason for its guidance and its truth, this was as worthy an ideal as rhetoric could hope to have stated on its behalf.[60]

Fénelon was read in England, as were Lamy, Rollin, and

[60] Pulpit rhetoric was the subject of much debate in France at the time, and in one of the finer ironies of the era we find none other than Antoine Arnauld (*Réflexions sur l'éloquence*, 1700) taking the side of Balthasar Gilbert against Guibaud Dubois and François Lamy (the Benedictine, not Bernard, the Oratorian), defending the use of imagination and emotion in sacred oratory.

On the general subject of rhetoric in seventeenth-century France, see P. Kuentz, "Bibliographie pour l'étude de la rhétorique," *XVIIᵉ Siècle* 80–81 (1978): 133–142, with a "Glossaire" by Jacques Morel, pp. 144–146; Peter France, *Rhetoric and Truth in France: Descartes to Diderot* (Oxford: At the Clarendon Press, 1972); and the excellent chapter in Wilbur S. Howell, *Eighteenth-Century British Logic and Rhetoric* (Princeton, N.J.: Princeton University Press, 1971), pp. 503–535.

the others, but the discussion in that country on philosophy and rhetoric was entirely overshadowed by the work of its erstwhile lord chancellor, Francis Bacon (1561–1626). A man who has suffered much from his reputation in the history of science, Bacon was at base a kind of British Peter Ramus, above all concerned with "clearing away the rubble of ages," canvassing the deficiencies of learning, and getting on with the task of "filling up" its parts. Though clearly attuned to the new experimentalism ("nature under constraints," as he called it), he had few clues as to its conduct; his *Novum Organum* (1620), in the end, was the tired instrument of the Schools. His legacy, rather, is the magisterial *On the Advancement of Learning* (1605), later enlarged and rewritten in Latin as *De dignitate et augmentis scientiarum* (1623), a work that Vico took very much to heart.[61]

The place Bacon finds for rhetoric in that work—a full-scale map of learning and its needs—is a niche called the "Illustration of Discourse" (6.3), itself but a part of the art of "transmitting," which in turn is the fourth part (after discovering, judging, and retaining) of Logic, the doctrine of reason and understanding (5.1; 6.1–3). This ordering of the subject—purely as a theory of communication—is fully Ramist, as is his treatment of the Topics under the heading of logical invention (5.2–3). What is not conventional is his insistence that invention is of two kinds—that of arguments (discovering what we already know), for which the Topics offer ample service, and that of the "arts" or branches of learning, on which the whole of current Logic is mute:

That this part of knowledge is wanting stands plainly confessed. For in the first place, Logic says nothing, nor takes any thought, about the invention of arts, whether mechanical or what are termed liberal, or about eliciting the works of the one or the axioms of the other;

---

[61] The references that follow are to the English version of the *De augmentis*, taken largely from Bacon's own *On the Advancement of Learning*, in volumes 4 and 5 of *The Works of Francis Bacon*, ed. James Spedding, Robert Leslie Ellis, and Douglas Denon Heath (1857–1874; reprint, New York: Garrett, 1968).

... Moreover, they who have written about the first inventors of things or the origins of sciences have celebrated chance rather than art, and represented brute beasts, quadrupeds, birds, fishes, serpents, as the doctors of sciences, rather than men.... And if you like better, according to the Greeks, to ascribe the first inventions to men, yet you would not say that Prometheus was led by speculation to the discovery of fire, or that when he first struck the flint he expected the spark; but rather that he lighted on it by accident, and (as they say) stole it from Jupiter. (5.2)

Bacon goes on to argue, of course, that the method of induction, which he has laid out in detail in his *Novum Organum*, is the way to new knowledge, the path that men have naturally followed in making their discoveries and constructing their devices. Nor is there need, he continues, to discuss judgment in induction apart from that of discovery, "for here the same action of the mind which discovers the thing in question judges it; and the operation is not performed by help of any middle term, but directly, almost in the same manner as by the sense" (5.4). All this, he says, he has made plain in his *New Organon*. It is doubtful that Vico truly grasped the issues of that book, though he does refer to it on occasion; these chapters of the *De augmentis* alone—which could rightly be quoted in full— with their talk of work and experiment, of imagination and ingenuity, of the simultaneity of insight and judgment, were sufficient to set him thinking, and they enlarged his mind in a way that few other notions of his forebears did.[62]

Bacon differed from the Ramists in another crucial way. Rhetoric is indeed the art of communicating the truths of reason, he held, but not all audiences are the same, much less

[62] See, for example, the section "De certa facultate sciendi" in the *De Italorum sapientia, Opere* 1.180–185, which is quite unintelligible apart from these chapters in Bacon, being so largely a restatement of their principal ideas. In the many pages written on the relation of Vico to Bacon, including the sparkling study by Enrico De Mas, "Bacone e Vico," *Filosofia* 10 (1959): 505–559, emphasis has fallen on the mature Vico, whose borrowings were less direct than those of his earlier writings. As Lord Verulam would say, I put down the study of the relation of Bacon and the early Vico as a major deficiency of learning.

the subjects of discourse. "For the 'one and only method,' with its distribution of everything into two members, it is needless to speak of it; for it was a kind of cloud that over-shadowed knowledge for awhile and blew over" (6.2). Thus Bacon rejects the cornerstone of Ramism and sets in its place a diversity of method, governed by a principle well known to students of Vico: "The method used should be according to the subject-matter which is handled" (6.2).[63] Moreover, man is not a disembodied mind; he is a tangle of reason and passions struggling for control of the will. Imagination is the swing faculty; if it can be allied with reason the day will be carried for the good. It is the noble task of the orator, through the ornament of words, to forge this alliance. Thus "Rhetoric is subservient to the imagination, as Logic is to the under-standing; and the duty and office of Rhetoric, if it be deeply looked into, is no other than to apply and recommend the dictates of reason to imagination, in order to excite the ap-petite and will" (6.3).

The Royal Society thought otherwise. Though founded to honor Bacon's principles, it was quick to forget his subtleties.[64] When fellows of the society, in 1663, wrote up its definitive charter of incorporation, they were careful to say that in all scientific reports made by its members, "the matter of fact shall be barely stated, without any prefaces, apologies, or rhetorical flourishes; and entered so in the Register-book." Thus Thomas Spratt could report in his history of the Royal Society of 1667 "a constant Resolution, to reject all the am-plifications, digressions, and swellings of style; to return back to the primitive purity, and shortness, when men deliver'd so

[63] "Methodus sit subjectae materiae quae tractatur accommoda," which comes out, significantly transmuted, in Vico's famous axiom: "Le dottrine debbono cominciare da quando cominciano le materie che trattano" (*Scienza nuova seconda, Opere* 4, §314). This axiom, which has its roots in Aristotle (*Eth. Nic.*, 1.1–4), is not among those treated by De Mas, "Bacone e Vico," pp. 533–536.

[64] On the Royal Society and its view of rhetoric, see Howell, *Eighteenth-Century British Logic and Rhetoric*, pp. 448–502.

many *things*, almost in an equal number of *words*."[65] Had not the great Thomas Hobbes (1588–1679) in his *Leviathan* (1651) shown that speech is nothing but the marks of our thoughts and the signs of their connections, there to "transfer our mental discourse, into verbal; or the train of our thoughts, into a train of words" (1.4)? "The light of human minds," he had written, "is perspicuous words, but by exact definitions first snuffed, and purged from ambiguity; *reason* is the *pace*; increase of *science*, the *way*; and the benefit of mankind, the *end*. And, on the contrary, metaphors, and senseless and ambiguous words, are like *ignes fatui*; and reasoning upon them is wandering amongst innumerable absurdities; and their end, contention and sedition, or contempt" (1.5). As for the "wit" so celebrated by the rhetors, it is nothing but a kind of "celerity of imagining" and the "steady direction" of thought to some approved end. It is central to poetry, useful in adorning history, and indispensable in those hortatives and pleadings in which disguise, not truth, is required; but in science or any rigorous search for truth, where "judgment does all," it is fully without place (1.8).[66]

If Hobbes's meaning had been in any way unclear, it could no longer be at century's end when the position was restated in bristling prose by the society's own John Locke (1632–1704). Doubtless he spoke for his entire generation, for the philosophers, the savants, and the men of the new learning if not for the masses, the barristers, the rhetoricians, and the divines, when he gave these assessments in his imposing *Essay concerning Human Understanding* (1689):

Since wit and fancy find easier entertainment in the world than dry truth and real knowledge, figurative speeches, and allusion in language, will hardly be admitted, as an imperfection or abuse of it . . . If we would speak of things as they are, we must allow that all the art of rhetoric, besides order and clearness; all the artificial and figurative application of words eloquence hath invented, are for noth-

---

[65] Ibid., pp. 481, 486.
[66] *The English Works of Thomas Hobbes*, ed. William Molesworth (London: Bohn, 1839), 3.19–20, 36–37, 56–59.

ing else but to insinuate wrong ideas, move the passions, and thereby mislead the judgment; and so indeed are perfect cheats. (3.10.34)

Men who have a great deal of wit, and prompt memories, have not always the clearest judgment or deepest reason. For *wit* lying most in the assemblage of ideas, and putting those together with quickness and variety, wherein can be found any resemblance or congruity, thereby to make up pleasant pictures and agreeable visions in the fancy; *judgment*, on the contrary, lies quite on the other side, in separating carefully, one from another, ideas wherein can be found the least difference, thereby to avoid being misled by similitude, and by affinity to take one thing for another. This is a way of proceeding quite contrary to metaphor and allusion; wherein for the most part lies that entertainment and pleasantry of wit, which strikes so lively on the fancy, and therefore is so acceptable to all people, because its beauty appears at first sight, and there is required no labour of thought to examine what truth or reason there is in it. The mind, without looking any further, rests satisfied with the agreeable mass of the picture and the gaiety of the fancy. And it is a kind of affront to go about to examine it, by the severe rules of truth and good reason; whereby it appears that it consists in something that is not perfectly conformable to them. (2.11.2)[67]

So it was that inventive wit, taken so deftly from rhetoric by Peter Ramus, ended her career with logic, a discarded mistress. Or was Pope's metaphor the better?

> For wit and judgement often are at strife
> Though meant each other's aid like man and wife.[68]

THE AGE OF SPLENDOR AND WIT

Stolen, then jilted by logic, rhetoric's "logical" arts of invention and arrangement had a modest career in the seventeenth century. Their companion arts of *verba*, meanwhile, namely *elocutio* and *pronuntiatio* (*memoria* having become

[67] *An Essay concerning Human Understanding*, ed. Alexander Campbell Fraser, 2 vols. (Oxford: At the Clarendon Press, 1894).

[68] *An Essay on Criticism* (1711), lines 81–83. Wit, I am reminded by Donald Kelley, was associated with logic in the sixteenth century, *witcraft* being an old word for logic.

part of Ramus's *dispositio)*, rather enjoyed their freedom. *Pronuntiatio*, that least likely of rhetoric's traditional offices, achieved stature as a vigorous, fully independent art in the course of the so-called elocutionary movement, the unfortunate label (having nothing to do with *elocutio* or style) under which British and eventually American authors, with French inspiration, developed conventional instruction on voice and gesture into a full-scale science of oral interpretation.[69] Cicero had indeed called delivery the "dominant factor in oratory" and cited Demosthenes' opinion that it is the first, second, and third most important thing about speaking (*De or.* 3.56.213). Yet the few pages he gave to the subject are a pale shadow of the elocutionists' tomes, and even Demosthenes would have blushed at the care they took in providing precepts and examples for good speaking. If the *Vacationes Autumnales sive De perfecta oratoris actione et pronunciatione* (1620) of Louis de Cressolles (1568–1634), 353 of whose 706 pages treat of gestures and expressions, marked the extent to which the subject of *corpus* could be elucidated, that of *vox* received its consummate handling in the *Course of Lectures on Elocution* (1762) of Thomas Sheridan (1719–1788), six of whose seven discourses are occupied with this subject.

The elocutionists may have claimed that in naming their art as they did, they were but indicating the unity of language, voice, and gesture necessary to any adequate theory of speech and drama. In point of fact, through an unfortunate synecdoche, elocution came in time to be seen, above all in Britain and America, as the whole of rhetoric, a confusion that some of the elocutionists took no pains to avoid.[70] Throughout continental Europe meanwhile, above all in its Catholic countries, a similar confusion had come to surround *elocutio* in

[69] See the chapter in Howell, *Eighteenth-Century British Logic and Rhetoric*, pp. 143–256. In naming their art, the elocutionists relinquished the Anglicized version of the traditional Latin title for delivery, *pronuntiatio*, which by this time had come to stand for correct phonation, in favor of a variant of *elocutio*, thus avoiding one confusion by creating another.

[70] Ibid., pp. 233, 243.

its technical sense, style. In part this occurred through the development of an elaborate, exaggerated form of oratory to which scholars have applied a term from art history—*baroque*—and in part it occurred through an appropriation by stylists of that facility of "ingenuity" or "wit" traditionally used in the discovery of rhetorical arguments. In both these developments, related and frequently linked, we have the occasion for that scruff rejection of wit and eloquence for which John Locke is the premier spokesman, as well as for that effort of rear-guard rescue whose effects are so startling in the work of Giambattista Vico.

Though its sources were many, baroque eloquence may surely be traced to the reforming spirit of the Council of Trent (1545–1563), whose decrees both directed and implied a rededication to the mysterious and the spiritual, and to the reforming zeal of the Society of Jesus, whose members pressed the renewal in all forms of life and culture. The tendency to excess so plainly manifest in the newly built churches of the day was equally to be found in the language, emotions, and style of delivery of the sermons spoken within. In secular rhetoric as well, whose paramount concern had long been language and style, force of argument as a mark of eloquence was largely replaced by full and ornate expression. The Jesuit *Ratio studiorum*, drafted in 1586 and revised in 1599, established in all the society's schools a rigorous cycle of preuniversity linguistic studies—three years of Latin and Greek grammar, followed by a year of prerhetorical literary study (*humanitas*) and a year of rhetoric proper.[71] During the final year of this basic training, daily dictations, repetitions, and exercises, filled out with monthly assignments of poems and

---

[71] Cf. *Ratio studiorum et Institutiones scholasticae Societatis Jesu per Germaniam olim vigentes*, ed. G. M. Pachtler (Osnabrück: Biblio-Verlag, 1968), 2.144–148, 155–200, 350–449, esp. 398–413. In the draft of 1568, the entire lower school is said to be concerned with the *studia humanitatis*, defined as embracing grammar, history, poetry, and rhetoric; by 1599, this term is reserved for the year of literary studies that follows grammar and precedes rhetoric, though the principles of these arts continue to figure in its curriculum—those of grammar being summarized, those of rhetoric introduced.

orations and an annual program of public performances (declamations, lectures, poetry readings, an occasional drama or mock trial), were set out with studied precision to ensure, by year's end, a "perfect eloquence" in oratory and poetry, one that would serve both utility and beauty of expression (*quae . . . nec utilitati solum servit, sed etiam ornatui indulget*). This was to be done in part by memorizing precepts and absorbing erudition—orations and poems during the week, history and more "recondite" matters on Saturdays and holidays.[72] But mainly it was to be done through practice and exercise: imitating a passage in a poet or orator; describing a scene or an action; saying the same thing in a new way or converting one poetic form into another; translating Greek into Latin or Latin into Greek; composing epigrams, inscriptions, and epitaphs; excerpting felicitous phrases from the ancients; finding for a given subject the right rhetorical figure.

These were all exercises suggested in the *Ratio*, and they were none of them, arguably, at odds with the classical aims of Ciceronian rhetoric that the Jesuits sought to embrace. As the seventeenth century wore on, however, the manuals of rhetoric that came into use—Père Pomey's *Novus candidatus rhetoricae* (1659) and later Père Jouvancy's *Candidatus rhetoricae* (1711)—show clearly what had become of classroom instruction. The topical *loci*, which once helped an orator find possible lines of argument, were now a kind of rhetorical checklist from which one culled as much material as possible. Similarly, the art of amplification, which in Quintilian (*Inst.* 8.4) defined ways to intensify an effect by making a subject appear more impressive, was now used simply to make a speech longer. "We are said to amplify something," writes Jouvancy, "when we express in words as many things as it

---

[72] Among the *recondita* that may be taught (always "within measure") are hieroglyphs, emblems, epigrams, epitaphs, odes, elegies, heroic poems, tragedies, information on the Roman and Athenian senates and militaries, and on their gardens, homes, clothing, dining habits, triumphal marches, and sibyls—the sort of thing, in short, that one finds strewn throughout the *Scienza nuova*. Cf. *Ratio studiorum*, ed. Pachtler, 2.411.

contains or have an affinity with it."[73] In his manual, amplification is given a section of its own, forming a bridge between
those on *inventio, dispositio,* and *elocutio,* and one entitled
Progymnasmata, an adaptation of Aphthonius concerned
principally with exercises in enlarging a theme. The magnil-
oquence of Cicero, always the Jesuit model, thus loses its
moorings in argumentation, and rhetoric becomes a mere theory of ornate form.

Since the Jesuit program was widely copied, we may assume
that many if not most of the European youth of the century,
including the many who did not proceed to higher learning,
were formed in this manner. The formalism it implied, however, was not nearly so troublesome as that of the popular
subrhetorical literature of the day and that of the burgeoning
poetic and aesthetic theories that attempted to construe it.
The phenomenon was truly European in reach, though the
events that provoked it and the names by which it was known
differed from culture to culture. In England it was known as
euphuism, after the didactic romance *Euphues* of John Lyly
(1554?–1606), a work that had much currency among the
courtiers of the time. In Spain, where the poetry of conceits
of Luis de Góngora (1561–1627) was in vogue, it was known
variously as *gongorismo* or *conceptismo,* while in Italy its
name was *marinismo,* after the lyrical poet Giambattista Marino (1569–1625), or simply *secentismo,* after the period. And
in the France of Louis XIII, where a little practice and a reading
of René Bary's *L'esprit de cour, ou Les conversations galantes,
divisées en cent dialogues* (1662) or a viewing of Gabriel Gilbert's *La vraye et fausse prétieuse* (1660) could turn any unschooled woman into a *femme précieuse* fit for polite society
in the fashionable salons, it was called *préciosité.* By whatever

---

[73] "Amplificare quidpiam dicimur, quoties ea quae insunt in ipsa re, aut
affinitatem habent cum illa, exprimimus dicendo" (*Candidatus rethoricae*
[Paris, 1714], p. 137). He writes further on that page: "Cum Isocrate, artem
illam intelligo, qua ex parvis ampla (unde amplificationis nomen deductum
est), ex angustis extensa et lata (ex quo dilatatio nuncupatur), ex compressis
diffusa et explicata fiunt."

name, it was a phenomenon wholly concerned with style, one that sought to say (or do) things in an unusual or unnatural way, and thus to surprise, astonish, or dazzle. The style could be elaborate and intricate, or it could be sharp, concise, and witty; but always it aimed to be subtle and tense, affected and artificial, to take the plain and simple statement and turn it into language (or gestures) that strained syntax and imagery.

To name the phenomenon *baroque*, with all the associations that that word evokes, is perhaps shortsighted and can even mislead, and thus such critics as E. R. Curtius choose simply to call it *Mannerism*, a style of thought and writing that, like the classicism to which it is counterpart, is a constant in European literature.[74] Curtius also finds that we must speak of the Mannerism of this period as one of both form and substance, concerned equally with conceiving and writing, thinking and speaking. This is certainly true of the tradition of Spanish and Italian writers whose collective works at midcentury form a veritable canon of the theory of conceitism (*conceptismo, concettismo*). Though the *Examen de Ingenios* (1575) of Juan Huarte (1529?–1588) is sometimes invoked as precedent, it is the *Agudeza y arte de ingenio* (1642; 2d edition, 1649) of Baltasar Gracián (1601–1658) that is its classical and most popular statement, while in Italy the *Delle acutezze* (1639) of Matteo Pellegrini (1595–1652), the *Trattato dello stile e del dialogo* (1646) of Sforza Pallavicino (1607–1667), and the *Il cannocchiale aristotelico* (1654) of Emmanuele Tesauro (1592–1675) are its best representatives.[75] The

---

[74] *European Literature of the Latin Middle Ages*, trans. Trask, pp. 273–301.

[75] The full title of Pellegrini's work is *Delle acutezze, che altrimenti spiriti, vivezze, e concetti volgarmente si appellano trattato.* The editions of Tesauro's work carry various subtitles, that of its fourth (1664) being *Idea dell'arguta et ingeniosa elocutione, che serve à tutta l'arte oratoria, lapidaria, et simbolica esaminata co' principij del divino Aristotele.*

Basic reading on the theorists of conceit are still Croce's *I trattatisti italiani del "concettismo" e Baltasar Gracián*, Memoria letta all' Accademia Pontaniana (Naples: A. Tessitore, 1899), reprinted in *Problemi di estetica e contributi alla storia dell'estetica italiana* (Bari: Laterza, 1910), pp. 309–345, and his *Storia dell' età barocca in Italia* (Bari: Laterza, 1929). A more generous

object of praise in these works is the conceit—the refined idea and subtle expression so different from everyday thought and patter. Not of one form, conceits must nonetheless always be novel; they must taunt and challenge, and thus frequently are expressed as striking, intricate metaphors or as brief, witty remarks. At their best, they exhibit a quality of sharpness or acuteness (*agudeza, acutezza*) that can only come from an alert, imaginative mind, one with a well-honed facility for seeing connections between separate and apparently unrelated things. This is the facility of wit (*ingenio, ingegno*).

The idea of *ingegno* occupies so large a place in the development of Vico's science that we will need to return to it, as well as to the authors who speak of it (for it is a very old idea), in the chapter that follows. Here it is enough to notice how it caught the fancy of the seventeenth century. "The word 'wit,' *ingegno*," writes Croce with contempt, "was now repeated much more frequently than in the preceding century; wit was hailed as presiding genius of Rhetoric; its 'vivacities' were lauded to the skies; '*belli ingegni*' was a phrase seized upon by the French, who rendered it as '*esprit*' or '*beaux esprits.*' " Croce finds in it an apt theory for the "empty style" of the century's "decadent authors."[76] This is of less interest to us than that it was a way of life held up to its age as ideal, for that could only mean, for most, a complete estrangement between thought and language. Discretion may be taught, perhaps even discernment, and one may learn the rules of logic and clear reasoning. But one either is or is not imaginative, has wit or does not have it, sees connections or misses them utterly. To expect of the age that its every participant

---

view of the theorists is offered in two excellent papers by Joseph A. Mazzeo, "A Seventeenth-Century Theory of Metaphysical Poetry" and "Metaphysical Poetry and the Poetic of Correspondence," *Renaissance and Seventeenth-Century Studies* (New York: Columbia University Press; London: Routledge and Kegan Paul, 1964), pp. 29–59. See also the monograph of Klaus-Peter Lange, *Theoretiker der literarischen Manierismus: Tesauros und Pellegrinis Lehre von der "acutezza" oder von der Macht der Sprache*, Humanistische Bibliothek, Abhandlungen, vol. 4 (Munich: Fink, 1968).

[76] *Aesthetic* (rev. ed., 1922), pp. 189–190.

both think and speak "acutely" was more than it could endure. The brightest did so masterfully while the rest collapsed into affectation, all quite possessed with the exercise itself.

We have our summary in the Cyrano of Rostand. It is Paris in 1640, the Hôtel de Bourgogne, where the popular Montfleury is to give a theatrical performance in the courtyard. Citizens, tradesmen, musketeers gather, flowers and refreshments are sold, pickpockets work the crowd, the *précieuses* take their seats in the boxes above, while the fops strut about below, ogling and scheming. One of them, Christian, despairs upon seeing the lovely Roxanne: "I'm afraid she's too experienced, too subtly cultured, for a plain and timid soldier such as I am. I have no claim to wit; no courage to address her. I'm bewildered by this fancy language." As the lights go down, Cyrano suddenly appears, hat plumed, nose gleaming, drives the pompous Montfleury from the stage, and when the impresario complains of lost revenues, tosses him a weighty bag of coins. The Viscount de Valvert, engaged to Cyrano's own secret love, Roxanne, fails at a witticism about Cyrano's nose, at which the latter lets forth a cascade of conceits the bumbling Valvert might have used: "It must get in your cups; you ought to have a pitcher made for drinking. . . . Are you so fond of birds, that in paternal fashion you tender for their little feet a perch?" Unrepentant, Valvert eggs him into a duel, and the gallant Cyrano, the thrusts of his rapier as quick and sharp as the shafts of his words, runs him through, as predicted, at the final words of the ballade he composes during the fight. With the crowd hysterical with praise, a friend suggests to Cyrano that they steal off to eat. "I've no money," says Cyrano. "I've given my full monthly allowance to the impresario." "What a fool!" his friend declares. "But what a gesture!" Cyrano replies.[77]

Such was the century into which, in 1668, Giambattista Vico was born.

---

[77] *Cyrano de Bergerac*, act I, scenes 1–4; trans. Harold Whitehall. The reaction to *préciosité* came in the plays of Molière, beginning with *Les précieuses ridicules*, first acted in 1659.

THE *INSTITUTIONES ORATORIAE*

Vico was clearly out of sorts with his age. He fell on his head when he was seven, he tells us, and from the trauma of a long convalescence he "grew up with a melancholy and irritable temperament such as belongs to men of ingenuity and depth, who, thanks to the one [*per l'ingegno*], are quick as lightning in perception [*acutezze*], and thanks to the other [*per la riflessione*], take no pleasure in verbal cleverness [*arguzie*] or falsehood."[78] That is a line, one imagines—one of the first in his autobiography—Vico should not have disliked to see graven on his headstone, for it states not only the qualities by which he chose to think of his own spirit but also those by which he came to define the earliest nations in their first, labored steps to humanity. It is also a line that shows how profoundly he depended on the conceptions of his day, even as he contested and changed them.

Largely self-taught in language and literature, law and philosophy, Vico spent the years from 1686 to 1695 at a castle in Vatolla, continuing his studies and tutoring the family of Domenico Rocca. There he was cured, he says, of the poetry of clever deceit—"this deviance" (*sì fatto errore*), as he calls it— so popular in the Naples of his youth, and he returned to his city "a stranger in his own land," horrified to find it in the grip of a nothern chill, with Descartes the rage, metaphysics in rout, poetry constrained, and oratory in ruins. One could not hear an oration, he groused, "either animated by Greek wisdom in the treatment of manners or invigorated by Roman grandeur in stirring the emotions."[79] Winning the chair of eloquence in 1699, he declared war on the French and passed the rest of his days in the saving embrace of the ancients,

[78] Crescesse di una natura malinconica ed acre, qual dee essere degli uomini ingegnosi e profondi, che per l'ingegno balenino in acutezze, per la riflessione non si dilettino dell'arguzie e del falso" (Autobiography, *Opere* 5.3).

[79] "Non udivasi orazione o animata dalla sapienza greca nel maneggiare i costumi o invigorita dalla grandezza romana in commuover gli affetti" (Autobiography, *Opere* 5.21; see generally pp. 8–21).

teaching the Latin authors and defending the vision of classical rhetoric.

Seen within its age, Vico's *Principles of Oratory* is indeed reactionary.[80] The version of 1711, and still more that of

[80] The only sustained study of the *Institutiones* is in the much neglected work of Andrea Sorrentino, *La retorica e poetica di Vico; ossia, La prima concezione estetica del linguaggio* (Turin: Bocca, 1927), which finds in Vico's rhetoric "la germinazione prima dell'opera del genio" (p. 115). Whatever that volume's shortcomings—it is often sketchy, for instance, where probing is needed, and pedantic where a word would suffice—its central thesis, I find, is sound: Key tenets of Vico's eventual "new science" are already developed in significant degree as principles of rhetoric in his early course manual. Sorrentino, however, is concerned to follow the transformation of the principles into a mature (and revolutionary) aesthetic and linguistic theory, whereas I am more struck by the "logical" and "civil" character of Vico's rhetoric and thus its eventual use in a general theory of culture.

Attention to Vico as humanist rhetorician has also been given by more recent critics and historians: Antonino Pagliaro, "La dottrina linguistica di G. B. Vico," *Atti dell'Accademia nazionale dei Lincei, Memorie della Classe di scienze morali, storiche, critiche e filologiche*, ser. 8, 8 (1959): 379–486, reprinted as "Lingua e poesia secondo G. B. Vico" and "Omero e la poesia popolare in G. B. Vico," *Altri saggi di critica semantica* (Messina and Florence: D'Anna, 1961), pp. 299–474; idem, "Giambattista Vico tra linguistica e retorica," in *Giambattista Vico nel terzo centenario della nascita* (Naples: Edizioni scientifiche italiane, 1971), pp. 133–162; Karl O. Apel, *Die Idee der Sprache in der Tradition des Humanismus: Von Dante bis Vico*, Archiv für Begriffsgeschichte, vol. 8 (Bonn: Bouvier, 1963); Tullio De Mauro, "G. B. Vico dalla retorica allo storicismo linguistico," *La Cultura* 6 (1968): 167–183, reprinted in translation in *Giambattista Vico: An International Symposium*, ed. Tagliacozzo and White, pp. 279–295; Andrea Battistini, *La degnità della retorica: Studi su G. B. Vico* (Pisa: Pacini, 1975), a series of particularly astute essays.

Yet none of these commentators has considered directly the course manual of 1711, available in full only in the edition of Pomodoro (cited in note 5, above), or the variants, indicated by Nicolini (*Opere* 8.197–203), in the text of 1738. A brief, thoughtful analysis of the 1711 version was recently made by Alessandro Giuliani, "Vico's Rhetorical Philosophy and the New Rhetoric," in *Giambattista Vico's Science of Humanity*, ed. Tagliacozzo and Verene, pp. 31–46, an essay prompted by the work of Chaïm Perelman, and one whose perspective is largely my own. In that same symposium, Nancy S. Struever, "Vico, Valla, and the Logic of Historical Discovery" (pp. 173–185), extends to Vico the argument developed in her book, *The Language of History in the Renaissance: Rhetorical and Historical Consciousness in Florentine Humanism* (Princeton, N.J.: Princeton University Press, 1970); Hayden V. White, "The Tropics of History: The Deep Structure of the *New Science*" (pp. 65–85), shows compellingly the extent to which Vico drew from rhetorical theory in framing his theory of culture.

1738, is marked by a consuming "logical" bias. No less than Aristotle, whose thought he repeatedly invokes, Vico is taken with rhetoric as a form of argumentation. This is immediately clear in his treatment of amplification—that central concern of the baroque oration. "Amplification," writes Vico, "is a fuller, more elevated form of affirmation, which wins over an audience by stirring its emotions. It differs from argumentation in that the latter is concerned only with convincing an audience, whereas the former tries also to move it emotionally."[81] Remarkable here is the context: Vico's instruction on amplification is appended to a discussion of rhetorical proofs. The use of amplification, he held, must be weighed by the needs of discourse. Its purpose is not to embellish a speech, but to enlarge an argument so as to increase its effectiveness in those instances in which emotional motivation is of the essence. Emotion takes time to build, and in cases where it is central, such as in epideictic oratory, a more leisurely pace is required. Generally, though, the orator should prefer the leaner form of argument through maxims (*sententiae*), those brief, ingenious statements which relate data in an entirely fresh way and thus delight the mind with their incisiveness.[82]

---

[81] "Amplificatio est gravior quaedam affirmatio, quae motu animorum conciliat in dicendo fidem. Itaque eo differt ab argumentatione, quod illa dumtaxat fidem conciliat, haec praeterea animi motum ciet" (*Institutiones oratoriae*, p. 66). I read *conciliat* for Pomodoro's *conciliet*, and *praeterea* for his *practerea*.

[82] Cf. *Institutiones oratoriae*, p. 65: "Sententiae autem frequentandae, cum mentem rationibus capias: ea enim acumine gaudet et delectatur. At ubi animam affici necesse est, tunc amplificationibus res est segnius peragenda."

Though Vico can justify amplification as part of the argumentative process, he hesitates to recommend it, apparently because of baroque excesses. In referring it merely to emotion, moreover, he misses the opportunity, seized elsewhere (cf. pp. 82f., 101), to relate the choice of language to reasoning. This is the endeavor of Quintilian (*Inst.* 8.4.1–3), following Aristotle (*Rh.* 1403a), who speaks consistently of amplification *and* attenuation and treats them as means for enlarging or diminishing a *concept*. Both processes, he notes, are illustrated well by a passage in *pro Caelio*: "If a widow lives freely, if being by nature bold she throws restraint to the winds, makes wealth an excuse for luxury, and strong passions for playing the harlot, would this be a reason for my regarding a man who was somewhat free in his method of saluting her to be an adulterer?" (trans. W. E. Butler, Loeb ed.). The action

Such is the tone of Vico's entire manual. It is a lean, spare treatise, wholly focused on a single idea: Rhetoric is a form of argumentation in which choice of material (*res*) and selection of language (*verba*) are essential, equal, and interrelated functions. Deprived by Ramus of its "logical" operations, rhetoric had become increasingly a formal enterprise, a theory of ornate form or an art of communication. In the face of this trend, Vico recalls the full program of classical rhetoric, insisting with Aristotle that its relation to dialectic is its distinguishing and unifying feature. The definition of *rhetoric* favored by Quintilian (*Inst.* 2.15.34; 2.17.38)—*ars bene dicendi*—had long been robbed of its grandeur and now meant simply "to speak with style." Thus Vico reverts to the more ancient idea that "rhetoric or eloquence is the facility to speak persuasively."[83]

Rhetoric, for Vico, is a pragmatic enterprise. Like the general at war or the doctor at a patient's bedside, the orator is concerned with results. His task is to persuade, "to induce in the hearer a mind agreeable to the oration."[84] His métier is the debating of specific courses of action, matters that can be framed by the question, *quid sit agendum*. Abstract, theoretical questions (*universa argumenta*), such as the nature of law or virtue, are properly left to philosophers; rhetors are concerned with concrete issues, particularly ones that are neatly circumscribed (*questiones peculiares finitae*), such as whether peace should be offered to a treacherous enemy who violates treaties. Issues of this kind are proper to all types of oratory—forensic, political, and epideictic—but for Vico, as for Cicero, the forensic is paradigmatic, for in a court of law, the fate of

---

of the woman is enlarged to harlotry; that of the man diminished to exuberance.

[83] "Rhetorica sive eloquentia est facultas dicendi apposite ad persuadendum" (*Institutiones oratoriae*, p. 1; *Opere* 8.159). Said to have originated with Isocrates, the definition of *rhetoric* in terms of persuasion is found prominently in Aristotle (*Rh.* 1355b26) and Cicero (*Inv. Rhet.* 1.5.6; *De or.* 1.31.138). Cf. generally Quint. *Inst.* 2.15.1–22.

[84] "Persuadere enim est inducere in auditorem animum orationi conformem" (*Institutiones oratoriae*, p. 1; *Opere* 8.159).

an accused hangs fully on the ability of opposing attorneys to sharpen the issue in a way favorable to their interest. Vico, in fact, had little to say about political and epideictic oratory, and the paragraphs devoted to them in 1711 are absent from the manual of 1738.[85]

Distinct from philosophy through its greater concreteness, rhetoric nonetheless finds in philosophy its "most necessary instrument."[86] Wisdom and eloquence are naturally related, wrote Vico in the 1738 manual, but just at a time when the two were disjoined in the schools, professors of rhetoric, though now mere triflers in words, asked to be called "sages."[87] Vico was clearly possessed by the specter of an "empty" rhetoric. Unlike logic, he knew, rhetoric depends on a fullness of language, yet the fullness it commands should be wisdom, not fustian; argument, not bombast. Style must be governed from without, subject to a principle extrinsic to its own dynamics. Thus Vico recalled from antiquity, and made the focus of his treatise, the perspective in which the choice of style was decided by the needs of persuasion.

In a famous chapter on style (*Inst.* 12.10), Quintilian had restated the elements of persuasion identified by Aristotle (*Rh.* 1356a). To persuade, he wrote, the orator must charm (*delectare*), instruct (*docere*), and move (*commovere*) an audience. Whereas instruction is served by a "plain" style, one that sets forth arguments directly, something grander is needed for the gentleness that charms an audience and the force that stirs it emotionally. Which style, then, is to be preferred? Given a jury of wise men, wrote Quintilian, I should content myself with stating facts and marshaling proofs, as *exordia* of charm and emotionality are unlikely to influence those who are truly wise. Since juries are drawn from the people, however, such

[85] Cf. *Opere* 8.165–166, 201.

[86] *Institutiones oratoriae*, pp. 7–8; *Opere* 8.161–162. Of the subjects besides grammar that prepare for a rhetorical training, only philosophy is crucial, Vico argues, though that of Descartes and the neo-Aristotelians is of no use at all, a point he elaborates in the *De studiorum ratione*.

[87] *Opere* 8.197–198. The reference is to the Sophists.

embellishments are usually necessary. Circumstance must prescribe the proper combination of persuasive elements; thus the types of style are virtually countless.[88]

Recast by Vico in his own manual, these somewhat playful remarks of Quintilian take on a lofty, almost censorious tone:

> The elements of the orator's task are to charm, to instruct, and to stir emotionally. . . . Of these, . . . the first consists in tricks and the last in devices; in its arguments, however, eloquence has its superior strength. . . . The wise require nothing more of an orator than his arguments, for they are accustomed to follow truth because it is true. Eloquence, however, was made for the vulgar masses, for whom truth is disagreeable unless fitted with allurements and who will not do right unless swept away in a rush of passion. For them, consequently, an oration must be inflamed with emotion and made winsome through the orator's charm.[89]

This ungenerous view of charm and emotion yields some decidedly terse instructions. What occupied Aristotle for pages Vico compresses into two brief paragraphs. One may capture an audience with charm, he reasons, and twist it with emotions, but one holds it with the truth.[90]

From this perspective, earnest and high-minded, Vico proceeds with his instruction, keeping to the conventional practice of treating successively the "offices" concerned with the dis-

---

[88] Quint. *Inst.* 12.10.58–68. Cf. Arist. *Rh.* 1414a–b. Quintilian's account follows a lengthy discussion of the Attic-Asiatic controversy, in the course of which the question is raised as to whether there is such a thing as a "natural" style.

[89] "Quare oratoris muneris partes sunt delectare, docere, commovere. . . . Harum partium . . . primae insidiae sunt, postremae machinae; in argumentis autem generosa eloquentiae virtus consistit. . . . Nec quid sane amplius ab oratore sapientes requirunt: utpote, qui vera sequuntur, quia vera sunt. Sed quia eloquentia multitudini et vulgo facta est; quibus verum est ingratum, nisi illecebris jucundum quoque fiat; nec recte quidem faciunt, nisi quadam libidinis impotentia abrepti: idcirco moribus delinenda, affectibus inflammanda est oratio" (*Institutiones oratoriae*, p. 2).

[90] "Atque hoc pacto orator delectatione captat, veritate tenet, affectu contorquet auditores" (*Institutiones oratoriae*, p. 2; the paragraphs on the *argumenta conciliantia* and the *argumenta commoventia* appear on pp. 24–26). Aristotle's treatment of *ethos* and *pathos* as sources of persuasion fills the first seventeen chapters of book 2 of his *Rhetoric* (1377b–1391b).

covery and arrangement of arguments (*inventio* and *dispositio*), followed by that concerned with style (*elocutio*). Memory and delivery receive a sentence each at the end of the treatise; as natural capacities improved with practice, they have no need of precepts. While the arts of *res* and of *verba* are thus handled serially, Vico is plainly uncomfortable with any split between content and form, and seeks repeatedly in his text to show how language and ideas are linked in the argumentative process. To say that he "seeks" to show this, however, is nearly to misstate the matter. Concerned to stress the persuasive over the ornamental element in rhetoric, indeed to show rhetoric as a form or extension of dialectic (in Aristotle's sense of probable reasoning), and taking for this purpose as paradigm of rhetoric the proceedings of courtroom disputation, he is almost compelled to find in language an instrument of reasoning, even as his reflections on style proceed from an awareness of the social construction of language and thus of knowledge.

Vico won the chair in eloquence, it will be recalled, with a discourse on Quintilian's *De statibus causarum*, which he himself recognized as the chapter in rhetoric most like logic.[91] We should not be surprised, then, to find a discussion of rhetorical "issues" at the heart of his instruction on the discovery of arguments. A criminal trial, Vico says, is quite literally a faceoff between two human beings—an accuser and an accused— who share, however unwittingly (or unwillingly), a common social frame. The accuser states that the accused committed a crime; the accused rebuffs the charge, either by denying that he did it, or by denying that he did what the accuser says he did, or by denying that what he did was illegal or incorrect. Out of these three possible replies emerge the issues on which

---

[91] Cf. *Institutiones oratoriae* (1738), *Opere* 8.201: "Et ista de statibus caussarum inveniendis praecepta sunt vere logica." I owe this reminder to Giuliani, "Vico's Rhetorical Philosophy and the New Rhetoric," p. 28. On the nature of the juridical *causa* and its relation to philosophical reasoning, see Ennio Cortese, *La norma giuridica: Spunti teorici nel diritto comune classico*, 2 vols. in 1 (Milan: Giuffrè, 1962–1964).

the whole of juridical oratory turns: the factual issue of whether he did it (*an fecerit*); the conceptual issue of what he did (*quid fecerit*); and the normative issue of whether what he did was illegal or incorrect (*an jure ac recte fecerit*). The fate of the accused rests with the skill of his counsel to give shape to these issues through argument.[92]

The issue of fact (*status conjecturae*) is built on arguments regarding a motive for the action, the character of the accused, and simple evidence (*signa*). What he cannot deny, the accused must try to render insignificant.

If the action of the accused in incontrovertible, the definition of his action can be debated (*status definitionis*), and it is at this point that language—both that of the orators and that of the society of which they are part—becomes crucial in the proceeding. In matters of definition, Vico says, the same *loci* or sources of argument are available to both parties, and each tries for a definition that best conforms with common sense and the meaning of the term (*vis verbi*).[93] Analogies are adduced, examples of similar usage are brought forth—anything that will support one's own definition and defeat the opponent's. Here Vico stands on very ancient ground—language as a bridge between fact and law is an idea that returns to the very sources of legal oratory (Cic. *Inv. Rhet.* 1.8.11). To be sure, a law is itself language, but it is frozen language; its

[92] Cf. *Institutiones oratoriae*, pp. 31–38. Stated in their general form—*an sit, quid sit, quale sit*—the issues are valid for all rhetorical situations, but Vico prefers, as did Cicero (*Inv. Rhet.* 2.14–154), the juridical formulations. In the manual's later version, however, he takes note of the disdain in which rhetorical "places" are held generally, adding that the criticism of Aristotle's treatment as "excessive" is even more valid of the *De inventione*, whose authorship Cicero came to regret. Cicero, he says, felt that the treatise on juridical issues was the most useless of all since the "natural prudence" of any case comes to be known to anyone (cf. *Opere* 8.200). Vico's own emphasis was that one should rely more on prudence than on the precepts that guide it, a matter to be examined in the next chapter. On the classical instruction on "issues" and the "topics" that relate to them, see Lausberg, *Handbuch der literarischen Rhetorik*, §§79–254.

[93] Cf. *Institutiones oratoriae*, p. 33: "In statu finitivo loci utrique parti communes sunt: ut definiat uterque quam maxime potest ad communem sensum, et vim verbi accommodata."

words confront us as precedent and authority. A fact is equally stubborn, claiming a peculiarity that resists all classification. Both the law and the fact stand within the flow of living speech, which in turn reflects a society's *sensus communis*. The orator's task, as Vico says over and over, is to accommodate the law to the facts. Through judicial process the deed of the accused acquires its legal reality and so settles the fate of its doer.[94] Since language is the ward of society, it is to usage the orator must look to make his case—etymologies, synonyms, common patterns of thought and speech—seeking that linguistic bridge between the fact and the law which will be recognized as most "apt" (*prēpon*).

Clearly, the issue of defining the deed shades naturally into the issue of deciding whether the deed was right (*status qualitatis*). In seeking to interpret the deed socially—for that is finally what is at issue—the orator may proceed from legal texts or procedures, arguing either for equity or for strict legal justice, in which case the issue is a legal one (*status qualitatis legalis*); or he may appeal to the yet larger norm of reason itself, claiming it as the *lex generis humani* that absorbs, mitigates, or otherwise interprets the action, in which case the issue is dialectical (*status qualitatis rationalis*). In the former case, he will pit one law against another, or the law against the lawmaker, or the legal process against the case; in the latter, he will point to a reality beyond the law—natural instinct, the consensus of nations, the judgment of the "wisest heads"—as a more appropriate norm than it. In either case, there is the recognition that the mere words of a law are insufficient, that they are in need of the living voice of society to be told what, in this instance, they mean. Only a prosecutor

---

[94] In the prologue to his *Diritto universale* (1720–1722), Vico would write: "Jurisprudentia omnis ratione et auctoritate nixa est atque ex iis condita jura factis accommodare profitetur. . . . Itaque jurisprudentia universa coalescit ex partibus tribus: philosophia, historia et quadem propria arte juris ad facta accommodandi." This last art he went on to identify as rhetoric, then argued that the Roman jurisconsult combined the three skills of philosophy, history, and oratory. Cf. *Opere* 2.26–28. This extends a theme of the *De studiorum ratione*, *Opere* 1.101.

intent on inspiring reverence for law will look no further than its words. The defender of equity will seek out the meaning of the law (*sententia legislatoris*), will plead for public utility as the queen of justice, and will argue for use of a Lesbic rule, which fits itself to the surfaces it measures and does not require them to be bent to its. From this perspective, the documents of law are just one element in an interpretive process that begins from a concrete case and reaches finally into questions of values and moral and social choices.[95]

There is at base no separation between language and thought, words and things—this is the insight to which Vico was brought in pondering juridical disputation.[96] Indeterminate in themselves, facts require definition, and definitions themselves are made and remade within a social context. Similarly, the law in itself is largely mute and needs a voice to become supple and effective; beyond the words of law there is their meaning, and beyond all law there is equity, the mistress of "civil reason." If reflection on the *res* of discourse led to so keen an appreciation of language, we should not be surprised to hear Vico say, as he turns to the subject of *elocutio*, that style is "the most potent part" of rhetoric.[97] As with *res*, Vico's perspective on style is relentlessly dialectical. In many direct and subtle ways, he states again and again the leitmotif of his treatise: Things require language to be told what they are; language, however, is a social construct and depends for its validity on the common sense of society.

Vico divides his material conventionally under the headings of elegance, dignity, and composition, giving to the last of

[95] Cf. *Institutiones oratoriae*, pp. 34–38, where Vico's principal concern is the conflict between the spirit and the letter of the law. The comparison of equity with a Lesbic rule—a pliant tool used by craftsmen on the isle of Lesbos—derives from Aristotle (*Eth. Nic.* 1137b) and was a popular image in the late seventeenth century.

[96] A contemporary rethinking of the subject inspired by the work of Vico is the monograph of Theodor Viehweg, *Topik und Jurisprudenz* (Munich: Beck, 1953).

[97] *Institutiones oratoriae*, p. 74: "Nunc ad elocutionem gradum faciamus, quae potissima huius artis pars est; ita ut ab eloquentia nomen acceperit."

these only some perfunctory definitions and illustrations. Determining the elegance of words and phrases requires knowledge of their origin, their meaning, and their use, for "it is one thing to speak grammatically, another to speak as the Romans did."[98] This said, Vico turns to philology and constructs a history of the Latin language, setting off its periods like the ages of a man; he canvasses the ways in which language is used, finding in the comic poets the carriers of Vulgar Latin; and he speculates on the phenomenon of meaning, noting that no two words of the same era ever mean the same thing in exactly the same way, and that therefore, strictly speaking, there are no such things as synonyms.[99]

Vico makes this point in the course of discussing the integrity of speech. Words can be divided into those which mean less, those which mean more, and those which "fit" (*exaequant*) the thing signified; our speech is elegant when, to express the things in our mind, we choose the words that are "born" (*nata sunt*) to signify them. What seems to be leading to an argument for the "plain style" worthy of the most prosaic mind in the Royal Society turns suddenly into a blazing insight: While a great many of these words are exact or proper names, a good part of them are, of necessity, metaphorical. Often lacking the proper name for the things they wished to express, the first people were led naturally to invent metaphors and give them the same value as proper terms, whence they are called "native" or "popular" metaphors.[100] Standing with

[98] *Institutiones oratoriae*, pp. 74f.; *Opere* 8.170f.: "Aliud est grammatice, aliud latine loqui," to which he adds, "grammatici student, ut oratio rēcta sit; latini, ut elegans."

[99] *Institutiones oratoriae*, pp. 82f.; *Opere* 8.177: "Sed, quo rem teneatis rectius, sciatis oportet in nulla lingua reperiri ista, quae synonima vulgus appellat: nam nullum sane verbum est, quod idem ac aliud, aut saltem eodem modo significet, aut postremo eiusdem sint aetatis."

[100] *Institutiones oratoriae*, p. 83; *Opere* 8.178: "Elegantia, igitur, virtus orationis et quae in singulis verbis spectetur, ideoque minuta est et tam difficilima usu quam facillima visu est. Ea enim virtus subest in oratione, non extat, cum, ad explicanda quaeque mentis sensa, deligimus verba quae ad ea ipsa significanda, uti diximus, nata sunt. Ea autem sunt ut plurimum vocabula propria et, bona ex parte, translata ex causa necessitatis, quae, quod propria

the ancients, with Aristotle, with Cicero, and with all the poets and orators who had thought deeply on the matter, Vico states for his age the great truth missed utterly by Hobbes and by Locke: There are more things in the world than there are words (Arist. *Soph. el.* 165a11–12). Our experience is infinitely richer than our language. Language indeed is part of the indigence of our race. Thus the tropes and figures we devise are not mere ornaments; they are necessities of communication arising from the poverty of our language (Cic. *De or.* 3.38.155). Metaphor is not an abuse of language, for to speak in metaphor is not a matter of choice; we are condemned by nature to poetry.

Vico's handling of the tropes and figures—the use of language that forms the "dignity" of style—is in essence a development of this insight. He does not deny that tropes and figures can be ornaments of speech, but adornment is not their deepest source nor their primary purpose. Tropes (*verba translata*) are words with transferred meanings, words used in a sense other than the one that is primary or native to them. Given the richness of nature, every language lacks words to make note of certain items of experience, and to do so must take "alien" words and fill them with new meanings. Such transfers in meaning occur in four logically predictable ways: from one thing to something similar (*metaphor*); from cause to effect or vice versa (*metonymy*); from the whole to the part or vice versa (*synecdoche*); and from one thing to its opposite (*irony*). These are the primary tropes, from which all others derive or deviate.[101]

Vico's classification of the tropes, unlike his appreciation of their necessity, was not a legacy of the ancients, who indeed

---

deessent, populus primus invenit et eodem jure quo propria censuit: quare metaphoras nativas et populares appello."

[101] *Institutiones oratoriae*, pp. 101f.: "Tropi sunt qui vocem a propria ac nativa significatione ad impropriam et alienam deflectunt. . . . Invertitur autem significatio quadrupliciter, vel a toto ad partem, et contra, vel a causis ad effecta, et vicissim, vel a similibus, vel ab oppositis. Hinc quatuor primarii tropi, synecdoche, metonymia, metaphora, et ironia, ad quos caeteri omnes revocantur."

prepared their lists with an uncharacteristic abandon. Grouping the tropes under four primary types was an idea of Peter Ramus and likely came to Vico through the work of Gerard Jan Voss.[102] Why he should have adopted it, apart from the authority of Voss to which he frequently deferred, is not far to be sought. Since the transfers are explained in the categories of logic, it was yet another way in which the "logical" use of language, and thus the kinship of rhetoric and logic, could be highlighted. When indeed he came eventually to incorporate the theory of the tropes in his *New Science* (and for this reason, it seems plain, suppressed it in the later version of his *Rhetoric*), the title he assigned to the section was "Poetic Logic."[103]

The same reasoning was at work, I surmise, in his treatment of the "figures," understood generally as departures from the usual mode of expression. Though the ancients could see little difference between them, to Vico the "figures of thought" (*figurae sententiarum*) were greatly to be preferred to the "figures of speech" (*figurae verborum*).[104] Seizing upon the distinction implied in the phrases, he passed off the latter as empty artifices, concerned rather with appearance than with substance, while the former take part in the argumentative process itself. Figures of thought, he writes, "occupy the mind, not the ears"; they are "the limbs and the powers of the oration," adorning both the body and the soul of eloquence.[105]

---

[102] *Commentariorum rhetoricorum sive oratoriarum institutionum libri sex* (1605), 4.5.2; cf. P. *Rami Scholarum rhetoricarum, seu Quaestionum Brutinarum in Oratorem Ciceronis, libri XX* (Frankfurt, 1593), pp. 141–148. On this lineage, see the article of Andrea Battistini, "Tradizione e innovazione nella tassonomia tropologica vichiana," *Bollettino del Centro di Studi vichiani* 3 (1973): 67–81. Aristotle (*Poet.* 1475b) gives a similar fourfold division of the metaphor.

[103] Cf. *Scienza nuova seconda, Opere* 4, §§400–501. On the suppression of the section on the tropes and figures, see Nicolini's note, *Opere* 8.203.

[104] Quint. *Inst.* 9.1.10–18 discusses the debate among rhetoricians as to whether there is a distinction between the two kinds of figures. On the subject of figures generally, see Lausberg, *Handbuch der literarischen Rhetorik*, §§600–910.

[105] *Institutiones oratoriae*, p. 115: "Eiusmodi est figurarum, quae verborum dicuntur, natura, ut videatis earum artificium nihil solidi habere, et plus ostentare quam esse. . . . Haec [figurae sententiarum] sunt illa orationis lu-

Under this head he offers a dizzying array of types, from hyperbole and the rhetorical question to exclamation and the pregnant pause, all ordered to forms of rhetorical proof. Arguably the figures of speech could be fitted to this frame, but for Vico the distinction is firm and crucial. As the body in acting assumes various postures, so also the mind in speaking. These are the figures of thought, which are thus less ornaments of speech than actual mental procedures through which a judge or a jury is drawn into the reasoning process and made to "see" rather than hear the case being presented (Cic. *De or.* 3.52.202).

There are other ways in the *Rhetoric* in which Vico could show the dialectical value of oratory. He indicates, for instance, a range of *loci* shared equally by rhetors and logicians; he finds oratorical parallels for the classical forms of demonstrative reasoning and measures their value in terms of them; he repeatedly warns against a puffed-up style or a reliance on emotional appeal in place of clear and persuasive argument. Nothing he attempts in his text, however, makes his case so strongly or is quite so large with promise as the effort to relate the "conceits" of seventeenth-century rhetoric with the "maxims" or *gnomai* of Aristotle and the *sententiae* of the Roman orators, thereby effecting in a wonderfully ambiguous way a merging of psychology, philosophy, and linguistics that would, in his *New Science*, find such happy issue. To observe this process fully, however, requires the larger context of the nature and mechanics of civil life, which the chapter that follows endeavors to set forth.

As for the tenets of juridical disputation and the theory of the figures and tropes—the two matters we have so far followed in detail—their career in Vico is plain. Severely transformed, the latter would in time give structure to his surprising notions of the birth of humanity while the former would be pressed into service to explain the growth of jurisprudence.

---

mina, quibus non tam corpus, quam animus eloquentiae distinguitur; quae non aures, sed mentes occupant, et cum magnam in se artem contineant, nulla indigent tamen. In his formis omnes artus et vires orationis consistunt."

In his several early attempts to write a science of humanity, Vico adhered to the ancient notion of a *scientia rerum et verborum*, wherein *res* included the institutions of society and the ideas embodied within them, and *verba* defined its languages, symbols, and myths. This was a distinction he naturally embraced when he first set forth a "new science" in the *De constantia jurisprudentis* of 1721 and one he retained in 1725 (with the titles *idee* and *lingue*) when he reworked his material into a full-fledged *Principi di una scienza nuova*.[106] The impossibility of separating the subjects so sharply, he tells us, led to the new arrangement of the *Scienza nuova seconda* (1730–1744), which combines the two inquiries under the general heading of "Poetic Wisdom"[107] Even there, however, the parts are undigested, and in its preliminary statement of "principles" we find, fragmented and reassembled, the theory of metaphor and the tropes (§§173–237) set neatly beside the theory of judicial interpretation (§§238–329)—the former then fitted to the birth and growth of language (§§400–501), and the latter serving to show the development of reason and law (§§947–74).

Beyond these particular conjunctions, however, there is the promise of rhetoric itself—the classical rhetoric of Vico, at least, if not that taught generally in his time. The contest of rhetoric and philosophy, like that of our literary and scientific traditions generally, has assumed over the centuries any number of forms and variations, the positions of its participants by no means uniform or predictable. At its sharpest, the argument has turned on what may be called the intellectualistic bias, the tenets of which are roughly these: Truth is at base integral and the path to it single and univocal; truth will

---

[106] Cf. the *De constantia jurisprudentis, Opere* 2.341, and the *Scienza nuova prima, Opere* 3, §44.

[107] Cf. the Autobiography, *Opere* 5.73: "Nella *Scienza nuova prima*, se non nelle materie, errò certamente nell'ordine, perché trattò de' principi dell'idee divisamente da' principi delle lingue, ch'erano per natura tra lor uniti, e pur divisamente dagli uni e dagli altri ragionò del metodo con cui si conducessero le materie di questa Scienza, le quali, con altro metodo, dovevano fil filo uscire da entrambi i detti principi: onde vi avvennero molti errori nell'ordine."

emerge if only we strive to think clearly and speak plainly. Correspondingly, the validity of ancient cultural forms rests in their hidden metaphysical verities, which to be seen must be freed from the subterfuge of metaphor and myth. The mind of the rhetor recoils at these notions. His art is one of dialogue and adjustment, precedents and examples, maxims and common wisdom. The demand of oratory is that the particular be regarded at all cost; speech to be effective must be peculiarly adaptive, selecting from among the possible lines of argument only those most capable of commanding assent. It deals in matters of deliberate human action, the truth of which must be established through language. In cases of law, the reality of a deed is only then constituted when set within the context of justice and social values. In political debate, a proposed action becomes real only when fitted by its supporters within a polity's sense of its heritage and its dreams. In these instances, moreover, language—particular, chosen words and images—participates in the making of truth. The legal status of the accused is established through argument, and one case becomes precedent for the next. Political action is shaped through debate, the outcome of which is the basis for future deliberations.

There are in these claims not only the refusal of the univocity of truth, but also a challenge to the intellectualistic notion of the origin of mind. Properly reflected upon, the principles of discourse contain in themselves the seeds of historical consciousness, if not of a full and proper historicism, such that one may doubt whether Vico, apart from the tradition of rhetoric, could ever have written a science of humanity.

CHAPTER 3

PEDAGOGY: INGENUITY AND PUBLIC LIFE

> Let us equal the ancients in wisdom and eloquence as we surpass them with our science.
>
> Vico, *De studiorum ratione*

"The power of civil education is such that it is doubtful whether man's nature is anything more than it. For we are by our birth almost like wax, whence arise among the nations the great variety of customs and institutions." Though he might well have made them part of the *New Science*, where indeed we encounter them in so many implicit ways, Vico set these words at the beginning of his *Principles of Oratory*.[1] There he was canvassing in customary fashion, before giving the precepts of rhetorical art, the endowments of nature that help to make a good orator. A sonorous voice and a straight back help, he wrote, as do a quick mind and a lively fantasy. But none of nature's gifts is more critical, he thought, than that of a "civil education"—simply growing up as part of a city's life, coming to know its streets and its buildings, learning its language and its lore, its history and its ways, and in time being trained in its schools, especially in the company of one's peers. There is nothing, he concluded, that can instruct one better in that

[1] "Ad naturam equidem civilem institutionem retulerim. Cujus tanta vis est, ut cum hominum indoles cerea ferme sit, quare tanta inter nationes morum est, atque institutionum diversitas, dubitare liceat, an natura hominum nihil aliud sit, nisi ipsa institutio" (*Institutiones oratoriae*, in *Opere di Giambattista Vico*, ed. Francesco Sa. Pomodoro, 8 vols. [Naples: Morano, 1858–1869], 8.6).

sensus communis which is the norm of all prudence and eloquence.

Of the many pages written about the roots of Vico's science, relatively few have been given to the relentless concern for pedagogy and civil life that informs, from the beginning of his life to its end, Vico's letters, orations, and other writings of the "school." Croce was embarrassed to look here, finding a more worthy start in those dramatic but contorted paragraphs on knowledge at the beginning of the *De Italorum sapientia,* and for the last seventy years or so critics have largely followed him in this view, taking as the mainstay of the *Scienza nuova* a transmuted form of that early epistemology, a subject in which Vico had little or no training and, after 1712, apparently no interest. For it is plain, in a way that few things in Vico are, that he advanced to his theories on the birth of humanity by holding fast to the classical (and humanist) ideal of the public servant as "sage," as man of learned eloquence, and by following out the implications of that vision as he roamed the fields of philology and law.

Vico's interest in the vitality of civil life, and in the form of education that assured it, was very nearly a point of obsession. Endlessly he inveighed against a "voiceless wisdom" (Cic. *Inv. Rhet.* 1.2.2) and an empty rhetoric. Societies fell apart when wisdom and eloquence became disjoined, when philosophers like the Cartesians forgot how to communicate and when rhetoricians like the Mannerists played games with language and sought merely to be clever, not true. The sign of utter social decadence, Vico noted—in a magnificent image adapted from Cicero (*Rep.* 1.17.28)—is that men, despite the great throng and press of their bodies, live in a deep solitude of spirit.[2] Despite his own penchant for solitude, there was

[2] *Scienza nuova seconda, Opere* 4, §1106. See also his early formulation of this image, as a portrayal of fallen humanity, in the Sixth Oration, *Opere* 1.59: "Collectivities of men may appear to be societies, but the truth is that with all the massing of bodies there is a thoroughgoing isolation of souls" ("Hominum coetus in speciem societates videntur, re autem ipsa in corporum frequentia summa est solitudo animorum").

nothing Vico so abhorred as a society of isolated individuals. Whether original brutishness or ultrasophistication caused it made no difference: Solitude of spirit was a cultural disease. He went so far at one point, in fact, as to suggest a kind of state curriculum and civil religion not unlike that of Rousseau. If Descartes's passion was indubitability, and Hobbes's was security, that of Vico was *civitas*, the well-functioning republic in which men acted as citizens.[3]

VITA ACTIVA VERSUS VITA CONTEMPLATIVA

In part, it must be said, Vico here was simply being true to a professional task by joining a humanist *paragone*. The contest of the active and contemplative lives, one of several such themes of a rich humanist literature, was first played out in some famous chapters in the *Nicomachean Ethics*.[4] Though Aristotle says quite pointedly in that work that the life of the mind is itself an activity, his preferring it to life in the *polis* was sufficient for him to earn a reputation, like Plato his mentor, as a champion of the contemplative life. Cicero, on the other hand, was the undisputed paladin of the active. The discussion of celestial spheres that opens the *De republica* (1.10–19) grinds to an embarrassed halt, and the dialogue continues on a "serious" and "immediate" subject, the State. "There is no other occupation," Cicero had said in the preface, "in which human virtue approaches more closely the august function of the gods than that of founding new States or

---

[3] *De studiorum ratione, Opere* 1.119. Two excellent attempts to see the unity of Vico's pedagogical and scientific thought are those of Enrico DeFalco, *L'ideale educativo secondo le "Orationes," il "De nostri temporis studiorum ratione," l' "Autobiografia," e il "Carteggio"* (Naples: S. Viti, 1954); and A. Robert Caponigri, "Umanità and civiltà: Civil Education in Vico," *Review of Politics* 31 (1969): 477–494.

[4] Arist. *Eth. Nic.* 1095b13–1096a10; 1177a12–1179a13; cf. *Pol.* 1325b14–33. Cf. Pl. *Resp.* 499a–d. On the humanist *paragone* literature, see Paul Oskar Kristeller, *Renaissance Thought II: Papers on Humanism and the Arts* (New York: Harper Torchbooks, 1965), pp. 53–56.

preserving those already in existence." Conversely, "nothing of all that is done on earth is more pleasing to that supreme God who rules the whole universe than the assemblies and gatherings of men associated in justice, which are called States."[5]

These last words Cicero put in the mouth of Scipio Africanus, conqueror of Hannibal, who spoke them in a dream to his grandson Scipio the Younger, telling him of the rewards that awaited the stateman's labors. It was likewise Scipio who was made to say earlier in the dialogue that "he was never doing more than when he was doing nothing, and never less alone than when alone."[6] The statement was originally that of Theophrastus, a disciple of Aristotle, who intended with the paradox to argue the superiority of the contemplative life by showing it to be one of intense activity and communality. Lost in contemplation, the scholar communes with all great thinkers before him, wrestling with their arguments and their opinions in a common search for the truth. For Cicero, as for many an "activist" after him, it was a way in which philosophical and literary studies could be justified as a legitimate use of a statesman's leisure. In the *De officiis*, his great celebration of political life written in the years of enforced retirement following the victory of Caesar, Cicero sharpened the paradox by fitting it entirely to the civic ideal: The statesman in solitude achieves the activity of which Scipio spoke by training his study on affairs of state and through his pen contributes to the soul of the republic as his active involvement helped build its body. Thus, to the ideal of the informed orator, who even in his activity continues to study (*De or.* 3.33.135–136), Cicero adds the ideal of the engaged recluse,

---

[5] "Neque enim est ulla res, in qua propius ad deorum numen virtus accedat humana, quam civitatis aut condere novas aut conservare jam conditas" (*Rep.* 1.7.12). "Nihil est enim illi principi deo, qui omnem mundum regit, quod quidem in terris fiat, acceptius quam concilia coetusque hominum jure sociati, quae civitates appellantur" (*Rep.* ["Somnium Scipionis"] 6.13.13).

[6] "Africanum avum meum scribit Cato solitum esse dicere . . . numquam se plus agere, quam nihil cum ageret, numquam minus solum esse, quam cum solus esset" (*Rep.* 1.17.27).

who even in his leisure continues to ponder the matters of state (*otium de negotio*).[7]

So elusive was the paradox of Scipio, however, that it could equally support a quite different conclusion. And in truth, throughout the Middle Ages it was far more frequently invoked, often in combination with Plotinian Neoplatonism, to bear out the claims of a monastic life of pure contemplation than to endorse the life of involvement for which Cicero so ably spoke.[8] Ambrose and Jerome, Abelard and Thomas could all find in the solitary ways of the monk or scholar that intense, tireless activity which made of contemplation, for Plato, Aristotle, and all their followers, the consummate human pursuit. Nor was the ideal without a voice during the Renaissance. In his *De remediis utriusque fortunae* (1366), Petrarch set over and against the idle leisure that good fortune can bring, the active, demanding leisure of the scholar, a theme he had worked some ten years before in a graceful exposition of Scipio's paradox, *De vita solitaria* (1356).[9] In the century that followed, Francesco Filelfo (1389–1481) and Giovanni Pontano (1426–1503) in Naples continued to praise the solitary life in the colloquial style of Petrarch, while in the Florentine Academy of Marsilio Ficino (1443–1499) and his colleagues Cristoforo Landino (1424–1504) and Giovanni Pico della Mirandola (1463–1494) the ideal of scholarly reflection was fitted within a fully developed scheme of Platonic ideas to which man's spirit, though never quite equal, is nonetheless directed.[10] This is a perspective that is never entirely absent

[7] Cf. Cic. *Off.* 3.1.1–4.

[8] See Hans Baron, "Cicero and the Roman Civic Spirit in the Middle Ages and the Early Renaissance," *Bulletin of the John Rylands Library* 22 (1938): 3–28.

[9] *De remediis* 1.21.

[10] Cf. Arnaldo Della Torre, *Storia dell'Accademia Platonica di Firenze* (Florence: Carnesecche, 1902); Paul Oskar Kristeller, "The Platonic Academy of Florence," *Renaissance Thought II*, pp. 89–101; idem, "Renaissance Platonism," *Renaissance Thought: The Classic, Scholastic and Humanist Strains* (New York: Harper Torchbooks, 1961), pp. 48–69; idem, *The Philosophy of Marsilio Ficino* (New York: Columbia University Press, 1943); idem, "The Active and Contemplative Life in Renaissance Humanism," forthcoming.

from Renaissance thought and even so staunch an advocate of *virtù* as Jean Bodin (1530–1596) does not fail, a century on, to offer a Neoplatonic frame for his political advice: The desire for self-preservation brings on at first the actions of violence and domination with which history is plainly rife, leading in time to activities of moral and intellectual excellence; but, just as nature is eager for repose, so also the spirit of man is led finally beyond even actions of virtue to "things grasped only with the mind," wherein it finds its "final peace and highest felicity."[11]

Nevertheless, it is not the love of contemplation but a fresh, even passionate concern for the glories of civic life that, in the minds of many interpreters, is the distinguishing feature of the Renaissance era.[12] The civic buoyancy and spirit of enterprise that accompanied the rise of new republics in fifteenth-century Italy could rightly be expected, when measured by scholars of humanist training, to yield a renewed appre-

[11] "Quoniam natura quietis est appetens, planum est eas virtutis actiones ad quietem aliquando dirigi oportere, quo fit ut homo paulatim a curis et hominum societate distractus solitudinem quaerat, ut tranquillitate naturae consentanea fruatur. . . . His veluti gradibus ad ea fertur, quae sola mente percipiuntur, id est, ad animorum immortalium vim ac potestatem, quousque pernicibus alis sursum abripiatur, ac suae originis primordia repetens, cum Deo penitus conjungatur: in quo finis humanarum actionum et quies extrema, summaque foelicitas consistit" (*Methodus ad facilem historiarum cognitionem*, in *Oeuvres philosophiques de Jean Bodin*, ed. Pierre Mesnard [Paris: Presses universitaires de France, 1951], pp. 119–120; see the translation of Beatrice Reynolds, *Method for the Easy Comprehension of History* [New York: Columbia University Press, 1945]).

[12] Baron, "Cicero and the Roman Civic Spirit"; idem, *The Crisis of the Early Italian Renaissance: Civic Humanism and Republican Liberty in the Age of Classicism and Tyranny*, 2 vols. (Princeton, N.J.: Princeton University Press, 1955; 3d ed., 1 vol., 1966); Eugenio Garin, *Der italienische Humanismus* (Bern: Francke, 1947); 2d ed., *L'umanesimo italiano: Filosofia e vita civile nel Rinascimento* (Bari: Laterza, 1952); Eugene F. Rice, Jr., *The Renaissance Idea of Wisdom* (Cambridge, Mass.: Harvard University Press, 1958), where the renewed concern for the *vita activa* is shown to be reflected in a rather continuous process of secularization in the idea of wisdom from the early quattrocento through the French humanism of Pierre Charron; cf. the review article by Hans Baron, "Secularization of Wisdom and Political Humanism in the Renaissance," *Journal of the History of Ideas* 21 (1960): 131–150.

ciation for the active life. This clearly occurred in Florence, where several of its ablest leaders were simultaneously distinguished humanists, whose writings and orations were concerned to recast the traditional themes of the primacy of the will over reason and of the study of man over the study of nature into a vigorous "civic humanism." Coluccio Salutati (1331–1406), for thirty years chancellor of Florence, celebrated fully the practical temper and bracing political skill he found to be embodied in Cicero, a theme his successor as chancellor, Leonardo Bruni (1369–1444), developed at length in a popular biography, *Cicero novus* (ca. 1415), a work intended to repair the slighting the Roman had received—or so he alleged—in Plutarch's *Lives of Cicero and Demosthenes*.[13] What these soundings implied was soon made explicit in two companion works of the 1430s—the *Della famiglia* of Leon Battista Alberti (1404–1472) and the *Della vita civile* of Matteo Palmieri (1406–1475). "Man is born to be useful to man," wrote Alberti; because he combines rational understanding with a capacity for virtuous action he is a "mortal but happy god."[14] This spirit of industry and helpfulness is construed by Alberti above all within the context of the family or *gens*, the society formed by ties of blood and affection, while in the work of his friend Palmieri it becomes a program of *honestas* for the whole of civil life. For Palmieri, Florence is the Republic of Rome brought back to life, and its survival can only be assured by that commitment to civic involvement which is, on his account, much superior to any form of solitude. In a conscious adaptation of Cicero, a soldier fallen at Campaldino brings to Dante in a dream the very

[13] Cf. Baron, "Cicero and the Roman Civic Spirit," p. 21. For Salutati, see Eckhard Kessler, *Das Problem des frühen Humanismus: Seine philosophische Bedeutung bei Coluccio Salutati* (Munich: Fink, 1968), pp. 91–103.

[14] "L'uomo nacque per esser utile all'uomo" (*De iciarchia*, bk. 2, *Opere volgari di Leon Battista Alberti*, ed. Cecil Grayson, 3 vols. [Bari: Laterza, 1960–1972], 2.243). "Per tanto troppo mi piace la sentenzia di Aristotile, il quale constituì l'uomo essere quasi come uno mortale Iddio felice, intendendo e facendo con ragione e virtù" (*Della famiglia*, bk. 2, *Opere volgari*, 1.132; cited by Rice, *Renaissance Idea of Wisdom*, pp. 46, 48; cf. Cic. *Fin.* 2.13.40).

message given by Scipio to his grandson: "There is no better work among men than to provide for the well-being of the homeland, preserve the cities, and maintain the unity and harmony of a well-ordered community. Those who do these things shall, before all others, take their place in these divine realms as if in their own home and shall live here in peace for all eternity with the other elect; for this is the place from which the saviors of republics have come to earth and the place to which they must, finally and forever, return."[15] Rome lives again, and with it the values of family, state, and society by which Cicero set its course.

If the civic humanism of Florence can anywhere lay claim to being generally descriptive of the Renaissance, then surely it is in a set of impressive pedagogical essays and treatises that fill the fifteenth and sixteenth centuries.[16] In a host of early quattrocento teachers and writers, the ideal of a liberal education as basic to civic endeavor is represented in every major center of northern Italy—Venice, Padua, Verona, Mantua, Ferrara, Bologna, and Florence—and in the late fifteenth century and the following is circulated throughout Europe in the works of Agricola, Erasmus, Budé, Sadoleto, and Vives. Behind them all stand a trio of Italian educators, nearly contem-

---

[15] "Nulla opera fra gli uomini può essere più ottima che provedere alla salute della patria, conservare le città, e mantenere l'unione e concordia delle bene ragunate moltitudini, nelle quali cose chi si esercita, innanzi ad ogn'altro, in queste divine sedie, come in loro propria casa, eternalmente con gli altri beati contenti viveranno, perocché questo è il luogo donde sono venuti i conservatori delle repubbliche in terra, ed al quale debbono infinite ritornare" (*Della vita civile* [Milan: Giovanni Silvestri, 1825], pp. 279–295, at 295).

[16] See William Harrison Woodward, *Vittorino da Feltre and other Humanist Educators* (Cambridge: At the University Press, 1897); idem, *Desiderius Erasmus concerning the Aim and Method of Education* (Cambridge: At the University Press, 1904); idem, *Studies in Education during the Age of the Renaissance, 1400–1600* (Cambridge: At the University Press, 1906); Eugenio Garin, *L'educazione in Europa (1400–1600): Problemi e programmi* (Bari: Laterza, 1957), together with two volumes of annotated texts: *L'educazione umanistica in Italia* (Bari: Laterza, 1949), and especially *Il pensiero pedagogico dello umanesimo* (Florence: Giuntine and Sansoni, 1958); Gregor Müller, *Bildung und Erziehung im Humanismus der italienischen Renaissance* (Wiesbaden: Steiner, 1969).

porary in age, whose several pedagogical writings and efforts fairly embody the civic ideal: Pier Paolo Vergerio (1370–1444), Guarino da Verona (1374–1460), and the most famous of all, Vittorino da Feltre (1378–1446), whose "Casa Giocosa" in Mantua offered a model humanist training for the minds, bodies, and spirits of an aristocratic elite. At the core of the training was that cycle of "liberal studies worthy of a free man," as Vergerio put it, quoting Seneca (*Ep.* 88.2). Their end, however, was not in themselves but in the fuller life of the republic. "We remember that Aristotle [*Pol.* 1337b15] would not have these studies absorb the entire interests of life: for he kept steadily in view the nature of man as a citizen, an active member of the state. For the man who has surrendered himself absolutely to the attractions of letters or of speculative thought follows, perhaps, a self-regarding end and is useless as a citizen or as a prince."[17]

It was precisely in this spirit that Vico thought and wrote some three centuries later. He could claim with pride that he was a man of "solitary tastes and habits" who "lived in his native city a stranger," that he was not even in the habit of calling for his mail at the post office, and that adversities were for him occasions for "withdrawing to his desk as to his high impregnable fortress";[18] yet in the vocabulary of his pedagogical and scientific writings there is no word more opprobrious than *solitudine*, a notion as vile to him as *servitus* was to Spinoza, *fanatisme* to Voltaire, or *Unmündigkeit* to Kant. He could speak without regret of a nine-year retreat to Vatolla, but one of the earliest discoveries he made in his au-

---

[17] "Liberalia studia vocamus, quae sunt homine libero digna." "Verum Aristoteles quidem voluit liberalibus scientiis non nimis indulgendum, nec immorandum esse; ad perfectionem, civilem hominum vitam negotiosamque respectans. Nam qui totus speculationi ac litterarum illecebris deditus est, is est forsitan sibi ipsi carus, at parum certe utilis urbi aut princeps est, aut privatus" (*De ingenuis moribus et liberalibus studiis adulescentiae*, ed. Attilio Gnesotto, *Atti e Memorie dell'Accademia di Scienze, Lettere ed Arti in Padova* 34 [1918]: 75–156, at 111, 128; trans. Woodward, *Vittorino da Feltre and Other Humanist Educators*, pp. 102, 110).

[18] Autobiography, *Opere* 5.22, 63, 79.

todidactic seclusion was that "the philosophical writings of Cicero, Aristotle, and Plato, all worked out with a view to the good ordering of mankind in civil society, caused him to take little or no pleasure in the moral philosophies of the Stoics and Epicureans. For they are each a moral philosophy of solitaries: the Epicurean, of idlers enclosed in their own little gardens; the Stoic, of contemplatives who endeavor to feel no emotion."[19] Such are the ways of the uncivilized, he argued, of the godless masses after the Deluge, "lawless and impious, wandering like vagabonds wherever their ability led them through the great forest of the world, all humanity lost, language confused, dissolved into a brutal, uncertain, and—because uncertain—often wicked lust, rotting in an idleness brought on by the abundance of fruit that nature gave them, like wild beasts, each separated from the next, not knowing their own kind and thus leaving their dead unburied on the ground."[20] It was from such aimless, feral wandering that providence had delivered mankind.[21] Could any philosophy that furthered an ethic of solitude be trusted? Solitude was the very *nihil* from which arose that most marvelous of all structures, civil society, and it was the chaos that stood ready to engulf a civilization grown rigid through abstract principles and inflexible institutions. Solitude was not a thing to be envied, much less a life to be claimed as ideal; it was to be

[19] "Le opere filosofiche di Cicerone, di Aristotile e di Platone, tutte lavorate in ordine a ben regolare l'uomo nella civile società, fecero che egli nulla o assai poco si dilettasse della morale così degli stoici come degli epicurei, siccome quelle che entrambe sono una morale di solitari: degli epicurei, perché di sfaccendati chiusi ne' loro orticelli; degli stoici, perché di meditanti che studiavano non sentir passione" (Autobiography, *Opere* 5.12). This judgment persists to the *Scienza nuova seconda*, *Opere* 4, §130.

[20] "Questi uomini exlegi ed empi, andando vagabondi, dove lor portava il talento, per questa gran selva del mondo, perduta ogni umanità, con lingua incerta, sciolti in una brutta e incerta e, perché incerta, spesso nefaria libidine, e marcendo nell'ozio, cagionato dall'abbondanza de' frutti che dava lor la natura, a guisa di fiere, tutti soli, non riconoscevano i loro, i quali perciò lasciavano morti sopra la terra insepolti" ("Sinopsi del *Diritto universale,*" *Opere* 2.10).

[21] Cf. *Scienza nuova prima, Opere* 3, §30; *Scienza nuova seconda, Opere* 4, §2.

shunned as the foe of civil order, held off as the undoer of all culture and learning. It alone was just punishment for calumniators, such as the anonymous gentleman from Leipzig who had so carelessly reviewed the *New Science*—he should, Vico thought, "take his departure from the world of men and go live with the wild beasts in the African desert."[22]

THE *QUERELLE* OF ANCIENTS
AND MODERNS

Vico entered the debate on the active and contemplative lives through another, related, and equally old academic contest—that between the ancients and the moderns. This is the explicit theme of the two great Inaugural Orations—the *De studiorum ratione* of 1708 and the *De mente heroica* of 1732— from which are suspended, as from two mighty pylons erected on the bedrock of humanist concerns, the entire edifice of his scientific writings.

As its title suggests, the *querelle des anciens et modernes* was first recognized and named in France.[23] When Charles Perrault in 1688 began publishing his famous *Parallèle des anciens et des modernes* (4 volumes, 1688–1696)—a theme treated more compendiously by Fontenelle that same year (*Digression sur les anciens et les modernes*)—he was but extending to the realm of letters and the arts a subject that had seemed natural to scientists for some decades. Though personally convinced that writers and artists in the enlightened age of Louis XIV were at least the equals if not the superiors

[22] "Fa una grave esortazione a costui, che . . . esca dal mondo degli uomini e vada a vivere tralle fiere ne' diserti dell'Affrica" (Autobiography, *Opere* 5.69). Cf. *Vici vindiciae*, *Opere* 3.314–318.

[23] Hippolyte Rigault, *Histoire de la querelle des anciens et des modernes* (1856; reprint, New York: Franklin, n.d.); Hubert Gillot, *La querelle des anciens et des modernes en France* (Paris: Champion, 1914); John B. Bury, *The Idea of Progress* (London: Macmillan, 1920); Richard F. Jones, "The Background of *The Battle of the Books*," *Washington University Studies* 7, Humanistic series, no. 2 (1920): 99–162; idem, *Ancients and Moderns: A Study of the Background of the "Battle of the Books,"* Washington University Studies in Language and Literature, no. 6 (Saint Louis, 1936).

of their ancient counterparts, Perrault was prepared to acknowledge that progress in the arts, based as they are on talent and taste, was less easily established than that of the mathematical disciplines. And indeed, critics such as René Rapin in France (*Réflexions sur la Poétique d'Aristote et sur les ouvrages des Poètes anciens et modernes*, 1674–1675; *Réflexions sur la Philosophie ancienne et moderne*, 1676) and William Wotton in England (*Reflections upon Ancient and Modern Learning*, 1694) found in the argument for modern Homers and Vergils a case bordering on credulity.

To claim progress even in the areas of science, however, required a measure of boldness. It had been the constant if not invariant judgment of the ages that the universe was in a state of perpetual decline; that Nature had lost the novelty and freshness of her youth; and that her creative powers, like those of a woman who had too often given birth (Lucr. *De rer. nat.* 2.1150–1152), were fading and wasting. Likewise history was held to be decaying, steadily receding from a Golden Age at the dawn of civilization—frequently associated with four great monarchies, the Assyrian, the Persian, the Greek, and the Roman (Dan. 7:1–28)—such that each successive generation is a yet paler reflection of a glorious antiquity, whose accomplishments in all forms of culture and learning were not so much paradigmatic as simply overwhelming. Our fate as moderns, consequently, in the famous image of Bernard of Chartres (d. ca. 1130), was to stand like dwarfs on the shoulders of giants, enjoying from that vantage the wider vision that the stature of the ancients could afford.[24]

[24] Cf. John of Salisbury, *Metalogicon* 3. 4: "Dicebat Bernardus Carnotensis nos esse quasi nanos gigantium humeris insidentes, ut possimus plura eis et remotiora videre, non utique proprii visus acumine, aut eminentia corporis, sed quia in altum subvehimur et extollimur magnitudine gigantea." See F. E. Guyer, "The Dwarf on the Giant's Shoulders," *Modern Language Notes* 45 (1930): 398–402; George Sarton, "Standing on the Shoulders of Giants," *Isis* 24 (1935): 107–109; R. E. Ockenden, "Standing on the Shoulders of Giants," *Isis* 25 (1936): 451–452; Raymond Klibansky, "Standing on the Shoulders of Giants," *Isis* 26 (1936): 147–149; Joseph de Ghellinck, "*Nani et gigantes,*" *Archivium latinitatis medii aevi* 18 (1945): 25–29; Robert K. Merton, *On the Shoulders of Giants* (New York: Free Press, 1965); Edouard

As with every good simile, however, its force could be blunted and even reversed, and during much of the Middle Ages and the Renaissance down to the *querelle* of the seventeenth century there was an increasing tendency to do just that.[25] Standing on the shoulders of the ancients may ensure an advantage in vision and perspective that the ancients could not claim— so argued Peter of Blois (1130–1200)—and it even implied, in Dante's judgment (*Monarchia* 1.1.1–4), a moral obligation to reach beyond them in the pursuit of truth. That nature was exhausted and history in decay seemed decreasingly plausible as marvel followed marvel in technology and art. Alberti stood in awe before the cupola in Florence and thereafter wrote in a letter to Brunelleschi that tired old Nature was surprisingly vigorous, a judgment that Pico and later Vives turned into a hearty celebration of nature and mind. Likewise to students of culture and politics, the theory of a fall from a Golden Age became too narrow to account for the subtleties they found. Thus in his *Discorsi* on Livy, written in the 1510s, Machiavelli put in its place the equally mechanical, but far more supple, theory of social *virtù*, which, though constant in level throughout human history, is divided among the nations in different ways at different times (book 2, preface).[26] Bodin followed him in 1566, giving a full chapter of his *Methodus* to refuting the theory of the four great monarchies, arguing instead for the alternating rise and fall of civilizations, a notion that Loys Le Roy, in his *De la vicissitude ou variété des choses* (1575), would popularize as the "cyclical" view of history.

Jeaneau, "*Nani gigantum humeris insidentes*: Essai d'interpretation de Bernard de Chartres," *Vivarium* 5 (1967): 79–99, reprinted in Italian translation with an introduction by Francesco Lazzari as *Nani sulle spalle di giganti* (Naples: Guida, 1969).

[25] August Buck, "Aus der Vorgeschichte der *querelle des anciens et des modernes* in Mittelalter und Renaissance," *Bibliothèque d'Humanisme et Renaissance* 20 (1958): 527–541; Hans Baron, "The *querelle* of the Ancients and the Moderns as a Problem for Renaissance Scholarship," *Journal of the History of Ideas* 20 (1959): 3–22. Giacinto Margiotta, *Le origini italiane de la querelle des anciens et des modernes* (Rome: Editrice studium, 1953), treats fifteenth-century Italy with a focus on Benedetto Accolti.

[26] Cf. Eduard Wilhelm Mayer, *Machiavellis Geschichtsauffassung und sein Begriff virtù* (Munich and Berlin: Oldenbourg, 1912).

Odd as it may seem today, finding cycles in history was a decisive blow for modernity, for if it implied that a culture could decline it also taught that one in decay could gather its strength and rise again, and that no culture, of whatever condition, need fear the unfailingly debilitating judgment of a distant, glorious past. Bolder still was an idea of Aulus Gellius (ca. 123–ca. 169), everywhere quoted in the Renaissance, that "truth is the daughter of time."[27] It was a favorite notion with Leonardo and Galileo and with others who had reason to suspect the wisdom of the ancients, and from it came the conclusion, drawn first by Giordano Bruno and more forcefully by Francis Bacon, that it is rather we, the moderns, with our greater experience and accumulated knowledge, who may rightly be called the ancients of the race. "For the old age of the world," wrote Bacon, "is to be accounted the true antiquity; and this is the attribute of our own times, not of that earlier age of the world in which the ancients lived."[28]

So it seemed also to Vico, speaking in his lilting swansong, *On the Heroic Mind*, delivered in 1732 at age sixty-four. "This world is still young," he told his youthful listeners, himself tired and sickly, "almost wasted away by the rigors of intellectual work." Only the cramped minds of petty scholars would deny this, he added.

To go back no further than the last seven centuries, four of which were overrun by barbarism, how many new inventions there have been, how many new sciences and arts discovered! The mariner's

[27] *Noctes atticae* 12.11.7: "Alius quidam veterum poetarum, cuius nomen mihi nunc memoriae non est, Veritatem Temporis filiam esse dixit." Cf. Buck, "Aus der Vorgeschichte der *querelle*," p. 536. On the concept in Bruno, see Giovanni Gentile, "Veritas filia temporis," *Il pensiero italiano del Rinascimento*, 3d ed. (Florence: Sansoni, 1940), pp. 331–355; Eugenio Garin, "La storia nel pensiero del Rinascimento," *Medioevo e Rinascimento: Studi e ricerche* (Bari: Laterza, 1954), pp. 195–201. See generally Erwin Panofsky, "Father Time," *Studies in Iconography: Humanistic Themes in the Art of the Renaissance* (New York and Oxford: Oxford University Press, 1939).

[28] *Novum organum* 1.84, in the *Works of Francis Bacon*, ed. James Spedding, Robert Leslie Ellis, and Douglas Denon Heath (1857–1874; reprint, New York: Garrett, 1968), 4.82. Bacon's Latin is in 1.190: "Mundi enim senium et grandaevitas pro antiquitate vere habenda sunt; quae temporibus nostris tribui debent, non juniori aetati mundi, qualis apud antiquos fuit."

compass, ships propelled by sail alone, the telescope, the barometer of Torricelli, Boyle's air pump, the circulation of the blood, the microscope, the alembic of the Arabs, Arabic numerals, indefinite classes of magnitude, gunpowder, cannon, cupolas in churches, movable type, rag paper, clockwork—each one a striking achievement and all of them unknown to antiquity. Hence there have come novelties in ships and navigation (and thereby a new world discovered and geography how marvelously expanded!), new observations in astronomy, new methods of timekeeping, new cosmographical systems, innovations in mechanics, physics, medicine, a new anatomy, new chemical remedies (which Galen so greatly desired), a new method of geometry (and arithmetic markedly speeded up), new arts of war, a new architecture, such an availability of books that they are as common as dirt now, such abundance of them that they grow wearisome. How is it that the nature of human genius is so suddenly exhausted that we must give up hope of any other equally goodly inventions?[29]

Though one may marvel at the richness of the account, to list the accomplishments of the race was an unremarkable deed, being the habitual practice of Renaissance humanists from Alberti to Bacon. But Vico's purpose was not merely descriptive; he meant also to demonstrate and to exhort. In his *Novum Organum* (1. 84–85, 129), Bacon had rehearsed the feats of mankind in order to stress the haphazard way they had

[29] "Mundus enim juvenescit adhuc. Nam septingentis non ultra abhinc annis, quorum tamen quadringentos barbaries percurrit, quot nova inventa? quot novae artes, quot novae scientiae excogitatae? Acus nautica, navis solis instructa velis, tubus opticus, Turricelli machina, machina pneumatica Boylis, sanguinis circulatio, microscopium, tubus Arabum stillatorius, arabicae numerorum formae, informia magnitudinum genera, pulvis pyrius, tormentum bellicum glandignivomum tholus templorum, typi literarii, charta lintea, horologium: singula quaeque optima maxima, et omnia antiquis prorsus incognita. Unde ortae nova navalis et nautica (quibus novus terrarum orbis detectus, et geographia mirum quantum adaucta!), nova astronomiae observata, novae temporum rationes, nova mundana, nova mechanicae, nova physicae, nova medicinae systemata, nova anatome, nova spargirica (Galeno tantopere desiderata), nova geometriae methodus (et arithmetica facta longe expeditior), nova bellica, nova architectura, tanta librorum facilitas quae vilescit, tanta copia quae fatiscat. Quomodo tam repente humani ingenii natura effoeta est ut alia inventu aeque egregia sint desperanda?" (*De mente heroica, Opere* 7.19; trans. Elizabeth Sewell and Anthony C. Sirignano, *Social Research* 43 [1976]:901).

been achieved; how much surer it would be—and how much more fruitful—if men would follow the plodding, systematic ways of his new experimental method. Vico's concern is quite otherwise. He celebrates discovery as surprise, as the almost random conjunction of accident and genius:

The sublime Galileo first observed the planet Venus "distinct with its duplicate horn" and discovered marvels in cosmology. The towering Descartes observed the trajectory of a stone thrown from a sling, and thought up a new physics. Christopher Columbus felt a wind from the Western Ocean blowing in his face, and in the light of Aristotle's hypothesis that winds arise from land masses, he guessed at other lands beyond the high seas and discovered the New World. The great Grotius paid serious attention to that one remark of Livy's: "Peace and war have each their own laws," and produced admirable volumes entitled *De jure belli et pacis*.[30]

It is not analysis, not logic, not "method" that invents new arts and discovers new sciences; it is the exertion of the "heroic mind," the almost godlike power possessed by each individual, there to be cultivated and developed through study, and made to reveal its divine origin through works of greatness for the "blessedness of the human race." For over thirty years Vico had taught the principles of eloquence, had conducted his inquiries into the history of poetry, language, religion, and law, and had combined them all into several versions of what he once called, in Roman fashion, a "jurisprudence of humanity." From his researches in human affairs Vico could find no unilinear march of progress; newness in history seemed to him rather more cyclical than progressive. But what novelties there were came from the alertness of acute minds, were flashes of insight that saw the connections that everyone else had

[30] "Sublimis Galilaeus Venerem corniculatam observavit; et de mundano systemate admiranda detexit. Observavit ingens Chartesius lapidis a funda jacti motum; et novum systema physicum est meditatus. Christophorus Columbus ventum ab Occidentali oceano in os sibi adspirantem sensit; et, eo Aristotelis argumento—ventos e terra gigni,—alias ultra oceanum esse terras conjecit, et novum terrarum orbem detexit. Magnus Hugo Grotius unum illud Livii dictum: 'Sunt quaedam pacis et belli jura' graviter advertit, ac *De jure belli et pacis* admirabiles libros edidit" (*De mente heroica, Opere* 7:19–20; trans. Sewell and Sirignano, p. 902).

missed. "So you see," Vico exhorted his students, "I ask of you things greatly surpassing the human: the near-divine nature of your minds—that is what I am challenging you to reveal. . . . Take fire from the god who fills you. . . . Prove yourselves to be heroes by enriching the human race with further giant benefits."[31]

CIVILITY AND RATIONALITY

In the great oration of his early career, *On the Study Method of Our Time*, Vico had made the same point, but in the sharper, testier voice of a young university professor: "It is undeniable that the inventions made in modern times, in which we are so immeasurably superior to the ancients, such as the cannon, the ship propelled by sails alone, the clock, suspended church domes, antedate the time when 'analysis' became a routine procedure." Brunelleschi, he argued, endured the scoffs of every technician in erecting his cupola on four pendant points, while the unfortunate P. Perot of our day built a ship after the plans of the most acute analytical geometry only to see it sink like a rock upon launching. Just as music composed by a mathematical formula gives no pleasure, so perhaps machines designed by "analysis" are of no practical use.[32]

Why, we will ask, did Vico so stubbornly resist the validity of a new mathematical tool that was everywhere being hailed for its elegance and utility, the more so in an area—engineering and mechanics—in which its claims would be dramatically and repeatedly sustained? With this inquiry we are at the heart of Vico's early thought and encounter that vital center from which even his most developed theories would proceed.

[31] "Videte quantum a vobis humana conditione majora peto, ut postulem a vobis divinam prope vestrarum mentium celebrari naturam! . . . Aestuate deo, quo pleni estis. . . . Vos heroas asserite, aliis genus humanum ingentibus commodis ditaturi" (*De mente heroica, Opere* 7.9, 20; trans. Sewell and Sirignano, pp. 888, 902).

[32] "Nam certe a nostris inventa, quibus potissimum longe praestamus antiquis, aeneum ignitae pilae tormentum, navis unis instructa velis, horologium et pensilia hemisphaeria templorum ante omnem vulgatam analysim prodiere" (*De studiorum ratione, Opere* 1.87; cf. generally pp. 87–88).

In a less guarded moment than that of a public address—
a letter to Francesco Saverio Estevan written twenty years
later—Vico spoke bitterly of the "metaphysical criticism" of
the Cartesians,

which ends its instruction where it began, in skepticism, which in
the minds of the young, at a time when they are racked with the
greatest of passions and have souls of the softest wax, receptive in
the extreme to impressions of vice, jolts the common sense [*senso
comune*] which their home education has begun to form in them and
which is supposed to be made firm by reflective wisdom, the most
dependable rule vulgar wisdom has for civil prudence, which comes
to our aid when we act in the way in which all men of right sense
do. But skepticism, putting in doubt the truth that unites men, dis-
poses them to follow their own sense [*senso propio*], each according
to his own pleasure or advantage, and thus recalls them from civil
community to the state of solitude—and not the solitude of the gentle
animals, which are able to live peacefully together in flocks and herds,
but that of the huge, fierce ones, which live scattered and alone in
their dens and lairs; and the reflective wisdom of the educated, which
is supposed to guide the vulgar wisdom of the masses, gives them
instead the cruelest shove so that they rush headlong forward and
perish.[33]

There is no secret to Vico's jeremiad. Estevan had written to
praise the oration he gave at the funeral of the marchesa
Angiola Cimini, and had asked how it had been received by

[33] "Delle critiche, altra è metafisica, che va finalmente a terminare donde
incomincian ad insegnarsi, cioè nello scetticismo, che nelle menti giovanili,
quando più tempestano di violentissime passioni ed hanno l'animo come di
mollissima cera per ricever altamente le impressioni dei vizi, stordisce il senso
comune, del quel avevan incominciato ad imbeversi con l'educazion ico-
nomica e doveva loro fermarsi dalla sapienza riposta, del quale non ha la
sapienza volgare regola più certa per la prudenza civile, la qual allora ci
assiste quando operiamo conforme operano tutti gli uomini di senzo diritto.
Ma lo scetticismo, mettendo in dubbio la verità, la qual unisce gli uomini, li
dispone ad ogni motivo di propio piacere o di propia utilità che sieguano il
senso propio, e sì dalle communanze civili li richiama allo stato della solitudine, nonché degli animali mansueti, c'hanno pur talento d'unitamente
vivere ne' greggi e negli armenti, ma di fieri ed immani, che vivono tutti divisi
e soli nelle lor tane e covili; e la sapienza riposta degli addottrinati, che
doverebbe reggere la volgare de' popoli, le dà le più forti spinte a precipitarsi
ed a perdersi" (letter of 12 January 1729 to Francesco Saverio Estevan, *Opere*
5.214).

the intelligentsia of Naples. For all I know, Vico answered, they are muttering behind my back as they did when my *New Science* was published, these fools of the new wisdom who know nothing of the nature of human society, composed as it is entirely of memory and fantasy, the work of prudence and eloquence, a world of language, religion, oratory, history, and poetry—everything whose study they condemn in the name of their almighty criterion of clear and distinct perception, according to which they pronounce my work "unintelligible." But such work, he averred, of which he thought his *New Science* a premier example, was *precisely* the work of understanding, of *intelligere*, of seeing everything in a subject that is to be seen and of seeing it as a whole, and so making men wise.[34]

Notwithstanding his polemic unfolding of the *verum/factum* principle, Vico's objection to Descartes was not scientific, and only derivatively epistemological. In the first instance it was "moral" or "civil"—applied beyond the narrow realm in which it was helpful, Cartesian analysis would wreck public life. From early in his career Vico had joined battle with the "ethic of solitude" of the Epicureans, off in their Garden, "blissful in the belief in their own happiness," as Cicero had quipped (*De or.* 3.17.64). The same implications he came also to see in the method of Descartes, made pedagogically serviceable by Arnauld—that through it students would be rendered incapable of civic life. Intellectual giants they might

---

[34] Ibid., pp. 212–218. While faithful to its substance and spirit, my summary of Vico's letter does not reflect the ease with which he moves—on the strength of the premise that "eloquence is nothing but wisdom speaking"— from a discussion of the nature of human society to that of the structure of a good oration to that of the marks of true erudition (such as he understands his *New Science* to be). Of any and all of these he may be speaking when he writes toward the beginning of his letter: "Pochissimi sono mente [*sic*], la qual bisogna come di architetto . . . per giudicare de' lavori dell'eloquenza; la quale fa uso con dignità di tutte le parti del saper umano e divino, e da un punto come di prospettiva ne dee vedere, e tra esso loro e nel tutto, la convenevolezza, che fa tutto il bello dell'eloquenza, che si chiama 'decoro.' " Few documents attest so clearly the unity of his pedagogical and his scientific work or show how gracefully he moved between the two areas of concern.

become, but they would be mute, unimaginative fools in the forum, the courtroom, and the pulpit. They would in fact be dangerous mutants of the effete "solitaries" of yore: quietly pressing the vagaries of life into neat little labeled boxes; losing even the most obvious cases at court for lack of the skill to make them plausible; letting an ailing man go unattended until the "truth" of his illness became acutely clear; solving problems in the mechanical arts quickly and simply with pat mathematical formulas instead of *seeing* their solution, after a draining effort of imagination, with the visual designs of Euclid. As protectors of the commonweal, these dry, smug "sages" of analysis would be worthy followers of their master, who presumed to found an entirely new metaphysics by responding in advance to a few solicited objections to his work instead of defending it openly in the academies.[35] Cartesian analysis—both its logical and its mathematical form—worked contrary to the skills of effective public action and implied a spirit utterly repulsive to the mind of a jurist; for this reason, plainly and consistently, Vico rejected it. Bacon's method, on the other hand, he could tolerate, even affirm, for to him it was a science of ingenuity, based in the imagination, in the art of experimentation, of trying literally to recreate the processes of nature, and thus could only support the analogous arts of politics and rhetoric necessary for civil life.[36]

[35] Letter of 27 October 1721 to Fr. Bernardo Maria Giacco, *Opere* 5.173–176, at 175: "Come troppo accortamente volle che seco si usasse da' leggitori della sua *Metafisica* Renato delle Carte, il quale per questa unica altra strada previdde poter fondare una filosofia tutta nuova da' suoi riposti ritiri, senza pubblicamente professarla nell'academie." Vico is referring to objections to the *Meditations* submitted by Hobbes, Arnauld, Gassendi, and others on the basis of a manuscript circulated by Mersenne, and published together with Descartes's replies in the work's first edition in 1641.

[36] Though Vico does speak of Bacon's "inductive method" (e.g. *Scienza nuova seconda, Opere* 4, §499), it seems clear that he understands (and treasures) it as an "inventive" or experimental procedure. See the *De Italorum sapientia*, in *Opere* 1.180–185, where it is presented, following Book 5 of the *De dignitate et augmentis scientiarum*, as "topics" or the art of discovery; and the conclusion of the work, *Opere* 1.191, where it is set forth as the model of the *verum/factum* principle: "id pro vero in natura habeamus, cuius quid simile per experimenta faciamus"; and the *Vici vindiciae*, in *Opere*

The *querelle* of ancients and moderns that Vico joined, therefore, was not that of Perrault and Rapin, of Wotton and William Temple. He was not concerned to argue the progress of knowledge—a point he thought largely moot[37]—and still less to compare classical and contemporary representatives in this field or that. The *querelle* he entered was the far older, more basic and consequential contest of eloquence against logic, of wisdom against science, of the vitality of a culture against the strength of its mind. It was a continued engagement of the battle so vividly reported in the satire of Henri d'Andeli (thirteenth century): the grammarians of Orléans, the ancient poets and authors at their side, marching valiantly if desperately against the logicians of Paris, in whose train walked the combined forces of the technical arts and the professions.[38] For Vico, however, this was no mere regionalist struggle, no mere war of the north against the south—though at one critical juncture in his oration *On the Study Method of Our Time* he did take the bait of Dominique Bouhours and indulged a taste for the geopolitics of culture ("geopoetics"?) then so much in fashion:

If there is any truth in the statement, which is the subject of a famous debate, that "genius is a product of language, not language of genius," we must recognize that the French are the only people who, thanks to the subtlety of their language, were able to invent the new philosophical criticism which seems so thoroughly intellectualistic, and analytical geometry, by which the subject matter of mathematics is, as far as possible, stripped of all concrete, figural elements, and reduced to pure rationality. . . . We Italians, instead, are endowed with a language which constantly evokes images. We stand far above

---

3.303, where it is related to the *ingenium*, the "divinum omnium inventionum parentem"; and the *De mente heroica* in *Opere* 7.18, where the reading of Bacon is recommended to the heroic mind as an impulse to advance the sciences and add to the inventions of our "still young" world.

[37] Cf. *De studiorum ratione*, *Opere* 1.77: "Enimvero omne, quod homini scire datur, ut et ipse homo, finitum et imperfectum. Quod si nostra cum antiquis tempora comparemus, reique literariae utrinque pensemus utilitates et damna, eadem nobis ratio cum priscis fortasse constiterit."

[38] Henri d'Andeli, *The Battle of the Seven Arts*, ed. and trans. L. J. Paetow (Berkeley: University of California Press, 1914).

other nations by our achievements in the fields of painting, sculpture, architecture, and music. Our language, thanks to its perpetual dynamism, forces the attention of the listeners by means of metaphorical expressions, and prompts it to move back and forth between ideas which are far apart. In the keenness of their perception, the Italians are second only to the Spaniards.[39]

By the point in his discourse when he pronounced this summary there was no need for Vico to remind his audience that, for him, keen perception (*acutezza*) and vivid language are the sources of all freshness and novelty in a culture as well as the guarantee of its future. It was enough for him to restate his theme in pedagogical form by turning national pride into a trenchant admonition: "Let us not be merely more exact

[39] "Si eius disputationis, summis dignae philosophis, illa pars vera est: linguis ingenia, non linguas ingeniis formari, hanc novam criticam, quae tota spiritalis videtur, et analysim, quae matheseos subjectum, quantum ex se est, omni prorsus corpulentia exuit, uni in orbe terrarum Galli vi suae subtilissimae linguae excogitare potuerunt ... Nos vero lingua praediti, quae imagines semper excitat; unde uni Itali pictura, sculptura, architectura, musica omnibus orbis terrarum nationibus praestiterunt, quae, actuosa semper, auditorum mentes in res longe dissitas et remotas vi similitudinum transfert; unde Itali post Hispanos acutissimi nationum" (*De studiorum ratione, Opere* 1.95).

It was Bouhours's essay, "Le bel esprit" (the French correlate of *ingegno*), inserted in his prickly *Entretiens d'Ariste et d'Eugène* (1671), that touched off this French-Italian epi-*querelle*—part of that larger battle of ancients and moderns which we have been considering, but more immediately an extension of the literary debate over "wit" and the *acutezze* that we will turn to presently. Various authors of prominence were drawn into it, including Ludovico Muratori and Gian Giuseppe Orsi, the latter's *Considerazioni sopra un famoso libro francese intitolato "La maniera di ben pensare"* (1703)—a reply to the 1687 work in which Bouhours sharpened the polemic—being the likely impulse to Vico's own reflections (see Andrea Sorrentino, *La retorica e la poetica di Vico; ossia, La prima concezione estetica del linguaggio* [Turin: Bocca, 1927], pp. 85–105; Mario Fubini, "Vico e Bouhours," *Stile e umanità di G. B. Vico,* 2d ed. [Naples: Ricciardi, 1965], pp. 135–146). Vico returned to the theme in his *Institutiones oratoriae* (1711), p. 96 (*Opere* 8.186), and in 1731 wrote yet a final paragraph on the matter, this one intended to round out his comments on the inventive genius of the early nations and to give point to his claim that the telescope, the cupola, sailing ships, and the other items on his list of recent inventions were the happy issue of "idiots and barbarians" in the age of "returned barbarism" at the close of the Middle Ages, not the products of refined analytic intellects of his own "human" age (cf. *Scienza nuova seconda, Opere* 4, §§498, 1245–1248).

and true than the ancients while allowing them to be more eloquent; let us equal the ancients in wisdom and eloquence as we surpass them with our science."[40]

THE SAGE AS PEDAGOGICAL IDEAL

The pedagogical focus on public life, and the corresponding ideal of the sage, underwent rapid and dramatic development in Vico's early thought from the time he began delivering his inaugural orations in 1699 to the point at which they achieved their acme, and his ideas their maturity, in the *De studiorum ratione* of 1708.[41] That development has been described by Gentile, with characteristic grace and insight, as the reorientation of Vico's thought from a largely Neoplatonic "return to unity" to a more broadly based "descent to multiplicity."[42] This is clearly the course it follows, even if we are reminded by a reading of the *Heroic Mind*, with its peculiar demand that the near-divine faculties of mind be applied to the benefit of public life, that elements of Neoplatonism remain in Vico's thought throughout his career in a fertile, dialectical tension with his more assured Ciceronianism, even as his *New Science* was intended to be, by his own description, both an "ideal eternal history" of the course the nations run and a "history of human ideas" as they actually came to be in the institutions of mankind.[43]

Temet nosce. "Know thyself!" Such is the advice Vico offers his listeners in the First Oration. This ancient injunction is

[40] "Ut ne . . . nostri veriores antiquis, et nobis eloquentiores antiqui: sed ita sapientia et eloquentia aequemus, ut scientia superamus antiquos" (*De studiorum ratione, Opere* 1.96).

[41] On the origin and purpose of the annual inaugural oration and Vico's obligation as professor of eloquence to deliver it, see Nino Cortese, "L'età spagnuola," in *Storia della università di Napoli,* ed. Francesco Torraca (Naples: Ricciardi, 1924), pp. 225f., 386ff. See also Emilio Santini, *L'eloquenza italiana dal Concilio Tridentino ai nostri giorni,* vol. 2, *Gli oratori civili* (Palermo: Remo Sandron, 1928), pp. 97–113.

[42] Giovanni Gentile, *Studi vichiani,* 3d ed., ed. Vito A. Bellezza (Florence: Sansoni, 1968), pp. 17–99, esp. 79–90.

[43] *Opere* 4, §§391, 393.

quickly converted into "Know thy soul," which in turn is made to mean, "Know that thy soul and all its faculties are of divine origin and character." The power of the imagination in fashioning images and creating new forms truly asserts its divine origin, Vico argues, while the ease with which a child recapitulates its culture by absorbing within two or three years' time its entire treasury of words and actions—to recount which a lexicographer would need to write countless volumes!—confirms the godlike power of memory. What is true of these faculties is equally so of seeing, hearing, inventing, relating, inferring, and reasoning. "In short, all the gods that antiquity painted in the heavens to account for any benefit conferred upon human society—all these gods are none other than you yourselves."[44] Ignorance is as alien to the soul as smoke to the eyes and a stench to the nose. If one is conscious of the divinity of his faculties, nothing but a lack of resolve can stand in the way of his mastering within a brief space of time the entire cycle of literary studies.

This Platonic vision of God and the soul—a theme we find in a vigorous tradition from Plotinus and Augustine, through Bonaventure and Scotus, to Ficino, Bruno, and Campanella—receives in Vico's Second Oration a decidedly Stoic nuance. We are not alone in the pursuit of truth, but are caught up with all other finite beings in a universe of structure and order in which each creature has the law of its being inscribed in its natural inclinations. The world of nature is spontaneously obedient to its law while in the company of men there are a surprising number who play the fool, drawn away by malice, luxury, sloth, or imprudence from the way of reason and virtue on which they are naturally set, and thus cast into a pitiful war each against himelf, more dire and dangerous than that of any two enemies (Pl. *Leg.* 766a). The wise, on the other hand, are citizens with God in a city unto themselves whose law is none other than divine reason and whose bliss

---

[44] "Ut hanc rem omnem brevi complectar, dii omnes, quos ob aliquod beneficium in hominum societatem collatum coelo appinxit antiquitas, vos estis" (*Opere* 1.12).

is the spontaneous reward of those who, in following reason, know with certainty, thus contemplating God, and act with integrity, thus imitating him.

In the image of right-thinking minds united with God there is more than a hint of Cartesian ideas, even as the text of the first two orations is amply supplied with free adaptations of Descartes's writings. Vico was pleased to suppress all this in his summary of the orations in the Autobiography, for beginning with his Third Oration in 1702 his thought began the gracious turn from an emphasis on individual purity to one on social complexity, a turn that would issue, in 1708, in the great palinode, De studiorum ratione.[45] In seeking to interpret this change, one biographer has called attention to the War of the Spanish Succession, brought on by the death of Charles II in 1700, while another finds merit in reading the De studiorum ratione, particularly its section on jurisprudence, against the arrival in Naples in 1707, after years of social unrest, of the victorious Austrian Hapsburgs.[46] Whatever the cause, Vico embarked around 1702 on a course of social and political conservatism that he would never again repent of, one in which the wisdom of ages is surer than science, the ways of society more probable than true, and life better served by the effective tools of ingenuity and rhetoric than the ham-handed rules of reasoning and logic.

The topics of orations three through six—the integrity of the republic of letters (1702), the relation of *honestas* and *utilitas* (1703), the *paragone* of the military and literary lives (1705), and the compendious mastery of the entire cycle of learning (1706)—are completely stylized humanist themes; yet in the course of working them through Vico moves ever more surely toward that vision of society and its ideal participants which informs the De studiorum ratione. His Third Oration,

---

[45] Autobiography, Opere 5.27–33.
[46] See H. P. Adams, Giambattista Vico (London: Allen and Unwin, 1935), pp. 78–82; Biagio De Giovanni, "Il De nostri temporis studiorum ratione nella cultura napoletana del primo Settecento," in Omaggio a Vico (Naples: Morano, 1968).

which could serve quite well as the Hippocratic Oath of the professoriat, gives point to the psychology of evil so vividly presented in the previous oration by listing with painful explicitness the varieties of academic sham and chicanery. It is a stirring call for tolerance and open-mindedness, for honest and civilized criticism, and for cautious and guarded judgments in complex and unclear matters. Scholars, it asserts, are not mere individuals but citizens of a republic of letters, which demands of its members candor, sincerity, and genuine cooperation. Its heroes are men of *bona fides*; its traitors, self-important fools—willful critics, stubborn sectarians, and impostors of all sorts. "Banish all obstinacy from your souls," Vico pleads, "and take on the candor proper to upright men. Hold fast to your opinions until something more plausible [*verisimilior*] has been shown. To unlearn something is not shameful, for to err is not something voluntary. Obstinacy is a matter of choice, whereas error derives from the feebleness of our nature."[47]

These claims of the republic of letters become, in the two orations that follow, those of the body politic at large. The clash of *honestum* and *utile*, of the virtuous and the advantageous—the theme so diligently worked by Palmieri in book 4 of *Della vita civile*—is the subject of Vico's Fourth Oration, and for him it is one of a false dichotomy. The use of material goods may indeed present gnawing dilemmas, he argues, but products of soul and intellect yield their greatest personal benefits when directed to virtue:

For the services that result from the powers of mind and soul are not like buildings or estates or even life itself, which cannot be simultaneously expended and enjoyed, but are of such a remarkable kind that they are lost by those who keep them and held by those who bestow them—kept, indeed, in the very act of being given. For

[47] "Abigatis, quaeso, istam ab animo pervicaciam: et propriam boni viri ingenuitatem induite. Tandiu in aliqua sententia sistite, quandiu alia verisimilior non commonstretur: non est turpe dediscere, quando non est voluntarium errare. Pervicacia ab electione est, error ab imbecillitate naturae" (*Opere* 1.33).

it is both clever and true to say of such things that those who hoard them are impoverished, while those who squander them are rich. Defending cases, curing diseases, giving counsel on what should or should not be done—which of the parties may enter these services in his ledger, the one who receives them or the one who gives them? But if this is so, then it follows necessarily that whoever endeavors to extend the bounds of his services will yield more handsome profits. What wider intention could one have, however, than to wish to assist as many people as possible, which in the end is the only ready way in which mortals, one more than the other, approach God, whose nature it is to assist all men?[48]

If the conception of wisdom, on one scholar's account, evolved over two hundred years of Renaissance history from that of a private, intellectual virtue to that of a public, moral virtue, Vico reenacts that development in the space of a few brief years.[49] The approach to God through use of one's divine mental faculties gives way to the ideal of other-regarding action, based to be sure on the powers of mind and spirit, but caught up within a larger moral framework in which all conflict between virtue and advantage is dissolved.

The absorption of apparently conflicting terms within a moral vision that can embrace them both is likewise the logic of Vico's Fifth Oration, where the popular sixteenth-century *paragone* of "arms and letters" is debated. That military and

---

[48] "Sed in rebus, quae totae ab animo sunt et intellectu consistunt, quo genere ingenuae artes scientiaeque continentur, affirmare ausim nedum honestatem ullam esse, a qua utilitas secreta ac disjuncta sit, sed nullam earum posse maximas parere utilitates, nisi quae sit directa ad honestatem et ordinata. Nam officia, quae a mentis opibus animique proveniunt, non sunt eiusmodi, ut vita, fundus, aedes, quas qui insumit non utitur, qui utitur non insumit; sed res eius miri generis sunt, ut qui eas tenent, non habeant: qui donant, hoc ipso quod donant, conservent, et argute ac vere earum avaros inopes, liberales dixeris copiosos. Et vero caussarum patrocinia, morborum curationes, agendorum fugiendorumque consilia uter in suis rationibus referat is, qui accepit has res, an qui dederit? Quod si ita se res habet, necessario illud conficitur: quo quis eiusmodi officiorum finem sibi ampliorem proponit, uberius eorum facere compendium necesse sit. Quis autem amplior finis, quam velle juvare quamplurimos; quo uno homines alius alio propior ad Deum Opt. Max. accedit, cuius ea est natura, juvare omnes?" (*Opere* 1.42–43).

[49] Cf. Rice, *Renaissance Idea of Wisdom*, pp. 149–215.

literary excellence are correlative forms of a culture's strength had already been argued, if with reservations, by Machiavelli (*Istorie fiorentine*, 5, introduction), and with this position Vico is fully at one. However, that the warrior-prince be as diligent in the study of geography and history as he is in the training of his bodily skills (*Principe*, 14) is a bit of advice more cautiously received. Unlike the Prince, Vico's commander has "glory" as his aim, not simple victory, and thus undertakes his studies less for a strategy of war than for the conduct of peace. For war is a process of law, Vico says, a surrogate judicial proceeding; lacking the means of redress that civil law has with its system of courts, the law of the nations (*jus gentium*) must look to war to avenge the wrongs of broken treaties and trampled human rights. Vico, clearly, has been reading his Grotius, and finds the *De jure belli ac pacis* as useful to this oration as the *Meditations* of Descartes were to the first.[50]

Man holds a double citizenship, one by nature, another by birth. Heaven is the limit of the former, whereas the latter is confined within definite boundaries. Each is constituted by its own laws, the former by the law of nations and the latter by commands from the people, the senate, and the ruler. Agreements are concluded in each sphere, treaties in the former and contracts in the latter. If a private individual is obliged by a contract or breaks the law, we have definite legal procedures for dealing with him. But if a nation breaks a treaty or offends the law of nations, what remedy is there for protecting human rights? War and arms. If, therefore, the priests of civil law profess true not counterfeit philosophy; if only those republics founded by wise men are best constituted by law; if Cicero, the most authoritative philosopher of all, placed the single brief book of the Twelve Tables before the entire corpus of philosophical writings, on the basis that

[50] On the influence of Grotius on Vico's orations, see Nicola Badaloni, *Introduzione allo studio di G. B. Vico* (Milan: Feltrinelli, 1961), pp. 310–338. An overview of Vico's relation to the thought of Grotius is offered by Dario Faucci, "Vico and Grotius: Jurisconsults of Mankind," in *Giambattista Vico: An International Symposium*, ed. Giorgio Tagliacozzo and Hayden V. White (Baltimore: Johns Hopkins University Press, 1969), pp. 61–76, to which a useful bibliographical note is appended.

the *jus gentium* is as superior to civil law as the entire human race to a single state; should we not all the more think that the wisdom of war making, which is the practical science of human law [*humani juris prudentia*], is of use in pursuing supreme glory?[51]

This curious bit of reasoning, eclectic and wholly singular, is vintage Vico, the kind that fills the whole of his writings. Important here is not the traditional, unrefined notion of *jus gentium*, which Vico will later develop into a key idea of his *New Science*, but the use of jurisprudence as an all-embracing concept in which war making has its standing. If war is to *jus gentium* what the court is to civil law (Grotius), then war is the jurisprudence of universal law, and the commander is its jurisconsult; and if jurisconsults of civil law are "priests of the law" who profess "true not counterfeit philosophy" (Ulpian) and if *jus gentium* is much the superior of civil law (Cicero), then the wars the commander as jurisconsult makes are principal regulators of human affairs and so have their part in the attainment of glory.[52]

Being at base a jurisconsult, to lead in war and rule in peace under provisions of the *jus gentium*, the commander is truly a sage of mankind whose training must include every discipline

---

[51] "Duplex homini civitas: quarum unam natura dedit, alteram nascendi conditio; illa coelo, haec certis finibus terminatur; utraque suis legibus constituta; illam fas nationum, hanc populi, senatus regisve jussa fundarunt; in utraque commercia, ibi foederibus, heic contractibus agitantur. Si quis privatus ex contractu obligatus sit, vel in legem fecerit, jus cum eo nostrum certis actionum formulis experimur; si quis autem populus in fas committat, vel foedus franget [*sic*], quodnam conservandi humani juris affulget remedium? Bella et arma. Si igitur juris civilis sacerdotes veram, non simulatam philosophiam profitentur; si respublicae legibus optime constitutae non sunt, nisi quas sapientes fundarunt; si unum XII Tabularum libellum universis philosophorum bibliothecis Cicero gravissimus philosophus anteponit: cum tantum praestet gentium jus civili, quantum uni civitati universum genus humanum; quantum sapientiam rei bellicae, quae est humani juris prudentia, usui esse ad perfectam gloriam existimabimus?" (*Opere* 1.51–52).

[52] On the Renaissance use of Ulpian's topos and its adaptation by Vico, see the articles of Donald R. Kelley "Vera Philosophia: The Philosophical Significance of Renaissance Jurisprudence," *Journal of the History of Philosophy* 14 (1976): 267–279; "In Vico Veritas: The True Philosophy and the New Science," *Social Research* 43 (1976): 601–611.

that wisdom embraces. Sharpened and turned into a general statement, this vision is the same that fills the pages of Vico's Sixth Oration. At issue now is no mere offense against the law of nations but the universal predicament of human estrangement; its cure, as before, is the full cycle of studies called wisdom, beginning with grammar and culminating in jurisprudence. Man in his essence is *mens*, *animus*, and *sermo*, but through the corruption of his nature his mind has been dulled and made rigid, his spirit turned base and cruel, his speech become halting and ineffective. The very faculties meant to unite mankind are the forces of its disarray. Mankind is entrapped in a gaggle of opinions (the willfulness in each man's soul laying hold of the shadow of truth within him as Truth itself) and a babble of tongues (vulgar and ambiguous speech compounding the problem that a confusion of languages begins). Our only hope lies in the pursuit of wisdom, to acquire the disciplines in a quick and orderly fashion and to turn them to good use through social involvement.

Vico was not the only of our writers to put the Bishop of Hippo to secular purpose, but he was surely among the most persistent. Wisdom as the purge of fallen man is the vision that would guide, in one form or another, his sundry attempts to fashion a science of civilization. This is a theme to be traced in the chapter that follows. For now it is enough to notice how and with what passion Vico asserts the social end of education. Wisdom, he writes, has three ultimate tasks: "to restrain by eloquence the ferocity of fools, to turn them from error through prudence, and to bring them benefit through virtue, in this way to give, each with his own particular talents, ardent support to society."[53] Thus one is to follow the entire course of studies that the repair of our nature dictates, from grammar and languages to logic and science, and beyond that to prudence and eloquence. Not to push on to human prudence falls short of wisdom's demand, solving perhaps the

[53] "Tria ipsissima sapientiae officia: eloquentia stultorum ferociam cicurire, prudentia eos ab errore deducere, virtute de iis benemereri; atque eo pacto pro se quemque sedulo humanam adjuvare societatem" (*Opere* 1.60).

deficiencies of tongue and mind but ignoring the most basic of all, those of spirit. The summary of all prudence is jurisprudence, fed equally by moral and civil doctrine, and combined with eloquence to bring order and justice to mankind. Such is wisdom at its peak, the "truest, most excellent, and most honorable aim of our studies." Whoever does not pursue his studies for the sake of wisdom—the improvement of man's nature in society—but chooses instead to engage in his discipline for its own sake, such a one confuses the end with the means of education.[54]

LIFE AS TORTUOUS AND UNCERTAIN

The note on which the Sixth Oration ends—the social aim of education—is the all-consuming theme of the seventh, the *De nostri temporis studiorum ratione*, by far Vico's longest and most original. The *ratio studiorum* at issue in the work is not the well-tried one of the Jesuits, though it, too, would be the subject of critique, but the upstart version of Descartes, to whose *Discours de la méthode* (1637) the work is intended as answer. For this reason, the word *ratio* seems best, if imperfectly, rendered as "method" (but not "methods," the plural form in which it is frequently seen in English). As Vico conceives it, it is less a program or curriculum of studies than an orientation or approach to learning, with a sense of direction and a conception of means, and a more or less clearly stated idea of what it means to be educated. So understood, a *ratio* is less a pedagogical principle than a cultural statement, less a theory of knowledge than a conception of society. It is on such a basis that Vico undertakes to compare the ancients and the moderns, pitting against the cool, solemn, independent life of rational process the pliant, gregarious, language-based program of *paideia*.

[54] Cf. *Opere* 1.66: "Qui ad sapientiam igitur humanem beatitudinem parentem literarum studia non ordinarit, solvit fortasse linguae aut mentis poenas, animi non absolvit. Quare complures sunt doctissimi homines, qui tamen ambitione circumaguntur, de fluxa eruditionis gloriola anxii vivunt, invidia doctiorum uruntur. Id eo fit, quia quae studia ad sapientiam comparandam sunt media, sibi fines proposuerunt."

Vico crafts his discourse masterfully, setting forth at the outset, in classical rhetorical mode, his opponent's strongest case, the better to do it in at the moment in his argument when its fatal flaw is most apparent. A *ratio*, Vico says, consists of *instruments* that precede the task of learning, *aids* that accompany it, and an *aim* to be achieved at the end. On every account our modern method seems superior: its instruments are formidable—the microscope, the telescope, the compass, geometry, chemistry, pharmacology, and the twin Cartesian inventions of "analysis" and "criticism," the latter forming the "common instrument of all our arts and sciences"; its aids are prodigious—printed books, organized universities, masterpieces to guide our arts, and systematic treatises (*artes redactae*) for subjects the ancients entrusted to common sense; and as for its aim, only one thing is kept in view, one is pursued, one is honored by all: Truth. If I were to set out to extol such an aim, Vico adds slyly, I would only arouse wonder: "Who would think to disparage it?"[55]

Who indeed but a classical humanist, who seeks in the schools less a foothold for science than an entry to life, and who finds in that life realities more tortuous than certain, contours more responsive to the open hand of rhetoric than to the closed fist of logic? The aim of a study method, writes Vico, "should circulate, like a bloodstream, through the entire body of the learning process. Consequently, just as the blood's pulsation may best be studied at the spot where the arterial beat is most perceptible, so the aim of our study method shall be treated at the point where it assumes the greatest prominence."[56]

That point is a section entitled "Disadvantages of Our Modern Study Method in the Fields of Ethics, Civil Doctrine, and Eloquence from the Viewpoint of the Purpose at Which It

[55] *Opere* 1.78–80, at 80: "Atque in his ferme omnibus literarum studiis ad unum hodie spectatur finem, veritatem; quam si laudare instituam, illa dignus sim admiratione: quis unquam vituperavit?"

[56] "De fine autem, quia per eam, uti sanguis per totum corpus, diffunditur; quemadmodum sanguinis motus, ubi sensibiliores arteriae sunt, observatur; ita, inquam, de nostrae studiorum rationis fine, ubi is magis emineat, disputabimus" (*Opere* 1.78).

Aims," beyond question the heart of Vico's discourse as indeed of his entire early work. As in the learning process itself, concern for the aim of education flows quietly through the whole of Vico's discourse, being at base the source of every critique he makes of modern instruments and aids; but when he turns from a discussion of the physical sciences to consider what in his day were still called the "moral" disciplines—ethics, politics, and jurisprudence, applied and brought to life through the art of rhetoric—the pedagogical aim of "truth" stands plainly exposed and must be confronted directly:

Since, in our time, the only aim of our studies is truth, we devote all our efforts to the investigation of physical phenomena, because their nature seems unambiguous; but we fail to inquire into human nature, which, because of the freedom of man's will, is most indeterminate. As a result of this emphasis, our youth are seriously compromised: they are unable to engage in the life of the community with sufficient prudence, nor do they know how to infuse their speech with a knowledge of human psychology or to permeate their utterances with passion. When it comes to prudence in civil life, it is well for us to keep in mind that human events are dominated by opportunity and choice, which are extremely subject to change [*incertissimae*] and which are strongly influenced by simulation and dissimulation—both preeminently deceptive [*fallacissimae*] things. As a consequence, those whose only concern is truth [*qui unum verum curant*] have great difficulty in finding means to a goal and even greater in attaining their ends. A course of action in life must consider the importance of specific events and their cirumstances, many of which may be extraneous and trivial, some of them bad, some even contrary to one's goal. It is therefore impossible to assess human affairs by the inflexible standard of abstract right; we must rather gauge them by the pliant Lesbic rule, which does not conform bodies to itself, but adjusts itself to their contours.[57]

[57] "Quia unus hodie studiorum finis veritas, vestigamus naturam rerum, quia certa videtur: hominum naturam non vestigamus, quia est ab arbitrio incertissima. Sed haec ratio studiorum adolescentibus illa parit incommoda, ut porro nec satis vitam civilem prudenter agant, nec orationem moribus tingere et affectibus inflammare satis sciant. Et, quod ad prudentiam civilis vitae attinet, cum rerum humanarum dominae sint occasio et electio, quae incertissimae sunt, easque, ut plurimum, simulatio et dissimulatio, res fallacissimae ducant, qui unum verum curant, difficile media, difficilius fines

This passage is remarkable in a number of ways, not least of all because it would later be restated, in triumphant form, in several much debated paragraphs of the second *New Science*, where Vico proclaims that the science of man he has achieved is more certain than that of nature and more real than that of mathematics.[58] Of whatever kind he conceived that science to be, however, it was surely not the intuitively assured, deductive knowledge of Cartesian method that he is here criticizing. More important, however firm and reliable our knowledge of man at the cultural or macrohistorical level, human life at the level at which we are compelled to deal with it was never thought to be—as the impassioned letters and orations of his later life make plain—anything other than tortuous, robust, fickle, and uncertain. Thus the pedagogical force of the passage remained untouched: Youths who are trained to ban from their minds the rubble of common experience and to think deductively and methodically from a single, self-reliant truth could never be more than "learned fools" (*docti imprudentes*) in the affairs of public life. To be publicly effective, one needed to be flexible, adaptable, and above all concrete, able to find the often circuitous means to proper ends. This required, Vico argued, less a training in science, which seeks to reduce the largest possible number of physical effects to a single cause (*unam caussam*), than one in prudence, which ferrets out the greatest possible number of causes that may have produced a single event (*unum factum*) and conjectures which of these is the correct one.[59]

Defining the realms of science and prudence and seeking

---

earum assequuntur; et suis consiliis frustrati, alienis decepti, quam saepissime abeunt. Quando igitur vitae agenda ex rerum momentis et appendicibus, quae circumstantiae dicuntur, aestimantur: et earum multae fortasse alienae ac ineptae, nonnullae saepe perversae, et quandoque etiam adversae suo fini sunt; non ex ista recta mentis regula, quae rigida est, hominum facta aestimari possunt, sed illa Lesbiorum flexili, quae non ad se corpora dirigit, sed ad corpora inflectit, spectari debent" (*Opere* 1.91).

[58] *Opere* 4, §§2, 331, 349.

[59] *De studiorum ratione*, *Opere* 1.91: "Atque adeo hoc scientia a prudentia distat, quod scientia excellunt, qui unam caussam, per quam plurima naturae effecta perducunt; prudentia vero praestant, qui unius facti quam plurimas caussas vestigant, ut quae sit vera, conjiciant."

their proper adjustment is so constant a theme in our literature, claiming a place at least from the time that Socrates and Callicles first argued the matter, that we should not be surprised to find the subject resumed in Vico. What does surprise is the passion with which he defends the priority and scope of prudence. The intolerance of the *unum verum*, which suppresses all that cannot logically relate to it, evokes in reaction a defiant insistence on the *unum factum*, with whose vagaries one is to deal effectively. Out of this confrontation come the marks of Vico's pedagogical counterideal: against scholarly seclusion, life in the forum; against the austerity of logic, the fullness of eloquence; against the harsh criteria of the scientist, the pliant standards of the sage.

With this conception of the aim of our studies, Vico conducts his critique of modern instruments and aids, trying to show their deleterious effects on prudence and eloquence—the arts of civic effectiveness—and seeking to narrow the realm in which they might legitimately claim to be valid. Basic to his argument in both its forms is the assertion of probability as the kind of knowledge that is our most usual lot, and of plausibility as the measure by which we must constantly seek to establish and communicate it.

The *verum* to which Vico objects as the aim of formal training is, of course, the apodictic, self-justifying truth of Cartesian method, the kind of truth "of which we can be certain even when assailed by doubt."[60] That there can be

---

[60] "Etenim critica id nobis dat primum verum, de quo, vel cum dubitas, certus fias" (*De studiorum ratione, Opere* 1.79). On Vico's criticism of the Cartesian ideal and his counteremphasis on the *verisimilia*, see especially the essays of Ernesto Grassi, "Vom Wahren und Wahrscheinlichen bei Vico," *Kantstudien* 42 (1942–1943): 48–63; *Verteidigung des individuellen Lebens: Studia humanitatis als philosophische Überlieferung* (Bern: Francke, 1946), pp. 106–116, 144–176; "Critical Philosophy or Topical Philosophy? Meditations on the *De nostri temporis studiorum ratione*," in *Giambattista Vico: An International Symposium*, ed. Tagliacozzo and White, pp. 39–50; "The Priority of Common Sense and Imagination: Vico's Philosophical Relevance Today," *Social Research* 43 (1976): 533–575; "Can Rhetoric Provide a New Basis for Philosophizing? The Humanist Tradition," *Philosophy and Rhetoric* 11 (1978): 1–18, 75–97; *Die Macht der Phantasie: Zur Geschichte abend-*

such a truth Vico does not question; even in criticizing the logic of "methodical doubt" and the consequent principle of the *Cogito*, Vico posits mathematics as a realm in which a true, self-validating science is possible, one in which (as Galileo had first said) we can achieve a certainty equal in its intensiveness to that of God's own knowledge, precisely because (as Hobbes had recognized) its principles are of our own making.[61] Beyond the pale of number and measure, however,

---

ländischen Denkens (Königstein/Ts.: Anthenäum, 1979), pp. 239–264; *Rhetoric as Philosophy* (University Park: Pennsylvania State University Press, 1980). Also of interest is the introduction of Maria Goretti to her translation of the *De studiorum ratione*, published as *La difesa dell'Umanesimo: Il "De nostri temporis studiorum ratione"* (Florence: Le Monnier, 1958); and the luminous pages of Hans-Georg Gadamer, *Wahrheit und Methode*, 2d ed. (Tübingen: Mohr, 1965), pp. 16–21.

[61] Cf. *De Italorum sapientia, Opere* 1.131–141; First *Risposta, Opere* 1.207–208, at 208: "Formata questa idea di vero, a quella riduco l'origine delle scienze umane, e misuro i gradi della lor verità, e pruovo principalmente che le matematiche sono le uniche scienze che inducono il vero umano, perché quelle unicamente procedono a simiglianza della scienza di Dio, perché si han creato in un certo modo gli elementi con definir certi nomi, li portano sino all'infinito co' postulati, si hanno stabilito certe verità eterne con gli assiomi, e, per questo lor finto infinito e da questa loro finta eternità disponendo i loro elementi, fanno il vero che insegnano; e l'uomo, contenendo dentro di sé un immaginato mondo di linee e di numeri, opera talmente in quello con l'astrazione, come Iddio nell'universo con la realità. Per la stessa via procedo a dar l'origine e'l criterio delle altre scienze e dell'arti." See further the First *Risposta, Opere* 1.217; Second *Risposta, Opere* 1.258.

The literature on Vico's theory of knowledge is particularly large. Robert Flint included a lengthy discussion of the subject in his enduringly valuable monograph, *Vico* (Edinburgh and London: Blackwood, 1884), pp. 86–111; but the impulse to its modern discussion was furnished by the opening chapters of Croce's *La filosofia di Giambattista Vico* (Bari: Laterza, 1911), best read with his historical essay of the same period, *Le fonti della gnoseologia vichiana*, Memoria all'Accademia Pontaniana nella tornata del 10 marzo 1912 (Naples: Giannini, 1912). Among the best studies of the subject to appear since that time are: Elio Gianturco, "Suárez and Vico: A Note on the Origin of the Vichian Formula," *Harvard Theological Review* 27 (1934): 207–210; Arthur Child, *Making and Knowing in Hobbes, Vico, and Dewey* (Berkeley and Los Angeles: University of California Press, 1953): Karl Löwith, *Vicos Grundsatz "verum et factum convertuntur": Seine theologische Prämisse und deren säkulare Konsequenzen* (Heidelberg: Winter 1968); Isaiah Berlin, "A Note on Vico's Concept of Knowledge," in *Giambattista Vico: An International Symposium*, ed. Tagliacozzo and White, pp. 371–377; idem, "Vico's Theory of Knowledge and Its Sources," *Vico and Herder* (New York: Viking, 1976), pp. 99–142; Rodolfo Mondolfo, *Il "verum-factum" prima di Vico*, Studi vichiani, 1 (Naples: Guida, 1969).

we are left to deal with lesser forms of truth, ones that do not contain their own guarantee, but must appeal for their validity to a standard beyond themselves, and not rarely to the rule of "common sense." Yet Descartes would give such truths no standing: "Criticism places upon the same plane of falsity not only false thinking, but also those secondary verities and ideas based on probability alone, and commands us to clear our minds of them."[62] To follow such a command, Vico asserts, would be the despair of most knowledge and the ruin of all prudence. As a pedagogical process "criticism" stands convicted by its own intolerance; its method is an impossible center of the curriculum, and its "truth" an inadequate aim of learning.

"Nature is full of incertitude."[63] In countering Descartes with so abrupt a pronouncement Vico does not mean to issue a challenge. The uncertainty that surrounds us is not a mystery to unravel, not a mass to be reduced through patient, persistent analysis. Uncertainty is the context of our actions, the framework of our endeavors, the environment in which we must, by and large, live out our lives. To assert that life in society is full and robust, marked by variety, fickleness, and surprise, and thus requires of one who would deal with it a mind that is supple and quick, not methodical and deductive, is unremarkable; but to say as he did, above all in the age in which he wrote, that nature at large is flux and change, so much more than what the modernists could capture in their tidy little mathematical systems, seems forced and desperate. The irony, of course, is that Vico would come to his own new science by seeing method in the madness of history and patterns within the flux of society; yet the point bears repeating that he arrived at this vision only through a sturdy insistence on the "tortuosities" of life and a corresponding reliance on

[62] "Critica . . . quae, quo suum primum verum ab omni, non solum falso, sed falsi quoque suspicione expurget, vera secunda et verisimilia omnia aeque ac falsa mente exigi jubet" (De studiorum ratione, Opere 1.81).

[63] "Natura enim incerta est" (De studiorum ratione, Opere 1.82).

the traditional tools—prudence and eloquence—by which one copes with them.

To the extent that Vico actually argues his claim for the elusiveness of nature and for the merely probable presentations—the *verisimilia*—it makes to our minds, he does so by reference to the skeptics of the New Academy, whose ideas were known to him through the works of Cicero: "Both Stoics and Epicureans came out in support of only one side of an argument; Plato inclined toward one or the other side, depending on which appeared to him more probable; Carneades, instead, was wont to embrace both of the sides of any given controversy."[64] As is his habit, Vico makes known a preferred opinion by claiming Plato as its author. Here he attributes to Plato the attitude known to be that of Carneades (Cic. *Acad.* 2.3.99) and imputes to the latter the purely "negative dialectic" (*ratio contra omnia disserendi*: *Nat. D.* 1.5.11) more accurately asserted of Arkesilaos or of the skeptic tradition generally.[65] However strained his references, Vico's meaning is nonetheless plain: If it is folly to take all positions, or no

[64] "Et Stoici atque Epicurei unam duntaxat disputationis partem propugnabant. Plato in alterutram, quae verisimilior videretur, inclinare: Carneades autem utrumque complectebatur oppositum" (*De studiorum ratione, Opere* 1.83).

[65] The skepticism recorded by Cicero was neither that of Pyrrho, an early philosopher about whose life and thought little is known, nor that of the later Pyrrhonians, represented in the writings of Sextus Empiricus, but a tradition of the Athenian Academy itself, part of the conscious and sustained attempt to define the legacy of Plato. Founded by the Scholarch Arkesilaos (315–241 B.C.), Academic Skepticism achieved its most subtle statement in Carneades of Cyrene (213–129 B.C.), whose twin principles of "probability" in nature and "plausibility" in discourse Vico embraces here. Carneades' influence in Rome dates to 156 B.C., when he came as an envoy to the senate and displayed his dialectical skills (cf. *De or.* 2.3.155; *Tusc.* 4.3.5). His probabilism is defended in the *Academica* (1.12.43–46; 2.31.99ff.) by the literary, if not the historical, Cicero, while at the outset of the *De natura deorum* (1.5.12) Cicero claims the position as his own: "Non enim sumus ii quibus nihil verum esse videatur, sed ii qui omnibus veris falsa quaedam adjuncta esse dicamus tanta similitudine ut in iis nulla insit certa judicandi et adsentiendi nota. Ex quo exstitit illud, multa esse probabilia, quae quamquam non perciperentur, tamen, quia visum quendam haberent insignem et inlustrem iis sapientis vita regeretur." Cf. Charles B. Schmitt, *Cicero Scepticus* (The Hague: M. Nijhoff, 1972).

stand at all, it is preposterous to assume, as the moderns do, that mathematical physics is "the authentic voice of Nature herself." Though mention is made of the philosophical position he will later elaborate in some famous passages of his *De Italorum sapientia*—that theorems of physics, unlike geometrical axioms, are indemonstrable, in that we do not create them ex nihilo—the argument Vico uses here has a more practical turn. Geometrical method, he argues, having an illusion of completeness, stifles the process of philosophical contemplation that the universe—its forms enclosed within God's being—naturally evokes. The force of these sentiments, which had a history in the Renaissance and which would come to be felt in full only later in Vico's discourse, is to restore texture and subtlety to the physical universe and to require in response a full, active, labored effort from man. We should cultivate the study of physics, Vico concludes, "in order to curb our pride," our longing to know leading us toward the Supreme Being, who alone is Truth.[66]

The finally pedagogical basis for Vico's arguments for the incertitude of nature and life, and for the consequent probabilities with which we must deal, comes clearly to the fore when he turns to consider two areas of endeavor—medicine and mechanics—which are neither nature nor life, but lie somewhere between the two. Illness, Vico reasons, is not a diseased body but an ailing man, and no one ailing man is ever like another. A machine is not an application of physics but an accommodation of man to his physical surroundings. Thus medicine and mechanics are not extensions of science; they are, like law, arts of living, ways of being with one's environment. Like justice, health and utility are virtues of accommodation.

As we have seen above, Vico's perspective on mechanics is that no deductive science, however subtle or acute, had ever produced a useful machine, nor would it ever; only a draining effort of imagination, fed by the visual art of plane geometry,

[66] Cf. *De studiorum ratione, Opere* 1.84–85.

could lead to a true invention. Though slightly more com-
promising, his view on medicine is yet more revealing, for in
stating it he is able to join issue with a longstanding controversy in his home city. In reaction to the modern "Galenists"
and to the apparently exotic pharmacological remedies by
which they proposed to attack the very "roots" of disease,
the more empirical (and thus more skeptical) school of *Investiganti* in Naples held out for a more traditional "art of
healing," akin to what today would be called "preventive
medicine."[67] It is the latter's views that Vico makes his own.
To look for the causes of disease rather than the symptoms
of illness, Vico writes, is to forgo the aim to preserve and
restore health. A Cartesian-based medicine relies on the certainty of clear and distinct diseases, sharply set off from equally
clear health. The ancients, however, who felt the causes of
disease to be "deeply hidden and uncertain" (*satis occultae
incertaeque*), knew that men cannot be divided so easily into
"sick" and "healthy," but that each man enjoys a state of
health that is in constant flux and is manifested by an ever-
changing set of symptoms. The art of medicine practiced by
the ancients, therefore, put great stress on preventing illness,
especially through gymnastics and dietetics; and as symptoms
of malfunctioning turned up, they did not wait for the disease
to reach a "critical point" so that its cause could be assigned,
but took steps to accommodate the changes in one's physical

[67] The Accademia degli Investiganti, whose history has been traced in ex-
acting detail by Max H. Fisch, "L'Accademia degli investiganti," *De Homine*
27–28 (1968): 17–78, was founded in Naples in the middle of the seventeenth
century and survived in various forms and reincarnations until 1744, the year
of Vico's own death. The new experimental sciences, represented in the works
of Gassendi, Harvey, Boyle, and others, occupied the center of its interest,
with medicine in particular a popular subject of debate. Most famous of its
members was Lionardo Di Capua, whose two works on pharmacology and
medicine, the *Parere* of 1681 and the *Ragionamenti intorno alla incertezza
dei medicamenti* of 1689, are reflected in Vico's text. Despite his acquaintance
with various members of the academy, Vico was himself a member only
during the final years of his life. In addition to Fisch's work, see Nicola
Badaloni, *Introduzione a G. B. Vico* (Milan: Feltrinelli, 1961), which devotes
its first 164 pages to the academy, pages 124–147 being given to the work
of Di Capua. Fisch treats Di Capua in pages 44–53.

condition. We may look to the moderns for the explanation of disease, but our healing should be of the traditional kind.[68]

Beyond the fairly narrow world of number and measure—the proper domain of *res extensa*—we encounter a universe that is complex and manifold, with surprising contours and ever shifting forms, showing us causes that are neither unfailingly true nor patently false, but typically merely probable. To this assertion about the nature of things, Vico adds a claim about the men who must deal with them: Only rarely are we the *res cogitans* of Descartes's dreams, and only usefully so when inhabiting the world of mathematical forms; typically, indeed necessarily, we are sentient and feeling participants in the world, frequently biased and uncritical. To be effective in a world such as this, we must know more than to judge probabilities; we must also know to make them plausible.

"These doctrinaires judge human actions as they *ought* to be, not as they usually are, done more or less at random. Satisfied with abstract truth alone, and not being gifted with common sense, unused to following probability, they do not bother to find out whether their opinion is held by the generality and whether the things that are truths to them are also such to other people."[69] As important as the structure of life, Vico argues, is the way in which it is perceived by its actors and observers. Unlike mathematical truths, which contain their own warrant and thus have their force whether spoken aloud

[68] *De studiorum ratione, Opere* 1.89–90, which concludes: "Caussas cum recentioribus, quia explicatiores sunt, explicemus; magni tamen signa et judicia faciamus; et Conservatricem antiquorum, sub qua Exercitatricem et Diaetariam comprehendo, aeque ac nostram Curatricem, excolamus." Similarly, *De Italorum sapientia, Opere* 1.146, where Vico is speaking of the inutility of universals, the source of all "sects" in philosophy, medicine, and jurisprudence: "In re medica, qui recta per theses pergunt, magis contendunt ne corrumpantur systemata, quam ut sanentur aegroti." I cannot resist adding that reading Vico brings to mind the "Cartesian" doctor of our own day who sends away the patient with a common cold, bidding him return when it turns into pneumonia, since *that's* something he can treat.

[69] "Ipsi de rebus judicant, quales esse oportuerit, et res, ut plurimum, temere gestae sunt. Et cum sensum communem non excoluerint, nec verisimilia unquam secuti sint, uno vero contenti, quid porro de eo homines communiter sentiant, et an iis quoque vera videantur, nequicquam pendunt" (*De studiorum ratione, Opere* 1.92).

or held in private, probabilities achieve strength only through discourse. The truth of probabilities must be argued, must be set against other apparently valid perceptions and made to compete for acceptance. In such a contest, the tradition of perceptions, and thus social expectation, is critical. "Barristers," Vico notes, "often struggle more with cases that are true but do not seem to be so than with ones that are false but plausible." "Is it not significant that an orator whose only concern is the bare truth [*unum verum*] gets stranded in cases in which another speaker extricates himself by paying attention to probabilities [*verisimilia*] as well as to facts?"[70]

However high a scientific ideal, indubitable truth cannot be the sole or even the primary aim of an education that trains one for service in this world. That aim can be wisdom alone. "Science is concerned with the highest truths," Vico writes; "wisdom with the lowliest." The wise man is one who derives the highest truths from the unimportant ones, "who, through all the obliquities and uncertainties of human actions and events, keeps his eye focused on eternal truth, manages to follow a roundabout way whenever he cannot travel in a straight line, and makes decisions in the field of action which, in the course of time, prove to be as profitable as the nature of things permits."[71] What Vico prescribes here as the path of the sage he will one day declare, scientifically, to be the course the nations run when they rise from their lowliest beginnings to the wisdom of their full perfection.

---

[70] "Nam saepe oratores magis caussa laborant vera, quae nihil verisimile habeat, quam falsa, quae credibili ductu constet." "Quid illud, quod in quibus caussis haerebit orator, qui unum verum curat, in iisdem sese expediet, qui verisimilia praeterea consectatur?" (*De studiorum ratione, Opere* 1.81, 82f.).

[71] "Scientia ad summa, sapientia ad infima vera spectat . . . Sapientes, qui per agendorum obliqua et incerta ad aeternum verum collimant, quia recta non possunt, circumducunt iter; et consilia expediunt in temporis longitudinem, quantum natura fieri potest, profutura" (*De studiorum ratione, Opere* 1.91f.). On the Renaissance precedents for this form of sageness, see again Rice, *Renaissance Idea of Wisdom*, esp. chaps. 4 and 6. Cf. as well the works of Hans Baron and the paper of Walter Ullmann, "The Rebirth of the Citizen on the Eve of the Renaissance Period," in *Aspects of the Renaissance*, ed. Archibald R. Lewis (Austin: University of Texas Press, 1967), pp. 5–25.

CIVIL LIFE AS PRUDENT
AND ELOQUENT

The man of public affairs—the "wise citizen"—is a man of effective discourse. The aim of his discourse is plausibility. The instrument of plausibility is the faculty of ingenuity. These are the theses Vico defends as he unfolds his pedagogical ideal.

If the truths that are the makings of civil life are only rarely the truths that survive the scrutiny of clear and distinct perception; if indeed they are so very largely the truths of verisimilitude, opinions that are widely and generally held to be true but that cannot justify their truth of themselves; and if, finally, the force of such truths in civil life depends on their being *made* true for those whose assent is critical to a proposed civic action, then it follows that philosophical "criticism" should not be the first, and cannot be the only, instrument of learning taught to our youth. Finding probable truths and rendering them plausible can only be the work of an acute mind and a lively fantasy, for whose training the arts of topics and rhetoric stand ready.

No argument Vico makes against "analysis" and "criticism," not any logical, ontological, or epistemological assertion, is set forth so passionately and consistently as the claim, appearing again and again in his writings from beginning to end, that Cartesian method is worthless and wrong because of the blunting effect it has on the eloquence needed in civil life. This fact is almost never remarked by scholars, and to our misfortune, for Vico's insistence on the point leads in his *New Science* to its final, unresolved issue: What validity does a fully "human" culture have, and can it rely, as is its tendency and occasionally its boast, on reason alone? If consciousness and articulateness are the marks of modernity, does it need, can it indeed tolerate, the rounded shapes and suggestive tones of metaphor? Vico was a far way from this dilemma when he was defending against Arnauld the fuller, richer program of traditional education, yet in his notion of the sage and of the kind of spirit the sage was to take on he had the fundament for all he would eventually say about the source of novelty and freshness in a culture.

Typically in the early works, the sage who is to lead is set above and apart from the masses (*rudes*) who are to be led. At times the masses are portrayed, as in Machiavelli, Bovillus, and Bodin, as fools (*stulti*) governed by whim and chance; at times they are the material spirits of Plotinus, tainted by contact with the body and thus driven by its powerful appetites, or the fallen souls of Augustine and his followers, with minds made dull by sin; at still other times, they are simply the *vulgus* of ancient emphasis, caught up in the drama of civic urgency in which science has little to say. Always, however, they are a crowd without direction, needing the word of the sage to see and to act.[72]

The sage who is to speak and thus to lead is one who must see visions in the midst of change, must find analogies between matters that lie far apart and are apparently unrelated, and must draw all things together in expressions that are both sweeping and concrete, images that are sharp and forceful, go right to the point, are never trite or repetitious, and so move men to social action. Is analytic geometry any schooling for a man who must do that? Consider, Vico urges, the plight of "analysis," with its severe, abstract, apodictic form, moving forward by a constant and gradual series of small, closely catenated steps, looking neither to the left nor the right, stating every little truth even when it is perfectly obvious to the listeners, rushing over others that are logically valid but too challenging to laymen who have difficulty following a long chain of reasoning, all of it stated in algebraic figures that are even less concrete than the lines and letters of Euclid. Premature training in that kind of mathematics would be the ruin of our youth and eventually our culture; "it numbs all that is most exuberant in youthful natures; it obscures their imagination, enfeebles their memory, renders their perception [*in-*

---

[72] See, for example, the Second Oration, *Opere* 1.15–25; Sixth Oration, *Opere* 1.57–61; *De studiorum ratione*, *Opere* 1.86, 92–94.

gegno] sluggish, and slackens their understanding [*intendimento*]. And these four things are all most necessary for the
culture of the best humanity: the first for painting, sculpture,
architecture, music, poetry, and eloquence; the second for
learning languages and history; the third for inventions; and
the fourth for prudence."[73]

Analysis might be tolerated in education were it not for the
misfortune of its greatest strength: it takes the challenge out
of mathematics by yielding its answers too easily, and thus
makes the mind go slack. "In its concern for facility," Vico
writes, "method obstructs inventive minds; in its care for truth
it destroys inquisitiveness. Geometry sharpens the mind [*acuit
ingenium*], not when it is taught methodically [*methodo traditur*], but when it is discovered and applied by ingenuity amid
many diverse and disparate experiences."[74] Vico objects to

[73] "Il quale assidera tutto il più rigoglioso delle indoli giovanili, lor accieca
la fantasia, spossa la memoria, infingardisce l'ingegno, rallenta l'intendimento, le quali quattro cose sono necessarissime per la coltura della miglior
umanità: la prima per la pittura, scoltura, architettura, musica, poesia ed
eloquenza; la seconda per l'erudizione delle lingue e dell'istorie; la terza per
le invenzioni; la quarta per la prudenza" (Autobiography, *Opere* 5.14; cf.
also *De studiorum ratione, Opere* 1.86). As late as 1737 Vico took the
occasion of the fourth annual opening of the Accademia degli Oziosi to press
his theme anew: The geometric method of the Cartesians may be superior
to the Scholastic method, he told his colleagues, but "it is so subtle and
compact that if you miss a single proposition you miss the whole argument"
("metodo geometrico . . . è così sottile e stirato che, se per mala sorte si spezza
in non avvertire ad una proposizione, è niegato affatto a chi ode d'intender
nulla del tutto che si ragiona") (*Opere* 7.34).

The object of Vico's scorn was plainly the method of the Port Royal Logic,
set forth in detail in part 4 of Arnauld's text, chapters 9 and 10 of which
showed the defects in Euclid's procedure, leading up, in chapter 11, to "The
Method of the Sciences Reduced to Eight Principal Rules." Vico was less sure
than Arnauld as to the quiet competence of the new method. Referring to
its many pompous notations—"See Axiom II," "Confer Postulate 3," "Q.E.D.,"
and the like—Vico scoffed: "True geometric method works quietly, without
making its presence felt; when it begins to make noise, that is a sign it's not
working, just as the frightened soldier in combat will do a lot of yelling but
inflict no wounds while the man of courage holds his tongue and deals the
mortal blows" ("Il metodo geometrico vero opera senza farsi sentire, ed, ove
fa strepito, segno è che non opera: appunto come negli assalti l'uom timido
grida e non ferisce, l'uomo d'animo fermato tace e fa colpi mortali") (Second
Risposta, Opere 1.272).

[74] "Nam methodus ingeniis obstat, dum consulit facilitati; et curiositatem

analysis, not because it ill serves geometry, but because it fails its traditional propaedeutical role in liberal education by insufficiently challenging the natural talents of the mind (*ingenia*). Working strictly with numbers and formulas, it merely tallies up its findings and watches the equations emerge. As a result, "perception is stricken by algebra, for algebra sees only what is right under its nose; memory is confounded, since when the second sign is found algebra pays no further attention to the first; imagination goes blind because algebra has no need of images; understanding is destroyed because algebra professes to divine [*indovinare*]."[75] The solution, Vico thinks, is to replace the ease of analysis with the labor of synthetic or "plane" geometry, the only "logic" the ancients taught children. Working with figures instead of numbers and symbols (*neque per numeros, neque per species, sed per formas*), students would find their reasoning power held in check, like a horse pulled up short in order to gather speed in racing, so that finally, straining their imagination to find structure in the figures, they might burst forth with the solution. Even in failure they would gain, for "even if a student's ingenuity were not cultivated in the process, at least his fantasy (which is the eye of ingenuity, just as judgment is the eye of the intellect) would be strengthened."[76]

The conflict between an abstract, "facile" analytic geometry and the visual, "labored" effort of Euclid led back, Vico knew, to the more basic struggle between Cartesian "criticism"— the philosophical or universal statement of analysis—and the

---

dissolvit, dum providet veritati. Nec geometria acuit ingenium, cum methodo traditur, sed cum vi ingenii per diversa, per alia, multijunga, disparata in usum deducitur" (*De Italorum sapientia, Opere* 1.185). Cf. *De studiorum ratione, Opere* 1.87. The interplay between *ingenium* and *acuere* is a subject of the next section.

[75] "E sì con l'algebra si affligge l'ingegno, perché non vede se non quel solo che li sta innanzi i piedi; sbalordisce la memoria, perché, ritruovato il secondo segno, non bada più al primo; abbacina la fantasia, perché non immagina affatto nulla; distrugge l'intendimento, perché professa d'indovinare" (Autobiography, *Opere* 5.14; translation slightly amended).

[76] "Ut si minus ingenium inter ediscendum excoleretur, phantasia firmaretur tamen, quae ita est ingenii oculus, ut judicium est oculus intellectus" (*De Italorum sapientia, Opere* 1.185).

ancient rhetorical art of "topics." The art of topics, we recall, was formalized by Aristotle in a work of that title as a means for "finding" those probabilities (*ta eikota: Rh.* 1357a32; cf. *An.Pr.* 70a3) or generally accepted opinions from which to construct a dialectical or rhetorical argument (*Top.* 100a18–100b30). As the rhetorical treatise developed among the Hellenists—a development best summarized in the *De inventione* of Cicero—topics assumed an identity, plainly restricted, as an operation distinct from the action of judgment. Topics would serve to find the lines along which to argue (and so assist the rhetorical task of *inventio*), while the quite separate art of "criticism" (or "dialectic," as the Stoics came to call it) would sift and arrange them in the most effective order (and so assist *dispositio*). Though remarkably ambivalent about their respective value and relationship, the entire tradition down to Ramus held out for the need of the two arts in building a rhetorical case. When Ramus dismembered rhetoric by transferring *inventio* and *dispositio* to logic, he robbed rhetoric of her topical and critical arts; but in moving them to logic he gave them an importance all out of proportion with their traditional significance: topics and criticism would be serially applied, and through their joint endeavor all valid reasoning, and thus all science, would be achieved.[77] Nonsense! thundered Arnauld in reply. "No one can truly say that when discussing a subject he has used the Topics to find the necessary arguments. Consult all the lawyers and preachers in the world, all the men who speak or who write—these always have subject matter enough at hand—and I question if one among them could be found who had ever thought of making an argument *a causa, ab effectu,* or *ab adjunctis* to establish any conclusion."[78]

---

[77] Cf. Ramus, *Dialecticae libri duo* (1543), epistle to the reader, in the rendering of the first English edition (1574): "I shall in fewe wordes shew the[e] the matter contayned in this booke, the methode and forme of the same, howe easye it is aboue all others to be apprehended, howe thou shalt applye it to all artes and sciences, and shortlie that no arte or science maye eyther be taught or learned perfectlie without the knowledge of the same."

[78] *La logique; ou, L'arte de penser,* ed. Pierre Clair and François Girbal

Vico entered the argument between Ramists and Cartesians hand in hand with Bacon, and in this alliance he took a crucial step toward the position that would mature in his new science. Bacon, we recall, adopted the Ramist ordering of *inventio* (and thus of topics) within logic, yet he did so in a fully personal way.[79] In inventing arguments, he held, we are concerned with finding and arranging knowledge we already possess, and for this task the art of topics is invaluable; in inventing new arts and new sciences, however, we must abandon the logic of argument in favor of the logic of induction (5.2), one in which the distinction between perception and judgment collapses, for here "the same action of the mind which discovers the thing in question judges it; and the operation is not performed by help of any middle term, but directly, almost in the same manner as the sense" (5.4). That is a procedure, presumably, in which the art of topics offers no help, yet Bacon did declare as "lacking" what he would call "Particular Topics," which are "mixtures of logic with the proper matter of each science," and promised to "construct a special work concerning them in the more important and obscure subjects of nature" (5.3). The result, he thought, would be no single method of discourse, such as that of Ramus or the Schoolmen, but a diversity of methods arising from the diversity of subject matter (6.2).

All these ideas make their way into Vico's text, including their ambiguity on the issue of topics. It is not a point on which one would have wished equivocation, for the distinction between topics and criticism becomes part of the very structure of the *New Science*:

Providence gave good guidance to human affairs when it aroused human minds first to topics rather than to criticism, for acquaintance with things must come before judgment of them. Topics has the

---

(Paris: Presses universitaires de France, 1965), p. 234; trans. James Dickoff and Patricia James, *The Art of Thinking* (Indianapolis, Ind.: Bobbs-Merrill, 1964), p. 237.

[79] The references that follow are again to Bacon's own rendering of his *De dignitate et augmentis scientiarum.*

function of making minds inventive, as criticism has that of making them exact. . . . Thus the first peoples, who were the children of the human race, founded first the world of the arts; then the philosophers, who came a long time afterward and so may be regarded as the old men of the nations, founded the world of the sciences, thereby making humanity complete.[80]

Read with other statements on the theme, above all in Vico's pedagogical works, this distinction between the "topical" and the "critical" ages of mankind seems mechanical and purely serial, the one having to do with "truth" in a way the other cannot. "The invention of arguments is by nature prior to the judgment of their validity," Vico writes in his discourse on *Method*. "Criticism is the art of true speech; topics, of speech that is copious. . . . We achieve truth through criticism, eloquence through topics." And more bluntly still: "Topics discovers and heaps up; criticism sifts the mass and chooses. Thus topical minds are more fertile but less true, while critical minds are truer but more sterile."[81]

Vico's meaning is finer and more subtle than these tradi-

[80] "La provvedenza ben consigliò alle cose umane col promuovere nell'umane menti prima la topica che la critica, siccome prima è conoscere, poi giudicar delle cose. Perché la topica è la facultà di far le menti ingegnose, siccome la critica è di farle esatte. . . . Così i primi popoli, i quali furon i fanciulli del gener umano, fondarono prima il mondo dell'arti; poscia i filosofi, che vennero lunga età appresso, e 'n consequenza i vecchi delle nazioni, fondarono quel delle scienze: onde fu affatto compiuta l'umanità" (*Scienza nuova seconda, Opere* 4, §498; cf. also §699).

[81] "Argumentorum inventio prior natura est, quam de eorum veritate dijudicatio. . . . critica est ars verae orationis, topica autem copiosae. . . . Nos autem . . . dicimus, ut critica veraces, ita topica nos fieri copiosos" (*De studiorum ratione, Opere* 1.82–83). "La topica ritruova ed ammassa; la critica dall'ammassato divide e rimuove: e perciò gl'ingegni topici sono più copiosi e men veri; i critici sono più veri, ma però asciutti" (Second *Risposta, Opere* 1.271). Vico's argument for the "natural" priority of topics is borrowed verbatim from Cicero (*Top.* 2.6; cf. Vico, Second *Risposta, Opere* 1.269f.), who was defending the usefulness of the art against the Stoics' one-sided concern for "dialectic." Quick to see parallels in history, Vico routinely compared the Cartesians of his day with the Stoics of old, and contemporary skeptics with either the ancient Academics or the Epicureans, depending on his context. The happy medium he found in "Plato," though the position he defended was rather that of the "prudential" Aristotle, renewed in the thought of Cicero and in the Roman tradition generally.

tional phrases reveal. As usual, he finds his meaning by returning to the full vision of dialèctical reasoning set forth in the works of Aristotle. Aristotle did leave behind in his *Rhetoric*, of course, many pages on those "particular topics" (concerned with specific kinds of oratory) that Bacon had thought wanting (*Rh.* 1.4–14), as well as a brief treatment of the commonplaces and general guides to building an argument that later treatise writers would add to and embellish and turn into the infamous topical "checklists" that became the scourge of Arnauld (*Rh.* 2.18–19).[82] What is most prominent in his text, however, is a concern for topics in the formal sense (*Rh.* 2.20–26), as a summary and application to rhetoric of the principles of dialectical reasoning stated in the *Prior Analytics* and developed in the *Topics* and the *De sophisticis elenchis*. Understood formally, topics is a complete form of reasoning, not a mere massing of impressions or heaping up of instances that the critical faculty must subsequently work through. All valid reasoning, Aristotle held, whether demonstrative or merely probable, takes one of two forms, induction or the syllogism (*An. Pr.* 68b10–14; *An. Post.* 71a1–10; *Top.* 104b10–19). So, too, in oratory: To the extent one gives reasons (*logoi*) in argumentation and does not rely simply on one's character or emotions, one either invokes significant examples (which form an imperfect induction) or uses enthymemes (imperfect syllogisms). The imperfection in these forms of reasoning lies not so much in the merely probable nature of their premises, for such is the nature of the matters on which the rhetor must reason, as in their brief or incomplete form; for the orator never says a word more than necessary, leaving it to his listeners to supply the elements in his argument that are obvious to all (*Rh.* 1356a36–1356b18, 1357a8–18, 1395b20–31). In this way he draws his listeners into the argumentative process itself, meeting them on ground that is common to them both (*Top.* 131a31), appealing never to abstract truth but always

[82] Cf. Cic. *Inv. Rhet.* 1.24.34–1.28.43, where the "general" topics of argumentation are summarized, and the whole of his *Topica*, which sets forth in detail all he had heard on the subject in the schools of the Greeks.

to the *sensus communis*, to "what is held generally or by most" (*An. Pr.* 24b11, 70a3; *Top.* 100a30; *Rh.* 1357a36), and so manages to persuade and lead them to action. This effort to find the "middle," a process strictly analogous to that of seeking the causes in demonstrative reasoning (*An. Post.* 90a5), is the proper task of topics, and it requires of its practitioners a constant application of alertness and imagination, no less an insertion of perception and judgment than that needed by the strictest logician.

Vico made all these ideas completely his own. Topics, he replied to a critic, is indeed the art of discovering the reasons and arguments to prove whatever is proposed,

but "argument" in this instance is not the "arrangement of a proof," as commonly assumed, what in Latin is known as *argumentatio*; rather, it is that third idea which is found to tie together the two in the issue being debated—what in the Schools is called the "middle term"—such that topics is the art of finding the middle term. But I claim more: Topics is the art of apprehending the true, for it is the art of seeing all the aspects or *loci* of a thing that enable us to distinguish it well and gain an adequate concept of it. For judgments turn out false when their concepts are either greater or less than the things they propose to signify: we cannot be certain we have dealt with something in all its essential respects if not all the possible pertinent questions have been asked.[83]

---

[83] "Dite che 'la topica è arte di ritruovare ragioni e argomenti per pruovar che che sia.' . . . Io pur diffinisco così la topica; ma 'argomento,' in quest'arte, non suona 'disposizione di una pruova,' come volgarmente si prende e da' latini '*argumentatio*' si appella; ma s'intende quella terza idea, che si ritrova per unire insieme le due della questione proposta, che nelle scuole dicesi 'mezzo termine'; talché ella è un'arte di ritruovare il mezzo termine. Ma dico di più: che questa è l'arte di apprender vero, perché è l'arte di vedere per tutti i luoghi topici nella cosa proposta quanto mai ci è per farlaci distinguer bene ed averne adeguato concetto; perché la falsità de' giudizi non altronde proviene che perché l'idee ci rappresentano più o meno di quello che sono le cose: del che non possiamo star certi, se non avremo raggirata la cosa per tutte le questioni proprie che se ne possano giammai proporre" (Second *Risposta, Opere* 1.268–269). Vico's reference is to the list of topical questions or inquiries (*an sit? quid sit? quanta sit? qualis?* and so forth) that he inserted, as useful in reading the "great book of nature," in the passage in the *De Italorum sapientia* that is here under discussion (cf. *Opere* 1.182).

With this Vico comes full circle in his argument. The mind formed by topics is superior to the Cartesian mind not merely because it is trained to find connections between disparate and apparently unrelated things, but also because it is "copious," will range widely, consider all possible aspects of a subject under debate, and so guarantee the possibility of truth. Only such a mind is equal to the tortuosities of life and the uncertainties in nature. It is a powerful mind, alert, imaginative, and quick, one that perceives and judges in one action, "almost in the same manner as by the sense," as Bacon had suggested. So convinced was Vico of the power of this mind that he singled it out as a faculty unto itself, a faculty similar to and yet distinct from intellect. He called it the *certa facultas sciendi*, the "faculty proper to knowing," and gave it its own name. That name is *ingenuity*.

INGENUITY AND THE *DICTA ACUTA*

Finding the "middle," making connections, and so advancing the cause of civil life, is the proper work of ingenuity.[84]

[84] The word I am rendering as "ingenuity" is, of course, Vico's *ingenium* (Italian, *ingegno*; French, *esprit*). Though at times used simply to mean "mind," or one's "natural talents," or even "human nature," Vico usually intends by it to signify that faculty of mind, distinct from intellect, by which one sees relationships, finds analogies, sees or creates similitudes, and so truly "knows." To render it as "genius," as some critics will, disguises its nature as a faculty of mind and gives too much emphasis to its purely creative or inventive function (which of course it has); it also makes the power seem remote or esoteric—the opposite direction in which Vico will take it in his *New Science*. To render it as "wit," on the other hand, which is its most common English equivalent, found throughout Vico's century (as indeed in my own text, when sources of Vico's ideas are discussed), would stress one-sidedly the aesthetic and linguistic context of the notion (as the source of novel concepts or striking expressions), a context, to be sure, that is positively critical to Vico's development, but one nonetheless that is narrower than that of civil life as a whole, whose entire operations are bound up with *ingenium*. I opt, then, for the flatter and somewhat vague "ingenuity," partly to protect the broad application that Vico gave the term, but also to allow for the specialized use of such related expressions as "ingenious," "ingeniousness," "genius," and "engineer." (Were I a braver man, I might render Vico's *"uomo ingegnoso"* as "civil engineer"!)

This is not a work that may be taken for granted, but one requiring sustained effort and the keenest, most acute perception. It is the work of "knowing" itself, such as we humans are given to know. "The faculty proper to knowing," Vico writes, "I call ingenuity, for through it one brings together and relates those things which, to persons not blessed with ingenuity, seem to have no connection at all. Whence man's ingenuity is in the world of arts and crafts, even as nature in the universe is God's."[85]

The Greeks, Vico claimed, paid no regard to this faculty of knowing and so made an unfortunate split between finding and judging.[86] Vico's claim is wrong by half, for while they surely distinguished perception and judgment, the Greeks' are the first voices we hear in the tradition so audible in Vico's own summary of the nature of ingenuity.[87] That poets, like

[85] "La particolar facultà del sapere dico esser lo ingegno, perché con questa l'uomo compone le cose, le quali, a coloro che pregio d'ingegno non hanno, sembravano non aver tra loro nessun rapporto. Onde l'ingegno umano nel mondo delle arti è, come la natura nell'universo è l'ingegno di Dio" (First *Risposta, Opere* 1.212).

[86] Cf. *De Italorum sapientia, Opere* 1.183: "Hoc dissidium inventionis et judicii non aliunde inter Graecos ortum, nisi quod facultatem sciendi propriam non attenderunt. Ea enim ingenium est, quo homo est capax contemplandi ac faciendi similia."

[87] The history of the Romantic notion of creative genius in antiquity and the Renaissance is traced by Edgar Zilsel, *Die Entstehung des Geniebegriffs: Ein Beitrag zur Ideengeschichte der Antike und des Frühkapitalismus* (Tübingen: Mohr, 1926). See also Jacques Barzun, *Romanticism and the Modern Ego* (Boston: Little, Brown, 1943), 3d rev. ed., *Classic, Romantic, and Modern* (Boston: Little, Brown, 1961); Milton C. Nahm, *The Artist as Creator: An Essay of Human Freedom* (Baltimore: Johns Hopkins University Press, 1956); E. N. Tigerstedt, "The Poet as Creator: Origins of a Metaphor," *Comparative Literature Studies* 5 (1968): 455–488. Ingenuity as an aesthetic concept is a recurrent theme in such texts as Croce's *Estetica come scienza dell'espressione e linguistica generale: Teoria e storia* (1902; 5th ed., Milan and Palermo: Sandron, 1922), trans. Douglas Ainslie, *Aesthetic as Science of Expression and General Linguistic*, 2d ed. (London: Macmillan, 1922); and Ernst Robert Curtius, *Europäische Literatur und lateinisches Mittelalter* (Bern: Francke Verlag, 1948), trans. Willard R. Trask, *European Literature and the Latin Middle Ages* (New York: Pantheon, 1953). As a rhetorical theme it is typically treated in the context of *inventio* and may be found in the various works cited in notes 7 and 11 of the previous chapter. For the Renaissance in particular, see Joel Elias Spingarn, *A History of Literary Criticism in the Renaissance*, 2d ed. (New York: Columbia University Press, 1908), now

lovers, are possessed of a divine madness (*mania*) and so share in the vision of final truth is an idea made current by Plato (*Phdr.* 265a–b; cf. 244a–249e). Released from the habits of mere ordinary men, they see through to the structure of things, and in their best of moments achieve that immortal perfection which befits true lovers of wisdom (249e). While more pedestrian, Aristotle's view is equally flattering: The poet's task is none other than to show the structure and meaning of human affairs, to take the complexities and uncertainties of history and reduce them to a form in which their necessary and probable connections are made manifest. "With the characters as with the incidents of a play," Aristotle writes, "the right thing is to strive always after the necessary or the probable; so that whenever such-and-such a personage says or does such-and-such a thing, it shall be the necessary or probable outcome of his character; and whenever this incident follows on that, it shall be either the necessary or the probable consequence of it."[88] No less than a cobbler of shoes or other craftsman, the poet is restless with nature as it is and anxious to improve upon it. The historian may rest with the facts of history and be content to report them in all their dizzying singularity, but not the poet. Using the same proper names that the historian uses, the poet weaves them into a plot and so makes of them a universal statement, one as to what such or such a kind of man will probably or necessarily say or do. "Hence poetry is something more philosophic and of graver import than history, since its statements are of the nature rather of universals, whereas those of history are singulars."[89]

---

superseded in significant part by Bernard Weinberg, *A History of Literary Criticism in the Italian Renaissance*, 2 vols. (Chicago: University of Chicago Press, 1961). Renaissance and early modern attempts to validate the imagination as part of the reasoning process are traced by Ernst Cassirer, *Das Erkenntnisproblem in der Philosophie und Wissenschaft der neuren Zeit*, 3 vols., 3d ed. (Berlin: Bruno Cassirer, 1922–1923), esp. 1.286ff., 316ff., 327f.

[88] *Poet.* 1454a33–40; trans. Ingram Bywater, *The Works of Aristotle*, ed. W. D. Ross, 12 vols. (Oxford: At the Clarendon Press, 1908–1952), vol. 11.

[89] *Poet.* 1451b5–7; trans. Bywater. Aristotle's distinction between the poet and the historian furnished a principal issue in the late Renaissance debate over the *ars historica*. Cf. Girolamo Cotroneo, *I trattatisti dell' "ars historica"* (Naples: Giannini, 1971), esp. pp. 121–168.

To reveal the ways of men and the pattern of human history, the poet seeks to make plausible to an audience the motivations and actions that bind men together, and in this he is at one with the orator. Poet and orator alike share the logic of persuasion (*Poet.* 1456a34; *Rh.* 1356a), beginning always from opinions that are seen to be probable, using language and demeanor to establish credibility. The orator may explain his sense directly while that of the poet must be borne in the action of his characters; yet the effectiveness of both depends on the images and language they choose. Their power rests in metaphor, which alone can give voice to experience, bring the prosaic to life, and show those connections between things which otherwise are not seen (*Rh.* 1404b–1405b; *Poet.* 1458a18–1459a7). The metaphor, says Aristotle simply, "is the one thing that cannot be learnt from others; and it is also a sign of genius, since a good metaphor implies an intuitive perception of the similarity in dissimilars."[90]

The universality that the poet achieves in characterization and plot is gained by the orator in *gnomai* or maxims (*Rh.* 1394a19–1395b19). Functioning roughly as a premise or the conclusion of an enthymeme, the maxim is a statement, not about a particular fact, but of a general kind, and concerns always a question of practical conduct, a course of action to be chosen or avoided. The maxim can be a proverb or a commonplace, it can be challenging or paradoxical, but always it must serve to give point to the argument and gain the nodding assent of the listeners. The advantage of the maxim to a speaker, Aristotle notes matter-of-factly, is that it is supremely suited to the lack of intelligence of the hearers, "who love to hear him succeed in expressing as a universal truth the opinions which they hold themselves about particular cases."[91] Appearing then as a general declaration of principles, the maxim invests a speech with moral character.

It is also to be counted, as is the enthymeme generally, with

[90] *Poet.* 1459a6–7; trans. Bywater. Cf. *Rh.* 1405a, 1412a.
[91] *Rh.* 1395b1–3; trans. W. Rhys Roberts, *The Works of Aristotle*, ed. Ross, vol. 11.

that class of acute or "smart sayings" (*ta asteia, dicta acuta*) through which an audience is easily and quickly instructed and so derives pleasure (*Rh*. 1410b–1413a). Being anything but trite or superficial (lest they give no information at all), sayings that are truly smart must nonetheless be immediately or readily understood. Their task is to make things "actual," plastic to the imagination, and thus intelligible. For this purpose the analogy or "proportional" metaphor is above all apt, for it combines familiar and foreign images in such a way as to bring an audience new visions. To heighten the sense of discovery and thus the pleasure of an audience, the speaker may set out from an initial deceit, leading his listeners to expect one thing, only to reveal another. Like riddles, wordplays, and other jokes of the kind, such sayings lead the mind to say, "How true it is! But I missed it" (*Rh*. 1412a). Indeed, all smart sayings gain by being in some way antithetical, even as they do by being brief, for "antithesis impresses the new idea more firmly and brevity more quickly."[92]

Neglected if not lost in the West until the sixteenth century, Aristotle's *Poetics* went unregarded by the Hellenist and Latin theorists, but the diffusion of his rhetorical doctrine is evident in the anonymous *Rhetorica ad Herennium* as in the writings of Cicero and Quintilian. In their concept of *sententia*, one of the most dexterous in all of traditional rhetoric, the Latins achieved a synthesis of the logical and the literary emphases in Aristotle's text, a notion that could unite the philosophic character of the "maxim" and the expressive character of the "smart saying."[93] As the term of the process of *inventio*, a *sententia* is both a thought and an expression, has equally to do with *res* and *verba*; it is in fact the proper and effective

---

[92] *Rh*. 1412b23; trans. Roberts. A saying that is *asteion* is "urbane" or "of the city," courteous, polite, smart, witty, elegant, the opposite of one that is *agroikon*—simple, naive, rude, or countrylike.

[93] On the notion of *sententia* in this specialized sense, see Lausberg, *Handbuch der literarischen Rhetorik*, §§872–879, and for its general usage see the survey under this term in his Latin index, §1244. For its more general, literary sense, see Curtius, *European Literature and the Latin Middle Ages*, pp. 57–61 and passim.

union of ideas and language. The ancients, Quintilian notes (in the kind of aside Vico loved to heed—and did), took *sententia* to mean "whatever they sensed or felt" (*quod animo sensissent*), and would say that they uttered their *sensa*, understood corporeally; we moderns, however, refer *sensus* to the mind as the "sense" or "meaning" of our concepts, and thus use *sententia* to mean a striking statement (*Inst.* 8.5.1). Though now quite diffuse in meaning, he continues, the *sententia* in its original and proper sense is a maxim or aphorism, what the Greeks called *gnome*—both Greeks and Latins deriving their names from the fact that such utterances resemble the decrees or resolutions of public bodies. For this reason, we must take care not to overuse them or put them in the wrong mouth, and must be certain they are not plainly untrue, as many are that are used by unscrupulous speakers who nonetheless vaunt them as "universal opinions" (*katholica*).[94]

Quintilian points here to the essence, and with it the power, of *sententia*; though pronounced in the context of an individual case, such as all instances of oratory are, the *sententia* has a universal character, an authority reflected stylistically in its brevity. Usually one sentence in length, a *sententia* literally punctuates a discussion or a paragraph, bringing it to a point and a close. Here thought and language interpenetrate, reinforcing one another. The last expression is the most thoughtful, and the last thought is the most expressive. Nowhere is this more evident than in that form of *sententia* to which the Romans gave particular emphasis, the judicial opinion. A "sentence" in court is both language and idea, both *verba* and *res*, each commanding authority. To "pass sentence" means both to "render judgment," thus bringing a process of reasoning and argument to a close, and to "make a statement," thus adding a text to the stock of public language in which a culture has its identity. As a spoken judgment (*judicatum*), a

[94] Quint. *Inst.* 8.5.7: "In hoc genere custodiendum est et id, quod ubique, ne crebrae sint, ne palam falsae (quales frequenter ab iis dicuntur, qui haec *katholika* vocant, et, quidquid pro causa videtur, quasi indubitatum pronuntiant), et ne passim et a quocunque dicantur."

sentence holds authority (*auctoritas*) and so orders the life of a people; as a norm of social existence, it becomes precedent (*praeiudicium*) for further cases of its kind, such that future plaintiffs must build their claims with reference to it. Certain statements of this sort, moreover, are particularly "sententious," not only in the sense of being pithy, but also in that of being weighty or trenchant. As such, they become part of folk wisdom, lines to which a people "instinctively" reaches when stating or explaining its social being.[95]

In their judicial sense, *sententiae* were collected in the Latin West in the great body of law that in time became known as the *Corpus juris civilis*, while in their wider meaning they joined with *exempla* (Aristotle's abbreviated induction) to form traditions of advice for good and prudent living and examples of human excellence and folly.[96] As conclusions about life and right living, the *sententiae* were products of discernment and

[95] On the judicial *sententia*, see Lausberg, *Handbuch der literarischen Rhetorik* §§92, 353. That public judgments of this kind, and particularly those of law, accumulate as a body of reliable wisdom has been richly represented in Western thought and attained a kind of climax in Edmund Burke's *Reflections on the Revolution in France*. In our enlightened day, wrote Burke, we tend to be "men of untaught feelings," heedless of the "just prejudices" that render a man's virtue his habit. Yet without such "prejudices"—by which he meant in the first place the established church and the monarchy—we would become "little less than the flies of a summer." "And the science of jurisprudence, the pride of the human intellect, which with all its defects, redundancies, and errors is the collected reason of ages, combining the principles of original justice with the infinite variety of human concerns, as a heap of old exploded errors, would be no longer studied . . . No part of life would retain its acquisitions. Barbarism with regard to science and literature, unskillfulness with regard to arts and manufactures, would infallibly succeed to the want of a steady education and settled principle; and thus the commonwealth itself would, in a few generations, crumble away, be disconnected into the dust and powder of individuality, and at length dispersed to all the winds of heaven" (Library of Liberal Arts edition [Indianapolis, Ind.: Bobbs-Merrill, 1955], pp. 108–109; cf. 98–99). There is no evidence I am aware of that Burke had occasion to read Vico's analysis of social decay, which makes all the more fervent one's hope that he has been caught up into Vico's circle in Paradise.

[96] See Curtius, *European Literature and the Latin Middle Ages*, pp. 57–61, where further reference is made to a collection of over 2,500 such aphorisms by Jakob Werner, *Lateinische Sprichwörter und Sinnsprüche des Mittelalters* (Heidelberg, 1912).

judgment, but they were remembered and passed on as samples of wit and quick thinking. Collected alphabetically as gnomic verses, they were taught for amusement and for sharpening the mind; in this sense they became stalwarts of *inventio*, partisans in its struggle against the measure and sobriety of *dispositio*, and so, too, of *ingenium* against *judicium*. To be thought "sententious" was not to be thought "judicious," or not necessarily so, and thus the man of wit or ingenuity was praised regularly for his cleverness, but not always for his truth.

This challenge to a clean and direct style of thought and expression by one that is intricate, surprising, or "mannered," has been a regular, if not continual, phenomenon in our literature and criticism, such that some choose to speak of classicist and Mannerist "strains" in the West, finding in them the inevitable ebb and flow of our culture.[97] While this can doubtless be sustained, the lines of the contest are nonetheless etched most clearly in the century in which Mannerism, now named, was called explicitly into question—the seventeenth. There at its sharpest is the argument over "wit" between stylists and logicians, which we observed at some length in the previous chapter, and there as well—indeed especially— is the debate among critics themselves over the nature and value of the "conceit" (*concetto*) and over the faculties of imagination and ingenuity that are said to produce it. Prepared for by the sixteenth-century discussions of the nature of poetry brought on by the rediscovery of Aristotle's *Poetics*, and more immediately by the works of the poets of "conceit" themselves—Luis de Góngora (1561–1627) in Spain and Giambattista Marino (1569–1625) in Italy—the conceitist debate issued in a cluster of works at midcentury and provoked in response a wave of neoclassicism whose force was particularly to be felt during Vico's own lifetime. Vico's own achievement, indeed, was first to fuse, then to transcend, Mannerist and neoclassicist thinking.

[97] This is particularly the thesis of Curtius, *European Literature and the Latin Middle Ages*, pp. 273–301.

By nearly common agreement, the *textus priscus* of conceitist theory is the *Agudeza y arte de ingenio* (1649) of Baltasar Gracián (1601–1658), the enlarged version of his earlier *Arte de ingenio, tratado de la agudeza* (1624).[98] The conceit, Gracián writes there, "consists in a splendid concordance, in a harmonic correlation between two or more knowable ex-

[98] Contained in *Obras completas*, ed. Arturo del Hoyo, 2d ed. (Madrid: Aguilar, 1960). On this work, see two articles by T. E. May, "An Interpretation of Gracián's *Agudeza y arte de ingenio*," *Hispanic Review* 16 (1948): 275–299, and "Gracián's Idea of the *concepto*," *Hispanic Review* 18 (1950): 15–41; cf. also Samuel Gili Gaya, "Agudeza, modismos y lugares comunes," in *Homenaje a Gracián* (Saragossa: Fernando el Católico, 1958), pp. 89–97. More generally, Hellmut Jansen, *Die Grundbegriffe des Baltasar Gracián*, Kölner Romanistische Arbeiten, new series, no. 9 (Geneva: Droz, and Paris: Minard, 1958); Monroe Z. Hafter, *Gracián and Perfection: Spanish Moralists of the Seventeenth Century* (Cambridge, Mass.: Harvard University Press, 1966).

The two classical poets of conceit are well represented by Dámaso Alonso, *Estudios y ensayos gongorinos*, 2d ed. (Madrid: Grecos, 1960); and by James V. Mirollo, *The Poet of the Marvelous: Giambattista Marino* (New York: Columbia University Press, 1963).

On conceitism and its theorists, see, besides Croce's *Estetica*, also his *I trattatisti italiani del "concettismo" e Baltasar Gracián*, Memoria letta all'Accademia Pontaniana nella tornata del 18 giugno 1899 (Naples: Stab. Tipografico nella R. Università, 1899), reprinted in *Problemi di estetica e contributi alla storia dell'estetica italiana* (Bari: Laterza, 1910), pp. 309–345, and his *Storia dell'età barocca in Italia* (Bari: Laterza, 1942). A more sympathetic, and more challenging, view appears in two essays by Joseph A. Mazzeo, "A Seventeenth-Century Theory of Metaphysical Poetry," *Renaissance and Seventeenth-Century Studies* (New York: Columbia University Press, 1964), pp. 29–43, and "Metaphysical Poetry and the Poetic of Correspondence," ibid., pp. 44–59. On the Spanish conceitists in particular, see Edward Sarmiento, "Sobre la idea de una escuela de escritores conceptistas en España," in *Homenaje a Gracián*, pp. 145–153. For Italy, Klaus Peter Lange, *Theoretiker des literarischen Manierismus: Tesauros und Pellegrinis Lehre von der "acutezza" oder von der Macht der Sprache*, Humanistische Bibliothek: Abhandlungen und Texte, vol. 4 (Munich: Fink, 1968). See also the texts collected by Ezio Raimondi, *Trattatisti e narratori del Seicento* (Milan: Ricciardi, 1960).

On the problem of defining the baroque, see René Wellek, "The Concept of Baroque in Literary Scholarship," *Journal of Aesthetics and Art Criticism* 5 (1946): 77–109; Helmut Hatzfeld, "A Clarification of the Baroque Problem in the Romance Literatures," *Comparative Literature* 1 (1949): 113–139; Giovanni Getto, "La polemica sul Barocco," *Letteratura italiana: Le correnti* (Milan: Marzorati, 1956); Frank J. Warnke, *Versions of Baroque: European Literature in the Seventeenth Century* (New Haven, Conn.: Yale University Press, 1972).

tremes expressed in an act of understanding. . . . Thus the conceit can be defined: it is an act of understanding that expresses the correspondence between things." The conceit then is at once a concept and the concept's expression, and in both forms it binds extremes and shows their correspondence. It is bright, like a vein of silver or a star in a darkened sky, brilliant, dazzling, or marvelous, anything but plain, raw, or unrefined. By nature it is "unnatural" for it finds and presents the connections among things that nature herself shields from dull or ordinary wits. Suited to any literary form, the metaphors it brings forth are not pedestrian or familiar, but sharp (*acuta*), even penetrating (*peracuta*), deserving a special name taken from those very qualities. They are *agudezas*, "acuities," the fitting product of an ingenious mind.[99]

Gracián had announced a new "art of ingenuity," one that would complement his own *Arte de prudencia* and supply a lack he found in ancient rhetoric, overly concerned with giving rules for judgment. Yet his own text went little beyond a few definitions and was given mainly to citing examples of acuities found in the works of Góngora and Marino (the "Góngora of Italy") and their more distant Latin forebears, especially Martial. A decidedly more restrained view of the conceit, and a fuller presentation of its theory, was to be found in the *Delle acutezze* (1639) of Matteo Pellegrini (1595–1652), a book Vico called "golden" (*aureus*), and in the writings of Sforza Pallavicino (1607–1667), a cardinal of the Church and historian of the Council of Trent whom Vico thought "most acute" (*acutissimus*). Yet in the process of being clarified, the fruitful ambiguity in Gracián's notion of the conceit—as both mental act and literary expression—was sacrificed, each critic

---

[99] *Agudeza y arte de ingenio*, Discurso 2: "Consiste, pues, este artificio conceptuoso, en una primorosa concordancia, en una armonica correlación entre dos o tres cognoscibles extremos, expresada por un acto del entendimiento. . . . De suerte que se puede definir el concepto: Es un acto del entendimiento, que exprime la correspondencia que se halla entre los objectos." Cf. Discurso 1: "Entendimiento sin agudeza ni conceptos, es sol sin luz, sin rayos, y cuantos brillan en las celestes lumbreras son materiales [comparados] con los del ingenio."

stressing one of these two dimensions. The formalism implied in the idea of an extraordinary and thus ingenious arrangement of words came to the fore in Pellegrini. The bond of "acuity," he held, is not between things that are extreme or disparate, nor even between things at all; it rests rather between things and the words that express them. Taken by themselves, the words of an expression and the things they signify are *dura materia*; only in the bond between them is the force of ingenuity evident. Metaphors that are true conceits—*acutezze, spiriti, vivezze* (the terms are synonymous to him)—are luminous and tense, have about them a quality that is "thrilling" (*mirabile*), their beauty delighting the ingenuity just as truth delights the intellect.[100] For Pallavicino, the "thrill" of the conceit is no less real, but it is merely guaranteed by the vividness of the metaphors, not produced by them. The delight is intellectual, resting in the observation that is expressed, and comes about when an unexpected insight occurs, or when one point is squeezed from another, or when the opposite of what is expected is drawn out of a proposition. An invalid conceit is one that is in fact trite, or rests on an equivocation, or affirms something that is inherently false.[101]

Though he earned no particular accolade from Vico, the critic whose thought was most like his and who developed most fully the theory of conceit was Emmanuele Tesauro (1592–1675). The ancients, he held, had indeed slighted ingenuity,

[100] *Delle acutezze*, chap. 3: "In un detto non è altro che parole, obietti significati, e loro vicendevole collegamento: le parole, sì come anche gli obietti, o cose, appartatamente considerate, sono dura materia: dunque l'acutezza si regge necessariamente dal legamento. Questo può considerarsi tra parole e parole: tra cose e parole: tra cose e cose, e in ciascuna di queste può essere artificioso, e anco essere senza artificio ... Così noi potremo diffinir l'accortezza dell'ingegno col proposito nostro, con felice trovamento del mezzo, per legar figuratamente in un detto con mirabile acconcezza diverse cose." Though appearing three years earlier than the first edition of Gracián's work, the *Delle acutezze* was apparently unknown to him, just as it is equally unlikely, though sometimes asserted, that Pellegrini plagiarized Gracián. Cf. Croce, *I trattatisti italiani del "concettismo" e Baltasar Gracián*, pp. 10–13; Edward Sarmiento, "Two Criticisms of Gracián's *Agudeza*," *Hispanic Review* 3 (1935): 23–35.

[101] *Trattato dello stile e del dialogo*, chaps. 10, 16, 17.

but in the *Rhetoric* of Aristotle we have a proper telescope by which to sight the principles of a full art of acute style, one that befits the whole of oratory, poetry, and symbolic expression.[102] The same troubling distinction between form and content, between representation that is figured and that which is plain or merely literal, burdens Tesauro's thought no less than that of his fellow theorists, yet from this initial assumption he rises to a position of some subtlety. Forms of metaphor, he argues, correspond exactly to the categories of logic; words, propositions, and arguments can all be figured and all are subject to the work of an ingenious mind. Arguments in particular are objects of ingenuity, taking form in rhetoric as a kind of extended metaphor. Following Aristotle, he calls such an argument an "urbane enthymeme" (*entimemo urbano*) or an "urbanely false syllogism" (*sillogismo urbanamente fallace*). Unlike the sophism, (the false syllogism of dialectic), which is falsity parading as truth, poetic's false syllogism is truth parading as falsity; it intends falsity in order to convey the truth. The "falsity" that it, like all metaphor, is, is like a transparent veil through which the truth is seen. The success of such transparency rests in its being sophisticated or "urbane"—Tesauro's rendering of Aristotle's *asteiōs* (*Rh.* 1410b20)—deriving from true wit or ingenuity, and resulting in the sustenance of society, not its destruction, the sad end of sophistry.[103]

Tesauro went further in his analysis, making of conceits the artful expressions not only of man, but also of God, the angels, and animals. Nature is indeed a book, he held, but it is written in metaphors and conceits, the work of a "witty creator" (*arguto favellatore*). "The notion that the world is a poem of God," writes Joseph Mazzeo,

---

[102] *Il cannocchiale aristotelico* (Turin, 1654), reissued in several editions with various subtitles, including this one of 1664: *Idea dell'arguta et ingeniosa elocutione, che serve à tutta l'arte oratoria, lapidaria, et simbolica esaminata co' principij del divino Aristotele*.

[103] *Il cannocchiale aristotelico*, 4th ed. (Rome, 1664), pp. 569–586. On the "urban enthymeme," see Lange, *Theoretiker des literarischen Manierismus*, pp. 103–113.

is old enough as a conception and, in various forms, goes back at least to Plotinus. However, the important difference for Tesauro is that the world is a "metaphysical" poem and God a "metaphysical" poet. He conceived *ingegno* as the faculty in man analogous to God's creative power. It is a small particle of the divine nature, for it can create "being" where there was no "being" before. As God created a "metaphysical" world, so the poet creates "metaphysical" poems.[104]

Tesauro could think of the universe as figured, for his notion of metaphor embraced not only verbal conceits but mute and mixed forms as well. Thus the sky is a grand mute conceit while thunder is an *acutezza* of the mixed type, picture and motto together.[105] Nature at large is an extended metaphor, challenging the poet to an elaboration of correspondences, a kind of aesthetic chain similar to the logical chain of the sorites.

A neoclassicist refinement, if not rejection, of these ideas occurred in the hands of two of Vico's contemporaries—Giovanni Vincenzo Gravina (1664–1718) and Ludovico Antonio Muratori (1672–1750), the latter a Modenese scholar and cleric whose monumental *Rerum italicarum scriptores* and *Annali d'Italia*, written during Vico's own most productive years, gave Italy the first real sense of its past; the former a classicist and legal scholar from Calabria, cofounder of the Accademia dell'Arcadia, whose bylaws he wrote, in Latin, on the model of the Twelve Tables of Roman Law, and who became in 1699 a professor *utriusque juris*—a man, in short, whose career Vico himself would have dearly loved as his

---

[104] "Metaphysical Poetry and the Poetic of Correspondence," p. 53. Cf. Tesauro, *Il cannocchiale aristotelico*, 4th ed., pp. 70–128, esp. 70–78, 87–94.

On the history of the metaphor of the "book of nature," see Curtius, *European Literature and the Latin Middle Ages*, pp. 319–326; and on that of *deus artifex*, with the corresponding image of the world as artifice, ibid., pp. 544–546. Already Augustine (*De musica* 6.29) had spoken of the "song of the universe" (*carmen universitatis*), a popular image in the Middle Ages, yet that of the world as poem appears to be of less certain origin. The ancient myths favored images of craftsmanship—the world as the work of a potter, a weaver, or a smith.

[105] *Il cannocchiale aristotelico*, 4th ed., pp. 89–90.

own.[106] If the conceitists took their start in the rhetorical doctrines of Aristotle, particularly that of the metaphor, the neoclassicists resumed contact with the theory of imitation that had marked the discovery of his *Poetics* in the late Renaissance. Poetry, wrote Muratori in his *Della perfetta poesia* (1706), is no less concerned with truth than are history and oratory, but it shows that concern through imitation, "filling the imagination of others with the most beautiful, strange, and wondrous images."[107] Ingenuity, he thought, is a most useful poetic tool, though as an intellectual activity its images are different from those of the imagination, which furnishes it with its raw materials; both, however, require the discipline of judgment, which either nature or study procure for us. Gravina's poetics, embodied in his popular *Della ragion poetica* (1708), are equally restrained, with great stress given to the civilizing power of good images:

Poetry is a sorceress, but a salutary one, a fever that clears away insanities . . . In vulgar minds, which are almost entirely engulfed in the fog of fantasy, the entrance is closed to the excitements of truth and universal ideas. In order for them to penetrate, they must be

[106] On the origin of neoclassicism in Italy, see Weinberg, *A History of Literary Criticism in the Italian Renaissance*; Baxter Hathaway, *The Age of Criticism: The Late Renaissance in Italy* (Ithaca, N.Y.: Cornell University Press, 1962). On its renewal in the eighteenth century, see Antonio Pironalli, *L'Arcadia* (Palermo: Palumbo, 1963). On Muratori, Fiorenzo Forti, *Ludovico Antonio Muratori: Fra antichi e moderni* (Bologna: Zuffi, 1953); Mario Fubini, *Dal Muratori al Baretti* (Bari: Laterza, 1954). For Gravina, Amedeo Quondam, *Cultura e ideologia di Gian Vincenzo Gravina* (Milan: Mursia, 1968), and *Filosofia della luce e luminosi nelle Egloghe del Gravina: Documenti per un capitolo della cultura filosofica di fine Seicento*, Studi vichiani, no. 3 (Naples: Guida, 1970), the latter being a supplement to Nicola Badaloni's excellent chapter on the Arcadians in his *Introduzione a G. B. Vico*, pp. 227–286. For the relation of the movement to Vico, see also Guido De Ruggiero, *Storia della filosofia*, pt. 4, *La filosofia moderna*, vol. 3, *Da Vico a Kant* (Bari: Laterza, 1943), pp. 99–104; Andrea Sorrentino, *La retorica e la poetica di Vico; ossia, La prima concezione estetica del linguaggio* (Turin: Bocca, 1927), pp. 265–281.

[107] *Della perfetta poesia* (Venice, 1724), p. 55: Poetry depicts the truth "col fine d'imitare e di recare con questa imitazione diletto, empiendo la fantasia altrui di bellissime, strane e meravigliose immagini" (cited by De Ruggiero, *Storia della filosofia*, p. 101).

displayed in a guise proportionate to the faculty of imagination, and
in a form able to be grasped adequately in these vessels; thus they
need to be clothed in material dress and converted into tangible attire,
the universal axiom dissolved into its particulars so that it spreads
out into them like a source through its rivers, and hides itself among
them like the spirit in the body.[108]

Similarly, "a fable is the essence of things transformed in
human minds; it is truth dressed up in popular guise: thus the
poet gives body to concepts both by giving life to the insensate
and by wrapping the spirit in body, converts into visible images the reflections aroused by philosophy, such that he is a
transformer and a producer—the function from which he acquired his name."[109]

Vico's mind grew large with these ideas, and in transmuted
form they gave him the frame he needed by which to take
hold of the labored, poetic origins of the race. Concerned
always with rhetoric in its logical form, as argumentation and
civil discourse, he accepted from Gravina and Muratori the
concept of poetry as a rational, truth-seeking enterprise, and
borrowed from the conceitists those elements of their theory
which supported this perspective. Poetry is indeed the great
civilizing sorceress, who encounters the vulgar in the fog of
fantasy and lifts them beyond it. That idea he could find in
the conceitists as well, in their poetic of correspondence, in

---

[108] *Della ragion poetica* (Florence, 1857), 1. 7: "La poesia è una maga, ma
salutare, e un delirio che sgombra le pazzie. . . . Nelle menti volgari, che son
quasi d'ogni parte involte tra la caligine della fantasia, è chiusa l'entrata agli
eccitamenti del vero e delle cognizioni universali. Perché dunque possano ivi
penetrare, convien disporle in sembianza proporzionata alla facoltà
dell'immaginazione, e in figura atta a capire adeguatamente in quei vasi: onde
bisogna vestirle d'abito materiale e convertirle in abito sensibile, disciogliendo
l'assioma universale nei suoi individui, in modo che in essi, come fonte per
li suoi rivi, si diffonda, e per entro di loro s'asconda, come nel corpo lo
spirito" (cited by De Ruggiero, p. 100).

[109] Ibid., 1. 9: "La favola è l'esser delle cose transformato in genii umani,
ed è verità travestita in sembianza popolare: perché il poeta dà corpo ai
concetti e con animar l'insensato ed avvolger di corpo lo spirito, converte in
immagini visibili le contemplazioni eccitate dalla filosofia, sicché egli è trans-
formatore e produtore, dal qual mestiero ottenne il suo nome" (cited by
De Ruggiero, p. 100).

their view of the conceit as the beguiling, enthralling bond of apparently dissimilar things. From Gracián came the stress on attaining difficult truths, from Pallavicino the emphasis on truths that are new and thus thrilling, and from Tesauro the notion of nature as a stubborn, even playful, mistress whose secrets, as Bacon had said in a different context, must be wrested from her by force. The power that does this is ingenuity—not the discursive power of reason but the faculty of insight—the power that finds and creates connections (*similitudines*), and so startles, uplifts, and brings men together. This notion he found in them all, conceitist and neoclassicist alike. From Tesauro, perhaps, came most: that the conceit is an "urbane enthymeme," a "false" argument through whose images the truth is transparent; that it arises less from art than from ingenuity and the "passions of the soul"; that God himself is a "witty speaker" whose own universe is written in conceits; that poets, artists, and all craftsmen improve on this nature, bringing order out of disorder, seeking out and establishing correspondences that were missed before; that, indeed, conceits are the trade of all ingenious minds, sane and insane alike, and may take form in words, mute signs, or some combination of these. All these ideas lay fertile in Vico's mind, and in time he combined them with others to produce, not a revolutionary aesthetic—a task left to Baumgarten and Baudelaire—but a grand new science of society. Before he was to do that, however, he developed the notions as part of his rhetoric and drew for his charges their pedagogical consequences.

Almost alone among Vico's concepts, that of ingenuity appears in his work with utter consistency, maintaining its essential meaning throughout the sundry applications it receives.[110] This is the more important since the notion is a

---

[110] This thesis of Luigi Pareyson, to which I fully subscribe, is presented in his remarkably limpid essay, "La dottrina vichiana dell' ingegno," *Atti della Accademia delle scienze di Torino* 83, no. 2 (1949): 82–115, reprinted in his *L'estetica e i suoi problemi* (Milan: Marzorati, 1961), pp. 351–377, and elsewhere. Among the many critics who appreciate the centrality of ingenuity

lodestone of his thought, drawing to itself so many of his original ideas. Ingenuity, Vico says repeatedly, is the "faculty of bringing together things that are disparate and widely separated."[111] It lays no claim to thoroughness or method, but is a capacity, as Petrarch had said of it, which is quick and decisive, penetrating and acute, ready and adaptive (*De remediis* 1.7). One does not need to call on ingenuity; one either has it or does not, sees connections or misses them utterly. Vico was a child of acute ingenuity, he claimed, and so, too, are children generally, if only we will recognize it and train them accordingly.[112] For ingenuity depends on the images of fantasy, a faculty most vivid and robust in youth, and on the power of memory, fantasy's twin, and they in turn take their start in sensations, the images of sense. But the point is more subtle than it seems, for sense and memory are not to be thought of as mere passive capacities, receiving and retaining impressions that imagination and ingenuity subsequently work through; sense, memory, imagination, and ingenuity are four virtually indistinguishable aspects of the single, prediscursive action of the mind. The notion is of capital importance, for Vico would eventually speak of the "vast imagination of those first men, whose minds were not in the least abstract, refined, or spiritualized, because they were entirely immersed in the senses, buffeted by the passions, buried in the body," and would hold that they, "like ingenious children entirely innocent of learning and language," were driven by a compulsion

in Vico's thought are Antonio Corsano, *Umanesimo e religione in G. B. Vico* (Bari: Laterza, 1935), superseded by his *Giambattista Vico* (Bari: Laterza, 1956); Franco Amerio, *Introduzione allo studio di G. B. Vico* (Turin: Società editrice internazionale, 1947); Antonino Pagliaro, "La dottrina linguistica di G. B. Vico," *Atti dell'Accademia nazionale dei Lincei*, Memorie, ser. 8, 8 (1959): 379–486, reprinted as "Lingua e poesia secondo G. B. Vico," *Altri saggi di critica semantica* (Messina and Florence: D'Anna, 1961). Of these, only Corsano seems to me to give the notion its full application.

[111] "Ingenium facultas est in unum dissita, diversa conjungendi" (*De Italorum sapientia, Opere* 1.179). Cf. the First *Risposta, Opere* 1.212f.; Second *Risposta, Opere* 1.252; *Institutiones oratoriae*, p. 5; *Vici vindiciae, Opere* 3.302–304; Letter of 12 January 1729 to Francesco Saverio Estevan, *Opere* 5.212.

[112] Autobiography, *Opere* 5.3, 13–15. Cf. *De studiorum ratione, Opere* 1.90–94.

of nature to fashion the first images of their humanity. For "those who perceive things with sharpened sense and a vigorous imagination grasp very little with their simple mind and sense all things passionately, just as children who are troubled will say everything almost violently."[113] A faculty is the facility to do something, indeed to do it quickly, Vico wrote in an earlier work, and "if the senses are faculties, they make the qualities of things they perceive, colors by seeing, savors by tasting, sounds by hearing, coldness and warmth by touching." And so, too, the imagination, called *memoria* by the Latins, which creates images of things only when we use it.[114] Through the activity of the senses and imagination, our encounter with external realities is made into an experience; things acquire sensual and imaginative forms and so become real for us. Within this encounter, the work of ingenuity is the critical activity, giving unity to our experience and so making us truly aware of it. The sharper our ingenuity, the keener is our perception, the more certain our knowledge. So fundamental is *ingenium* to being human, Vico adds, that the Latins used the word for human nature itself, a correspondence they drew either because it is man's ingenuity that sets the measure of things by determining what is fitting and suitable in life (*quid aptum sit, quid deceat*) or because it is by being ingenious that man, through his artifices and machines, becomes god of the crafted world even as God is the crafter of nature (*ut Deus sit naturae artifex, homo artificiorum Deus*).[115]

---

[113] "Vasta immaginativa di que' primi uomini, le menti de' quali di nulla erano astratte, di nulla erano assottigliate, di nulla spiritualezzate, perch'erano tutte immerse ne' sensi, tutte rintuzzate dalle passioni, tutte seppellite ne' corpi" (*Scienza nuova seconda, Opere* 4, §378). "Statuendum est . . . primos ingeniosos homines, omnis eruditionis omnisque linguae rudes, nihil aliud quam ingeniosos pueros fuisse. . . . Cumque natura ita comparatum sit: ut qui sensu praenimio et acri phantasia res percipiunt, ii mente puriore parum intelligant et omnia sentiant animo perturbato, ut pueri omnia fere vehementer, aliquo affectu commoti, proloquuntur" (*De constantia jurisprudentis, Opere* 2.363–378, at 365, 369).

[114] *De Italorum sapientia, Opere* 1.175–178.

[115] *De Italorum sapientia, Opere* 1.179. Cf. First *Risposta, Opere* 1.212; *Vici vindiciae, Opere* 3.303; *De mente heroica, Opere* 7.9.

Engineer and jurist, both building cities through ingenuity, the one their bodies, the other their souls: again Vico brings his argument around. In circling back to this point, as he does routinely, Vico makes clear the most trenchant aspect of ingenious knowing. Ingenious perception is truly an invention, an assembling and arranging of images that produces a genuinely novel vision. In geometry the vision is of lines and figures, and out of it comes a new theorem, an extension of the science. In physics (Baconian, to be sure) the vision is of the forces and systems of nature reproduced tangibly in devices and experiments of our making. In mechanics and engineering, it is a vision of nature remade, of the rearrangement of our environment to suit a social purpose, resulting in a bridge, a ship, a device to propel, or to count, or to improve vision, an entire new city, a new physical universe. And in oratory and law, it is a vision of how things should be, a course of action that will set things right or avoid their deterioration, a vision that joins past to future through current expectations, thus achieving plausibility, but one that does so through images that are familiar and foreign alike, thus opening to us new ways. Such images are those of metaphor, language that is sententious and acute.[116]

[116] This would be the place to trace out Vico's famous epistemological principle, "verum et factum convertuntur," not as an independent thesis that he later applies scientifically, but as a corollary to his early rhetorical and pedagogical writings. That Vico intended it to be understood in this way is evident in a number of places, including this one toward the end of the *De Italorum sapientia*: "In my discourse *On the Study Method of Our Time*, I upheld the position that difficulties in the study of physics can be overcome by the cultivation of ingenuity. This caused some people, wholly infatuated with the problem of method, to raise their eyebrows; but I stand on that position. In its concern for facility, method obstructs inventive minds; in its care for truth it destroys inquisitiveness. Geometry sharpens the mind not when it is taught methodically, but when it is discovered and applied by ingenuity amid many diverse and disparate experiences. Thus I advocated that it be taught not analytically, but synthetically; just as we demonstrate by relating elements, so let us not discover truths, but make them, that is, construct them with the mind." ("Idque adeo in dissertatione *De nostri temporis studiorum ratione*, physicae incommoda ingenii cultu vitari posse innui; quod aliquis methodo occupatus forte miratus sit. Nam methodus ingeniis obstat, dum consulit facilitati; et curiositatem dissolvit, dum providet veritati.

The Roman notion of *sententia*, we saw, was a conscious adaptation of Aristotle's *gnome*, or maxim, a concept in rhetorical logic, while the *acutezza* of the conceitists was directly inspired by the *to asteion* in Aristotle's discourse on style. Both Pellegrini (*Delle acutezze*, chapter 10) and Pallavicino (*Dello stile*, chapter 10) had thought the ideas related, but it was not until Vico's own work on rhetoric that the connection was fully exploited. It has been the common fate of the Greek, the Latin, and the Italian languages, he notes, that, after an age in which elegance in style was celebrated, another followed in which to speak *per sententias*, or *in concetti* as the Italians say, was prized, the point being to choose those sayings which showed most fully one's ingenuity.[117] Vico's statements are too terse to say for sure that he means here to criticize, as others in his age were doing, the overblown style of the century just passed, but that is certainly the conclusion to which the context of the passage, as indeed the tone of his treatise as a whole, leads one. To be an orator by wit rather than by tongue has a precise meaning in Vico, as these claims for oratorical ingenuity at the outset of his treatise make clear:

It must be sharp and quick-witted, able to go immediately to the heart of the issue at hand, seeing every facet there is to see about it and bringing them all together into a fruitful unity; it must be facile in expression, able to make the meaning in the thoughts and the thoughts in the words as lucid as glass; and it must be versatile, swifter than Proteus in moving from light to serious matters, from those gentle to those harsh, from those simple to those challenging, and from a style that is grand to one that is moderate, then plain.[118]

Nec geometria acuit ingenium, cum methodo traditur, sed cum vi ingenii per diversa, per alia, multijuga, disparata in usum deducitur. Et ideo non analytica, sed synthetica via eam edisci desiderabam; ut componendo demonstraremus, hoc est ne inveniremus vera, sed faceremus" (*Opere* 1.185).

[117] *Institutiones oratoriae*, pp. 90–91; *Opere* 8.182f.

[118] "Ingenium sit ad excogitandum acutum, ut quam celerrime, et in rei, qua de agitur, medullas penetret, et omnia, quae ad rem spectant, circumspiciat, eique feliciter uniat. Idem sit ad explicandum facile, ut in sententiis res, in verbis sententie pellucidius vitro perspiciantur; sit et versatile, quodque ad jocos, ad seria, ad lenia, ad aspera, ad facilitatem, ad vim, ad grandia, moderata, tenuia Proteo citius convertatur" (*Institutiones oratoriae*, p. 5).

What then is ingenuity *in concetti*? Though he quotes Pellegrini, Vico speaks here with Gracián and Tesauro, and through them with Aristotle himself. The strength (*virtus*) of ingenuity in a *dictum acutum* is the bond that connects two disparate things. The mere uniting of two ideas into a "simple enunciation" requires no ingenuity at all; an ingenious statement is one that combines two separate ideas with a third one in so suitable a way that the statement acquires enthymemic force. In this, ingenuity achieves power (*vis* or *acumen*), even as reason does in fashioning the perfect syllogism; the acumen of ingenuity rests in its successful finding of the "middle," in "that rare and novel ability to link two extremes in a particularly felicitous statement."[119]

A properly ingenious statement, then, shares in the power of logic, but in what does its felicity consist? How does it thrill and delight an audience? Aristotle thought it was because it could teach them many things quickly and easily; Pallavicino, because the things taught them are truly novel and thus fascinating. Pellegrini, however, thought it was the beauty of the statement itself rather than any discovery of truth that is the source of the thrill. Pellegrini, Vico says, has a point, for the orator is not simply a philosopher in disguise, he does not simply teach; through his images he leaves things unsaid, and so engages the ingenuity of his listeners, drawing them into the reasoning process with him, leading them to *see* rather than to receive mutely the point of his argument:

In producing a conceit, the orator effects a beauty that is left to the hearer to detect. For when a conceit is produced, there is concealed within it the rationale of its bond; the hearer ponders it, discovers the "middle," joins the extremes, reflects on the aptness, and so discovers the beauty that the orator has created, whence he thinks of *himself* as ingenious, thrilled by a conceit not as something produced by the orator but as something understood by himself.[120]

---

[119] "Hinc idem Peregrinius acumen seu ingenii vim definit 'felicem medii inventionem, quod in dicto aliquo diversas res mira aptitudine et per summam elegantiam colligat' " (*Institutiones oratoriae*, p. 93; *Opere* 8.183).

[120] "Orator autem, acuto dicto prolato, efficit pulchrum quod ipsi auditori

Thus the conceit, Vico concludes, gives a hearer more pleasure than a mathematical demonstration, for its beauty thrills his ingenuity while its truth is teaching his intellect. Thus, too, he concludes, a conceit should be brief—the briefer the better—so as to engage most fully the ingenuity of the listeners. The incisiveness of the thought is matched, indeed enhanced, by the conciseness of its expression. In the best moments of oratory, an acute, concise statement is set forth, catching up into its force both speaker and hearer, each claiming a surfeit of ingenuity.

Vico pressed his argument one step further. The French critic Dominique Bouhours had written a book on the art of clear thinking in which he took to task recent Italian literature, referring especially to the poetry of Torquato Tasso, as no better than the pretentious, puffed-up prose of French *préciosité*. In a vigorous reply, Gian Giuseppe Orsi had distinguished two types of verisimilitude, one of thoughts, another of words, the former leading to probability but not truth, the latter leading to neither. For Vico, the distinction he had drawn was between "truth appearing as falsity" and "falsity appearing as truth," and it was inadequate, for it marked as opposites what are merely two forms of *dicta acuta*, the former "unexpected" or paradoxical, the latter metaphorical or symbolic. The point, Vico adds, is that both involve latent truth and beauty, retrieved in an identical way. The paradox perhaps has a higher degree of thrilling to novelty, for it entails discovering connections between things previously thought opposed, whereas the symbol relates things that are merely diverse. Yet both have one and the same source: the truth that lay hidden and is laid bare quickly and easily when a novel, unusual link is found.[121]

---

detegendum relinquit. Nam, acuto dicto prolato, hoc est sub indicata ligaminis ratione, auditor eam vestigat, medium invenit, extrema confert, aptitudinem contemplatur; et ipse detegit pulchrum, quod orator effecit: unde ipse sibi ingeniosus videtur, et acuto dicto non tam ut ab oratore prolato quam ut *a se* intellecto delectatur" (*Institutiones oratoriae*, p. 95; *Opere* 8.185; my emphasis).

[121] *Institutiones oratoriae*, pp. 96–98; *Opere* 8.186–187. On the Bouhours-

What *are* properly distinguished, Vico continues, are *dicta acuta* and *dicta arguta*, the former the flower of rhetoric, the latter the bane of mankind. Properly understood, *concetti* are not those pithy, witty one-liners (*dicta arguta*) of the Mannerists by which an agile tongue dazzles and regales an audience, snaps back heads with laughter, and demonstrates his own cleverness; such conceits discover no truths, advance no civil ends. Rather, *concetti* are brief, sharp-witted statements (*dicta acuta*) having enthymemic force, with incisiveness equal to their conciseness, born of imaginative, ingenious minds intent on discovering the true; through them listeners see novel visions and discover new relationships, sinners are reduced to tears, implausible cases are won in court, legislation is gotten through intractable assemblies. Cicero had indeed once suggested that "for exposition and explanation *sententiae* should be pointed (*acutae*); for entertainment, bright and witty (*argutae*); for rousing the emotions, weighty and impressive (*graves*)," a sentiment Vico was pleased to echo by dropping its second clause.[122] But Cicero had also written at length on the use and abuse of jokes (*facetiae*) in oratory (*De or.* 2.54.216–71.289), finding a purpose for humor that was serious if not exalted. The tradition had largely followed him in this opinion, and Vico's own Emmanuele Tesauro had considered a joke wholesome for self and society alike.[123] But Vico would have none of it. *Acuta* derive from truth and succeed when they teach; *arguta* arise from playfulness and succeed when they deceive. As a species of the "ridiculous," a kind of obvious, harmless deformity (Arist. *Poet.* 1449a13–37), *arguta* are not precisely false; yet they are built on a reversal of expectations and in this sense are subverted maxims, frustrating the mind's innate desire for truth.[124]

Orsi controversy, which Vico also addresses in the *De studiorum ratione, Opere* 1.95f., see note 39 above.

[122] "[Sententiae] sunt enim docendi acutae, delectandi quasi argutae commovendi graves" (*De opt. gen. orat.* 1.2.5). Cf. *Institutiones oratoriae*, p. 100; *Opere* 8.189.

[123] Cf. Lange, *Theoretiker des literarischen Manierismus*, p. 154.

[124] Cf. *Institutiones oratoriae*, pp. 98–100; *Opere* 8.188: "Arguta dicta ab

Not only did Vico hold to this view throughout his life; he hardened in it some twenty years later after a critic of his first *New Science*, indulging a contemporary fashion, called its author "more ingenious than true."[125] How could the critic draw such a naive distinction? he asked. Had he not shown plainly in that very work how ingenuity is the source of all innovation and culture, and how laboriously it is gained and how quickly lost by men, being as they are "first stupid and rough, later docile and capable of being disciplined, then perspicacious, after which keen [*acuti*] and able to discover, finally shrewd [*arguti*], astute, and fraudulent?"[126] Philosophy, geometry, philology, jurisprudence—the whole of learning shows us how ludicrous it is to fight ingenuity with truth. The acuities of oratory, to cite only one such example, give the pleasure they do because they show relationships that only the ingenious can see. Witty remarks (*dicta arguta*), on the other hand, arise from a "feeble and narrow imagination" (*infirma brevique phantasia*) and out of a spirit of trickery. Led to expect one thing, the hearer is told another, and thus convulses with laughter. Laughter, however, Vico continues (following Aristotle and Cicero), rests in the *subturpe*, the "moderately base," and not for naught have the poets pictured *risores* as satyrs, halfway between men and animals. For through laughter one is rendered, in the Latins' fine phrase, "irresolute of mind" (*mente non constare*), and such mental weakness (*imbecillitas*) is the root of all folly. Whence the aim of philosophy is to strengthen the constancy of the wise.[127]

---

acutis longe alia sunt: acuta enim docent, arguta fallunt. . . . Acuto dicto audito, quis celeriter verum discit; at arguto dicto is expectatione fraudatur sua, et, dum verum expectat, nam is est intellectus humani ingenitus appetitus, detegit falsum."

[125] "Ingenio tamen magis indulget quam veritati," the most biting comment in a one-paragraph review appearing in the *Acta eruditorum Lipsiensia* and cited by Vico at the beginning of his twenty-five page response, *Vici vindiciae, Opere* 3.295. Locke, *Two Treatises of Government*, 1.1.1, had rendered the same judgment of Filmer's *Patriarchia*.

[126] "Prima stupidi, indi rozzi, poi docili o capaci ad esser disciplinati, appresso perspicaci, dopo acuti e valevoli a ritruovare, finalmente arguti, astuti, e fraudolenti" (*Scienza nuova prima, Opere* 3, §130).

[127] *Vici vindiciae, Opere* 3.304–306. Thus the melancholy portraits of Vico

PRUDENCE AND THE *ARTES REDACTAE*

The "constancy" of wisdom that philosophy aims to imbue is the highest ambition of the truly ingenious. For the man of public service in particular, who takes his measure from the *sensus communis* and whose arena of action is marked off by those *verisimilia* to which chance and choice give rise, such constancy is no calm possession or settled estate; it is the life of prudence itself, the unending struggle to understand and do right by the affairs of men. In its consummate form, as social authority, it coalesces in that "knowledge of all things human and divine" which the Greeks called wisdom and the Romans jurisprudence, and gives us in its finest practitioner— the sagelike jurisconsult—an image of the fully cultured human being. Such is the final and most passionate message of Vico's discourse *On the Study Method of Our Time.*

Vico makes his argument in the course of comparing, in the closing pages of his treatise, ancient and modern "aids" to learning. The modern advantage, he acknowledges, seems formidable indeed, for unlike the ancients we have printed books to circulate our ideas, organized universities to develop them, masterpieces to guide our arts, and systematic treatises (*artes redactae*) for areas of enterprise that the ancients left to common sense. What Vico offers here is a veritable catalog of humanist achievements in the reform of education, a reform that began with the very modest attempts by Guarino and Vittorino to bring order to the training of young boys and led, by 1599, to the imposing *Ratio studiorum* of the Jésuits, which gave form, schedules, and textbooks to all the disciplines of higher and lower learning. Having structure in the life of learning is, Vico recognizes, a mixed blessing, for the

---

that have come down to us, both the canvas and the Autobiography, receive confirmation. One does not imagine Vico enjoying a good knee-slapping joke. Cf. Benedetto Croce, "La dottrina del riso e dell'ironia in Giambattista Vico," *Saggi filosofici*, vol. 3, *Saggio sullo Hegel e altri scritti di storia della filosofia*, 3d ed. (Bari: Laterza, 1927), pp. 277–283, now extended and deepened by Salvatore Cerasuolo, "Le fonti classiche della dottrina del riso e del comico nelle *Vici vindiciae*," *Bollettino del Centro di Studi vichiani* 12-13 (1982- 1983): 319-332.

direction and purpose it brings to a student's work can result in a rigidity of spirit that runs counter to the flexibility needed for effective action in the public forum. What is more serious, in its effort to facilitate learning by putting the whole of the curriculum within the quick and easy reach of every student, modern pedagogy can actually obstruct education, dulling the very talents it is intended to train. To help our youth in the imitative disciplines, he notes, we set before them the masterworks of art (*optima exempla*)—the poetry of Vergil, the orations of Cicero, the paintings of Raphael—thereby blocking from view the model of nature itself (*optima natura*), the only guide the masters had to follow. "It is easy to add to inventions," as the aphorism has it, but to challenge our artists to the fullest we should have them contemplate nature alone, leaving the masterpieces for the epigones to study. Similarly in the humanities, we should run clear of the pap that pours from modern printing presses, whose only check on quality is contemporary fashion, a notoriously fickle guide, in favor of the classics of thought that had to be copied by hand and thus enjoy the judgment of the ages.[128]

Vico's curmudgeonly advice is in fact the expression of a consistent pedagogical ideal—the wise and prudent citizen who among the ironies and uncertainties of life will always be able to act effectively—an ideal he thought compromised by witless artistry and pedestrian reading. Nowhere did he find the ideal more threatened, however, than in the growing tendency to distill the arts of learning and living, which "the Greeks had left to prudence," into convenient little epitomes or preceptive manuals (*artes redactae*), aimed at ensuring the "quick and easy" mastery of their subjects. In truth, not even the Greeks were content with mere prudence in life. Socrates himself was abundantly concerned with *technē* (*Phdr.* 265d–277c), a notion to which Zeno gave point by defining an art as "a set of percepts exercised together toward some end useful in life." In the hands of the Latins, consciously or not, the

---

[128] *De studiorum ratione, Opere* 1.114–116.

definition underwent a subtle change, Zeno's "percepts" (*perceptiones*) being replaced over time by the more tangible "precepts" or "rules" (*praeceptiones*). Thus, when humanists of the Renaissance read in the *De oratore* of Cicero (1.42.187) that the law, no less than other subjects of inquiry and action, "once without order or correlation," should be reduced to an art (*redigere ad artem*), they felt enjoined to devise arts as they were then understood: as sets of rules for the accomplishment of socially useful purposes. To this they added their own concern, that the rules be put down methodically so as to facilitate and speed up the mastery of the art, and set about reducing the curriculum to order. The Jesuit *ratio* was only the most dramatically successful of these efforts. Singly and together, all school subjects from grammar to medicine were condensed and "put into order," and the host of textbooks that ensued, widely disseminated after the invention of printing, formed something of a College Outline Series of the era. An unmistakable trend toward superficiality resulted, and brought in its trail an inevitable reaction.[129]

One scholar startled by the epitomizing fashion was Francis Bacon, who counted it among the "peccant humours" that obstruct the advancement of learning. The "peremptory reduction of knowledge into arts and methods" arrests the growth of a science, making of it a body of knowledge that "may perchance be further polished and illustrated, and accommodated for use and practice; but it increaseth no more in bulk and substance."[130] Despite an initial ambivalence—arguing in his First Oration that the entire cycle of learning

---

[129] The history and development of this movement are well presented by Neal W. Gilbert, *Renaissance Concepts of Method* (New York and London: Columbia University Press, 1960) , pp. 4–13, 67–115. The various compendiums of Philipp Melanchthon, including his famous *Loci communes theologici*, were the outcome of this movement, as were the manuals of Peter Ramus; and even so late a text as Bouhours's *La manière de bien penser* (1687), while offering instruction "rather by example than by precepts," was yet declared to be a "thornless logic" and a "short and easy rhetoric."

[130] *The Advancement of Learning*, in *The Works of Francis Bacon*, ed. Spedding and Ellis, 3. 292. Cited by Gilbert, *Renaissance Concepts of Method*, p. 114.

could be mastered in a brief space of time (*ad omnem doc-trinarum orbem brevi absolvendum*), while holding in his fifth that no art of war, nothing short of prudence, could bring victory to a general, "for rules are precise and circumstances infinite" (*cum [leges] certae sint, et occasiones infinitae*)—Vico associated himself fully with the mind of Bacon. Yet he did so, typically, in a wholly singular way. Not the growth of knowledge but the health of a society was Vico's concern. To win at war is only one public function high in its demand for prudence; the entire range of civil endeavors requires a discretion that takes guidance from the countless particularities of events. Try as they may, the preceptive manuals are unequal to such detail, and worse still, they build a false confidence, fostering a habit of abiding by general maxims whereas in real life nothing is more useless. If criticism and analysis are blunt tools in the dealings of civil life, hapless visitors from the realm of the straight and the true, the *artes redactae* are enemies from within, meaning the best for young orators, lawyers, and other practitioners in the public forum, but giving them arts which are sapped of their vitality and essential flexibility. The point is not to abandon all hope in the face of an endlessly complex experience; such is the attitude of a cynical skepticism that Vico consistently resists. The point, rather, is to walk, even while surrounded by life's variety, "on the path of philosophy toward the contemplation of nature at its ideal best" (*per philosophiam ad ipsius optimae contemplationem naturae*).[131]

The prudence that is the constancy of wisdom takes shape

---

[131] "Qui enim omnia prudentiae in artem redigere conantur, principio inanem insumunt operam: quia prudentia ex rerum circumstantiis, quae infinitae sunt, sua capit consilia. . . . Quamobrem ut usui sint artes, quae prudentia constant, uti oratoria, poetica, historica, deorum compitalium instar sint; et tantum demonstrent quo et qua sit eundum: nempe per philosophiam ad ipsius optimae contemplationem naturae" (*De studiorum ratione, Opere* 1.99f.). That Vico's thought unfolds as a series of attempts, of which this is the first, to comprehend the relation of the *verum* and the *certum*, is the very plausible thesis of Guido Fassò, *I "quattro auttori" del Vico: Saggio sulla genesi della "Scienza nuova"* (Milan: Giuffrè, 1949).

Like Machiavelli before him, Vico takes the way of Cicero. His point of departure is a concrete issue. Why, he asks, do we moderns possess an immense number of books on law, as did the Romans after the promulgation of the *Edictum perpetuum*, whereas prior to that time the Romans had very few? His concern is to know how jurisprudence, which during the Roman Republic and early Empire was a streamlined "science of the just" with very few laws, should have become an "art of equity" with innumerable rules governing the most trifling of matters. Vico's thesis is that the transformation has occurred through the severing of the practice of law from its philosophy, the latter understood as an imposing theory or doctrine of state (*doctrina civilis*). For the ancient Romans, he argues, wisdom was preeminently a matter of ordering public affairs, and unlike the Greeks, who sought wisdom through discussion, the Romans tried to master the art of government by direct experience. Both the philosopher's knowledge of theory and the jurist's familiarity with positive legislation were combined in the person of the jurisconsult, and out of this experience came a lean, simple, and straightforward *jus civile*, first codified in the Law of the Twelve Tables.[133] The code was a unified system of sacred, public, and private law, with the public primary; the law of cults and auspices and the law of judicial proceedings were subordinate to public law and all were directed to the ordering and pres-

---

res inclinet, retinere aut ante possitis occurrere" *Rep.* 2.25.45; cf. 1.46.70; trans. George H. Sabine and Stanley B. Smith, *On the Commonwealth* (Columbus: Ohio University Press, 1929), p. 178. Cf. *Scienza nuova seconda, Opere* 4, §1405, an unpublished paragraph in which Vico adapts this notion.

[133] Cf. *De studiorum ratione, Opere* 1.101, and *De uno principio, Opere* 2.26–28. The jurisconsults Vico has in mind are Ulpian, Pomponius, Papinianus, Caius, and the others whose opinions are excerpted and organized by subject matter in the *Digest* or *Pandects* of Justinian. The first titles of the *Digest* ("De justitia et jure," "De origine juris et omnium magistratuum et successione prudentium," "De legibus senatusque consultis et longa consuetudine," etc.) contain, in Vico's view, the general principles (*ta Prota*) or philosophy of law, the balance being given to a summary of positive legislation. For this insight, he credits the author of the *Methodus juris civilis*, likely a reference to Nicolaus Vigelius's *Juris civilis totius absolutissima methodus* (Basel, 1561), one of the best known *artes juris redactae* of the time.

ervation of the state. To this end, the law was religiously guarded, inflexible and rigid; an aura of secrecy surrounded private law. If certain cases demanded special handling, the law itself was not changed, but the facts were adapted to the law by means of legal fictions and the issuance of privileges. Above all, the inflexibility ensured a flourishing eloquence, for while jurists struggled to preserve the sanctity of the law and the universal application of its provisions, orators endeavored to gain exceptions for their clients through an appeal to equity.

When the Empire was formed, public and private law began to be severed, and the latter assumed an unusual importance; for the emperors allowed the praetors to mitigate the severity of the law through equitable interpretations and to supply its defects with benignant sentences. Thus began the erosion of the "science of the just" in favor of praetorian *aequitas*, a process that was completed with Hadrian's *Edictum perpetuum*, which established the *jus honorarium* as the basis of jurisprudence in place of the Twelve Tables. With judicial proceedings now founded on equity, forensic oratory fell gradually silent, for no special eloquence was needed to win a case. And when, two centuries later, Constantine abolished the "formulary" system of judicial actions and made the "*extra ordinem*" procedure ordinary, the praetor became the unchallenged arbiter of all private law. As a consequence, facts were no longer adjusted to the law but the law, once inflexible and supreme, was now freely and openly adjusted to facts. With this, oratory was rendered totally mute, its place taken by innumerable books of law trying to deal with life's myriad situations. The science of the just had become fully an art of equity.

Which, then, is superior? Standing before an assembly dominated by professors and students of law, as indeed by public officials trained in the law, Vico could do little but speak from the modern vantage; yet in vaunting the advantages of a system in which "equity rules the courtroom," he felt drawn as a humanist to state the costs of modernity, and his opinions fell freely. In antiquity, he argued, the laws were few, sacred, secret, and inflexible, and orators were needed to soften their severity through appeals to equity. Today, jurisprudence is itself an art of equity, and our law groans under the great bulk of its books, trying to provide for every contingency in life. In consequence, the philosophy of law has been forgotten, jurisprudence attenuated, and eloquence compromised. Theory and practice, the tasks of the jurist and the orator, have been joined, but jurisprudence has been severed from philosophy; equity can now be attained without eloquence, but the sanctity of the law has been lost; equity now has precedence over *jus*, but reverence for law has diminished; private law is now prior to public law, but the common good suffers; the roles of jurist and orator are now combined, but the law, once a single jurisprudence, is now materially divided into public law, private law, and ecclesiastical law. One disadvantage of the modern system, however, indeed its principal failing, has no corresponding and mitigating advantage:

Since equity is tested by facts and facts are countless, containing often a multitude of points of very little importance, we have as a result an unbounded number of legal rules, dealing for the most part with extremely picayune and trifling questions. Being innumerable, such rules cannot all be complied with, and those dealing with unimportant matters easily fall into contempt, and detract from the sanctity of momentous ones.[134]

The forlornness of these words gives pause, for audible within them is an issue that Vico would contend with the rest

[134] "Quod cum aequitas ex factis spectetur, et facta infinita, et in iis quam plurima levissima sint, leges quoque innumeras et levissimis de rebus maxima ex parte conceptas habeamus. Atqui nec innumerae servari omnes possunt, et de levibus rebus jussae, facile, ut fit, contemnuntur, et leves contemptae gravissimis quoque detrahunt sanctitatem" (*De studiorum ratione, Opere* 1.109; cf. generally pp. 106–110). In this he was at one with Descartes: "A multiplicity of laws often furnishes excuses for evildoing, and . . . a State is hence much better ruled when, having but very few laws, these are most strictly observed" (*Discours de la méthode*, pt. 2, *Oeuvres de Descartes*, ed. Charles Adam and Paul Tannery, 12 vols. [Paris: Cerf, 1897–1910], 6.18; trans. Elizabeth S. Haldane and G.R.T. Ross, *The Philosophical Works of Descartes*, 2 vols. [Cambridge: At the University Press, 1911], 1.92).

of his days. What becomes of a culture when it actually achieves its highest aspiration—a law of natural equity—when it must no longer rely on the mysteries of its youth or learn to soften or adapt the harsh realities of its heroic years? Does its passion grow cold and its need for eloquence abate? Does it put aside its prudence like a shopworn tool or a toy of youth, now confident of the reasons of its being and satisfied with their forms and formulas? Torn as he was by the question, Vico seems genuinely to have preferred a "heroic" society, one that was perhaps more severe than true, but one that was alive with ingenious citizens struggling to find their separate ways in a society whose essential purpose was clear. Justice, he wrote, is "constant care for the common good," and the science of law is "knowledge of the best government." Such a government, he made clear, was the Empire of old and the monarchy of his own time, and only by knowing the nature and structure of these "best forms of nature" (and so being a philosopher) could any practitioner of law or other public official hope to grasp that "civil equity" (*aequitas civilis*) which is the backbone of a strong jurisprudence and the guarantee of a sound society. Just as the genius in imitation is to shun the masterpieces of art so as to take the best in nature (*natura optima*) as model, so the consummate jurist will reject even the best manuals of law in order to contemplate the ideal structure of state. Schooled in this way, he will know the demands of natural and civil equity alike, preferring the latter to the former, reconciling them when he can, concerned always to relate his definitions to the nature and power of the monarchy.[135]

Thus could Vico reconcile, to his own satisfaction, the contrary appeals of a "science of the just" and an "art of equity." And thus could he find for himself within his ideal university, as indeed within his own, a large and significant role:

Our ancestors, the founders of this university, showed clearly, by assigning the professor of eloquence the task of delivering every year a speech exhorting our students to the study of the principles of

[135] *De studiorum ratione, Opere* 1.110–111.

various sciences and arts, that they felt he should be well versed in all fields of knowledge. Nor was it without reason that the great man Lord Verulam, when called upon to give advice to King James of England concerning the organization of a university, insisted that young scholars should not be admitted to the study of eloquence unless they had previously studied their way through the whole curriculum of learning. For what is eloquence, in effect, but wisdom ornately and copiously delivered in words appropriate to the common opinion of mankind?[136]

To know one's history, the past of one's common sense, and be able to bring it alive in language—this pedagogical ideal became with these words Vico's own personal mission. What he would require of his students, or of anyone who aspires to a role in the public realm, he will first require of himself. Whether he saw in that mission at this point in his thinking anything larger than a university duty cannot be known for sure. What is plain is the bristling quality of his pages on jurisprudence, particularly in their face-off between former and current systems of law. There in brisk, summary form is his final word on the *querelle* of ancients and moderns; there, too, is a foretaste of his cultural theory. Present in those pages are all the essential themes he would shortly work out in rapid succession in the *De uno principio*, the *De constantia jurisprudentis*, and several versions of the *New Science*, and present as well are all the elements of uncertainty and ambiguity that persist in these later works. The first ages of man are a period of volatility and inventiveness, but they are severe and even brutal times. Our own times are mild and humane, but frequently effete and overly subtle. In our effort to reduce all

---

[136] "Quando sapientissimi majores nostri, qui hanc studiorum universitatem fundarunt, eloquentiae professorem omnes scientias artesque doctum esse oportere satis suo instituto significarunt, ut is anniversaria oratione studiosam juventutem ad omnia scientiarum et artium genera capessenda exhortaretur. Nec temere ter maximus ille vir Franciscus Verulamius, illud Jacobo Angliae regi dat de ordinanda studiorum universitate consilium, ut adolescentes, non omni doctrinarum orbe circumacto, ab eloquentiae studiis prohibeantur. Nam quid aliud est eloquentia, nisi sapientia, quae ornate copioseque et ad sensum communem accommodate loquatur?" (*De studiorum ratione*, Opere 1.119–120; cf. Bacon, *De dignitate et augmentis scientiarum*, bk. 2, *Ad regem*).

things to method and to norms agreeable to all (because invoked in Reason's name), we bring on that climate of delusion and isolation which causes a culture to decay. Enfolded in these thoughts is more than pedagogical caution; in them, in capsule, is an entire science of society. And finding it was a task on which Vico's ingenuity was already at work.

CHAPTER 4

CULTURE: WISDOM AND ELOQUENCE

> Wisdom among the gentiles began with the muse.
>
> Vico, *Scienza nuova seconda*

The conversion of pedagogical tenets into principles of culture, and of a vision of civic life into a full-scale science of humanity, begins in Vico many years prior to his first bold announcement, in 1721, that a *nova scientia tentatur*. If his own words may be believed, there was never a time in his life in which he was not attempting to reduce the whole of his learning to order, to find a principle or set of principles by which to bring unity and understanding to the body of curious knowledge about man and history that his task as humanist and teacher compelled him to confront.[1] Finding and relating his many false starts and incomplete attempts at a science of civilization, and identifying the classical and contemporary sources that prompted them, has become fair game in Vico studies, and there are few such inquiries that do not in some way advance our understanding of his remarkable mind. For if in its final form the *Scienza nuova* is a paradigm of cultural science, it is at least equally—and in its earlier stages more—"a crazy quilt of curious learning," "a dynamic encyclopedia of inter-disciplinary lore and superdisciplinary logic—a latter-day *speculum mundi*."[2]

Finding unity in Vico's own ideas is hardly less challenging

---

[1] Autobiography, *Opere* 5.77–78; cf. *De studiorum ratione*, *Opere* 1.77. Here as so often Vico's authority is Cicero, *De or.* 3.33–36.

[2] Donald R. Kelley, "In Vico Veritas: The True Philosophy and the New Science," *Social Research* 43 (1976): 601–611, at 601.

a task than the one he set himself in organizing learning. Of the many rubrics by which one may seek to take hold of his efforts, however, none are more plain, more reliable, or more useful than the two that fairly dominate his published works: wisdom and eloquence. The primacy of language in social life was the characteristic bias of traditional poetic and rhetoric, and nothing could so guarantee the vitality of civil life, it was held, than to join eloquent speech with true wisdom. "Eloquence is nothing but wisdom speaking," Vico liked to quote, and their proper union in a healthy society was the most frequent theme of his letters and orations, including the remarks he gave at the 1737 opening of the Accademia degli Oziosi, shortly before his retirement from teaching. "I hold the opinion," he said on that occasion, "that if eloquence has lost the luster it had among the Latins and Greeks while the sciences have made advances equal to or perhaps even greater than theirs, it is because our sciences are taught without any embellishment of eloquence."[3] One imagines that line raising a few sniggers, but it serves well to show how compelling an idea the union of wisdom and eloquence was in Vico's thinking. The same reasoning that led him to assert the primacy of language in social life, moreover, led him to see also in language, reconceived in the broad sense he came to give it, the key element in the formation of culture. In his use and reformulation of this ancient conviction lies much of the excitement of his discoveries and some considerable portion of his legacy.

LANGUAGE AND SOCIETY

In his *Ars poetica*, one of the most enduring and frequently glossed works in Western literature, Horace wrote:

While men still roamed the woods, Orpheus, the holy prophet of the gods, made them shrink from bloodshed and brutal living; hence the fable that he tamed tigers and ravening lions; hence too the fable

---

[3] "Porto opinione che, [se] ne' nostri tempi l'eloquenza non sia rimessa nel lustro de' latini e de' greci, quando le scienze vi han fatto progressi uguali e forse anche maggiori, egli addivenga perocché le scienze s'insegnano nude affatto d'ogni fregio dell'eloquenza" (*Opere* 7.34).

that Amphion, builder of Thebes' citadel, moved stones by the sound of his lyre, and led them whither he would by his supplicating spell. In days of yore, this was wisdom, to draw a line between public and private rights, between things sacred and things common, to check vagrant union, to give rules for wedded life, to build towns, and grave laws on tables of wood; and so honor and fame fell to bards and their songs, as divine.[4]

In some marginal comments on this passage, Vico noted that while Horace's chronology was wrong, his claim was correct. "First, or vulgar, wisdom was poetic in nature," wrote Vico, "and from poetic history are to be sought the origins of republics, laws, and all the arts and sciences that make civilization [*humanitatem*] complete." Thus the "*New Science* [of 1730], and especially its second book," is essentially "an extended commentary on this passage."[5]

And so it is. But the passage itself is but one in a long tradition of Greek and Roman authors, dating at least from Aristophanes and Isocrates, who held that speech, not reason, is the basis of culture; that poetic heroes, not philosopher kings, create human society.[6] The idea is stated most impressively by Cicero in *De inventione,* itself a summary of Hellenistic rhetoric. After speaking of "men scattered in the fields and hidden in sylvan retreats," he writes:

It does not seem possible that a mute and voiceless wisdom could have turned men suddenly from their [savage] habits and introduced

[4] "Silvestres homines sacer interpresque deorum, / caedibus et victu foedo deterruit Orpheus, / dictus ob hoc lenire tigres rabidosque leones. / Dictus et Amphion, thebanae conditor urbis, / saxa movere sono testudinis, et prece blanda / ducere quo vellet. Fuit haec sapientia quondam / publica privatis secernere, sacra profanis; / concubitu prohibere vago, dare iura maritis; / oppida moliri, leges incidere ligno: / sic honor et nomen divinis vatibus atque / carminibus venit" (*Ars P.* vv. 391–401; trans. H. Rushton Fairclough, Loeb ed.).

[5] "Prima sapientia vulgaris fuit poetica. Quare ab historia poetica sunt repetendae origines rerumpublicarum, legum omniumque artium ac scientiarum, quae humanitatem perfecere. Quod in *Novae scientiae,* secundae editionis, libro secundo praestitum est: qui liber est huius loci horatiani quidam perpetuus commentarius" (*Opere* 7.76).

[6] Cf., for example, Aristophanes, *Frogs,* vv. 1031–1036; Isocrates, *Nicocles,* 5–9. On this tradition, see Friedrich Solmsen, "Drei Rekonstruktionen zur antiken Rhetorik und Poetik," *Hermes* 67 (1932): 133–154.

them to different patterns of life. . . . [And] after cities had been established, how could it have been brought to pass that men should learn to keep faith and observe justice . . . unless men had been able by eloquence to persuade their fellows of the truth of what they had discovered by reason?[7]

Or, as he says most simply in *De oratore*:

What other power [than eloquence] could have been strong enough either to gather scattered humanity into one place, or to lead it out of its brutish existence in the wilderness up to our present condition as men and as citizens, or, after the establishment of social communities, to give shape to laws, tribunals, and civic rights?[8]

Fine humanist that he was, Vico himself, in his seminal Sixth Oration, set aside the rather trivial subquarrel between poets and rhetors over ascendancy in the realm of language (and thus in the founding of culture), combined elements from both the Horatian and Ciceronian versions, and offered his own reconstruction of the ancient topos:

For no other reason did the wisest poets imagine in their fables that Orpheus tamed beasts with the music of his lyre and Amphion moved stones with his singing, charming them into place of their own accord, and so built the walls of Thebes; and for these merits the lyre of the former and the dolphin of the latter were borne aloft and painted in the stars. These stones, these beams, these beasts are foolish men, and Orpheus and Amphion the sages who conjoined their theoretical knowledge of divine things and their practical knowledge of human things with eloquent speech, and by its compelling force led men from solitude into social bonds, that is, from love of self to respect for humanity, from inertia to industry, from unbridled freedom to

---

[7] "Ac mihi quidem videtur hoc nec tacita nec inops dicendi sapientia perficere potuisse ut homines a consuetudine subito converteret et ad diversas rationes vitae traduceret. Age vero, urbibus constitutis, ut fidem colere et justitiam retinere discerent . . . qui tandem fieri potuit, nisi homines ea quae ratione invenissent eloquentia persuadere potuissent?" (*Inv. Rhet.* 1.2.2–3).

[8] "Ut vero jam ad illa summa veniamus; quae vis alia potuit aut dispersos homines unum in locum congregare, aut a fera agrestique vita ad hunc humanum cultum civilemque deducere, aut, jam constitutis civitatibus, leges, judicia, jura describere?" (*De or.* 1.8.33). See, too, the *De republica*, where Cicero writes that virtue depends entirely upon its use and that the actual performance of statesmen, not the theoretical knowledge of the philosophers, gives us our sense of moral obligation and reverence toward the gods (1.2.2).

the obedience of law, thus uniting fierce and weak men under the stability of reason.[9]

For Vico, as for the tradition he represents, knowledge alone is impotent in the face of ferocity; only eloquence has the power to make men quit their independent ways and submit to the forces of civilization. To assert the primacy of language in culture, however, is not to decide how the language that civilizes is to be conceived or how it actually functions in the birth and growth of a people. "With the most agreeable tie of speech," wrote Cicero, "reason bound together men who had hitherto been solitary."[10] Poignant as the statement is, it fails to say how language relates to the reason whose instrument it apparently is, and whether there is any significant difference between speech and reason as we know them and the speech and reason that first drew men together in those remote, dark times we call the dawn of civilization.

From the vantage of his *New Science* Vico could eventually say, in fact, that most commentators on earliest times, ancients and moderns alike, had fallen victim in their accounts to one or both grievous "conceits" (*borie*) that afflict our refined

---

[9] "Nec sane alio fictis fabulis poetae sapientissimi Orpheum lyra mulxisse feras, Amphionem cantu movisse saxa, iisque sese sponte sua ad symphoniam congerentibus, Thebas moenisse muris; et ob ea merita illius lyram, delphinum huius in coelum invectum astrisque appictum esse finxerunt. Saxa illa, illa robora, illae ferae homines stulti sunt: Orpheus, Amphion sapientes, qui divinarum scientiam humanarumque prudentiam cum eloquentia conjunxerunt, eiusque flexianima vi homines a solitudine ad coetus, hoc est, a suo ipsorum amore ad humanitatem colendam, ab inertia ad industriam, ab effrena libertate ad legum obsequia traducunt; et viribus feroces cum imbecillis rationis aequabilitate consociant" (*Opere* 1.60–61). As to the "dolphin of Amphion," did Vico confuse Amphion with the sea goddess Amphitrite, persuaded by the dolphin to marry his master, Poseidon, who thereupon rewarded his sea servant with a constellation in his image? While the lyre of Orpheus became Lyra, Amphion was not, to my knowledge, honored in the heavens.

For Vico's final handling of the topos, see the *Scienza nuova seconda, Opere* 4, §§81, 523, 615, and especially 734, where Horace's chronology is corrected.

[10] "Hominesque antea dissociatos jucundissimo inter se sermonis vinclo [ratio] conligavit" (*Rep.* 3.2.3; trans. George H. Sabine and Stanley B. Smith, *On the Commonwealth* [Columbus: Ohio University Press, 1929], p. 197).

spirits, the one nationalistic, the other scholarly. The conceit of each nation is that it before all others invented the comforts of human life and that its remembered history goes back to the very beginning of the world; thus its chroniclers claim their kinsmen as the founders of humanity and are forever adjusting the chronology of the race to fit the events that are familiar to them. More serious is the conceit of the scholars, who assume that what they know is as old as the world itself; thus myths are made the repository of recondite truths, hieroglyphs become a code for mystic messages, Greek fables are turned into allegories, and sundry other anachronisms are committed. This annoying predisposition to make our own minds and histories those of the most primitive cultures is due, Vico claims, to a property of human thinking itself, such that "whenever men can form no idea of distant and unknown things, they judge them by what is familiar and at hand."[11] Such is the inexhaustible source of the errors about the principles of humanity, for when nations and scholars pondered the matter, "it was on the basis of their own enlightened, cultivated, and magnificent times that they judged the origins of humanity, which must nevertheless by the nature of things have been small, crude, and quite obscure."[12]

The errors Vico found were in part philological and in part philosophical in nature. Neither the Greeks nor the Romans, he wrote, had any regard for their origins, and Plato himself ascribed philosophic wisdom to the poetic theologians, an opinion that even the great Lord Verulam (*De veterum sapientia*) had shared. As to philosophic errors, the range of ideas projected by moderns on earliest times ran roughly between the extremes identified by Lactantius (*Div. Inst.* 6.10.13–

[11] "È altra proprietà della mente umana ch'ove gli uomini delle cose lontane e non conosciute non possono fare niuna idea, le stimano dalla cose loro conosciute e presenti" (*Scienza nuova seconda, Opere* 4, §122; cf. generally §§122–128, 361).

[12] "Perocché da' loro tempi illuminati, colti e magnifici, ne' quali cominciarono quelle ad avvertirle, questi a ragionarle, hanno estimato l'origini dell'umanità, le quali dovettero per natura essere picciole, rozze, oscurissime" (*Scienza nuova seconda, Opere* 4, §123).

18): that of the Epicureans, who held that men were driven by their fear of beasts to ally themselves with other men (e.g. Lucr. *De rer. nat.* 5.805–1116), and that of the Stoics, who saw in the rise of cities a social instinct natural to man (e.g. Cic. *Rep.* 1.25.39). The first of these views, cynical and hard-bitten, Vico found reflected in the work of Hobbes, whose "fierce and violent" men cast in their lot together to avoid the "war of each with all," while the second view, elitist and high-minded, he found repeated in Grotius and his fellow jusnaturalists, Pufendorf and Selden. In none of them, moreover, could he find a commitment to providence as the "architect" of the civil world, a principle he took to be axiomatic, even as "common sense" was the "rule" of humanity, and man's own free will its "fabricator."[13] These failings were such that a "new critical art" to establish the principles of humanity was called for, one that would merge in an appropriate manner the separate evidence of philology and philosophy.

Like many of Vico's ruling concepts, that of a "new critical art" as the combination of philology and philosophy has not one but several inspirations, resulting in a spectrum of meanings that Vico himself recognized.[14] Its most obvious source is the one Vico himself cites, the *De jure belli ac pacis* of Hugo Grotius, whose hermeneutical theory was drawn, Vico thought, from the rhetorical teachings on the issues of judicial cases (*de statibus causarum*). Vico made that claim in the introduction to his *Universal Law*, in the course of discussing jurisprudence as a composition of reason and authority. To be valid and effective, laws must be exact and public, thus carrying authority, but they must also have the warrant of reason. It was the genius of the jurisconsults, Vico argued, to be able

---

[13] Cf. *Scienza nuova prima, Opere* 3, §§45–47. Vico's canvassing of prior errors in the science of humanity appears in §§12–39, the book's first section, which is likely a summary of his unpublished and now lost *Scienza nuova in forma negativa*. Cf. the Autobiography, *Opere* 5.48f.

[14] Cf. the Autobiography, *Opere* 5.49, and *Scienza nuova seconda, Opere* 4, §§7, 143, 348, and especially 131–163, where the separate concerns of "philosophy" and "philology" are set forth.

to establish both reason and authority in the laws but also to accommodate them to the many actual situations to which they had to apply. The more recent schools of interpreters were not so successful. The "ancient" or Scholastic interpreters, followers of the so-called *mos Italicus* of Accursius and Bartolus, assuming perfect logical consistency in the *Corpus juris*, were ingenious in expounding the law's text, often in ignorance of its history and flagrant violation of its meaning, all in an effort to save its authority by showing its applicability to the increasingly complex situations it had to face in Europe. The "modern" or humanist interpreters, on the other hand, followers of the so-called *mos Gallicus* founded by Andrea Alciato, were above all concerned to know the history of specific provisions so that they might, in a hope that finally proved fatuous, reduce the law to the status of an art that it plainly had not achieved in the code of Justinian. The point, Vico thought, was not to trade one approach off against the other—not to abandon history for the sake of order or order for the sake of history—but to realize that authority is not capriciousness but a part of reason itself, just as the *certum* that is the child of authority is directly akin to the *verum* to which reason gives birth. Joined of themselves in human history, they are artificially separated by the disciplines that purport to study them, philology and philosophy; a valid science of humanity must be at once philological and philosophical, able to show that reason possesses authority and that authority has a warrant in reason. Grotius produced a methodologically sound work, Vico thought, and but for the probable character of his principles would have had a fine result.[15]

---

[15] Cf. *De uno principio, Opere* 2.26–33, esp. 31f.; *De constantia jurisprudentis, Opere* 2.267–268; *Scienza nuova prima, Opere* 3, §21. The first theoretical joining of the *verum* and the *certum* is in the *De uno principio, Opere* 2.82–84, at 83: "Certum vero est proprium et perpetuum juris voluntarii attributum, sub aliqua tamen veri parte."

Forever fond of combining clear and distinct opposites, Vico overdraws the contrast of the "philosophical" Scholastics and the "historical" humanists (see the Autobiography, *Opere* 5.7f., and *De studiorum ratione, Opere* 1.110).

The point in Grotius where reason and authority were most fully joined was in the concept of *jus gentium*, itself the outcome of a tradition of speculation that began in the formative period of Roman Law, continued with the jurisconsults, and led through the Jesuit jusnaturalists of Spain, especially Molina and Suárez, up to the triumvirate so often named by Vico—Selden, Pufendorf, and Grotius. The *jus gentium* arose out of praetorian diligence and practical necessity as the law of the "gentile" or non-Roman peoples in the expanding Roman state, in part to regulate relations between citizens and noncitizens, but especially to care for matters beyond the purview of the elitist *jus civile*. At first a mere supplement to the "law of citizens," in time it dwarfed it in size and appeal, for unlike the *jus civile*, patrician in provenance and prejudice, it came to be seen as more subtle, more diverse, and above all more "equitable" or rationally assured, a bias that was enhanced as it was gathered in from the provinces and recognized for what it had become: a law not only *of* the nations but *common to* them as well. When the jurisconsults undertook to rationalize the codes on the basis of Stoic natural-law theory, it was inevitable that they would find in the *jus gentium*, now perceived as "universal" and "impartial," a law that had sprung from nature itself, and thus one more closely allied with *jus naturale* than with *jus civile*, decidedly a positive law. Ulpian and Gaius, in fact, had all but made them identical (*Dig.* 1.1.6, 10). Concerned to establish an international *Law of War and Peace*, therefore, Grotius chose to admit as evidence not only the teachings of natural law but also the testimony of philosophers, historians, poets, and orators, "for when many at different times and in different places affirm the same thing as certain, that ought to be referred to a universal cause; and this cause, in the lines of inquiry which we are following, must be either a correct conclusion drawn from the principles of nature, or common consent. The former points to the law of nature, the latter to the law of nations."[16]

[16] "Sed quod ubi multi diversis temporibus ac locis idem pro certo affir-

Like every jusnaturalist before him, Grotius resolves at the start to hold strictly separate in his discourse the principles of nature and those of *jus gentium*, a determination that cracks and breaks fully apart as he takes up one after the other increasingly more complex issues. Between *jus naturale merum* and laws that are simply "common to many peoples separately" (the *jus gentium merum*, one might say) there are "precepts which are natural in a certain situation" (*praecepta quae pro certo statu sunt naturalia*) and tenets of the *jus gentium* "which contain the bond of human society" (*quae societatis humanae vinculum continent*); and the issues that truly count seem usually to be ruled by the wisdom of this large gray area.[17] It would be Vico's merit, of course, to take the last step and, on the theory that the nature of a reality is its history, merge the two systems into a *jus naturale gentium*, a name by which he wished to describe those first severe, poetic beginnings of just actions which, with time and application, evolve into the natural law of the philosophers.[18] In this way, too, his science was at once philological and philosophical.

A similar conclusion, though one of an altogether different

---

mant, id ad causam universalem referri debeat: quae in nostris quaestionibus alia esse non potest, quam aut recta illatio ex naturae principiis procedens, aut communis aliquis consensus. Illa jus naturae indicat, hic jus gentium" (*De jure belli ac pacis*, pr. 40; trans. Francis W. Kelsey, Carnegie Endowment for International Peace ed.).

[17] Ibid., pr. 17, 40; 1.1.14.1; 2.8.26. On the significance of Grotius, see especially J. N. Figgis, *Political Thought from Gerson to Grotius, 1414–1625: Seven Studies*, 2d ed. (New York: Harper, 1960).

[18] Cf. *De uno principio, Opere* 2.126–128, where the two are first combined, and *Scienza nuova seconda, Opere* 4, §§394–398 and passim, where the mature formulation appears. Vico's historicist theory is stated in his famous Element 14: "The nature of institutions is nothing but their coming into being at certain times and in certain guises" ("Natura di cose altro non è che nascimento di esse in certi tempi e con certe guise") (*Opere* 4, §147). Apparently to gain authority for his suggestion, Vico credits Vulteius with removing the comma between *naturali* and *gentium* in the latter's *De jure naturali, gentium et civili*, something that was not at all the case (cf. *De uno principio, Opere* 2.127). A compelling argument for Vico's joining philology and philosophy in this sense is that of Guido Fassò, *I "quattro auttori" del Vico: Saggio sulla genesi della "Scienza nuova"* (Milan: Giuffrè, 1949), esp. pp. 51–90.

spirit, was reached by the "Alciatani" or latter-day followers of the humanist legal scholar Andrea Alciato (1492–1550), whose own efforts, no less than those of the jusnaturalists, reached back through the medieval glossators to the jurisconsults themselves.[19] "Priests of the law" (*sacerdotes legum*), as they were wont to refer to themselves, the ancient jurists had posited in the evolved Roman Law the completeness and rationality of a science. Civil law and its "gentile" supplement had indeed taken root in sundry enactments, arose from particular circumstances and suited particular needs, but with time it reached out to embrace the whole of the civil world such that nothing, human or divine, did not fall within its interest or enjoy its ordering purpose. Thus could Ulpian say with bold simplicity that jurisprudence is the "knowledge of things human and divine" (*Dig.* 1.1.10: *divinarum atque humanarum rerum notitia*) and claim for it the status of "true philosophy" (*Dig.* 1.1.1: *veram nisi fallor philosophiam, non simulatam*). Though fed by a sober practical motive, the effort of classification that issued in time in Justinian's great work was equally the result of a scientific bias. From the great body of law, the jurists held, itself arranged under comprehensive titles, could be extracted the general principles on which they were convinced it rested, and these could be set down, as they

[19] The continuity of the jurisprudential tradition, in and through its several permutations, is the important thesis of Donald R. Kelley, "Vera Philosophia: The Philosophical Significance of Renaissance Jurisprudence," *Journal of the History of Philosophy* 14 (1976): 267–279, which refocuses the perspective set forth in his book, *Foundations of Modern Historical Scholarship: Language, Law, and History in the French Renaissance* (New York: Columbia University Press, 1970). A similar notion is found in Roderich von Stintzing, *Geschichte der deutschen Rechtswissenschaft*, vol. 1, *Bis zum Jahre 1650* (Munich and Leipzig: Oldenbourg, 1880). On humanist jurisprudence in particular, see further Domenico Maffei, *Gli inizi dell'umanesimo giuridico* (Milan: Giuffrè, 1956); Guido Kisch, *Erasmus und die Jurisprudenz seiner Zeit* (Basel: Helbing and Lichtenhahn, 1960), and "Humanistic Jurisprudence," *Studies in the Renaissance* 8 (1961): 71–87; Julian H. Franklin, *Jean Bodin and the Sixteenth-Century Revolution in the Methodology of Law and History* (New York: Columbia University Press, 1961), this last being a remarkably lucid statement of the rise of the *mos Gallicus* and its development through the work of Bodin.

came to be in the first books of the *Digest*, in systematic form, even as the fiftieth and last book of that work sifted and arranged the various definitions and maxims by which they had sought to order their interpretations. Such interpretations, they made clear (*Dig.* 1.3), were not the work of weak or undisciplined minds but followed a circumspect course that looked always beyond the text of the law (*verba legis*) to its spirit (*vis legis*) and beyond that to its reason or rational basis itself (*ratio juris*).[20]

Out of these same convictions came the effort of Scholastic interpreters, best known to us in the Gloss of Accursius (1182–1259), to accommodate the *Corpus* to the evolving social and economic arrangements of the Middle Ages through the simple internal logical analysis of its text. When the Law, like other ancient documents, came under the scrutiny of the new philology of the humanists, the result, presented most trenchantly in Guillaume Budé's *Annotationes in Pandectas*, was to reveal the many inconsistencies in Justinian's compilation and thus to show as forced and often erroneous the Scholastic opinions. A reforming spirit took hold among humanist jurists, led by Alciato in Italy and by Jacques Cujas and his colleagues at Bourges, who combined philological methods with the consuming philosophical and systematizing interest of the tradition in an effort to reduce the law truly to an art. The questioning of the ancients that this implied extended at first only to the form of Roman Law, not to its authority, and indeed efforts continued throughout the sixteenth century, now with the aid of historical vision, to give the vulgar traditions the same completeness and philosophical rigor that the *Corpus*, properly understood and arranged, was assumed to have. In the work of François Hotman and François Baudouin, however, the call for a truly comparative approach to law was sounded, a call that was heeded, even exceeded, in the writings of Jean Bodin (*Methodus ad facilem historiarum cognitionem*,

[20] On the scientific method and influence of the jurisconsults see William C. Morey, *Outlines of Roman Law*, 2d ed. (New York and London: Putnam, 1914), chap. 10.

1566; *Les six libres de la république*, 1576) and his Toulouse rival Pierre Grégoire (*Syntagma iuris universi*, 1582; *De republica*, 1596), in which a universal theory not only of law but of the entire human cosmos is attempted.[21] That this effort continues in Vico is evident to anyone who has even browsed the entire *corpus* of his writings. As his early pedagogical orations recapitulated in ten years' time the development in the idea of wisdom from a contemplative to an active virtue that had been carried out over three centuries, so a decade of scientific work—from his *De universi juris uno principio et fine uno* of 1720 to the *De constantia jurisprudentis* of 1721 to the *Principi di una Scienza nuova intorno alla natura delle nazioni* of 1725 and 1730—recapitulated some two centuries of effort (and arguably two millenniums) to evolve first an art of Roman Law, then a science of Universal Law, and finally a philosophy of human history itself. In this sense, Vico was the last and most intriguing of the Alciatani.

To these more particular contexts of Vico's "new critical art" must be added one that is perhaps most fundamental of all, and certainly the one that assumed a consistent prominence in his various attempts to present a science of humanity: using the history of Rome as scientific prototype for the growth and development of any culture. "I shall find my task easier," Vico had heard Scipio declare in the *De republica*, "if I place before you a description of our Roman State at its birth, during its growth, at its maturity, and finally in its strong and healthy state, than if I should follow the example of Socrates in Plato's

[21] See Kelley, "Vera Philosophia," pp. 277–279; Franklin, *Jean Bodin*, pp. 59–79. For an exposition of the *Methodus* see John L. Brown, *The Methodus ad Facilem Historiarum Cognitionem of Jean Bodin: A Critical Study* (Washington, D.C.: The Catholic University of America Press, 1939). Equally grand attempts at a universal history were being made by classicists of the day, notably Loys Le Roy, *De la vicissitude ou varieté des choses en l'univers* (1575). See Werner L. Gundersheimer, *The Life and Works of Louis de Roy* (Geneva: Droz, 1966); Kelley, *Foundations of Modern Historical Scholarship*, pp. 80–85; George Huppert, *The Idea of Perfect History: Historical Erudition and Historical Philosophy in Renaissance France* (Urbana: University of Illinois Press, 1970), pp. 104–117.

work and myself invent an ideal State of my own." And he had heard Laelius's praising response:

You have begun the discussion in accordance with a new principle which is not to be found anywhere in the works of the Greeks. For Plato . . . chose his own ground that he might construct a commonwealth according to his fancy. His was a noble state, no doubt, but incongruous with human life and customs [cf. Arist. *Pol.* 1266a31]. The other Greek philosophers discussed the kinds of states and their principles but failed to treat any concrete example and type of commonwealth. You, it seems to me, are likely to combine the concrete with the general.[22]

Similarly Machiavelli, despite a concern that the "envious nature of man" made the discovery and introduction of any new principles a dangerous event, determined in his *Discorsi* on Titus Livius to open a "new route," suggesting a programmatic reading of ancient Roman history that would lead to the establishment of states in the same manner in which medicine and law are practiced—by applying ancient successes.[23] A vestige of these practical concerns is still to be found in Vico, yet his interest in the course of Roman history runs deeply scientific. The experience of the best state is the civil equivalent of the artist's *natura optima* and is taken by him to have a rational guarantee that is not asserted of, though also not denied to, other cultures. Vico, of course, knew Rome best, his knowledge of other cultures, save Greece, being spotty and uncertain. Yet his assumption of the "constancy" of Roman history had less to do with any "conceit of the nations"

---

[22] "Facilius autem, quod est propositum, consequar, si nostram rem publicam vobis et nascentem et crescentem et adultam et jam firmam atque robustam ostendero, quam si mihi aliquam, ut apud Platonem Socrates, ipse finxero" (*Rep.* 2.1.3; trans. Clinton Walker Keyes, Loeb ed.). "Nos vero videmus, et te quidem ingressum ratione ad disputandum nova, quae nusquam est in Graecorum libris. Nam princeps ille . . . auream sibi sumsit, in qua civitatem extrueret arbitratu suo, praeclaram ille quidem fortasse, sed a vita hominum abhorrentem et moribus, reliqui disseruerunt sine ullo certo exemplari formaque rei publicae de generibus et de rationibus civitatum; tu mihi videris utrumque facturus" (*Rep.* 2.11.21–22; trans. Sabine and Smith, p. 164).

[23] *Discorsi* 1, intro.

than with his conviction that it was a complete culture, one that had achieved a complexity and universality that others had not, but also one that had patently run the entire gamut of the human *corso*, from barbaric and crude beginnings to a state of high refinement. Rome therefore emerged as at once the exquisite philological *certum* and the paradigmatic philosophical *verum*, its own course indistinguishable, in fact as in principle, from that "ideal eternal history" which any nation was destined to have. As the truth of its own *jus civile* was in time made plain and filled out by the *jus gentium*, so its history as a nation acquired in retrospect a universality that is immediately pertinent to a science of humanity.[24]

In all these ways Vico's new science was a merging of philology and philosophy, of history and theory, of the certain and the true. When he came to reflect on just what he had wrought, he could not settle on a single name by which to define his work, and so he gave it several. He had shown the basis and progression of the idea of providence under which humanity is formed, he concluded, and in this respect his *New*

---

[24] In the *De uno principio, Opere* 2.46, the civil equivalent of *natura optima* is the antediluvian state of man: "Haec esset naturalis honestas integra. Nam conformitas cum natura optima, ut in corpore vocatur 'corporis honestas,' 'corporis pulchritudo,' ita in animo dicitur 'animi honestas.'" By the time of the *New Science*, man's nature has been fully historicized and Vico has returned from Augustine's *civitas dei* to Cicero's *respublica romana*, where he had begun in the *De studiorum ratione*, as the model for his science. On Rome's having run the complete human *corso* and its consequent special character within his science, see the *Scienza nuova seconda, Opere* 4, §§1088–1096.

It seemed to him perfectly natural at one point to prepare as the conclusion for the work a "Pratica della Scienza," the opening of which states: "This entire work has so far been treated as a purely contemplative science concerning the common nature of nations. It seems for this reason to promise no help to human prudence toward delaying if not preventing the ruin of nations in decay"—a distinct echo of the *De republica* (2.25) (*Opere* 4, §§1405–1411, at 1405). For good reasons, very likely those stated by Max H. Fisch ("Vico's *Pratica*," in *Vico's Science of Humanity*, ed. Giorgio Tagliacozzo and Donald P. Verene [Baltimore: Johns Hopkins University Press, 1976], pp. 423–430), Vico chose not to use this conclusion. A translation of the *Pratica* by Fisch and Thomas G. Bergin appears in pages 451–454 of the same symposium.

Science was a "rational civil theology of divine providence." But he had also shown the necessary progression of human will in history, from its first bold assertions to its subjugation by reason, and in this sense had written a "philosophy of authority." Equally he had treated the development of human thought from its first crude acknowledgment of Jove to its full appreciation of every art and science, and thus his work was a "history of human ideas" and a "philosophical criticism" of the same. The governance of human actions was also his theme, followed from its start as a necessary consequence of the recognition of Jove to its refinement in the practices of auspices to its eventual perfection in the concepts of natural reason, and in this respect his book was a "natural law of the peoples." In sum, his science gave the "ideal eternal history" traversed in time by any and every nation as it rises from its heroic youth to its full perfection, and in this sense was also a "philosophy of universal history." In each of these forms, he claimed, its triumph was the same: to have shown at once the authority or actuality of history's reasons and the principles of history's certainties. His work, in short, was philology reduced to a science.[25]

As varied as the science may have been, "philology" in this equation was a constant. From start to finish Vico conceived of philology in its most traditional sense as the "history of things and words" (*historia rerum et verborum*), wherein *res* are the ideas and institutions of a society, above all legal and civil, and *verba* its languages, myths, and symbols. The impossibility of separating the two in any final way, Vico said, led him to recast the earlier version of his *New Science*, whose two major parts he had entitled *idee* and *lingue*, into the form he gave it in 1730 and thereafter.[26] Even in this later form, however, the combination was incomplete, its ninety-two "special" axioms or propositions (*elementi particolari*) divided neatly between those pertaining to language and myth

[25] See *Scienza nuova seconda, Opere* 4, §§385–399; cf. §§7, 342–360.
[26] Cf. the Autobiography, *Opere* 5.39f.

(23–63) and those treating of ideas and institutions (64–114), corresponding roughly to their separate discussions in book two, sections 1 and 2, on the one hand, and in book two, sections 3 through 9 and most of book four, on the other. Through the notion of "wisdom," a wisdom that was "poetic" in its origins and "esoteric" (*riposta*) in its evolved form, he sought to provide a banner under which both the scope of humanity as well as the "constant" or scientific nature of its course could be shown, all taking root in that "poetic metaphysics" in which humanity had had its birth. Through that phrase and its correlates, he felt, the final unity of *res* and *verba*, of thought and expression, of theory and action, and of sundry other dyads that these in turn suggest, could be made clear and defended. To reach that point, he would say in retrospect, required the reflection of some good twenty years—a reflection, I would add, on the structure of rhetorical discourse and on the development of great Western texts, above all the two poems of Homer and the "imported" laws of Solon. As it proceeded, Vico sought to grasp in ever more successful formulations the unity of wisdom and eloquence of which he was always, as humanist and teacher, persuaded. The constitution of wisdom in language, the deepest meaning of his "Poetic Wisdom," was the last and most dramatic presentation of that unity. Its novelty and excitement, which Vico himself was the first to enjoy, is only truly appreciated when set over and against two early and thoroughly traditional formulations: that of the transmission of wisdom through language, the subject of his Sixth Oration, and that of the discovery of ancient wisdom in language, the expressed theme of the *De antiquissima Italorum sapientia*.

SAPIENTIA CORRUPTAE NATURAE EMENDATRIX

As later in the scientific accounts, the union of wisdom and eloquence in the Sixth Oration is also set out against the background of human isolation. Solitude is the great constant in Vico's thought, not the physical solitude that many animals enjoy by nature and that even men will seek out as a source of refreshment and renewal, but solitude of spirit, the isolation of minds and feelings and the attendant collapse of language, a spiritual aloneness that can exist even within a massing of bodies however superficially joined through gestures and conventions. Solitude of this kind, Vico asserts ever more strongly, is the chaos of human existence, the antipode of civilization, the yawning abyss from whose jaws men have been rescued by drawing together in society and into which they threaten always to be returned. The causes and thus the remedies of such isolation vary in his thought, but to avoid or to repair it is very nearly a point of obsession. Not the price of civilization in psychological repression, but its cost through an extreme individualism is Vico's concern, and in this sense he is heir to the republicans of Greece and Rome and the precursor of the classical social theorists of the last century and our own.

"There is nothing," we read in the *City of God*, "so social by nature, so unsocial by its corruption, as this race." That God should have created but a single man, Augustine adds (in a lovely piece of his "symbolic logic"), only reinforces this idea, for in doing so he commended to us more effectually the unity of society and the bond of concord.[27] In its own solidarity mankind reflects and thus worships the unity of its creator, even as the individual of the race will put aside all distractions and seek to know only his soul and God. These powerful images of Plotinus, fitted by Augustine to the drama of sin and salvation, pass into the text of Vico, but there they are presented in a secularized version much akin to that of Descartes. Not estrangement from God but disunity among men is the predicament of history brought on by our folly, and it is through the works of wisdom that our nature will be restored. Though like brutes a bodily being, man in his

[27] "Nihil enim est quam hoc genus tam discordiosum vitio, tam sociale natura" (*De civ. D.* 12.28; cf. 12.22; trans. Marcus Dods, Modern Library ed.).

essence is *mens, animus*, and *sermo*, and through his corruption these very faculties, meant to hold men together, have become the instruments of disintegration. The unity of mind has been shattered by headstrong visions: "Every opinion has about it a certain shadow of the truth [*similitudo veri*] that the willfulness at work in our souls lays hold of as truth itself; thus each man has his own sense of things and there are, as the saying goes, as many opinions as heads."[28] There is not yet here, as there would be a short time later, that defense of verisimilitude as the driving force of socialization; only in clear and distinct ideas does mankind have its bond. So also in speech, conceived as the mere vessel of ideas, images that are rough or common and language that is elusive or challenging can only compound the confusion of diverse opinions:

For through its inelegance, language in countless instances fails the mind, abandoning it when it seeks help in explaining itself. Or by its rough and primitive mode of expression it distorts the mind's perceptions with inappropriate words: it sullies them with base and vulgar terms or it conceals them in ambiguous phrases, so that what is understood is different from what is spoken.[29]

To these defects of mind and tongue are joined the most pernicious of all, those of soul, created to be open and sharing but overpowered through sin by an overweening self-love. Thus the "gatherings of men may appear to be societies, but amid the throng and press of their bodies there is in fact a deep isolation of souls."[30]

---

[28] "Hinc notet hominem usquequaque corruptum, et primo linguae infantiam, tum mentem opinionibus involutam, animum denique viciis inquinatum comperiat. . . . opinionibus autem, cum unaquaeque a se habeat aliquam similitudinem veri, quam libido, ut cujusque fert animus, pro vero arripiat; inde suus cuique sensus est, et, quod vulgo dicitur, quot capita tot sententiae" (Sixth Oration, *Opere* 1.58f.). Cf. Descartes, *Meditations on First Philosophy*, 4.

[29] "Nam per infantiam innumeris in rebus lingua menti non succurrit, eamque, dum ad explicandum suam implorat opem, destituit; vel incondita ineptaque rusticitate sermonis mentis sensa fraudat verbis, quae dignitatem non habent; sive foedat turpibus sordidisque, sive fallit aut prodit ambiguis, ut aliorsum accipiatur quam loquitur" (Sixth Oration, *Opere* 1.59).

[30] "Hominum coetus in speciem societates videntur, re autem ipsa in cor-

The very specter of our corruption suggests its cure, Vico argues. It is wisdom, the purge and completion of the inner man (Pl. *Alc.* 124e), pursued fully in all its ramifications and in the order dictated by our own corrupt nature, that will supply our deficiencies and restore our humanity. For wisdom touches all that touches us—knowledge of things divine, prudence in things human, and speech that is both true and eloquent—such that to be wise is to know with certainty, to act correctly, and to speak effectively.[31] Basic to all wisdom is grammar, simply knowing to speak correctly. Bacon had thought grammar an antidote to the confusion of tongues (*De dig.* 6.1), and so Vico will make it the beginning of wisdom. Next must come the disciplines of knowledge itself studied in the order prescribed by our natural psychological development. Memory being strongest in children and language being a matter of memory, childhood is the time for languages, while in youth and into maturity a complete "science of divine things," understood as the knowledge of nature and of nature's God, is to be achieved, beginning with the *res naturales*, matter bound and thus fit for the lively imagination of youth, and rising through mathematics and mathematical physics, by which the mind is cleansed of images, into the pure realm of the *res spiritales*, the disciplines of the mind and God, metaphysics and theology. After science must come the wisdom of pru-

---

porum frequentia summa est solitudo animorum" (Sixth Oration, *Opere* 1.59).

[31] Wisdom as the combination of science and prudence, "cognitio rerum divinarum et humanarum rerum prudentia," appears most prominently in Cicero, *Tusc.* 4.26.57 and *Off.* 2.2.5, and is repeated by Augustine, *De civ. D.* 8.4, and later by Salutati and his fellow civic humanists (cf. Rice, *Renaissance Idea of Wisdom*, pp. 30–49). Vico adds eloquence to the realm of wisdom, at first as a separate *officium* together with science and prudence, but later and more typically as a synonym for *wisdom* that is "applied" or brought to life, as in his letter of 12 January 1729 to Francesco Saverio Estevan: "La vera eloquenza è la sapienza che parla, e la sapienza è l'aggregato di tutte le virtù e della mente e del cuore, onde naturalmente escono da se stesse e le più belle e le più grandi virtù della lingua; le quali tre spezie di virtù compiono il vero uomo, che tutto è mente illuminata, cuor diritto e lingua fedel interpetre d'amendue" (*Opere* 5.212). Cf. *De mente heroica*, *Opere* 7.36.

dence, the cure of the human spirit. Here the order of study reverses itself. Like the captain at sea who sails an unobstructed course to yonder shore with the guidance of celestial bodies, so the sage, instructed in the *divina* of a sound ethics, charts the way for fools in the world, who lack the capacity to see the boundaries of good and evil, the wellspring of all prudence. Through moral and civil doctrine the sage will pass to jurisprudence, the end of his studies, and with the aid of a true eloquence will effect that justice and social utility which are the aim of all education.[32]

We are a long way, it seems, from any novelty in this plan, much less any breakthrough in cultural science. Man in his bodiliness is fully disregarded, this part of his nature being spiritually inert, marking only his unity with the beasts of the earth. So also the things of the body, the drives and appetites that give us our initial direction, the emotions that are "felt" rather than known, the limbs and senses by which we build and work, the stances and gestures by which our meanings, often unconsciously, are expressed—none of these have any standing in this vision of wisdom, being rather, as trappings of the "perturbations" of our soul, its obstruction. A development of the psyche is assumed and a theory of psychological progression set forth, from the fantasy and its images to reason and its concepts; yet fantasy in this scheme is predicament, not promise, conceived as an adolescent misery, a vice of youth, its effect on the mind to be scrubbed clean as the ascent to true knowledge is made. Language on the contrary is positively valued, indeed it encases the scheme, grammar at the start, true and apt speech at the end. Yet language and knowledge, like theory and action, are never permitted truly to interpenetrate; language is not yet the maker of knowledge, still only its vessel, an art of learning as grammar, an art of communication as eloquence. Similarly, the realms of mind and spirit are set off like regions of being, estranged sectors of our existence, aided separately by science and prudence.

[32] Sixth Oration, *Opere* l.61–67.

Still and all, there are rudiments of Vico's new science to be found here and nowhere more clearly than in the very scheme of wisdom as the perfection of man. This first sketch of culture will return, transmogrified, as Vico's last, the disciplines of learning and technique taking root in a "poetic metaphysics," showing forth the manifold exertions of spirits that make up our true humanity. If the arts and sciences, fully articulated, are the pride of our maturity, the bristling statement of our finest hour, they were also there at our birth, Vico will reason, "poetic" in form, scarcely recognizable, but there nonetheless as forms of our earliest wisdom. In this, moreover, the further suggestion of his juvenile sketch of wisdom is made plain. The path of wisdom in Vico's oration is marked by a settled but tense relation between reason and fact, between the general and the particular. Rising from grammar, the most specific of all knowledge, it passes through languages to the airier regions of physics, metaphysics, and theology, then descends via ethics to jurisprudence and in conjunction with eloquence rejoins the masses in their quotidian concerns. The wisdom of a nation in Vico's *New Science* follows a similar but more ambiguous course, passing from the certainty of its heroic days to the stark and dizzying truth of its maturity, only to be thrown back through necessity and need on the resources of its youth. Therein, one may conclude, lies the tragedy of a culture, but also the force of its renewal.

SAPIENTIA ITALORUM ANTIQUISSIMA

Vico took a large step toward his eventual new science with his attempt, in 1710, to recover the wisdom of the early Italian people by establishing the original meaning of some of their key words and phrases. The *De antiquissima Italorum sapientia ex linguae latinae originibus eruenda* is the strangest of all his works, a true "anomaly" in the judgment of the nineteenth-century critic Carlo Cantoni, "which runs counter to the tendencies and principles of Vico's entire scholarly life and to the method he would later employ almost instinctively in his historical inquiries."[33] Cantoni's extreme view, which is matched in reaction by that of Croce and his followers in our own century, who concede the work an exaggerated importance, derives from the book's peculiar philosophical agenda—a hodgepodge of fascinating and fanciful ideas drawn from a score or more sources and served up as a finished metaphysics. Yet there is more in the work than that. In intention, it is a philologically based attempt to recover ancient wisdom, and as such points forward to the program of the *New Science*. In fact, it is a mere adjunct to the *De studiorum ratione*, giving greater, more polemic statement to certain of its central themes, and as such points back to the Inaugural Orations. Vico thought of it, it seems plain, as an answer to the *Meditations* of Descartes, just as he conceived his *De studiorum ratione* as a classical and humanist response to the *Discourse on Method*. Through a new philosophy built on language and etymology and exuding the spirit of oratory and civility he would slay the dragon of the north, vindicate the ancients in their assumptions, and cause all of Europe to stand up and take notice. This affective level of the book is laid bare in Vico's response to some published criticism; it is the arrogance of the Cartesians and their utter disregard for the work of erudition that disturbs him. Society functioned well, indeed it flourished, when truth was left to the mathematicians and the philosophers were content to make men alert, sharp-witted, and reflective. The Stoics confounded this arrangement and now the Cartesians have done the same, seeking only knowledge that is "demonstrated." The inevitable result is that verisimilitude parades as truth and the name "demonstration" is claimed for merely probable and even patently false reasoning, just as even the vilest of men have come to be called "sir."[34]

[33] "Questo libro forma una strana anomalia nella storia del pensiero di Vico; esso è contrario a tutta la sua vita scientifica, alle sue tendenze, ai principi e al metodo che quasi inconsciamente applicò poi nelle sue ricerche storiche" (*G. B. Vico: Studi critici e comparativi* [Turin: Civelli, 1867], p. 38).

[34] Cf. Second *Risposta*, *Opere* 1.273–274.

What would a philosophy of traditional purpose be? It would be the familiar *philosophia triplex* of old, "handed down by its teachers in a manner fitted to foster eloquence," not a philosophical theory "taught by such a method as to dry up every fount of convincing expression, of copious, penetrating, embellished, lucid, developed, psychologically effective, and impassionate utterance."[35] Attributed to Xenocrates, a pupil of Plato, the tripartition of philosophy into "rational," "natural," and "moral" branches was a cherished idea of the Stoics, appearing prominently in the works of Cicero (e.g. *De or.* 1.15.68) and especially Seneca (*Ep.* 89), and passed to the Christian Middle Ages through Augustine (*De civ. D.* 8.4) and his later confrere, Isidore of Seville (*Etym.* 2.24.3). The distinction is assumed as obvious throughout Vico's works and achieves a particular importance in 1730 when it provides the scaffolding for his mature presentation of the Poetic Wisdom of all nations. Out of the trunk of a crude metaphysics—the birth of man's spirit in the first dim awareness of God and itself—grow up as one branch of knowledge a poetic logic, morals, economics, and politics, and as another, poetic physics, cosmography, and astronomy.[36] So dynamic a notion of "first philosophy" and so complete a fusion of knowledge and language were well beyond Vico in 1710 when he sought to recover the wisdom of the early Italians, yet even then he was convinced that such wisdom, once recovered, would fall naturally into "rational," "natural," and "moral" branches, and would show forth that combination of reflection and eloquence which any flourishing society must have. Thus the plan of this early work, like the tree of knowledge in his final *New Science*, was in three parts. First would come metaphysics (the doctrine of God and soul), with logic as an appendix; then physics, with mathematics adjoined to it; and finally the su-

---

[35] "Et quando olim triplex philosophia ab iisdem tradebatur ad eloquentiam accommodate, unde a Lyceo Demosthenes, ab Academia Cicero luculentissimarum maximi oratores linguarum prodiere; hodie ea ratione docetur, ut in ea fontes omnis verisimilis, copiosae, acutae, ornatae, explicatae, amplae, moratae inflammataeque orationis sint exiccati" (*De studiorum ratione, Opere* 1.93).

[36] *Scienza nuova seconda, Opere* 4, §367.

preme, all-encompassing treatise on ethics. Vico prepared and published the metaphysics but never came to add the logic nor to write more than the draft, now lost, of a piece on the "equilibrium" of animate bodies, a subject doubtless inspired by the work of the Investiganti and intended as part of the physics. For this we may be grateful, for there is every reason to believe that he understood even less about these matters than he did about first philosophy. His métier was "ethics" in the broadest sense—the world of social arrangements—made known to us in philology, rhetoric, and jurisprudence, and this part of his enterprise was to consume, with unexpected result, his remaining thirty-four years.

The traditional philosophy Vico proposed to establish was not merely to lead to a reflective eloquence; it itself would be extracted from early linguistic forms. This is the further and yet more telling mark of Vico's *Ancient Wisdom of the Italians*. The roots of many Latin words and phrases are so learned, Vico argued, that they could not have derived from the vulgar usages of the masses, but only from the esoteric doctrine of philosophers, to wit, those of Ionia and Etruria. Plato in his *Cratylus* and Varro in his *Origines* had tried to penetrate the Greek and the Latin languages, respectively, so as to uncover their latent philosophical wisdom; he, too, would follow in course, careful, however, not to impose his own philosophical theories on the earlier age as they so obviously had.[37] Though plainly aware of the anachronistic impulse he would later identify as the "conceit of scholars," Vico nonetheless still lay victim to its root bias. The wisdom of the ancients that he would extract from their language was indeed to be their own, but it was assumed to be esoteric and refined, the kind he himself could recognize as philosophy.

To what purpose, then, did he ply etymology? At least from the time of Valla's *Elegantiae*, etymology as a means of historical scholarship had been an established part of humanist philology. Vico himself alludes to the works of Julius Caesar

---

[37] *De Italorum sapientia, Opere* 1.126; Second *Risposta, Opere* 1.244.

Scaliger and Francisco Sánchez, and throughout his writings makes liberal use of the *Etymologicon* of Gerard Jan Voss, a convenient collection of all known Latin etymologies from the classical authors down to those of Voss's own day.[38] As his notion of human origins changed, Vico's use of etymologies changed with it, yet not even those critics most fascinated by his word derivations would argue that an etymology for him was ever an end in itself, a philological *finis*, as it so plainly was for Valla and Voss and the tradition they represented. Etymologies in Vico function always as parts of a great puzzle, as means by which disparate items are bound together or things unknown produced from what is familiar or near at hand. In this sense Vico was an "old" etymologist in the manner of the ancient orators and jurists, seeking arguments in the origins of words. The way into wisdom, they had held, is not through an empty mind but through words and texts, and lacking a definitive authority to tell us their meaning, etymology and definition are the appropriate tools of interpretation. The *Digest* itself had concluded with a title on the meaning of words (50.16: *De verborum significatione*), and out of it grew over time a sturdy tradition of legal hermeneutics concerned less with establishing an historical fact than with reaching a term's "final" or philosophical meaning.[39] This is the tradition in which Vico stands, and nowhere more squarely than in the *De Italorum sapientia*. The ancients held a constructivist theory of knowledge, for in their usage *verum* and *factum* are identical in meaning. They also used *genus* and *formae* interchangeably, which puts the lie to the Scholastic interpretation of *genus* as "universals." What did they

---

[38] *De Italorum sapientia, Opere* 1.126. On the use of Vossius, see the fascinating article of Andrea Battistini, "Vico e l'etimologia mitopoietica," *Lingua e Stile* 9 (1974): 31–66, which offers a challenging reappraisal of Vico's etymological method as an extension of the classical rhetorical tradition. Battistini makes the surprising discovery that Voss relates *verus* to the Hebrew *davar*, which in turn is made to mean both *verbum* and *factum*, and suggests this as the likely source of Vico's famous equation of *verum* and *factum* (ibid., p. 53).

[39] On this tradition, see Kelley, "Vera philosophia," pp. 271–273.

mean by *effectus*? The "result of a production," surely, for *causa* and *negotium* were synonyms to them. Their theory of extension, moreover, is that of Zeno's "metaphysical points," borne out by their equating *punctum* with *momentum*, both indicating indivisibility. And so on it goes.

For being such a ramshackle work, the *De Italorum sapientia* evoked a quite gentle review. A critic in Venice found it bold in conception but finally unrealized—rather a "sketch of a metaphysics" than a developed treatise; so many of its points were merely pronounced or adumbrated, and above all the central thesis of the book remained unproven—that the etymologies of certain Latin words revealed a wisdom identical to that of the metaphysics set forth. Vico responded in character, with wounded pride, and the critic rejoined. An author of new and unheard of theories is required, the critic wrote, to treat his subject at length, not in the brief and obscure manner in which you have. We need to see proved, for example, that *verum* and *factum* are identical in meaning, that the Latins meant *forma* by *genus* and *negotium* by *causa*, and that "metaphysical points" are even mentioned, much less expounded, by the ancient authors. The problem lies in the etymological method itself, which only gives rise to endless wrangling. If you truly want to know the wisdom of the early Italians, why not dig up the ruins of Etruria? After all, it was the Etruscans who gave Rome their first laws and sacred rites. But that approach, replied Vico, would be even less certain, for ancient myths were purposely enshrouded in mystery, the better to secure their venerableness, and as for laws, the number of those derived from the Etruscans are relatively few compared with those imported from Greece![40]

[40] "Polemiche relative al *De antiquissima Italorum sapientia*," *Opere* 1.197–276, esp. 237f., 242–248. Vico might have heeded earlier than he did the advice of his beloved Bacon: "I by no means approve of that curious inquiry, which nevertheless so great a man as Plato did not despise; namely concerning the imposition and original etymology of names; on the supposition that they were not arbitrarily fixed at first, but derived and deduced by reason and according to significance; a subject elegant indeed, and pliant as wax to be shaped and turned, and (as seeming to explore the recesses of antiquity) not

HOMER AND SOLON

It is not the least irony in intellectual history that Vico progressed to his new science by disproving the substance of his own objections; not only would ancient fables be deprived of their esoteric character, but the Law of the Twelve Tables would be given indigenous origins. Vico did not join in any archaeological dig, nor did he abandon his fascination with etymologies, but he widened his philological concerns to include, among other things, the epics of Homer and ancient Roman Law, and through a series of curious conjectures and transmutations he came to see them, not as esoteric philosophic products, but as gradually evolving, imaginative efforts by peoples, at first separated, to form themselves into nations. Fitted out with the principles of rhetoric he had long contemplated, these insights in turn were made the basis for a theory of the poetic origins of the race, and combined with further data from the history of law they became a full-fledged, if lopsided, theory of human culture.[41]

If Vico's "mythopoetic" etymologies were forever bound to the speculative or "philosophic" part of his enterprise, his lifelong search for the true Homer and his parallel inquiry into the origins of Roman Law fitted squarely in the tradition of humanist philology. That tradition had taken form with Italian attempts of the sixteenth century, inspired by Aristotle's distinction between history and poetry, to produce usable *artes historicae*, and led on among the French, in an arc

without a kind of reverence,—but yet sparingly true and bearing no fruit" (*De dignitate et augmentis scientiarum* 6.1).

[41] The balance of this chapter deals in the main with the five books of Vico's *Scienza nuova seconda*, the current section with book 3 ("The Discovery of the True Homer") and the corollary to book 4 ("That the Ancient Roman Law Was a Serious Poem"), the next with book 2 ("Poetic Wisdom"), the following with book 4 ("The Course the Nations Run"), and the last with book 5 ("The Recourse of Human Institutions Which the Nations Take When They Rise Again"), yet into this structure are brought elements from Vico's earlier discussions of these themes as well as the "Principles" set forth in book 1 of the *New Science*, which pertain, as one might expect, in part to the whole of the work and in part to its separate theses.

that stretched roughly from Budé to Pasquier and Popelinière, to the foundations of modern historical scholarship.[42] Driving the movement as a whole was the simple respect for texts, and finally for words themselves, as manifestations of mind and thus as marks of human institutions and their development. That was a spirit that had infused the movement even in its earlier rhetorical or prescientific stage, one that speaks to us in the very title of its founding book, Valla's *Elegantiae latinae linguae* (ca. 1444). Cleansed of the encrustations of time, stripped of the barbarisms of later authors, Valla held, the language of the ancients would reemerge in its full vigor and pristine beauty. "For this reason," writes Garin, "he spoke of the *sacrament* of classical Latin as if he were dealing with a sacred being or a divine seal which embodies the first thought of man in its purity. For this reason, too, he established the rule that the word ought to be met with respect; that one ought not to do violence to language; that one ought to listen humbly and piously to the message of the living spirit that has become word."[43] Beyond the systematizing interest that

[42] The French phase of the tradition is treated with varying emphases in the books by Brown, Franklin, Kelley, and Huppert previously cited, while Girolamo Cotroneo, *I trattatisti dell' "ars historica"* (Naples: Giannini, 1971), and Eric Cochrane, *Historians and Historiography in the Italian Renaissance* (Chicago: University of Chicago Press, 1981), show the achievements of the Italians. A good systematic survey of the issues is offered in the work of Rüdiger Landfester, *Historia Magistra Vitae: Untersuchungen zur humanistischen Geschichtstheorie des 14. bis 16. Jahrhunderts* (Geneva: Droz, 1972). On the roots of the *ars historica* in the *praelectiones* of fifteenth-century humanists, see Charles Trinkaus, "A Humanist's Image of Humanism: The Inaugural Orations of Bartolommeo della Fonte," *Studies in the Renaissance* 7 (1960): 90–147. Classical statements on the subject at large are those of Friedrich von Bezold, "Zur Entstehungsgeschichte der historischen Methodik," *Aus Mittelalter und Renaissance* (Munich: Oldenbourg, 1918); and Arnaldo Momigliano, "Ancient History and the Antiquarian," *Journal of the Warburg and Courtauld Institutes* 13 (1950): 285–315, reprinted in his *Contributo alla storia degli studi classici*, 2 vols. (Rome: Storia e letteratura, 1955). See also Beatrice Reynolds, "Shifting Currents of Historical Criticism," *Journal of the History of Ideas* 14 (1953): 471–492, reprinted in *Renaissance Essays*, ed. P. O. Kristeller and P. P. Wiener (New York: Harper Torchbooks, 1968), pp. 115–130.

[43] Eugenio Garin, *Italian Humanism: Philosophy and Civil Life in the Renaissance*, trans. Peter Munz (Oxford: Blackwell, 1966), p. 54.

many in the tradition—notably Bodin and later Vico himself—
had or came to have in the fields of language, religion, and
especially law, there was the basic need felt to be true to a
text by reading it critically, to find the original meaning and
tenor of its words, to observe their conjunctions, the ways
they fit or did not fit together, to see the parts of the text and
its structure, and to discover in this way the mind, sentiments,
and human relationships of the author and his people. Pious
in intention, such work could lead to an unholy, disorienting
result. The most notorious success of the early critics, if for
no other reason than for the discomfort it caused in Rome,
was Valla's own debunking of the Donation of Constantine,
a feat that left philologists, antiquarians, and other socially
irrelevant types flush with the power of their profession for
centuries.

In league with this triumph, for scientific if not political
reasons, was Vico's "discovery of the true Homer," a success
in which the alleged discoverer, Friedrich August Wolf, was
anticipated by some seventy-five years. From our own sober
vantage it is difficult to appreciate the impact that was had
on the understanding of classical and preclassical times by the
detection in the Homeric poems of a variety of social experiences with differing degrees of complexity and sophistication, and the consequent realization that not one but many
hands over several generations were involved in their creation.
We should likely need to think, as an analogy, of the changed
understanding of authority in the Judeo-Christian tradition
caused by the identification of multiple traditions of thought
in the books of Moses and by finding in the synoptic Gospels
an array of literary forms traceable to differing social and
cultural situations. Yet such was Vico's discovery in Homer,
and its effect on his science was immediate, dramatic, and
irreversible. As hieroglyphs were presumed cryptograms, and
myths the embodiment of the high mysteries of theological
poets, the elevated founders of mankind, so the *Iliad* and the
Odyssey of Homer were assumed to be the work of a refined
spirit, a poet like our great poets, indeed telling a story through

stirring images, but thereby as well speaking truths as deep as the most recondite philosophic wisdom. As Plato was the "Homer of philosophers," so Homer was the "Plato of poets"— so Plutarch had judged in his *De vita et poesi Homeri*, and so, too, the tradition had thought. But if that is the case, Vico came eventually to ask, if Homer was truly a man of sublime intelligence and exalted spirit (*ex peculiaris naturae ingenio quodam divino*), the first of his kind after the long night of human barbarism, why such a long interval before another of his sort arose? That is simply not plausible. Vico put this brazen question in the very first chapter of his *De constantia philologiae*, the one he entitled "A New Science Is Attempted," and by the end of his discourse he had given an equally bold counterthesis: Homer was prince of the poets not because of a philosophic intelligence but because he was a man of rare ingenuity (*felicissimo ingenio praeditum*), born just after the first, poetic, age of the race when language was still impoverished, when the senses still reigned and reason was as yet still feeble.[44] An argument for this position he set forth in detail in the fourth and longest of thirteen "ercursuses" published the following year (1722), then summarized his findings as part of his theory of "heroic poetry" in the first edition of his *New Science* (1725). By 1730 he had come to see yet deeper into the nature of Homer, and realizing its impact on the theoretical conclusions of his work, turned his argument for the "true Homer" into the third of the five books of his second *New Science*.[45]

Vico would have done well to set his argument at the front of his work, for rather than being the "necessary consequence"

[44] *De constantia jurisprudentis, Opere* 2.313f., 375–378.

[45] I am fond of recalling that this was the first text of Vico translated into English (likely from the French of Michelet), and by no less a personage than Henry Nelson Coleridge, "The Third Book of Vico's *Scienza nuova*: On the Discovery of the True Homer," in his *Introductions to the Study of the Greek Classic Poets: Designed Principally for the Use of Young Persons at School and College*, 2d ed. (London: Murray, 1834), pp. 73–98. For Vico's earlier discussions of Homer, see *Notae in duos libros, Opere* 2.675–700, and *Scienza nuova prima, Opere* 3, §§288–305 and passim.

of his science, as he represents it to be, his discovery of the true Homer was in large part responsible for the new principles of humanity that his work puts forth. Was Homer ever a philosopher? Vico asks at the start. Grant him that he had to conform to the vulgar feelings of his day, so that he had to allow Ulysses to poison his arrows and the corpse of Hector to be dragged three times around the walls of Troy. Yet if poetry is to tame the ferocity of the vulgar, it is not the part of a wise man to cause them to take pleasure in their fierce and cruel ways, and Homer glories in the butchery and battles, paints heroes and gods who are fickle and inconstant, and makes the captain of the Greeks a man, Agamemnon, who needed to be compelled to do his duty. "Such crude, coarse, wild, savage, volatile, unreasonable or unreasonably obstinate, frivolous, and foolish customs . . . can pertain only to men who are like children in the weakness of their minds, like women in the vigor of their imaginations, and like violent youths in the turbulence of their passions; whence we must deny to Homer any kind of esoteric wisdom."[46]

Who was this Homer, then; where did he come from and when did he live? His poems breathe such separate spirits and are written in different styles; already Longinus had noticed that (*Subl.* 9.11ff.), and so thought the *Iliad* a work of his youth, the *Odyssey* a product of old age. But do the texts tell us more? The Homer of the *Odyssey*, Vico argues, was surely from the west of Greece and a little toward the south, quite a distance from the Troy of the *Iliad*, which is situated in Asia near the shore of the Hellespont. The shield of Achilles, moreover, is indeed engraved, but painting had not yet been invented in his time, whereas the palace of Alcinous was magnificent and his banquets sumptuous, perfumes were in use

---

[46] "Tali costumi rozzi, villani, feroci, fieri, mobili, irragionevoli o irragionevolmente ostinati, leggieri e sciocchi . . . non posson essere che d'uomini per debolezza di menti quasi fanciulli, per robustezza di fantasia come di femmine, per bollore di passioni come di violentissimi giovani; onde hassene a niegar ad Omero ogni sapienza riposta" (*Scienza nuova seconda, Opere* 4, §§780–787, at 787).

and linens were finer than the outer skin of an onion, all signs of the effeminacy of a later day. So many refined customs cannot be reconciled with the many wild and savage habits of the *Iliad*'s heroes; whence "we must suppose that the two poems were composed and compiled by various hands through successive ages."[47] Turn the matter around, Vico asks, and make Homer a man of the people, "lost in the crowd" of early Greeks; suppose this people to be crude, common, and unrefined, incapable of thinking philosophically or abstractly about themselves and their society, about what they valued, experienced, and knew to be true; suppose them then to be ruled by their senses and imagination, forced by a necessity of their nature to speak in images; suppose further that they sang of themselves and their deeds in the images to which they were compelled; that these songs were repeated by the bards, shaped, added to, embellished, combined one with the next; and that in time the Pisistratids, tyrants of Athens, divided and arranged the poems into two groups, each united by one of the great figures of their highest ideals, Achilles and Ulysses, and ordered the poems sung from that time onward by the rhapsodes at the Panathenaic festivals—suppose all these things, each supported by evidence philosophical and philological alike, and you will be forced to conclude that Homer was not a philosopher, that he was not even a man, or two men. "Homer was an idea or a heroic character of Grecian men insofar as they told their histories in song."[48]

By a similar but more trodden route Vico came to a new understanding of the Law of the Twelve Tables, the object of his most sustained research in the history of Roman Law.[49]

[47] "Sembrano tai poemi essere stati per più età e da più mani lavorati e condotti" (*Scienza nuova seconda, Opere* 4, §§788–805, at 804).

[48] "Omero sia egli stato un'idea ovvero un carattere eroico d'uomini greci, in quanto essi narravano, cantando, le loro storie" (*Scienza nuova seconda, Opere* 4, §873; cf. generally §§806–904). See also the interesting remarks of Bruce A. Haddock, "Vico's Discovery of the True Homer: A Case Study in Historical Reconstruction," *Journal of the History of Ideas* 40 (1979): 583–602.

[49] On this subject, see the lovely essay of Max H. Fisch, "Vico on Roman

Though Varro and Cicero had already cast doubt upon it, the legend of the Twelve Tables had come down to Vico and his age with the authority of Livy and Dionysius of Halicarnassus, was attested to by Pomponius in the *Digest*, and supported by a (pseudo)epigraphic letter of Heraclitus. The tables had arisen, the legend ran, as a patrician attempt to still the unrest of the plebs by giving them the written code of law they had long demanded. The plebs had wanted specially elected officials to prepare a draft, but the patricians instead dispatched an embassy to Greece to take counsel with the wisest heads and to bring back the codes of Solon, ancient sage and lawgiver of Athens. Upon their return, a commission of ten, the so-called Decemvirs, all patrician, were elected to draw up the new law, a task they completed with the help of Hermodorus, an exiled Ephesian living in Rome who helped them interpret the Greek codes. Ratified that year, 451 B.C., by the assembly of the centuries, the code was inscribed on ten bronze tablets and put up in the marketplace. A new decemvirate elected the following year added two tables more, and while a revolution was needed to deprive this second Group of Ten of the power to which they continued to cling illegally, the Law of the Twelve Tables survived as Rome's first written law, literally a monument to reason and sagacity erected in the public square.

So lofty a notion of the rise of Roman civility was rejected with difficulty, and Vico did so only gradually. The first hint

Law," in *Essays in Political Theory: Presented to George H. Sabine*, ed. Milton R. Konwitz and Arthur E. Murphy (Ithaca, N.Y.: Cornell University Press, 1948), pp. 62–88, to which the paragraphs that follow are in part indebted. See also the work of Benvenuto Donati, *Nuovi studi sulla filosofia civile di G. B. Vico* (Florence: Le Monnier, 1936); Arnaldo Momigliano, "Vico's *Scienza nuova*: Roman 'bestioni' and Roman 'eroi,' " *History and Theory* 5 (1966): 3–23, esp. 13–23; Dino Pasini, *Diritto, società e stato in Vico* (Naples: Jovene, 1970); and the recent essays of Donald R. Kelley, "Vico's Road: From Philology to Jurisprudence—and Back," in *Giambattista Vico's Science of Humanity*, ed. Tagliacozzo and Verene, pp. 15–29; "In Vico Veritas: The True Philosophy and the New Science," *Social Research* 43 (1976): 601–611; and "Vico and Gaianism: Perspective on a Paradigm," in *Vico: Past and Present*, ed. Giorgio Tagliacozzo, 2 vols. in 1 (Atlantic Highlands, N.J.: Humanities Press, 1981), 1.66–72.

he had of the tables' barbaric nature was apparently their "horrid and coarse" language, duly noted in his rhetoric of 1711.[50] Yet it was not until his *De constantia jurisprudentis* a decade later, the same work in which he first expressed doubts about Homer, that he abandoned the centerpiece of the legend—the dramatic visit to Athens. The Decemvirs were still considered real, however, and they had still enlisted Hermodorus, the son of a higher culture, to advise them on what should be set down in writing and to help them actually draft it.[51] By the time of his first *New Science* (1725), however, Vico had only scorn for this view, a sentiment that he later wrote up in an unpublished paper intended as an appendix to the 1731 version of that work. How much Athenian good taste, he wrote, does one encounter in the provision that "a sick debtor accused of his crime should be hauled before the praetor on an ass or in a wheelbarrow"? How much Greek delicacy in the legal procedure of *Tigni juncti* ("Joined timbers"), as though the contracting parties were turning themselves into arbors or trellises?[52] The Law of the Twelve Tables was brought into Rome at a time when Athens enjoyed its highest culture, boasting a Plato, an Alcibiades, a Xenophon. And what do we find? A law so coarse and uncouth that a debtor who refused to see the praetor voluntarily was dragged there by his creditor "with a twisted neck"; one so monstrous, cruel, and fierce that anyone who purposely set fire to another's fields was himself burned alive, and anyone harvesting another's crops or letting his cattle graze on a neighbor's lands at night was hanged. "These are laws all fit to come from the caves of the cyclopes, wandering beneath the mountains of wild and primitive Sicily in its most ancient days, not from

[50] *Institutiones oratoriae*, p. 76; *Opere* 8.172.

[51] *Opere* 2.564–580.

[52] "Non diciamo quanto sapesse del buon gusto ateniese quel capo: che ' 'l reo infermo, citato, egli sull'asinello o dentro la carriuola comparisse innanzi al pretore'! quanto esprimeva della dilicatezza dell'arti greche l'azione 'Tigni juncti,' come se allora gli uomini cominciassero a farsi le pergole e le capanne!" (First *Ragionamento, Opere* 4, §1430).

the city known to be the most refined in the world at that time."[53]

Look closely into the tables, Vico argues, and you will find there the remains of an agrarian law, Rome's second to be precise, not that of Servius Tullius who granted the workers mere "bonitary" or equitable ownership of their fields, but that which followed the struggles for justice of the plebs' own tribunes and ended with the concession of "quiritary" or true legal ownership of land. A powerful, basic, heroic struggle, that was, one that led on to the demand to be able to marry "under the auspices," and so to marry truly, and thus to have families, not mere progeny, and thus make wills and pass one's property on, and thereby be full and proper citizens of Rome.[54] The law that has come down to us in "Twelve Tables" is the record, assembled over time, of this grand, heroic struggle for civil liberty, originally a concession of the quiritary ownership of land, but eventually the guarantee of sundry other rights and privileges wrested by the plebs from the noble class after many contests and fights.[55] *Such* was the sagacity of the ancient Romans who drafted their "Twelve Tables," imputing their work to the authors of the critical agrarian law, the Decemvirs of old, even as the Athenians had had their Solon, who was no esoteric philosopher but a "sage of vulgar wisdom, party leader of the plebs in the first times of the aristocratic commonwealth at Athens," and perhaps no more than a poetic character for the Athenian plebeians themselves in their struggle for civil standing and rights.[56] Thus the law of ancient Rome was a "serious poem," even as its jurisprudence was "a severe poetry," like in form to the epics of Homer,

---

[53] "Le quali tutte sono leggi degne di venire dalle grotte de' polifemi, sparse per sotto i monti della, ne' suoi primi antichissimi tempi, fiera e selvaggia Sicilia, non dalla città la quale, in questi tempi, in buon gusto era la più riputata del mondo" (First *Ragionamento, Opere* 4, §1432).

[54] *Scienza nuova seconda, Opere* 4, §§73, 86, 88, 96, 102, 104–111, and generally 981–1003.

[55] *Scienza nuova seconda, Opere* 4, §§420–422; cf. *Scienza nuova prima, Opere* 3, §§87, 161–173.

[56] *Scienza nuova seconda, Opere* 4, §§414–422.

with which it has also shared a common abuse, disguised at first by the conceit of nations, then hidden by the conceit of scholars.

The same fate has befallen the poems of Homer as the Law of the Twelve Tables; for, just as the latter, having been held to be the laws given by Solon to the Athenians and subsequently taken over by the Romans, has up to now concealed from us the history of the natural law of the heroic gentes of Latium, so the Homeric poems, having been regarded as works thrown off by a rare and consummate poet, have hitherto concealed from us the history of the natural law of the gentes of Greece.[57]

SAPIENZA POETICA

A mind forever set on seeing things whole, sworn by profession and by personal choice to reduce the whole of its learning to unity, to draw each and every item of knowledge into a system in which both its principles and consequences would be manifest, could not but have been powerfully moved by discoveries such as these. If no majestic Homer had risen up among the Greeks to tell their noble tales; if no sagacious Solon had ever stood at the gates of Rome to give it its first written codes; if instead, Homer was "lost in the crowd" of brave but cruel peoples, all taken up with their senses and images, and the tables of ancient Rome were literally the "rudiments" of a simple agrarian society, then how much less abstract and esoteric, how much more entangled in the body and its passions were the minds of the true children of the race, those "theological poets" whose austere myths and severe rites had established the whole of humanity? This insight,

[57] "Tanto che lo stesso fato è avvenuto de' poemi d'Omero, che avvenne della legge delle xii Tavole: perché, come queste, essendo state credute leggi date da Solone agli ateniesi, e quindi fussero venute a' romani, ci hanno tenuto finor nascosta la storia del diritto naturale delle genti eroiche del Lazio; così, perché tai poemi sono stati creduti lavori di getto d'un uomo particolare, sommo e raro poeta, ci hanno tenuta finor nascosta l'istoria del diritto naturale delle genti di Grecia" (*Scienza nuova seconda, Opere* 4, §904; cf. §§154–157, 1037).

Vico said, cost him the labor of "twenty years of continuous hard thought," but when he came to it, from all we can tell, he did so in a way he thought all new arts and new sciences are discovered—in a blaze of ingenuity. He recalled the logic of discourse he had been maintaining for years in his lectures and pedagogical orations; he recalled Cicero's view that metaphors and tropes are necessary to life (*De or.* 3.38.155) since, as Aristotle had held (*Soph. el.* 165a11–12), there are more things in the world than there are words;[58] he remembered the line from Aristotle's *Rhetoric* (1395b1–4) that simple minds like to hear stated as universal truth the opinions they hold about particular cases,[59] and the lines from the *Poetics* (1451b5–7) that poetic statements, unlike those of history, have the nature of universals;[60] he remembered as well that poetic maxims, the *sententiae* ingeniously grasped in a flash, were thought by the ancients to be, as their name implied, rather felt by the senses than seized by the mind (Quint. *Inst.* 8.5.1).[61] These disparate, seemingly unrelated things he recalled, and all these he combined, in typically transmuted form, with his philological research and—in one of the most singular instances of *ingenium* on record—drew his famous conclusion: Poetry is the native tongue of the race, the clarion call of humanity's birth.[62] Poetry is not a product of mind, but the logic of the mind's development.[63] Not philosophy or human wisdom, but *poetic* wisdom was the wisdom of the ancients. Here, in a single phrase adapted from the Stoics, he had the perfect syn-

---

[58] *Scienza nuova seconda, Opere* 4, §§34, 456, 830; cf. *Scienza nuova prima, Opere* 3, §262.

[59] *Scienza nuova seconda, Opere* 4, §§209, 816; cf. *Institutiones oratoriae*, pp. 90ff., *Opere* 8.182–183; Second *Risposta, Opere* 1.274.

[60] *Scienza nuova seconda, Opere* 4, §§205–206, 403, 424, 494–498, 809; cf. *Scienza nuova prima, Opere* 3, §§261–265.

[61] *Scienza nuova seconda, Opere* 4, §§816, 819, 821, 825; cf. *De constantia jurisprudentis, Opere* 2. 363–365.

[62] *Scienza nuova seconda, Opere* 4, §§34, 199; cf. *De constantia jurisprudentis, Opere* 2.363–385; *Scienza nuova prima, Opere* 3, §§253–262, esp. 261, where the discovery, "dopo venticinque anni ormai che corrono di una continova ed aspra meditazione," is announced.

[63] *Scienza nuova seconda, Opere* 4, §§400–411.

thesis of wisdom and eloquence, of *res* and *verba*, for which he had striven his whole life.[64]

In its primary sense, of course, *poetic wisdom* means simply "wisdom that is made"; Vico is quite explicit in saying that the first men were "poets" in the Greek sense of "creators."[65] Never one to use central concepts univocally, however, Vico also considers the first men poets because "they spoke in poetic characters"—the discovery of this fact being the "master key" of the *New Science*.[66] The etymological meaning of "poetic wisdom" is thus conjoined with the traditional notion of the poet as creator of culture; the "self-making" that is poetic wisdom is in the first instance—as vulgar "metaphysics" and its corresponding "logic"—a matter of language.

Language, however, has now a fuller, more profound meaning than it had in the ancient topos. The earliest language, Vico argues, was fully nonverbal—the "mute" language of myth and fable and the (to him) "natural" signs of hieroglyphs and ideograms. The first human act was literally mute, wholly sensory and corporeal, scarcely imaginable. The descendants of Ham, Japheth, and Shem, scattered by the Flood throughout the earth, the offspring of promiscuous intercourse, were nursed by their mothers, then abandoned, left to wallow in

---

[64] *Scienza nuova seconda, Opere* 4, §§361–363, 375, 779; cf. *Scienza nuova prima, Opere* 3, §263. Vico first speaks of the "wisdom of poets" as that which establishes humanity in the *De constantia jurisprudentis, Opere* 2.383, crediting Horace with the idea: "Prima omnium fuerit sapientia poetarum, in fundandis rebuspublicis posita, ut tradit in *Arte* Horatius." In the *Scienza nuova prima, Opere* 3, §294, he repeats the idea, now calling the first sages "theological poets," the term used by Varro (but traceable to Panaetius and arguably to Aristotle) to describe the makers of myth, as distinguished from the "civil theologians," who establish the gods of the people, and the "natural theologians," who decide the true nature of the gods (cf. August. *De civ. D.* 6.5 and passim). Having discovered poetry to be vulgar, natural, and necessary, not refined or rare, Vico conflates poetic and civil theology into "poetic wisdom" or the "natural theology of the gentes" and sets it off sharply from "esoteric wisdom" or the "natural theology of the philosophers" (cf. *Scienza nuova seconda, Opere* 4, §§365–366).

[65] *Scienza nuova seconda, Opere* 4, §376.

[66] *Scienza nuova seconda, Opere* 4, §31.

their own filth, thus absorbing into their bodies the nitrous
salts by which they grew to the stature of giants—such are
the ancients on whose shoulders we, literally the dwarfs of
the race, stand.[67] These "stupid, insensate, and horrible beasts,"
all language and delicacy lost, having no mind at all but only
bodies and a "corporeal imagination," roamed the great forests of the world, which themselves were restless with dehydration, sending gradually to the sky the "dry exhalations"
that might some day ignite in the air. And when at last the
sky fearfully rolled with thunder and flashed with lightning,

thereupon a few giants, who must have been the most robust, and
who were dispersed through the forests on the mountain heights
where the strongest beasts have their dens, were frightened and as-
tonished by the great effect whose cause they did not know, and
raised their eyes and became aware of the sky. And because in such
a case the nature of the human mind leads it to attribute its own
nature to the effect, and because in that state their nature was that
of men all robust bodily strength, who expressed their very violent
passions by shouting and grumbling, they pictured the sky to themselves as a great animated body, which in that aspect they called
Jove, the first god of the so-called greater gentes, who meant to tell
them something by the hiss of his bolts and the clap of his thunder.
And thus they began to exercise that natural curiosity which is the
daughter of ignorance and the mother of knowledge, and which,
opening the mind of man, gives birth to wonder.[68]

---

[67] *Scienza nuova seconda, Opere* 4, §§369–375. That children who play
in dirt will grow up strong and healthy, if not to the stature of giants, was
a tenet of Neapolitan folklore popular in Vico's day (cf. Fausto Nicolini,
Commento storico alla seconda "Scienza nuova," 2 vols. [Rome: Storia e
letteratura, 1949], 1.127).

[68] "Quivi pochi giganti, che dovetter esser gli più robusti, ch'erano dispersi
per gli boschi posti sull'alture de' monti, siccome le fiere più robuste ivi hanno
i loro covili, eglino, spaventati ed attoniti dal grand'effetto di che non sape-
vano la cagione, alzarono gli occhi ed avvertirono il cielo. E perché in tal
caso la natura della mente umana porta ch'ella attribuisca all'effetto la sua
natura, . . . e la natura loro era, in tale stato, d'uomini tutti robuste forze di
corpo, che, urlando, brontolando, spiegavano le lore violentissime passioni;
si finsero il cielo esser un gran corpo animato, che per tal aspetto chiamarono
Giove, il primo dio delle genti dette 'maggiori,' che col fischio de' fulmini e

No mysterious imagination, reminiscent or otherwise, permitted Vico a glimpse of this first moment. No process of deduction or induction, no sober logic or experiment at all gave him access to it. If rhetoric is reasoning *inter rudes*, he reflected, then the logic of rhetoric applies as much to the first as to the most recent moment of our social existence. One must only make allowance, as Hobbes and Grotius and other "conceited" commentators did not, for the cruelty of time. *Veritas filia temporis*, he remembered; thus the truth of our ancestors was a crude, dim, even violent truth, grasped more with the body than with the mind. Hearing thunder sound in the heavens, they raised up their eyes, became aware of the sky, and "saw" it as a great animated body, Jove. In this action, no longer mere reaction but act of "poetic" imagination, of the transfer of meaning (*metapherein*) through the "ingenious" discovery of relationships heretofore unnoticed, the *grossi bestioni* quit their spiritual isolation, established communication and community, and became men. Through their "collective sense" (*sensus communis*) of Jove, life in society began. The rhetorical act, the art of speaking effectively *inter rudes*—of discerning new relationships, fashioning appropriate language, appealing never to abstract truths but always to the *sensus communis*, to "what is held generally or by most" (Arist. *An. Pr.* 24b11, 70a3; *Top.* 100a30; *Rh.* 1357a35), and so persuading men to civil action—this act of the rhetor is here generalized, made the common, universal, and necessary act of the ancestors of the race. And so, too, it remained, Vico argues, not a studied device, but a "necessity of nature" owing to the youth of mind and the poverty of language throughout the entire prephilosophical age of humanity.[69]

---

col fragore de' tuoni volesse loro dir qualche cosa; e sì incominciarono a celebrare la naturale curiosità, ch'è figliuola dell'ignoranza e madre della scienza, la qual partorisce, nell'aprire che fa della mente dell'uomo, la maraviglia" (*Scienza nuova seconda, Opere* 4, §377).

[69] *Scienza nuova seconda, Opere* 4, §§495–498, 830, 832–833. Cf. *De constantia jurisprudentis, Opere* 2.379; "Poesis necessitate naturae orta, quam hactenus omnes ex hominum consilio et arte natam putarunt." Thus did Vico

The first human act, then, was a fully mute poem, grasped by the body and expressed with the body. In this it was more childlike than the actions of children themselves. "Ingenuity," wrote Vico in 1710, "is the faculty by which we grasp similarities and make them. In children, whose nature is less corrupted by ingrained ideas and prejudices, we notice that this is the first faculty to develop, for they both see similarities, calling all male individuals 'father' and all women 'mother,' and make them, 'building little houses, harnessing mice to a tiny chariot, playing at odd and even, riding on a long reed' [Hor. *Sat.* 1.47–48]."[70] Vico retrieves and deepens this thought a decade later when he formulates "new principles" of the origin of poetry and draws the comparison he would repeatedly invoke thereafter. If humanity is more easily achieved by the ingenious; if the nature of ingenuity is to discover while that of reason is to perfect; if the senses are sharper and fantasy more vivid as the power of reason is weaker (brutes and women being superior to men in this respect); and if finally, as the adage has it, "minds [*ingenia*] are sharpened by necessity," then we can say that the first ingenious men, fully wanting (*rudes*) in learning and language, were nothing more than ingenious children.[71] Confronted with a new experience or object, children are compelled to invent, relating the novelty to what is familiar; their lack of language (*inopia verborum*)

---

decide, to his satisfaction, the ancient debate as to whether poetry is a matter of "nature" or "art" (i.e. human design). On this controversy, see Heinrich Lausberg, *Handbuch der literarischen Rhetorik*, 2 vols. (Munich: Hueber, 1960), §§37–41.

[70] "Ea enim ingenium est, quo homo est capax contemplandi ac faciendi similia. Nos quidem in pueris, in quibus natura integrior est et minus persuasionibus seu praejudiciis corrupta, primam facultatem se exerere videmus, ut similia videant; unde omnes viros 'patres,' foeminas omnes 'matres' appellant, et similia faciant, 'Aedificare casas, plostello adjungere mures / ludere par impar, equitare in harundine longa' " (*De Italorum sapientia, Opere* 1.183).

[71] *De constantia jurisprudentis, Opere* 2.363–365. A further principle tying ingenuity to warm and temperate climates—Vico's nod to the geopolitics of Bodin (*Methodus*, chap. 5)—is preserved in the *New Science*, but only as a marginal idea at the back of the book (cf. *Scienza nuova seconda, Opere* 4, §§1088–1091).

leads them naturally to metaphor.[72] So, too, with the ancestors, children of the race. When thunder rolled in the heavens,
a novelty whose cause was entirely beyond them, the dumbstruck brutes reached readily for the only image they had by
which to seize the experience, the mere sense of themselves
as great lumbering bodies that shouted in moments of passion;
and dumbstruck they stood, in awe of Jove's body above them,
their own silent posture a grand poetic sentence, man's first.[73]

Putting the rise of religion in the midst of lightning and
thunder was an unremarkable deed, having ample precedent
in Vico's time and continuing in our own in the theories of
Vico's compatriot, Raffaele Pettazzone.[74] The comparison
sometimes made with Boulanger, whose *L'antiquité dévoilée
par ses usages* of 1766 would also make much of the trauma
of the Great Deluge, is wrongly placed, however, for the *New
Science* breathes an entirely different spirit. "While for Vico,"
Frank Manuel notes well, "the creation of a religious idea

[72] *De constantia jurisprudentis*, *Opere* 2.365: "Hinc, si percurras tropos
omnes, et poeticos maxime, ab altera ex his duabus caussis natos esse com-
perias, nempe in verborum inopia vel a rerum similitudine: ut 'sitire agros,'
'laborare fructus,' quae certe, ut aliae innumerae tum graecis tum latinis, sunt
metaphorae rusticorum, vel a rebus quae magis sensus afficiunt."

[73] Vico's adaptation of the rhetorical doctrine of the *sententia* may be
followed through the *De constantia jurisprudentis*, *Opere* 2.370–374, and
the *Scienza nuova prima*, *Opere* 3, §§253–266, 309–316. *Sententia*, Vico
notes, is related to *sentire* and the first men, scarcely more than mere bodies,
thought and judged through their senses. Significantly, by 1738, and probably
much earlier, Vico had excised the part on the *sententiae* from his course
manual, having treated the matter more thoroughly in his published works
(see Nicolini's note, *Opere* 8.203).

[74] See Raffaele Pettazzone, *Dio: Formazione e sviluppo del monoteismo
nella storia delle religioni*, vol. 1, *L'Essere celeste nelle credenze dei popoli
primitivi* (Rome: Athenaeum, 1922), pp. xix–xx, 355–356, where Vico is
credited for having anticipated him in his principal idea. See also his *L'on-
niscienza di Dio* (Turin: Einaudi, 1955), pp. 39–40. A comprehensive study
of the concept of a sky god in ancient Mediterranean cultures is that of Arthur
Bernard Cook, *Zeus: A Study in Ancient Religion*, 3 vols. in 5 (Cambridge:
At the University Press, 1914–1940), the second and third volumes of which
are devoted to *Zeus God of the Dark Sky*, a deity that manifests itself amid
lightning and thunder. For examples of the theory in Vico's day, see Frank
E. Manuel, *The Eighteenth Century Confronts the Gods* (Cambridge, Mass.:
Harvard University Press, 1959), esp. chap. 4.

became the guiding force in man's self-humanization, for Boulanger the birth of false terrors of the next world and the
wasteful devotion of the whole of life to a contemplation of
doom was the great pall which had descended upon mankind."[75] Rescue and deliverance dominate the birth scene in
Vico, for in the image of the thundering heaven, man and
nature alike are caught up into a single rhetorical act, whose
outcome is called "sublime."[76] We must tread lightly here,
however, for there can be no thought of a mind in nature;
while positing animism as a universal historical necessity—
the *impossibile credibile* that civilized the feral wanderers—
Vico stays a long polemical distance from the Renaissance
notion of *anima mundi* and its lingering presence among his
contemporaries.[77] Yet in his description of mankind's birth
there is the unmistakable hand of Tesauro and his colleagues
for whom nature is a book, written in poetic conceits.

What appealed to Vico especially in the image of lightning
was the instantaneousness of it all, for it lent support to his
notion of ingenuity. The ingenious Demosthenes, he had written many years before, was master of the *hyperbaton*, speaking
now on this, now on that matter, seemingly without relation,
forever stretching his argumentation like a bowstring pulled
taut, until at once he released the force of his reasoning and
it crashed like a bolt of lightning on his listeners.[78] So also
nature *in initio*, its forces having gathered over a hundred
years' time while the earth dried out after the Flood and the
brutes themselves could grow to the stature of giants with
powerful senses and vivid imaginations, brought the whole of

[75] *Eighteenth Century Confronts the Gods*, p. 221.

[76] *Scienza nuova seconda, Opere* 4, §§376, 384, 387; cf. *Scienza nuova prima, Opere* 3, §258.

[77] *Scienza nuova seconda, Opere* 4, §378. Gustavo Costa, "G. B. Vico e la 'natura simpatetica,' " *Giornale critico della filosofia italiana* 3 (1968): 401–418, examines Vico's polemic against the surviving occult mentality in his age and shows the extent to which he was the exponent of a burgeoning experimentalism.

[78] *De Italorum sapientia, Opere* 1.181; cf. *Vici vindiciae, Opere* 3.307; and his early school writing, "De chriis," in *Opere di Giambattista Vico*, ed. Fausto Nicolini (Milan and Naples: Ricciardi, 1953), pp. 958ff.

its argument together in an instant, spoke literally in a flash, and so made the *rudes* see the truth that bound them together. And they in response spoke ensemble, craning their necks upward as one, and in that dumb, mute action spoke humanity's first word, a soundless gesture of recognition.

Is the conceit then nature's or is it man's? In truth it is both. In a moment of stirring oratory, Vico held, when the beauty of a conceit overwhelms the spirit as its truth impresses the mind, both speaker and listener are caught up in a rush of ingenuity, each making connections that were not made before, their spirits fused by the freshness of the language, their minds and finally their wills made one. So here, too, analogously to be sure, the first dim seeing of Jove is an event in which body through language becomes conscious, the poetry of a thundering sky evoking in response the poetry of giants made men, struck dumb with awe. What occurs is an exchange in metaphor, the image of providence in a thundering heaven passing into the bodies of awe-struck men. The physical universe of *deus artifex*, itself a poem, everywhere written in conceits, becomes in the bodies of clustered men a poet, henceforth a maker of self; the passive ingenuity of the universe comes to life in the mind (however unrefined it yet is) and the spirit (however passionate and violent it may be) of man, and man, now standing erect, becomes the *artifex* of his own existence. "As God is artist of nature, so man is god of the arts." What is true of man's maturity is majestically true of his birth, for in that instant he is poem and poet alike, his awe-struck posture itself an image of reverence before a violent but provident Jove.

Providence, then, as the grand mute gesture of awe-struck beasts, is the *principium* or beginning of humanity, our first "metaphysical concept," entirely active and poetic, out of which would evolve over time the entire edifice of human wisdom, known to us now as the world of arts and sciences. Implied in this concept, moreover, are two further "principles" of first philosophy, equally old and equally poetic, arising spontaneously with the worship of Jove: taking one woman to wife and burying one's dead. Truth, Vico held, begins with certainty, which is to say—"specificity" or focus. In their bestial state the brutes roamed the world "aimlessly," living promiscuously "with an uncertain lust," not distinguishing "their own" from other creatures of the wild, and so leaving their dead unburied upon the ground.[79] Their lives in a word were "common" (*comune*), wildly unfocused (*incertissime*), and thus fully beyond truth (*fallacissime*). All this is reversed by the voice of Jove. As lightning marks the close of the earth's own desperate dehydration, so the vision of Jove in a thundering sky arrests the pointlessness of feral wandering, literally stops the giants in their tracks, brings them to their senses, and establishes authority. Authority comes about with the dawn of consciousness (*coscienza*) itself, the brutes now sensing themselves with reference to a provident deity. So begins the knowledge of certainty, the *certum*, and out of this initial certainty, Vico thinks, arise two others spontaneously: knowing one's children by living monogamously, and knowing one's kind in burying the dead.[80]

[79] Cf. the "Sinopsi del *Diritto universale*," *Opere* 2.10, and the *Scienza nuova seconda, Opere* 4, §321: "In good Latin *certum* means particularized, or, as the schools say, individuated; so that, in over-elegant Latin, *certum* and *commune*, the certain and the common, are opposed to each other" ("[Certo] in buon latino significa 'particolarizzato' o, come le scuole dicono, 'individuato'; nel qual senso *certum* e *commune*, con troppa latina eleganza, son oppositi tra loro").

[80] Cf. *Scienza nuova prima, Opere* 3, §§61–78, at 74: "Dalle quali cose il diritto naturale delle prime genti . . . nacque e si custodì da tutti e tre i principi da' quali noi sopra proponemmo essere uscita tutta l'umanità. De' quali il primo fu la giusta oppinione universale che vi sia provvedenza. Il secondo, che gli uomini con *certe* donne, con cui abbiano comuni religioni, leggi e lingue, contraggano giuste nozze per fare *certi* figliuoli, che possano essi educare nelle religioni, istruire nelle leggi natie, per le quali questi debbano dimostrare i loro *certi* padri coi nomi, coi patronimici, e così abbiano a perpetuare le nazioni. . . . Il terzo, che si seppellissero i morti in *propie* terre a ciò destinate, onde le sepolture gli *accertassero*, con le genealogie o serie degli antenati, il sovrano dominio delle loro terre, che essi riconoscessero dagli auspici de' loro dei, coi quali i loro primi ceppi l'avevano da prima occupate" (my emphasis; cf. *Scienza nuova seconda, Opere* 4, §§333, 502–505, 529–531).

I am taking a liberty in this presentation that the reader must understand. In the strictest sense, the idea of a provident Jove is the sole concept of Vico's

Like that of providence, the ideas of "fidelity" and "humanity" (from *humare*, to bury, Vico argues) were at first pure actions, mute gestures, principles of an entirely "poetic" metaphysics—pairing off and remaining so; burying the dead as one's own. Only later would worship, marriage, and burial be given the panoply of symbols, songs, and rites that the histories of nations reveal to us, and only much later still would their truth be grasped abstractly in the "natural theology of the philosophers." Truly "first" philosophy, however, was the "natural theology of the gentes," its tenets grasped in the way men formed their original lives together, fearing a single, provident god, keeping one woman as wife and thus knowing one's children, and burying and honoring one's dead. These particular human customs, these *certa* of man's existence, arose spontaneously from the original act of consciousness, the recognition of Jove in a thundering sky, and banished forever an aimless, promiscuous uncaring life in the wild. As our original, founding certainties, they are the core of our first philosophy, the tenets of "poetic metaphysics." As the defeat of unspecificity and chaos, they are the start of that wisdom which in time would lead from mere consciousness to science (*scienza*), knowledge of the true. They are thus the beginning of our language, the rise of our mind, the onset of our life in common. In a word, they are the "principles" of our humanity.

How did Vico hit upon these principles? He did not hit upon them at all. They are available, he asserts, in a philosophically assured philology. First put aside that unfortunate

"poetic metaphysics," while that of marriage, implying a sense of restraint and responsibility, is the founding tenet of "poetic morals," and the practice of burial, with grave sites establishing dominion over land, the beginning of "poetic economics." Yet these ideas are also linked in his text as the irreducible principles of humanity, and thus of his science, and it is this emphasis, which dominates the earlier versions of his work, which I have chosen to adopt. In doing so I am obscuring a subtlety in his work that should not be lost: that all metaphysics, like all knowledge, derives from a single principle, not "Being is being" or any such abstract proposition, but the infinitely concrete and immediate idea, "There's a shouting Jove up there who is trying to tell us something."

notion of John Marsham, John Spencer, and Otto van Heurn, entirely unsustainable, that the earliest nations intermingled and so passed their languages, rites, and laws from one to the next. The Egyptians were an inland people, as were the Chaldeans, and the Chinese are found writing hieroglyphs thousands of years before they had commerce with other nations. And the Hebrews, of course, as Flavius Josephus and Lactantius attest, lived unknown to all the gentile nations. "The fact is that all the nations sprung from Ham and Japheth first developed their native languages inland, and [only] then, having descended to the sea, began to deal with the Phoenicians, who were famous for navigation and colonies along the shores of the Mediterranean and of the Ocean."[81] Yet "every nation had its Jove," Varro alone counting forty of them, each worshiped with a different name.[82] Out of piety or fear of its Jove came shame, and thus marriage, the foundation of all morality, while knowledge of one's own led to burial of the dead, whose graves established ownership of land and thus the beginning of economy.[83] In brief, all nations have some religion, all contract solemn marriages, all bury their dead. This fact has an importance that exceeds its mere statement. Did not Aristotle allow that in matters of civil reasoning arguments should be drawn from opinions generally accepted, those held by all, or by the majority, or by the most notable and illustrious thinkers (*Top.* 100a–b; *Rh.* 1357a30ff.); did not Cicero seek a course for the Republic "which has ever been chosen by the best of men" (*Rep.* 1.2.3); did not Gaius make universally valid the laws that were common to the many nations of Rome (*Dig.* 1.1, 9); and did not the great Grotius of our own enlightened times seek the beginning of an international

---

[81] "Tutte le nazioni provenute da Cam e Giafet si fondarono prima le lingue natie dentro terra, e poi, calate al mare, cominciarono a praticar co' fenici, che furono celebri ne' lidi del Mediterraneo e dell' Oceano per la navigazione e per le colonie" (*Scienza nuova seconda, Opere* 4, §63; cf. generally §§44, 45, 48, 50, 54, 55, 62).

[82] *Scienza nuova seconda, Opere* 4, §§62, 193, 380.

[83] *Scienza nuova seconda, Opere* 4, §§402–405, 529–531; cf. *Scienza nuova prima, Opere* 3, §§57–78.

law in the customs and practices of the various nations, on the principle that something affirmed as certain at different times and in different places must be attributed to a "universal cause" (*De jure belli ac pacis*, pr. 40)? Indeed, Vico concludes, it is axiomatic that "uniform ideas, born among peoples unknown to each other, must have a common ground of truth."[84] These similarities in customs are not mere accidents or coincidences; they are the ingenuity of humanity writ large, "judgments without reflection" shared by the entire human race, and as such form the certainty of human choice and the "common sense" of men.[85]

It all stands to reason as well: Children born of free sexual unions may be abandoned by their parents, "exposed to be devoured by dogs," and if humanity does not rear them no one will teach them religion, language, or any other human custom. If human bodies remain unburied on the earth "as food for crows and dogs," fields, too, will remain uncultivated and cities left uninhabited, and "men will go about like swine eating the acorns amidst the putrefaction of their dead."[86] Civilization is of a piece, and so, too, its ruin, an unbroken chain, one action linked to the next; without the certainties of marriage and burial, all other uncertainties follow in train, untilled lands, vacated cities, unspoken words, broken laws, forgotten rites—until all humanity retreats again into the small, private ambience of solitudinous existence. Providence, marriage, burial—on these there is agreement "between the vulgar wisdom of all lawgivers and the esoteric wisdom of the phi-

---

[84] "Idee uniformi nate appo intieri popoli tra essoloro non conosciuti debbon avere un motivo commune di vero" (*Scienza nuova seconda, Opere* 4, §144; cf. §333).

[85] *Scienza nuova seconda, Opere* 4, §141. The link of "common sense" with Vico's notion of ingenuity is traced by Luigi Pareyson, "La dottrina vichiana dell'ingegno," *Atti della Accademia delle scienze di Torino* 83, no. 2 (1949): 82–115, esp. 101–115. For a discussion of the idea within the final *New Science* itself, see Leon Pompa, *Vico: A Study of the "New Science"* (Cambridge: At the University Press, 1975), pp. 21–41 and passim.

[86] "Gli uomini a guisa di porci anderebbono a mangiar le ghiande, colte dentro il marciume de' loro morti congionti" (*Scienza nuova seconda, Opere* 4, §§336–337, at 337).

losophers of greatest repute," such that they must be the very "bounds of human reason." "Let him who would transgress them beware lest he transgress all humanity."[87]

Once Vico began seeing connections, he continued to see them everywhere, fitting them relentlessly within that scheme of the growth of the human spirit, from ingenuity to reason, which he took to be as true of the "children" or founders of a nation as it was of his own eight children and the hundreds more he taught. Creatures of pure sense at the start, they passed through a period of startling ingenuity in which connections were drawn imaginatively between things unknown and things familiar to them, until gradually, through the development of reason, they learned to grasp them abstractly in true philosophical genera.[88] Not merely metaphysics, the mother of the disciplines, had a poetic phase, but all her many progeny as well, the sciences of nature and society alike. As metaphysics was created in the actions of men's earliest life in common—in worship, marriage, and burial—so, too, the other disciplines: morals by creating heroes, economics by founding families, politics by establishing cities, physics by fathoming the divine origins of things, cosmography by peopling the universe with gods, astronomy by carrying the planets from earth to heaven, chronology by setting a beginning to time, and geography by naming familiar places.[89]

What is immediately obvious in this canvassing of Poetic Wisdom is that all the disciplines in their primitive form, despite their familiar names, are stated as kinds of civil en-

---

[87] "Conchiudiamo tutto ciò che generalmente si è divisato d'intorno allo stabilimento de' principi di questa Scienza: che, poiché i di lei principi sono provvedenza divina, moderazione di passioni co' matrimoni e immortalità dell'anime umane con le seppolture; e 'l criterio che usa è che ciò che si sente giusto da tutti o la maggior parte degli uomini debba essere la regola della vita socievole (ne' quali principi e criterio conviene la sapienza volgare di tutti i legislatori e la sapienza riposta degli più riputati filosofi): questi deon esser i confini dell'umana ragione. E chiunque se ne voglia trar fuori, egli veda di non trarsi fuori da tutta l'umanità" (*Scienza nuova seconda, Opere* 4, §360).

[88] *Scienza nuova seconda, Opere* 4, §§211–212.

[89] *Scienza nuova seconda, Opere* 4, §367.

deavor; even the physical sciences in their poetic beginnings were so many attempts of the earliest peoples to "locate" themselves spatially, temporally, and—as we would say—ontologically. Vico's very point is that ideas and institutions are impossible to separate, and that in the earliest times theory and practice were one and the same. Thus his *New Science*, he says, "comes to be at once a history of the ideas, the customs, and the deeds of mankind."[90] All are of a piece, reflecting and revealing, separately and together, the poetic nature of their authors. Moreover, the three civil sciences— morals, economics, and politics—though equally poetic, reveal a progression in social complexity, a process of differentiation, from marriage to families to cities; they are thus treated by Vico serially, and so made to show, above all else, the gradual development of the "greater nations" (*gentes majores*) in Greece and Rome.[91] This conforms not merely with his general principle that "doctrines must take their beginning from that of the matters of which they treat," but also with his more specific assertion that "the order of ideas must follow the order of institutions."[92] And that order is clear and invariant—"first the forests, after that the huts, then the villages, next the cities, and finally the academies"—conforming in turn to the evolving nature of the peoples—"first crude, then severe, then benign, then delicate, finally dissolute."[93] Name any custom, state any idea, recall any law or form of government,

---

[90] "Di tal maniera questa Scienza vien ad essere ad un fiato una storia dell'idee, costumi e fatti del gener umano" (*Scienza nuova seconda, Opere* 4, §368).

[91] *Scienza nuova seconda, Opere* 4, bk. 2, secs. 3–5.

[92] "Le dottrine debbono cominciare da quando cominciano le materie che trattano" (*Scienza nuova seconda, Opere* 4, §314). "L'ordine dell'idee dee procedere secondo l'ordine delle cose" (*Scienza nuova seconda, Opere* 4, §238). The latter axiom echoes a famous line in Spinoza, *Ethica*, 2, prop. 7: "Ordo et connexio idearum idem est ac ordo et connexio rerum."

[93] "L'ordine delle cose umane procedette: che prima furono le selve, dopo i tuguri, quindi i villaggi, appresso le città, finalmente l'accademie" (*Scienza nuova seconda, Opere* 4, §239). "La natura de' popoli prima è cruda, dipoi severa, quindi benigna, appresso dilicata, finalmente dissoluta" (*Scienza nuova seconda, Opere* 4, §242). Need I add that delicacy and dissoluteness, on Vico's account, are equal opportunities within the mild age of the academies?

any religious practice or god, anything that man makes at all, Vico boasts, and I will show its necessary place on that continuum from poetic to esoteric wisdom which any and every nation has followed, is following, and will always follow. Vico marks off that course routinely into three ages—the divine, the heroic, and the human—distinctions that Herodotus had traced to the Egyptians, and that Varro in turn had repeated analogously.[94] But as the above citations reveal, he will also speak of four stages of growth, sometimes of five, and occasionally even more. Important is not the number of such stages but the inexorable law that they describe: Before a culture can achieve sciences that are deliberate and methodologically self-conscious, grasped by an intellect that is refined and in categories that are properly abstract, it must first have invented by a compulsion of its nature, which delights in uniformity but commands as yet a spirit that is troubled and agitated and an imagination entirely corporeal, those myriad customs and images through which it states, with increasing consciousness, what it is and is becoming. This is the world of Poetic Wisdom.[95]

Beyond that first dim glimpse of a provident Jove in which men discovered their humanity, wisdom is made with ever increasing complexity and articulateness. Habits are formed and become customs, relationships are established and solemnized, fields are tilled and access to the necessities of life secured, rites are elaborated and laws emerge, families increase and are combined, and guardianships established, cities are founded, and in time men push out to the seas and beyond—Vico's nations, we recall, always take root inland, the better to defend his thesis that each culture, always and everywhere, is an autochthon, living its poetic and most of its heroic years in splendid isolation, its customs and languages thus fully indigenous.[96] Throughout it all, men are seized by wonder, the natural consequence of that first moment of awe before

[94] *Scienza nuova seconda, Opere* 4, §52.
[95] *Scienza nuova seconda, Opere* 4, §§218–219.
[96] *Scienza nuova seconda, Opere* 4, §303.

a thundering sky, and so are led to state, in the only way they can, the connections among things that they sense or create. That way is poetry, the way of image. Though bound to particulars and concrete instances, men sense uniformities and so create images of general or universal meanings. Thus arise emblems, blazonings, symbols, and thus, too, metaphors, myths, and fables, the entire world of folklore and poetry in the narrower, articulate sense.

This transcendent impulse of culture, its spontaneous, pre-reflective need to state its existence linguistically, is a leitmotif of Vico's *New Science*, arguably its principal theme. The evidence of this abounds, Vico held, and he presented it on page after page of his text. Swinging a scythe three times was a "natural" way for an agrarian people to signify three years; and when Idanthyrsus, king of the Scythians, replied to a bellicose Darius the Great with five real words—frog, mouse, bird, plowshare, and bow—could it mean anything else than that he, Idanthyrsus, was a son of Scythia, as frogs seem to spring from its earth in the summer rains; that he grew up there, as mice make their home where they were born; that he was subject only to God or auspice birds; that he had made the lands of Scythia habitable with the plowshare and would defend them with the bow as their supreme commander?[97] As with symbols, so, too, with names. The Greeks called their first communities *phratriai* after *phreatia*, cistern, doubtless because it was the sharing of water that brought families together; and the walls of Rome over which Remus jumped were surely a hedge, the bounds of cultivated land, from which came *munire viam*, to build a road by strengthening the hedges, which in time yielded *moenia*, walls, as if for *munia*, from *munire*, "which keeps the sense of fortifying."[98] Grand as it all is, however, such evidence of cultural self-statement is as nothing compared with the gods and heroes the nations made, for in their theogonies, Vico finds, they truly recorded the

[97] *Scienza nuova seconda, Opere* 4, §§431, 435.
[98] *Scienza nuova seconda, Opere* 4, §§526, 550.

major steps of their development, their most urgent sense of themselves. This is above all true of the gods of the "greater gentes" or noble classes of Greece and Rome, the birth of which is used by Vico to punctuate his account of the growth of poetic morals, economics, and politics.[99] In turning the sky into the body of Jove, the brutes did more than create their humanity; they stated their sense of selves as large crude beings filled with passions. And so, too, for the other eleven deities that the nobles progressively made: the chaste Juno, wife and sister of Jove, who arose with the solemnization of marriage "under the auspices"; the nubile Diana, goddess of the living springs, brought to life as the first human need, a dependable source of water, was secured; thereafter her brother and fellow hunter, Apollo, god of civil light, who sits upon the now-secure mountaintop and from his Parnassus sends forth the Muses of the noble arts; so, too, Vulcan, who conquered the forests with fire, Saturn (sown fields), and Cybele or Vesta (cultivated land); in time came Mars and Venus, as altars and hearths had to be defended, and when the multitude of *famuli* or slaves mutinied with the practice of their servile arts, Minerva sprung from the brow of Jove, which the plebeian Vulcan had split with an ax, and soon thereafter Mercury was fashioned, who carried law to the plebs and so restored order; and last of all came Neptune with his trident, created by the peoples as they took to the sea for war and adventure.[100]

There is a logic at work in all this, Vico holds, a specific, definable process of reasoning, but one not at all like that expected of the refined minds of our own human age. It is poetic logic, the logic of poetry. As with Poetic Wisdom at large, *poetic logic* is a term with two meanings, and Vico intends them both. On the one hand, it is "logic that is made," and in this sense it is the story of the mind's development, a record of the growth of consciousness. On the other hand, it signifies a logic bound to images, to language and concepts

[99] *Scienza nuova seconda, Opere* 4, §317.
[100] *Scienza nuova seconda, Opere* 4, §§502, 511, 528, 533, 549, 562, 589, 604, 634.

of a specific sort. Vico's point is that language and mind develop together and that they in turn—as witness the fabulous debris of ancient symbols, words, and myths—are tied to evolving social and cultural forms. Like all logics, therefore, the "poetic logic" of man's early age has both a formal and a material aspect. It describes at once a process of thought and the linguistic categories in which that thinking is done. The form of this logic is topical reasoning, a variant of the *res* of rhetoric, while its matter is a variant of rhetoric's *verba*, the "imaginative universals" embraced in the four principal and most "logical" tropes—metaphor, metonymy, synecdoche, and irony.[101]

From the start Vico believed that the principles of wisdom lay within us. His first university oration (as indeed his last) called simply for the development of one's "near-divine mind," a bias he never truly abandoned. By the time of his Sixth Oration in 1706 the works of mind, tongue, and spirit alike were seen to be the instruments of humanity, a perspective that persisted to the *De uno principio* of 1720; but there was no thought yet of their changing fundamentally in form. A year later came the dramatic conversion to historicism, and now the path to wisdom was thought to proceed along a series of natural developments that Vico felt could be viewed in the

[101] Vico begins his section on Poetic Logic thus: "That which is metaphysics insofar as it contemplates things in all the forms of their being [*generi dell'essere*], is logic insofar as it considers things in all the forms [*generi*] by which they may be signified. Accordingly, as poetry has been considered by us above as a poetic metaphysics in which the theological poets imagined bodies to be for the most part divine substances, so now that same poetry is considered as poetic logic, by which it signifies them" ("Or—perché quella ch'è metafisica in quanto contempla le cose per tutti i generi dell'essere, la stessa è logica in quanto considera le cose per tutti i generi di significarle—siccome la poesia è stata sopra da noi considerata per una metafisica poetica, per la quale i poeti teologi immaginarono i corpi essere per lo più divine sostanze, così la stessa poesia or si considera come logica poetica, per la qual le significa") (*Scienza nuova seconda, Opere* 4, §400). The "genera" of a poetic metaphysics are formed imaginatively and expressed tropologically, and it is this process of "concept formation," suggested to Vico by his pedagogical and rhetorical principles, that we must now trace out.

way a child's mind and language matured, a parallel he drew
most clearly in the first edition of his *New Science*:

As by nature individuals at first sense and later reflect, reflecting first
with souls torn with passions, then finally with pure minds, so the
human race had first to sense the modifications of bodies, then reflect
on those of souls, and finally on those of abstract minds. Herein we
have the telling reason that every language, as copious and learned
as it may be, encounters the hard necessity of explaining things
spiritual in relation to things corporeal.[102]

Obscure as this passage is, it is in some measure more revealing
than the shortened but more eloquent version Vico put in a
famous paragraph of his last *New Science*, where we read that
the night of thick darkness enveloping antiquity is illumined
by the indubitable truth that we have made our own civil
world and may thus find its principles within the modifications
of our own human mind.[103] "Modifications of the soul" was
a phrase of Malebranche, used in his debate with Arnauld
over the knowability of the soul—whether we truly know it
or merely sense it internally.[104] Vico does not join that issue,
but seems merely to want to assert the highlights of a historical
psychology. Our minds are inescapably bound to our bodies,
and our knowledge is itself a descendant of sense, which was
once entirely corporeal, a development we may appreciate by
watching the growth of a child. What Aristotle said of the

[102] "Che, come gli uomini particolari naturalmente prima sentono, poi
reflettono, e prima riflettono con animi perturbati da passioni, poi finalmente
con mente pura; così il genere umano prima dovette sentire le modificazioni
de' corpi, indi riflettere a quelle degli animi e finalmente a quelle delle menti
astratte. Qui si scuopre l'importante principio di quello: che ogni lingua, per
copiosa e dotta che ella si sia, incontra la dura necessità di spiegare le cose
spirituali per rapporto alle cose de' corpi" (*Scienza nuova prima, Opere* 3,
§298).
[103] *Scienza nuova seconda, Opere* 4, §331.
[104] See the remarks of Antonio Corsano, *Giambattista Vico* (Bari: Laterza,
1956), pp. 219–221. For a fuller statement of Malebranche's position, see
John H. Randall, Jr., *The Career of Philosophy*, vol. 1, *From the Middle
Ages to the Enlightenment* (New York: Columbia University Press, 1962),
pp. 425–433.

individual is thus radically true of the race in general: *Nihil est in intellectu quin prius fuerit in sensu.*[105]

A mind in its infancy, Vico held, is a remarkable instrument driven by two powerful capacities. On the one hand it has, like any human mind, an "almost divine nature" and "is naturally impelled to take delight in uniformity."[106] On the other, it is fully immersed in the body, necessarily bound by what is particular and immediate, incapable of reflecting or "bending back" on its activities, and thus unable to abstract the materials with which to form philosophical universals or "intelligible class concepts."[107] The combination of these irreducible tendencies, like opposite charges across an open circuit, yields the universe of Poetic Wisdom, the "poetic falsity" that is "metaphysically true."[108]

What can it mean to think through the body, to reason with a mind that is torn with passions and immersed in the senses? It means to reason as a rhetor must reason when speaking *inter rudes*, arguing among the simple who cannot take in a complicated argument. It means first to canvass a situation in its full extent, trying to see it in all its many aspects and selecting from among them those which are most trenchant and persuasive. It means also to enlarge on particulars, to state as general maxims the opinions one's listeners hold about their own situations. And it means finally to catch up one's argument in stirring images, in language that can so much embrace oneself, one's listeners, and the shared situation that all are impelled to act effectively and as one. Such reasoning

---

[105] *Scienza nuova seconda, Opere* 4, §363. The formula is doubtless medieval in origin, and was likely developed from Aristotle's *On the Soul* 432a7–8. Cf. Nicolini, *Commento storico*, 1.122–123.

[106] "La mente umana è naturalmente portata a dilettarsi dell'uniforme" (*Scienza nuova seconda, Opere* 4, §204; cf. §816).

[107] *Scienza nuova seconda, Opere* 4, §§209, 218–219, 819, 821, 825.

[108] *Scienza nuova seconda, Opere* 4, §205. Cf. the *De studiorum ratione, Opere* 1.97, where the poet is said to teach "by delighting" and "through fictions," while the philosopher teaches "severely," such notions to be compared with Vico's later remarks in the *De mente heroica, Opere* 7.13f., and his annotations on Horace's *Ars poetica, Opere* 7.54, 74, which speak of poetic falsities as sublimely or metaphysically true.

is an art to the rhetor, Vico held, but to minds *ab ovo*, buried in the body, it is a compulsion of nature. They have no *copia rerum et verborum* that they artfully sift, yet they sense what is trenchant in their social experience and enlarge such particulars by rendering them spontaneously in stirring images. Observe the birth of Jove, "the greatest fable" the poets created. Jove is not a metaphysical god; he is God contemplated "under the attribute of his providence," the poetic enlargement of a finite but dramatic experience. Jove was created as a thundering voice in the sky, a giant body observing a cluster of frightened men. Out of this particular experience, moreover, came a god of enduring providence, as the founding metaphor was preserved and extended. Thus the auspices were born and the practice of divination, all referred to the provident Jove, and Jove himself acquired over time the additional titles of best (*optimus*), strongest (*fortissimus*), and greatest (*maximus*). In this wise, through a natural process of imagination, a particular experience of sense became a universal institution and an idea of general application. Having thus the character of universality, though not as the term of a logical abstraction, these imaginatively enlarged particulars deserve, Vico thought, a special name—"imaginative universals" (*universali fantastici*). Such is the fate, in a mind drunk with history, of Aristotle's "maxims" and "poetic universals."[109]

As it was with Jove in the beginning, so it was with all the

[109] *Scienza nuova seconda, Opere* 4, §§365, 379–381; cf. §§209, 933–934. The logic of Vico's "imaginative universals" is plainly an adaptation of Aristotle's rhetorical and poetic doctrines and may be followed through the *De constantia jurisprudentis, Opere* 2.363–378, and the *Scienza nuova prima, Opere* 3, §§253–266, 309–316, into the paragraphs of the final *New Science* cited above. Elsewhere in the work he shows their basis in "topical" reasoning (§§494–498, 699) and relates them explicitly with rhetorical "maxims" (*massime*: §816) and "poetic sentences" (*sentenze poetiche*: §825), which are "concetti di passioni vere" and distinguished from the "sentenze di filosofi." Amid a sizable literature on the subject, see Mario Fubini, "Ancora dell' 'universale fantastico' vichiano," *Stile e umanità di G. B. Vico*, 2d ed. (Milan and Naples: Ricciardi, 1965), pp. 201–204; and Antonino Pagliaro, "Lingua e poesia secondo G. B. Vico," *Altri saggi di critica semantica* (Messina and Florence: D'Anna, 1961), pp. 394–411.

gods and heroes of the ancients, each a "poetic character" (*carattere poetico*) embodying a treasured aspect of a culture's experience. Thus to Achilles the Greeks attached all the properties of heroic valor and its corresponding habits—quick temper, punctiliousness, wrathfulness, implacability, violence—while to Ulysses they attached all feelings of heroic wisdom—wariness, patience, dissimulation, duplicity, deceit; and they themselves in a particular respect, as Grecian men telling their histories in song, became in the process a grand heroic character—the poet Homer.[110] So, too, Solon, possibly a character for the Athenian plebs "under the aspect" of demanding their rights, even as Aesop, whom we find still speaking in comparisons (rather than in the maxims of the later Sages), was a poetic character of the plebs in their more ancient days.[111] The many contests of song?—Apollo besting the satyr Marsyas, and later conquering Linus; the sirens who lull sailors to sleep and after which slay them; Circe, who turns the comrades of Ulysses into swine with her enchantments—all these portray the politics of heroic times, lost struggles for a share in the auspices for which the plebeians had to pay in blood.[112] The pantheon of every nation is the same, a temple of figures such as these, congeries of related values and experiences. Throughout all this we discover without fail the remarkable logic of simple or unschooled minds, which make universals of the particulars they value in things, writing them large in forceful images. Such was the logic of the ancestors, a logic of "a sensory topics, by which they brought together those properties or qualities or relations of individuals and species which were, so to speak, concrete, and from these created their poetic genera."[113]

But Vico could not rest with explaining the mere form of poetic development; with that exuberance which is the greed

[110] *Scienza nuova seconda, Opere* 4, §§809, 873.

[111] *Scienza nuova seconda, Opere* 4, §§414–416, 424–426.

[112] *Scienza nuova seconda, Opere* 4, §§646–649.

[113] "Ch'i primi autori dell'umanità attesero ad una topica sensibile, con la quale univano le propietà o qualità o rapporti, per così dire, concreti degl'individui o delle spezie, e ne formavano i generi loro poetici" (*Scienza nuova seconda, Opere* 4, §495; cf. generally §§34, 412–429, 494–498).

of ingenuity he pressed on with a theory of the very structure of poetic history. From the beginning of his rhetorical instruction he had taught that the tropes of speech, as the forms of figured language, were logically reducible to four principal types according to the way they transferred meaning—from one thing to something similar (metaphor), from cause to effect or vice versa (metonymy), from the whole to the part or vice versa (synecdoche), and from one thing to its opposite (irony). By 1738, and probably much earlier, the treatment of the tropes had disappeared from his Rhetoric, having now been absorbed by the Science into the section that he had come to call "poetic logic." More than absorbed, the tropes are rather ingested in the work, like sundry other rhetorical principles, sustaining the science but being themselves transformed in the process. In consequence, they not only appear in the work as one of its signal themes but can also be traced, as one author has done brilliantly, into the "deep structure" of the science as well.[114]

Already in his Rhetoric, Vico had exploited the claim of Cicero (De or. 3.38.155) that in many instances of civil life metaphor is a necessity, not a mere ornament, of communication; judicial process itself consists largely in a struggle for the words in which to grasp the changing contours of human experience, which are forever eluding our concepts and formulas. In the earliest times, Vico argues, this anxiety of namelessness was absolute. The earliest men were literally speechless and thus forced to be inventive. When the thunder sounded in the heavens, moreover, the only images they commanded were those of the modifications of their own bodies, dimly perceived. The recognition in the sky of their bodily actions led to a transfer of these images and thereby to the creation of Jove, first in mute gestures and eventually in speech. Thunder sounds but they hear a voice, a voice like theirs yet louder,

[114] Hayden V. White, "The Tropics of History: The Deep Structure of the New Science," in Giambattista Vico's Science of Humanity, ed. Tagliacozzo and Verene, pp. 65–85, which develops a theme set forth in his Metahistory: The Historical Imagination in Nineteenth Century Europe (Baltimore and London: Johns Hopkins University Press, 1973).

larger, more powerful; the voice metaphorically identified is made through metonymic reduction into a being who acts, and around this being are clustered, through synecdoche, all the attributes and actions that pertain to a giant, powerful, shouting god: Jove is born and with him the idea and rites of providence. Thus history began tropologically, the rise of mind revealing itself as a process of naming, of appropriating the alien through things familiar. The making of mind was a poetic construction, a construct of images assembling themselves through the logic of the tropes.[115]

If, therefore, the logic of topics and of topical reasoning is adapted by Vico to explain the process of primitive thought, the logic of the tropes is used to show the emergence of that thought in language and the outcome it has in imaginative genera; in such a way could Vico unite, as he had insisted on so firmly in his rhetorical instruction, the *res* and *verba* of culture. In the article referred to above, Hayden White takes the matter yet further: Vico uses the tropes to demonstrate not merely the formation of language but the entire *corso* of the nations in all their intellectual and social forms as they proceed from the divine to the heroic to the human age. In the *New Science*, White argues, the development of consciousness from metaphorical identification to metonymic reduction to synecdochic construction to ironic statement is strictly analogous to transformations in social structure from the rule of the gods to the rule of the aristocrats to the rule of the people to a state of lawlessness. The initial age in which men project

---

[115] *Scienza nuova seconda, Opere* 4, §§401–409, which begins with the assertion that " 'Logic' comes from *logos*, whose first and proper meaning was *fabula*, fable, carried over into Italian as *favella*, speech. In Greek the fable was also called *mythos*, myth, whence comes the Latin *mutus*, mute" (" 'Logica' vien detta dalla voce *logos*, che prima e propiamente significò 'favola,' che si trasportò in italiano 'favella'—e la favola da' greci si disse anco *mythos*, onde vien a' latini '*mutus*' "). The Greek notion of *logos* as both speech and reason is traced by Max Heinze, *Die Lehre vom Logos in der griechischen Philosophie* (1872; reprint, Aalen: Scientia, 1961); and by Anathon Aall, *Der Logos: Geschichte seiner Entwicklung in der griechischen Philosophie und der christlichen Literatur*, 2 vols. in 1 (Leipzig: Reisland, 1896–1899).

upon gods their own sensed human attributes and thus live
in fear of themselves is followed by the age of the heroes in
which, through a metonymic reduction, the mere act or accident of the established class ruling the plebs, who have come
to the asylums for protection, is taken for the agency of rule;
the passage from this age to the human is marked by a shift
in perception to a synecdochic mode whereby the plebeians
claim for themselves the attributes originally ascribed to the
gods and later claimed by the nobility, and is consolidated by
an ironic consciousness in which the distinction between image and reality is appreciated. Thus Vico's dialectic, White
argues, is not that of the syllogism (thesis, antithesis, synthesis)
but of "the exchange between language on the one side and
the reality it seeks to contain on the other."[116]

Whether Vico's history unfolds with quite this tropological
neatness, the terms of its dialectic are undoubtedly those of
language and society. The structure of language in which a
society coheres reaches across history as well, binding men
over time as it binds them in place, and a change in society
necessarily involves a change in its language. The rhetorical
parallel again shows the way. The debate arising from an issue
of social urgency leads over argument to a judgment or sentence, a statement of authority that establishes order and joins
men socially; no mere external instrument, the language of
this outcome becomes part of the social fabric itself, a precedent for future issues of the kind, a "prejudice" (*praejudi-
cium*) with which further claimants are compelled to deal. So
also in the construction of poetic wisdom—one image seeds
the next; one word, one symbol, one myth leads to another,
not through any logical extrapolation but through an endless
social dialectic between public language on the one hand and
a culture's changing sense of itself on the other. Jove is an
image of the brutes' own lumbering, passionate bodies, but
through it they are reduced to men who know their kind, and

---

[116] "The Tropics of History," pp. 77f. White's point is well taken, but he
appears to confuse the terms of Hegel's dialectic with those of the syllogism
(major, minor, conclusion).

out of the monogamous unions to which this leads comes forth the chaste goddess Juno, whose cult in turn embroiders the practice of the auspices and makes of them the legitimate form in which to contract and solemnize marriage. Through such a process—a kind of poetical sorites—symbolic systems and mythical structures are established, great chains of images that stretch over time and give a culture standing and identity.

SAPIENZA RIPOSTA

But men do eventually develop prose, and the poetic tropes, once necessary modes of expression and being, become mere figures of speech.[117] The mind unfolded, man moves from his natural ambience of simile and metaphor, of poetic universals, to the land of genera and species, capable of formulating abstract principles for areas of inquiry and industry for which previously he had only a tradition of imaginative trials and errors, expressed in tropological form. He moves on, for instance, from a civil equity based on authority to a natural equity based in reason, from customs that are pious and punctilious to ones that are truly dutiful, taught to each man by his own sense of right.[118] In sum,

man is properly only mind, body, and speech, and speech stands as it were midway between mind and body. Hence with regard to what is just, *the certain* began in mute times with the body. Then when the so-called articulate languages were invented, it advanced to ideas made certain by spoken formulae. And finally, when our human reason was fully developed, it *reached its end in the true* in the ideas themselves with regard to what is just, as determined by reason from the detailed circumstances of the facts.[119]

---

[117] *Scienza nuova seconda, Opere* 4, §409.
[118] *Scienza nuova seconda, Opere* 4, §§912–921, 947–953.
[119] "Insomma—non essendo altro l'uomo, propiamente, che mente, corpo e favella, e la favella essendo come posta in mezzo alla mente ed al corpo— *il certo* d'intorno al giusto cominciò ne' tempi muti dal corpo; dipoi, ritruovate

What leaps from the page in this text, which comes at the very end of Vico's account of the course of humanity and is intended as its summary, is that human rationality in its highest form—recondite or esoteric wisdom (*sapienza riposta*)—is conceived on the model of a mature jurisprudence. Unfailingly in his work Vico accepts the high jurisprudence of the Roman Empire, the peak of the first human *corso*, as his image of the best humanity, while the model of humanity tending to decay—the dark underside of cultural maturity—he takes from tendencies in the returned humanity of his own mild times—Cartesian rationalism and linguistic Mannerism. Descartes's "barbarism of reflection" has of course its ancient parallel—Stoic rigidity—even as Baconian experimentalism is the modern equivalent of the best jurisprudence; yet these are inserted by Vico to fill in his landscape, never to etch its lines.

What does it mean to be rational in the manner of a developed jurisprudence? There is a concluding line to the text just cited that tries to describe such truth: "This truth is a formula devoid of any particular form, called by the learned Varro the formula of nature [*formula naturae*], which, like light, of itself informs in all the minutest details of their surface the opaque bodies of the facts over which it is diffused."[120] Vico had first invoked Varro's phrase in the introduction to his *Diritto universale*, where he cites the idea in context. If he were establishing a state, Varro wrote, he would cast the many idols of Rome on the dustheap in favor of a single, incorporeal, infinite God *ex formula naturae*. Vico applauds the idea and says that his work will show that natural law is

---

le favelle che si dicon articolate, passò alle certe idee, ovvero formole di parole; finalmente, essendosi spiegata tutta la nostra umana ragione, *andò a terminare nel vero* dell'idee d'intorno al giusto, determinate con la ragione dall'ultime circostanze de' fatti" (*Scienza nuova seconda, Opere* 4, §1045; my emphasis).

[120] Ch'è una formola informe d'ogni forma particolare, che 'l dottissimo Varrone chiamava '*formulam naturae*,' ch'a guisa di luce, di sé informa in tutte le ultime minutissime parti della lor superficie i corpi opachi de' fatti sopra i quali ella è diffusa" (*Scienza nuova seconda, Opere* 4, §1045).

that very formula, the "idea of the true" that shows us the true God, who is the principle of all religion and law.[121] The *Universal Law* is indeed an effort of this kind, but it is subverted from the start by a contending notion that would in time engulf Vico's work: it is the idea of the jurisconsult as sage of mankind whose duties required him to be, at one and the same time, historian of law, philosopher of law, and jurist, able to show as a unity the authority of the law, its warrant in reason, and its applicability to the facts at hand.[122] Work of this kind was praised by the Romans as *jurisprudence*, a term that defined both a process of thought and the texts that were its result. The jurisconsults themselves, as we saw, were wont to call it "true philosophy," a claim that seemed sustained in the compilation of Justinian. Here was a work encyclopedic in scope, treating of persons, things, and the actions that united them, encompassing all things human and divine, construing the civil world in cause and effect, and operating according to its own method and principles of interpretation. It was moreover the result of a painstaking process, building up over time and taking into its founding "law of the citizens" the uniform provisions of the "law of the nations" that had come to make up the Empire. Small wonder then that it came to be seen by interpreters down to Vico himself as *ratio scripta*, reason itself written down.[123] Such is the model for that "formula of nature" which Vico now describes as a light that informs in all the minutest details the opaque bodies of the facts over which it is diffused.

The rationality of such a law is equity. Equity is the principle of "mild law," "connatural with civilized nations," one that does not insist on the literal application of a code however harsh that may be, but looks always to the facts of a case and

---

[121] *De uno principio, Opere* 2.33. Varro's statement is in Augustine, *De civ. D.* 4.31.

[122] *De uno principio, Opere* 2.26ff.

[123] Again, see Kelley, "Vera Philosophia," and his later application of the idea to Vico, "In Vico Veritas: The True Philosophy and the New Science," *Social Research* 43 (1976): 601–611.

takes for law "whatever impartial utility dictates."[124] Our "princes" of natural-law theory, Vico writes, because they begin with nations reciprocally related in the society of the entire human race, assume that a rationality of this kind was understood by the nations from the start.[125] By such a conceit they impute the natural law of philosophers to the fierce and cruel ancestors of the race. To understand *their* rationality, one must push the brain down into its stem, bury it again in the body, and make it rise slowly to the head through the tongue.

The natural law of the peoples begins in the habits of the "greater gentes," the noble classes with their serfs or *famuli*, who rule their "families" with a law of force. This law is harsh, particular, but certain, secured by the auspices that the "fathers" control.[126] Language is the fulcrum, the point at which change is levered. So long as the law is held secret, authority is embodied in the nobles speaking to each situation; once written down, as the plebs demanded, it assumes some distance from the ruling class and acquires the ability to become a general statement of justice. Here begins the idealization of law, its slow conversion into principles or ideas of universal application. The Law of the Twelve Tables is the faintest shadow of this long and weary process, the result, Vico notes, of many hard contests between plebs and nobles over the rights of citizenship, the struggle for a law whose reason would break the force of heroic caprice and erect an equitable standard for all. The result is a clear advance, called by Livy the "fountainhead of all equitable law" (*fons omnis aequi iuris*), and by Tacitus its "consummation" (*finis omnis aequi iuris*).[127] Yet its equity is mere civil equity (*aequitas civilis*), a severe code written with the interests of state in

---

[124] *Scienza nuova seconda, Opere* 4, §§323, 327.

[125] *Scienza nuova seconda, Opere* 4, §§318, 329.

[126] *Scienza nuova seconda, Opere* 4, §§250–257, 917, 923.

[127] *Scienza nuova seconda, Opere* 4, §1001. On the heroic struggle for a written law, again see Momigliano, "Vico's *Scienza nuova*: Roman 'bestioni' and Roman 'eroi,' " pp. 13–23.

mind, its rationality no longer "arcane" or divine, but not yet "natural" and open.[128] Thus a heroic jurisprudence arises, a period of superstitious observance of the words of law, an observance so scrupulous that "the laws march straight through all the facts."[129] As in the earliest times when "bloody religions under divine governments" were used to guard marriage and the boundaries of fields in order to arrest promiscuity, so now the nobles protect their estates by keeping for themselves the solemn nuptials and by reserving to the jurists the right to interpret the laws; the secrecy of law is replaced by an arcane jurisprudence. Thus ensues the contest of tongue against code, orator against jurist, the latter guarding the strictnesss of the law's letter, the former appealing for exceptions in light of a higher principle. This process comes to term under the emperors. The institutions of citizenship are extended to the underclass, the laws common to the nations severally are brought into the written code, and the code itself is interpreted by the mild jurisprudence of natural equity in which, by the "light and splendor with which natural reason illuminates them," the laws are benignly bent to the requirements of each case.[130] Such is humanity at its fullest, civility in its true and proper form, the mere authority of the certain yielding to the rationality of the true.

Formal philosophy, Vico posits, was the happy byproduct of a society of this kind. "It must have been from observing that the enactment of laws by Athenian citizens involved their coming to agreement in an idea of an equal utility common to all of them severally that Socrates began to adumbrate intelligibile genera or abstract universals by induction." And again, "Plato, reflecting that in such public assemblies the minds of particular men, each passionately bent on his private utility, are brought together in a dispassionate idea of common utility (according to the saying that men individually are swayed

[128] *Scienza nuova seconda, Opere* 4, §949.
[129] "Con osservarne superstiziosamente le lor parole, facevano camminare le leggi diritto per tutti i fatti" (*Scienza nuova seconda, Opere* 4, §950).
[130] *Scienza nuova seconda, Opere* 4, §§981–1003; cf. §§319–329, 1086.

by their private interests but collectively they seek justice), raised himself to the meditation of the highest intelligible ideas of created minds, ideas which are distinct from these created minds and can reside only in God."[131] With man's coming of age, the direction of mind thus reverses itself. No longer compelled to enlarge particulars into those imaginative genera in which life has its certainty, men are now able to grasp particulars within properly philosophical categories. The logic of topics is superseded by the logic of criticism; cities arise, and with them the academies.[132]

Vico does not tell us how this change comes about; he does say, however, that it is signaled linguistically by the development of ironic statement. Irony as a trope, Vico argues, is based on a conscious distinction between truth and falsity: one thing is spoken while its opposite is intended. An ironic statement "is fashioned of falsehood by dint of a reflection that wears the mask of truth." Such a capacity was entirely beyond the founders of the race who, like children, were naturally truthful, unable to reflect and thus unable to feign anything.[133] Irony, moreover, implies a split between tongue and brain, the rise of distance between language and the reality it seeks to contain. Irony is the conscious trope, and the con-

---

[131] "Egli è necessario che Socrate, dall'osservare ch'i cittadini ateniesi nel comandare le leggi si andavan ad unire in un' idea conforme d'un'ugual utilità partitamente comune a tutti, cominciò ad abbozzare i generi intelligibili, ovvero gli universali astratti, con l'induzione, ch'è una raccolta di uniformi particolari, che vanno a comporre un genere di ciò nello che quei particolari sono uniformi tra loro." "Platone, dal riflettere che 'n tali ragunanze pubbliche le menti degli uomini particolari, che son appassionate ciascuna del propio utile, si conformavano in un'idea spassionata di comune utilità (ch' è quello che dicono: 'gli uomini partitamente sono portati da' loro interessi privati, ma in comune voglion giustizia'), s'alzò a meditare l'idee intelligibili ottime delle menti criate, divise da esse menti criate, le qual'in altri non posson esser che in Dio, e s'innalzò a formare l'eroe filosofico, che comandi con piacere alle passioni" (*Scienza nuova seconda*, *Opere* 4, §§1040–1041; cf. §§499, 1043, 1101).

[132] *Scienza nuova seconda*, *Opere* 4, §§219, 498, 821, 934.

[133] "L'ironia certamente non poté cominciare che da' tempi della riflessione, perch'ella è formata dal falso in forza d'una riflessione che prende maschera di verità" (*Scienza nuova seconda*, *Opere* 4, §408).

sciousness it implies extends to the other tropes as well. Metaphor, metonymy, and synecdoche are now seen as figured, not literal statements, and the poetic characters lose the mark of univocity that they necessarily had in the beginning.[134] Metaphor may remain a necessity of communication (as Vico continued to argue in his school writings), but that necessity is now conscious; and in addition it can now simply adorn.

With this there arises that most enduring of all issues, one that dogged Vico—as it must anyone who thinks deeply on the history of things human—to the end. What is the relation of poetry to philosophy, of mythical times to the age of man? The gods and rites, the customs and laws, the symbols and fables are indisputably certain; but are they also true? One's first impulse is to discard the question as meaningless, as the critic of Vico's *De Italorum sapientia* wished to put aside the issue of truth in the art of topics. Topics, he claimed, relate to perception, an act of the mind that precedes judgment, and only judgments can be true or false. So equally, if mankind's first poetic actions, as Vico asserts, were "simple apprehensions," perceptions that preceded reflective consciousness, the issue of their truth never arises. Vico would reject this claim as he did that of his early critic, for he also held that perceptions of this kind, as instances of a "common sense" of things, were also judgments, "judgments without reflection" to be sure, but judgments nonetheless.

Vico did not give this matter separate or sustained consideration; he was so taken with his discovery of the poetic origins of the race that he gave an increasing prominence in the versions of his science to making that case and showing its implications. The "human age," once his sole occupation, was correspondingly de-emphasized, and so, too, the issue of its relation to human origins. In another sense, however, the issue was constantly before him, for to make a new claim about the origins of humanity is necessarily to take a stand

[134] *Scienza nuova seconda*, Opere 4, §403, cf. *Scienza nuova prima*, Opere 3, §265.

on their relation to modern consciousness. His entire work was intended as a refutation of the "conceit of scholars," who put their own refined wisdom in the near-brute minds of the ancestors. The poets are the sense of the human race, he stressed, while the philosophers are its intellect.[135] In that striking synecdoche we have an appropriate context in which to consider his further claim, often repeated, that myths are "true narrations."

Vico is both terribly concrete and maddeningly elusive on the topic. His text fairly abounds in images by which he tries to explain his meaning, and each reinforces the central assertion that there is a fundamental difference in continuity between traditional and modern man. They are related not only as the sense to the intellect of the race, but also as children to adults, as those who live by their wit, forever seeing or making connections, and those who live by reason, abstracting the general from particulars by drawing distinctions. They share a sense for the uniform, a natural capacity for the universal, yet the one can establish genera rationally while the other must create them imaginatively; they share a common humanity, yet the actions of the one cohere in what is set, authoritative, and certain, while those of the other are defensible by reasons that in principle are open to all. There is then an inevitable tension in Vico's text, the accent falling at times—and typically at the critical junctures—on continuity in history, as when he chooses to present Poetic Wisdom in the framework of contemporary disciplines, but far more frequently on the traits of mind and behavior that separate the ages. The dragon to be slain was the frightful habit of turning primitives into philosophers and their colorful stories into ciphers for recondite truths; so his task was to show, above all else, how impossibly philosophical were those gross, sensate beasts of yore.

In calling myths "true narrations," therefore, Vico means first and above all to distinguish them from later kinds of

---

[135] *Scienza nuova seconda, Opere* 4, §363.

speaking.[136] The myths are no devices or instruments, and certainly no hoaxes, for they are the product of childlike minds. Like children, the ancestors were incapable of deception, for they could not make the distinctions necessary to feign.[137] Thus neither could they manage the mental steps necessary to dress up as a story the "plain" statement of a metaphysical or moral truth. There is no such gap between language and meaning in the childlike mind; myths are not tales that are "spun" but stories told in language that is immediate and natural, and we should be as loathe to translate them into prose as we would be to reduce an ancient urn to a modern cooking utensil.

More than the stories of truthful men, who lacked even the ability to deceive, the myths are also histories narrated truly. Vico means actually to say that we can read in the myths the histories of the ancient peoples; that while the obscenities and crudities attributed to the gods and heroes were surely the accretions of a later, decadent age, the original myths were "all true and severe and worthy of the founders of nations."[138] We must understand, however, that these histories are necessarily told poetically: Castelvetro had understood the priority of history over poetry but had failed to see the poetic origins of history itself.[139] In the first instance this means that the myths are materially or representationally false, their proper material being, more truly than Aristotle knew, the "credible impossible" (*impossibile credibile*): "It is impossible that bodies should be minds, yet it was believed that the thundering sky was Jove."[140] The thunder was only just that—thunder— no voice of a provident god, just as the air has no wings and

---

[136] *Scienza nuova seconda, Opere* 4, §401.

[137] *Scienza nuova seconda, Opere* 4, §408; cf. §817.

[138] "Ma questi duri scogli di mitologia si schiveranno co' principi di questa Scienza, la quale dimostrerà che tali favole, ne' loro principi, furono tutte vere e severe e degne di fondatori di nazioni" (*Scienza nuova seconda, Opere* 4, §81; cf. §§221, 708, 814, 846).

[139] *Scienza nuova seconda, Opere* 4, §812.

[140] "Egli è impossibile ch'i corpi sieno menti (e fu creduto che 'l cielo tonante si fusse Giove)" (*Scienza nuova seconda, Opere* 4, §383; cf. §401).

the sea carries no trident. These are material impossibilities and no generosity or empathy will ever make them real. In their "simplicity and doltishness" mythical men believe the impossible, the world made animate by "a powerful deceit of imagination"; but by their very image they lead themselves beyond credulity to true humanity, thus achieving the principal end of poetry—to teach the ignorant *vulgus*.[141] For in worshiping their Jove, the ancestors do not wish merely to note the experience, as Hobbes thought words marked thoughts, but seek to contain it imaginatively, to grasp it truly in a name. Born of a nature that at once craves the universal and is bound to particulars, Jove is an image that survives the moment and becomes a statement of what the brutes now are—children of a provident deity; and the actions undertaken in consequence, divination and the practice of auspices, are referred back to Jove as are all similar experiences of being watched over or otherwise directed. Jove becomes thereby an imaginative class concept in which their lives have standing, and a poetic statement in which their history is told.

Not only providence, but all the ideas and institutions of the nations, Vico thought, or at least their most significant, took shape in this way. Contracting marriage, clearing the forests, securing the necessities of life, conquering the seas, achieving a heroic valor, even telling their histories in song were both realized and stated in the grand "poetic characters" of myth. This, Vico said, is the "master key" of his *New Science*, and he uses it indeed, in page after page of his work, on the gates of every pantheon in the Mediterranean world.[142] Almost invariably his ideas are compared with the euhemeristic theories of his century, to which they bear a superficial resemblance, but in fact they break the constraints of that vision. Myths for Vico are not divinized persons and events, a recording for eternity of actual grand moments of history; they are the language in which a culture both states and achieves

---

[141] *Scienza nuova prima, Opere* 3, §258.
[142] *Scienza nuova seconda, Opere* 4, §34.

its existence. As in stirring moments of oratory an ingenious image *becomes* social reality, the image in which an audience now understands itself and will act, so myths in a culture's life are instances of self-expression in terms of which a people now knows who it is. Such images moreover are not static but enter a dialectic with the society that created them, giving rise to consequent actions and being themselves enlarged or revised. Looked at after the fact, as a body of collected literature, the fables of course bear the imprint of this process, their strongest figures showing most clearly the major achievements and values of a culture. There is much to be criticized in Vico's use of myths—that his principles are applied too leadenly, that meanings are forced and details brushed aside, above all perhaps that every cycle of myths is assumed to describe an identical development—but the charge of euhemerism is one that Vico can survive.[143]

And when philosophy arrives, is myth then embarrassed and the innocence of its makers revealed? "As much as the poets had first sensed in the way of vulgar wisdom," Vico writes, "the philosophers later understood in the way of esoteric wisdom; so that the former may be said to have been the sense and the latter the intellect of the human race." This is immediately construed with two further statements. "The human mind does not understand anything of which it has had no previous impression (which our modern metaphysicians call 'occasion') from the senses. Now the mind uses the intellect when, from something it senses, it gathers something which does not fall under the senses."[144] Vico then proceeds

---

[143] Vico's break with euhemerism is well presented by Manuel, *Eighteenth Century Confronts the Gods*, pp. 147–167, esp. 160–164, an essay nonetheless that emphasizes myth as a literature, not a process of culture.

[144] "Quanto prima avevano sentito d'intorno alla sapienza volgare i poeti, tanto intesero poi d'intorno alla sapienza riposta i filosofi; talché si possono quelli dire essere stati il senso e questi l'intelletto del gener umano; ... la mente umana non intenda cosa della quale non abbia avuto alcun motivo (ch'i metafisici d'oggi dicono 'occasione') da' sensi, la quale allora usa l'intelletto quando, da cosa che sente, raccoglie cosa che non cade sotto de' sensi" (*Scienza nuova seconda, Opere* 4, §363).

to lay out, in some two hundred pages, the poetic metaphysics, logic, physics, morals, and other vulgar wisdoms that the ancestors made, and he concludes:

We have shown that poetic wisdom justly deserves two great and sovereign tributes. The one ... is that of having founded gentile mankind. ... The other ... is that the wisdom of the ancients made its wise men, by a single inspiration, equally great as philosophers, lawmakers, captains, historians, orators, and poets, on which account it has been so greatly sought after. But in fact it made or rather sketched them such as we have found them in the fables. For in these, as in embryos or matrices, we have discovered the outlines of all esoteric wisdom. And it may be said that in the fables the nations have in a rough way and in the language of the human senses described the beginnings of this world of sciences, which the specialized studies of scholars have since clarified for us by reasoning and generalization.[145]

Then the poets were philosophers in spite of themselves? That, Vico would say, is a "conceited" question, but since you persist in it, let me speak to the issue from your vantage point. You wish to find physical, moral, or metaphysical truths in the myths. Here is a physical interpretation that uses *my* scientific principles: *Chaos* to the poets was the confusion of human seeds during the period of notorious promiscuity; that same word later, its proper idea obscured, gave a reason (*motivo*) to philosophers to reflect on the confusion of seeds in the whole of nature and likewise gave them the occasion (*aggio*) to express this with the name "Chaos." So, too, Jove, a

---

[145] "Ed ecco la sapienza poetica dimostrata meritar con giustizia quelle due somme e sovrane lodi: delle quali una certamente e con costanza l'è attribuita, d'aver fondato il gener umano della gentilità; ... l'altra, ... che la sapienza degli antichi faceva i suoi saggi, con uno spirito, egualmente grandi filosofi e legislatori e capitani ed istorici ed oratori e poeti, ond'ella è stata cotanto disiderata. Ma quella gli fece o, più tosto, gli abbozzò tali, quali l'abbiamo truovati dentro le favole, nelle quali, com'in embrioni o matrici, si è discoverto essere stato abbozzato tutto il sapere riposto; che puossi dire dentro di quelle per sensi umani essere stati dalle nazioni rozzamente descritti i principi di questo mondo di scienze, il quale poi con raziocini e con massime ci è stato schiarito dalla particolare riflessione de' dotti" (*Scienza nuova seconda, Opere* 4, §779).

thundering sky to the poets, gave reason and occasion to Plato to reflect on the nature of the ether that penetrates and moves all things and to cap his examination with the motto: *Jovis omnia plena*. And here is a moral interpretation: The fable of Titan the giant, his liver and heart eternally ravaged by the eagle, which for the poets meant the terrible and frightening superstition of the auspices, was appropriately taken by philosophers to signify the remorse of a guilty conscience. And finally, metaphysics: The heroes of the poets who were born of the auspices of Jove and thus thought to be of divine origin gave occasion and opportunity (*occasione ed aggio*) to the philosophers to reflect on their own heroes, who were found to be of a divine nature endowed with corresponding power, and Jove himself, who was named by the few giants who were able to find anger in the thundering heavens, was carried over (*trasportato*) to the Jove who gives to a few the fortunate talent to become philosophers.[146] Do not look for philosophy among the poets, Vico means to say, and do not seek to correlate their ideas with the refined and disciplined notions of the sciences. The poets are the founders of humanity, not its explicators, and they achieve their task by seeing the connections that were not seen before and so creating the images in which men have their coherence and their life. The wisdom they command is not esoteric, recondite, or hidden, the kind that yields only to scrutiny and patient analysis; but it is wisdom nonetheless. It is the wisdom of certainty, wisdom that is made, the certain knowledge of things human and divine, and but for it there would be no metaphysics, for there would be no men worshiping their god; no ethics, for there would be no men regulating their lives; no politics and economics, for there would be no men building cities and arranging their lives in common; no physics or astronomy, for there would be no men certain of their bodies, their homes, and the patterns of the sky; no logic, for there would be no

---

[146] *Scienza nuova prima, Opere* 3, §§298–301; cf. *Scienza nuova seconda, Opere* 4, §688, and dozens of other places in the "Poetic Wisdom."

poetic characters, no universal images; no wisdom at all, for there would be no awe and no wonder. Let Polybius then watch his tongue, Vico concludes. If all men were wise, Polybius had scoffed, there would be no need of these superstitions (Polyb. *Hist.* 6.56.6–10). Polybius should know, Vico says, that "if there had not been religions and hence commonwealths, there would have been no philosophers in the world, and if human institutions had not been thus conducted by divine providence, there would have been no idea of either science or virtue."[147]

CORSO AND *RICORSO*

But can a society of just and wise leaders, of mild and equitable laws, of a populace that is open and civil ever be achieved; and if so, can it long be sustained? To a man of Vico's disposition, questions such as these could not have seemed bilious or perverse; and to a man of his learning the answers of the forebears were ready to hand. "Hard as it may be for a state so framed to be shaken, yet, since all that comes into being must decay, even a fabric like this will not remain forever, but will suffer dissolution." So Plato had judged of his own ideal republic, and equally Polybius, reflecting on the histories he had surveyed, took such demise as axiomatic: "There being two ways by which every kind of state is liable to decay, the one external and the other internal to the state itself, we can lay down no fixed rule about the former, but the latter is a regular process."[148] Other classical authors averred

---

[147] "Che se non vi fussero state religioni, e quindi repubbliche, non sarebber affatto al mondo filosofi, e che se le cose umane non avesse così condotto la provvedenza divina, non si avrebbe niuna idea né di scienza né di virtù" (*Scienza nuova seconda, Opere* 4, §1043). This is a regular refrain in Vico, appearing in the *De constantia jurisprudentis* (*Opere* 2.277) and in each version of the *New Science*, and always at its close. Cf. *Scienza nuova prima*, §§269, 476; *Scienza nuova seconda, Opere* 4, §§179, 334, 1043, 1110.

[148] *Resp.* 546a; trans. Francis MacDonald Cornford, *The Republic of Plato* (London: Oxford University Press, 1914), pp. 268ff. Polyb. *Hist.* 6.57.1–2; trans. W. R. Paton, Loeb ed. Cf. Polyb. *Hist.* 38.21.3.

the same, and when the thought of the ancients was revived in Renaissance writings the circularity of culture was again made popular, albeit in a new key. Machiavelli found in the world of nations a constant level of excellence or *virtù*, which changing national temper and external conquest, both ruled in part by fortune, were forever redistributing among them. Bodin posited a similar cycle in his *Methodus*, though less from any sense of foreboding than from the need to arrest the steady descent from a distant Golden Age, and Louis Le Roy thought the vicissitudes of nations were tied plainly to their ability to sustain financially an intellectual elite.[149]

What surprises, then, is not that Vico himself would accept cultural circularity in his work, but that he should wait so long to give it any emphasis. It appears already in the first edition of the *New Science*, but only as an historical possibility. Culture at its peak is a vigorous civil society in which religion and law, supported by a fully developed metaphysics and ethics, flourish; but if philosophical divisiveness, skeptical indifference, or atheistic cynicism cause the erosion of these certainties, all other institutions will in time decline, leading to the collapse of the polity itself and its merciful conquest by a stronger power, thus returning it to an "heroic" form in which the rule of reason, which makes equals of weak and strong, is replaced by the law of the victorious and the vanquished.[150] Yet this is all stated nonchalantly in the work, the accent falling squarely on the magnificent ascent of a culture to its *acme* or state of perfection (*stato di perfezione*) in which positive religion and law are supported by a rational theology and ethics and made replete by the other sciences and arts in all their dazzling variety.[151] In the second *New Science*, by

---

[149] *Discorsi* 1.6; 2, preface, and passim; cf. E. W. Mayer, *Machiavellis Geschichtsauffassung und sein Begriff virtù* (Munich and Berlin: Oldenbourg, 1912). *Methodus ad facilem historiarum cognitionem*, chaps. 6–8; cf. Brown, *The Methodus . . . of Jean Bodin. De la vicissitude ou variété des choses en l'univers*, esp. bks. 10–12; cf. Huppert, *The Idea of Perfect History*, pp. 104–117.

[150] *Scienza nuova prima, Opere* 3, §247.

[151] *Scienza nuova prima, Opere* 3, §10–11.

contrast, a pervasive gloom takes hold as cultural demise is brought into the theoretical structure, made part of that ideal eternal history of the rise, progress, maturity, decadence, and dissolution of nations, a course each nation would follow "even if there were infinite worlds being born from time to time throughout eternity."[152] Vico sets this all down in a memorable axiom: "Men first feel necessity, then look for utility, next attend to comfort, still later amuse themselves with pleasure, thence grow dissolute in luxury, and finally go mad and waste their substance."[153]

Why, one must ask, did Vico come to emphasize so late in his career what has been aptly referred to as his least original idea? One is tempted, in the fashion of the day, to look first into his feelings. If a starving Le Roy could make a culture founder on the penury of its scholars, could not an embittered Vico deliver his Cartesian betters into the hands of an inexorable Fate? As plausible as that thesis might be, there are readier reasons available in the philology and philosophy of his developing science itself as well as in the pedagogical interests that consumed him to the end, and by following these out we may come to see his theory of *ricorso* as more than the hackneyed idea it is at first blush.

One reason Vico came to stress the theory is that he had actually observed a recourse of human institutions and felt he could confirm it with his science. Brief as it is, the entire "book" dedicated to the subject in his second *New Science* is given to showing the repetition in Europe after the barbarian invasions of the sundry institutions of early Rome. Key to this was the parallel he saw between the origin of fiefs in the early Middle Ages and the rise of the ancient clienteles. The fundamental civil benefits sought by the vassals pledging fealty

---

[152] "Si avrà la storia ideale delle leggi eterne . . . , se ben fusse . . . che dall'eternità di tempo in tempo nascessero mondi infiniti" (*Scienza nuova seconda, Opere* 4, §1096).

[153] "Gli uomini prima sentono il necessario, dipoi badano all'utile, appresso avvertiscono il comodo, più innanzi si dilettano del piacere, quindi si dissolvono nel lusso, e finalmente impazzano in istrappazzar le sostanze" (*Scienza nuova seconda, Opere* 4:241).

to the barons (eventually called *beneficia*, Vico notes)—initially mere protection from starvation and from a hostile environment—were precisely those sought by the clients of the Roman nobles. This dramatic parallel was no accident, Vico asserts, and can be confirmed by a hundred others of its kind; so one last time we are treated to a marvelous piece of mad ingenuity. As the hordes swept down and laid waste to what civilized ways a dissolute Empire had managed to conserve, frightened survivors betook themselves to "high or hidden places" to hear Mass and perform other offices of piety, even as the still impious, unchaste, and nefarious wanderers of old had sought asylum in the "monastic commonwealths" established by the first god-fearing men. The mingling invaders of the fifth century surely reverted to communicating in mute gestures, even as the runs of the corsairs marked a return to heroic raids. More remarkable were the return of institutions during the growth of feudalism itself. True rustic fiefs were formed by an agrarian law like that of Servius Tullius; the *nexi* freed by the Petelian Law reappeared as the liege men bound (*legati*) to the vassals; mancipations returned as the vassal placed his hands between those of his lord in fealty; *dominium directum* and *dominium utile* corresponded exactly to the quiritary and bonitary ownerships of old; and so forth. Even technical terms had a recourse: *servitium* for *opera*, the work of a peasant; *seniores* for *patres*, the patrons or protectors of the serfs; *vassalus* for *vades*, both linked to the Greek *bas*; and of course *feudum* for *clientela*, which learned feudists, Vico notes, will use interchangeably. Such parallels continued right down to the opening of schools in the universities of Italy and the teaching of the Roman laws contained in the books of Justinian, laws therein based on the natural law of human gentes, such that "minds now more developed and grown more intelligent were dedicated to the cultivation of the jurisprudence of natural equity, which makes the common people and the nobles equal in civil rights, just as they are equal in human nature."[154]

[154] "Ma finalmente, con gli Studi aperti nell'università d'Italia, insegnandosi

Was this recourse of institutions a historical necessity or was it a mere quirk of fortune? Even so powerful an instance of cultural circularity required a measure of philosophical confirmation, and Vico could supply it, he felt, by reflecting on the "returned age of man" in which he himself was living; for by reasons both practical and theoretical he had grown to doubt the power, and certainly the stamina, of an open, rational society. The stricter, more severe one's reasoning became, the drier and more sterile one's spirit seemed to grow. One need only observe the dour Cartesians who were now the models of learning. Similarly language, now rich, complex, and intricate, seemed to have lost the purity and power of a simpler, less conscious day, its erstwhile role in the struggle for conceptual clarity now having yielded to the lure of instant glory in the artistry of Mannerism. These developments held no surprise, Vico felt, for he thought he could find in rationality itself, or more precisely in the rationality of the critical intelligence, the source of its own undoing. As irony marked the onset of a full humanity, so, too, it displayed the fallibility of such an age. An ironic consciousness is one capable of science, for it knows to distinguish the true from the false; but by that same capacity it can also deceive, saying one thing and meaning another, and by this same route can come eventually to deceive itself, claiming that what it knows, in the quiet of its inner self, is right, rational, and correct despite any willingness or ability to state it in words or in actions or through any human risk at all. And so it pulls back into smugness, a desperate self-reliance. Similarly, an ironic consciousness is one capable of adornment, luxury, and pleasure, for it necessarily distinguishes the literal from the figured and

---

le leggi romane comprese ne' libri di Giustiniano, le quali vi stanno concepute sul diritto naturale delle genti umane, le menti, già più spiegate e fattesi più intelligenti, si diedero a coltivare la giurisprudenza della natural equità, la qual adegua gl'ignobili co' nobili in civile ragione, come lo son eguali in natura umana" (*Scienza nuova seconda, Opere* 4, §1086; cf. generally §§1046–1087). Linking fiefs with ancient clienteles was an old idea deriving from medieval debates, continuing into the Renaissance, on the origins of feudalism. See Donald R. Kelley, "De origine feudorum," *Speculum* 39 (1964): 207–228, and the further literature cited there.

thus the plain from what is mannered. It has put some distance between language and thought and so can savor an image for its beauty and the arts for their splendor, no longer requiring that they teach or ennoble. Through this same action, however, it renders language precarious; severed through irony from the intention of mind, language can become self-absorbed, its images sought for their own sake. No longer asked to be acute or insightful or even to communicate a truth at all, language can descend to verbal coyness, a patter of witticisms intended only to titillate, cajole, or to parade a personality.[155]

Thus the very triumph of refined humanity, the separation of language and thought of which natural, "poetic" man was incapable, puts society in jeopardy. Without the authority of images on which an earlier age could rely spontaneously, the bond of society rests in the consensus that reason is to forge. Vico sensed the precariousness of this arrangement, for he argued that in even the best of circumstances a hearty eloquence must accompany abstract truth, inflaming the people to do the things they know by reason to be true.[156] To one who had spent the better part of a career defining the role of language in the formation of culture that must have seemed a dismal suggestion. Had eloquence lost its logical, truth-seeking function and become merely hortatory, following fast on the heels of science? Having so brilliantly rewritten the first half of the ancient topos—that eloquence alone can establish society—was Vico now content to repeat its second

[155] While irony is treated by the ancients quite casually as simply another rhetorical possibility (e.g. Quint. *Inst.* 8.6.54–56), it assumes in Vico the ominous character of "calculated falsity" or deceit, a distinctly "human" posture unavailable to the childlike, spontaneous, "naturally truthful" poets and heroes (*Scienza nuova seconda, Opere* 4, §§408, 817). In this it is similar in structure to the *dicta arguta* so roundly condemned by Vico in his course manual and especially in the *Vindiciae*. See also Croce's note, "La dottrina del riso e dell'ironia in Giambattista Vico," *Saggio sullo Hegel e altri scritti di storia della filosofia,* 3d rev. ed. (Bari: Laterza, 1927), pp. 277–283.

[156] *Scienza nuova seconda, Opere* 4, §1101.

half slavishly—that once society matures, eloquence is needed to persuade men of the truth of what they have discovered by reason?

It would be handy at this point to follow Croce and other neo-Idealist interpreters in arguing that Vico, in an unfortunate confusion, made historical-chronological eras of universal forms of the spirit. Imagination could thus be spared, and with it the sundry linguistic forms through which it operates, and the entire apparatus assured a permanent role in the functioning of culture.[157] But Vico was far too attuned to the rhythm of history, far too conscious of the dialectic of social and linguistic development, far too engaged with the actual rise and demise of cultures to permit such a rendering of his thought. More plausibly, one might appeal to the unfinished character of the *New Science*, far more concerned with the birth of humanity than ever it was with its maturity; and one might recall the obvious fact, often remarked, that for all their "haughty, avaricious, and cruel" ways it was "heroic" spirits that Vico admired and praised effusively in his final academic address (1732); and one might further insist that in the portrait of a culture served equally by reason and eloquence there is something too trite—while in the image of a nation of ironists, each man knowing "the truth," there is something more novel and genuine—for us ever to believe that Vico considered a fully mature culture anything more than an illusion.

In the end, I suspect, Vico compromised. Not wishing to abandon the architectonics of cultural development he had

---

[157] Benedetto Croce, *La filosofia di Giambattista Vico* (Bari: Laterza, 1911), esp. chaps. 3–4. Vico does remark in passing that "poetic speech . . . continued for a long time into the historical period" (*Scienza nuova seconda, Opere* 4, §412) and that the "three languages [mute, symbolic, articulate] began at the same time" (§446)—passages which Pagliaro, *Altri saggi di critica semantica* (Messina and Florence: D'Anna, 1961), pp. 421–424, 474, sees as an inchoate "phenomenology of language," in contrast to the chronology of language that Vico developed at length. Croce, however, treats them as mere signs of Vico's confusion.

arrived at with such pain, he nonetheless erected humanity on a kind of cultural fault that, with the slightest shift in balance, would bring the edifice down entire. Thus humanity at its peak retained in its structure as acute a tension as that which marked its formative days, and history itself could be made to move, nearly with the regularity of tides, between eras that are stirring but slightly frightening, when men see visions that are large, paint images that are sweeping but not subtle, take great ingenious leaps in science and social experiment, but without regard for effects and implications; and eras that are cautious and refined, but vaguely effete, when every step is measured and every action conscious, when politeness and civility hold sway, to the point of social despair.

This moment of rending in a fully mature culture is the one Vico chose to emphasize in the closing pages of his *New Science*. The tolerance of natural equity leads readily to a new individualism as each man looks first to his own interest and ease; philosophy turns corrupt and descends to skepticism, and eloquence grows cynical and false.[158] If no leader from within or conqueror from without arrives to take charge— the twin cures Machiavelli had seen—then providence has at hand an extreme remedy:

For such peoples, like so many beasts, have fallen into the custom of each man thinking only of his own private interests and have reached the extreme of delicacy, or better of pride, in which like wild animals they bristle and lash out at the slightest displeasure. Thus no matter how great the throng and press of their bodies, they live like wild beasts in a deep solitude of spirit and will, scarcely any two being able to agree since each follows his own pleasure or caprice. By reason of all this, providence decrees that, through obstinate factions and desperate civil wars, they shall turn their cities into forests and the forests into dens and lairs of men. In this way, through long centuries of barbarism, rust will consume the misbegotten subtleties of malicious wits that have turned them into beasts made more

[158] *Scienza nuova seconda, Opere* 4, §§951, 1001, 1102.

inhuman by the barbarism of reflection than the first men had been made by the barbarism of sense.[159]

In setting down, even in so mechanical a way, a theory of cultural circularity, Vico brought his own thought full circle. The *Practic* of his science that he once thought to add to his work was indeed superfluous, for through the bold statement of his science itself he could best warn his age of its self-destructive tendencies. The failure of the Cartesians to understand his *New Science*, he wrote in a letter of 1729, was itself a sign of cultural decay. That work had been meditated as a metaphysics that rose to contemplate the mind of the human race and thus God through the attribute of his providence, the attribute by which the entire race contemplates him; had been examined with a criticism of the very authors of the nations themselves, which alone can certify what the writers say of them, who began to appear only ten or so centuries later; and had been conducted with a method that penetrated the origin of human customs, a method that was yielding important results at every try. Yet in this age that prides itself on metaphysics, criticism, and method, the work has been condemned as "unintelligible." Can one expect it to be understood when training in Greek and Latin is shunned, when Roman Law is ignored, and the study of orators, poets, and historians is condemned? When the principle of verisimilitude, the rule that governs what seems to be true to all or the greater part of humanity, is rejected in favor of the

[159] "Che—poiché tai popoli a guisa di bestie si erano accostumati di non ad altro pensare ch'alle particolari propie utilità di ciascuno ed avevano dato nell'ultimo della dilicatezza o, per me' dir, dell'orgoglio, a guisa di fiere, che, nell'essere disgustate d'un pelo, si risentono e s'infieriscono, e sì, nella loro maggiore celebrità o folla de' corpi, vissero come bestie immani in una somma solitudine d'animi e di voleri, non potendovi appena due convenire, seguendo ogniun de' due il suo proprio piacere o capricci,—per tutto ciò, con ostinatissime fazioni e disperate guerre civili, vadano a fare selve delle città, e delle selve covili d'uomini; e, 'n cotal guisa, dentro lunghi secoli di barbarie vadano ad irruginire le malnate sottigliezze degl'ingegni maliziosi, che gli avevano resi fiere più immani con la barbarie della riflessione che non era stata la prima barbarie del senso" (*Scienza nuova seconda, Opere* 4, §1106).

criterion of clear and distinct perceptions, by which each man is led to trust his own private sense of things?[160]

Whom, then, are we to believe? Arnauld, who rejects the *ars topica*; or Cicero, who claims it as the source of all his eloquence?

[160] Letter of 12 January 1729 to Francesco Saverio Estevan, *Opere* 5.210–218.

CONCLUSION

We perceive that you have entered upon a new style
of discussion, one that is nowhere employed in the
writings of the Greeks.

Laelius to Scipio, in Cicero, *De republica*

The question arises effortlessly, almost of its own accord: If
the cast of Vico's thought was so definitely that of Renaissance
humanism, especially of its defenders of the *vita activa*; if the
principles of his science were so clearly drawn from the ancient
tradition of rhetoric, renewed and deepened by seventeenth-
century critics; if the essential form of his science was borrowed from Roman jurisprudence, embellished by the offerings of the great system builders of his day; if, in short, Vico
was so literate, so read, so drunk with tradition—then in what
sense could he claim his science to be "new"?

Part of the answer, surely, resides in the very putting of the
question. Vico's *New Science* was first of all new by virtue of
its comprehensiveness. In intention and reach, it was more
than a canvassing of the disciplines of all learning, as Bacon's
De dignitate et augmentis scientiarum strove to be; more than
an account of pagan gods and rituals, as found in the *De
theologia gentili* of Vossius; more than a sketch of traditional
cultures, as the many volumes of Rollin's *Histoire ancienne*
contain; more even than the great attempts by Le Caron,
Bodin, and Grégoire in one tradition, and by Grotius, Selden,
and Pufendorf in another, to reduce the whole of law to a
universal system. Vico's science was both all and none of these
things. It was an attempt to see all parts of a culture together,
and to see them through their conditions, their causes, and
their development. It was as if Vico wished to take the whole
of Hoffmann's *Lexicon universale*, which he possibly owned
and apparently consulted with some frequency, and recast it

into a structure so elegant and coherent that each part would speak to the other.

The comprehensiveness Vico achieved was rather more intensive than extensive, for he largely missed the flood of ethnological and other materials that were then being gathered in distant lands and would pour into Europe during the late eighteenth and early nineteenth centuries. He did take note on occasion of well-known figures or practices of the East, but without any real knowledge of who or what they were, and showed particular fascination for the American Indians, whose customs and beliefs were beginning to be reported upon by traders and missionaries. His knowledge of them, however, came from passing references in standard works, above all Justus Lipsius's commentary on the *Germania* of Tacitus, which in turn was the principal if not exclusive source of his knowledge of the ancient Germans. Vico's real philological base was formed by the seven Mediterranean and adjacent cultures whose chronologies he sketched at the front of his *New Science*— the Hebrews, Chaldeans, Scythians, Phoenicians, Egyptians, Greeks, and Romans—and only for the last two of these did he command any significant body of facts. Granted all these limitations, his work was nonetheless comprehensive in an original way. No aspect of a culture was beyond his interest, and each fact was embraced with the confidence that it would not threaten but confirm his science, and by becoming a part of it would become itself so much richer and more significant than what it could ever be in isolation. Words, symbols, laws, cults, social habits, implements, buildings, economic patterns, structures of power and authority—they all had meaning for Vico, and he set about making them speak their truth with an almost intimidating fury.

This thirst for detail had its inevitable effect on the growth of his text. Mario Fubini has shown how the language of Vico's writings became ever more concrete as his science progressed.[1] This runs counter to what we have come to expect

---

[1] "La lingua del Vico," *Stile e umanità di Giambattista Vico*, 2d ed. (Naples: Ricciardi, 1965), pp. 83–134.

of a great thinker, whose text grows typically "purer" and more abstract as special theories become general theories or as terms that were once fresh and daring become established or even household words. Galileo and Newton progressed in this way, as did Descartes and Kant, Darwin and Marx, Freud and Einstein. Nietzsche perhaps is the exception, but he made no conscious attempt to draw his ideas into a universal system. Such, however, was Vico's plain purpose, yet he became ever more greedy for facts as he proceeded in his work. Compared with his final *New Science*, the *De uno principio* is a lean, spare text, its language never drifting far from that of the school issues of Roman Law that form its substance, and even the first *New Science* falls something short of the exuberance of its last version. Moreover, points in his work that one might expect to be remote or abstract are among his most vivid. Axioms are frequently expressed as metaphors, summaries are rhapsodic or filled with examples, and even the beginning of his final *New Science* is an extended commentary on an elaborate frontispiece, far more intricate than that of Hobbes's *Leviathan*, by which he hoped to capture the substance of his ideas.

Because of this, some have wished to see in Vico a kind of failed jurist or impossible scientist who in his fervor or frustration turned his work into a sort of transcendent vision in the manner of Dante, the poet whom, next to Homer, Vico admired most.[2] Considered in its broadest strokes, his science has indeed a Dantesque character. The cycles of history are bound to a pattern of human exertion and folly, and through them men are cleansed and renewed if not redeemed—a process that, at an appropriate remove, shows forth the hand of a powerful if fully immanent providence. Yet the intensity of his work is not found here, but at a much lower level of inquiry. The ecstasy we feel in Vico is neither visionary nor poetic, but truly scientific, embedded in literally dozens of separate but related analyses in which one fact is joined to

---

[2] The most extreme instance of this, perhaps, is Norman O. Brown's *Closing Time* (New York: Random House, 1973).

the next, then they in turn joined to another until at once an entire structure of intelligibility is erected before us. Throughout this process, facts and instances are not dissolved into the science, but neither are they given independent status, assumed to have a "simple location" in a particular here and now. Like the monad of Leibniz, an event in Vico's civil world is not an atom that persists beyond an infinite division, but a unit in multiplicity; it is a certain order or sequence of action, a whole that tends to profusion, a present forever big with the future. To speak of society as a structure of events, then, is to say that it is a continuous multiple series of changes, such that each is a function of the other. This process is an intelligible one, Vico held, for the events enjoy a constant relatedness, even as the monads of Leibniz's universe are set in a "preestablished harmony." The task of his science, accordingly, was to probe and express ever more completely the forms of this relatedness, an effort, plainly, that could only profit from a steady supply of fresh data. He announced this task by naming his work, in the year of its critical turn, a *constantia jurisprudentis*, by which he meant the "consistency" or final coherence of the "jurisprudent," that is, the knower of human and divine institutions.[3] From that point onward he took it upon himself to show the entire civil world as an intelligible whole, not by reducing its complexities, like so many species, to simpler, known genera, but by attempting to show the regular process that guided their formation.

With this notion of "comprehensiveness" we arrive at a second and more significant novelty in Vico's work, the one he himself recognized and took pride in—that of having broken the double "conceit" of nations and scholars and so having set the science of man on a new course. For it was not sufficient to Vico's achievement that he attempt to see all parts of a culture together; he needed to grasp them in a particular way, a novelty we may begin to take hold of by extending to

---

[3] Cf. *Notae in duos libros*, *Opere* 2.615.

the development of modern physical science generally the analogy with Leibniz we have just found useful to draw.

It is the well-known thesis of Ernst Cassirer that physical science as a theoretical enterprise entered its modern phase through two major conceptual shifts. The first involved a conquering of the age-old distinction between heavenly and earthly bodies, held to be different in material and form and assumed to operate according to entirely separate principles, and the consequent reversal of the notion of a "natural" or "privileged" place in the universe. Gilbert's theory of magnets, extended by Kepler's concept of inertia, put an end to these traditional distinctions, and in place of the teleological and often animistic theories by which heaven and earth were thought to be linked came the regulative law of force, mathematically expressed, which described the regular movements of all cosmic bodies. More trenchant still was a shift in the concept of substance, understood as the object of science. As revealed in the formula *agere sequitur esse*, substance was conceived traditionally as the form beneath change, such that to know how something behaved, actually or potentially, required that its essential difference from all other entities be established. This logic of classification—the reflection of a universe conceived as a body of "contrary opposites"—yielded slowly during the Renaissance to what Cassirer has called a "logic of function." A new awareness of degree, variance, and process in nature weakened the notion of essential form, and in time the object of science itself shifted from that of *distinguishing* entities to that of defining the constant, mutual relationship between them. Reaching its term in the Newtonian laws of motion, the shift was made plain in the calculus of Leibniz and its effect on the notion of science consolidated. In contrast to analysis, which sought the reduction of figures to discrete units, the calculus aimed at discerning the constant relationship of two elements throughout an infinite series of changes. The implication of this for the theory and logic of science was that the familiar principle of identity—the reduction of multiple phenomena to the unity of substance—had now to be

right to brand a "conceit," Vico developed a notion of humanity as process (*nascimento*), as a set of ideas and institutions coming to be at certain times and in certain guises.[5] Positing a fundamental difference between early and mature humanity, Vico nonetheless joined the two by means of an invariant law of psychological progression, from the bold ingenuity of youth to the restrained rationality of maturity. Phylogenesis, as we now say, recapitulates ontogenesis. In and of itself, the idea was neither entirely original nor terribly subtle. Yet it provided a way in which to give a direction or tendency to human development without insisting that humanity be conceived as essentially any one of its several forms; on the contrary, to know what man is truly required on this view that man be grasped genetically, as a being in time.

Had he rested with this analysis alone, had he left human culture to be grasped simply by the stages of psychological growth and sophistication, Vico would have fallen victim to a leaden form of thinking indeed, a kind of psychologism such as we find, for example, in Hobbes. What is sense perception? Hobbes had asked. Nothing but original fancy, caused by the pressure of external things upon our eyes, ears, and other organs thereunto ordained. And what is imagination? Decaying sense. And thoughts? A train of imaginations. And words? The marks of our thoughts. Thus language in Hobbes was made the servant of mind, and mind in turn was conceived as a kind of instrument of verbal computation, which adds and subtracts names until the object of thought is "produced."[6]

In Vico the matter is entirely reversed, and herein we have the most fundamental novelty of all in his work. Mind does not precede language, but arises with it, and both in turn are the necessary outcome of social urgency, the result of a spontaneous attempt, gradually made conscious, to grasp a startling experience through images that are familiar. At first mere

---

[5] *Scienza nuova seconda, Opere* 4, §147.

[6] *Leviathan*, in *The English Works of Thomas Hobbes*, ed. William Molesworth (1839; reprint, Aalen: Scientia, 1966), 3.1–38.

gestures, or actions taken in common, the ordering images become in time articulate and complex, even as the institutions from which they are initially indistinguishable grow large and diverse. This elaborate universe of meaning, always restless and changing, remains intact so long as those who inhabit it continue to have a common sense of things; indeed whole areas of experience may in the process achieve the status of refined, quasi-independent arts and sciences. But let the founding sense of things be overturned by events, or let the struggle for a public consensus give way to a tyranny of private opinions, and the structure will weaken and totter, and possibly collapse.

Still audible in these ideas are the principles of rhetorical theory and practice from which they ultimately derive, yet in them as well are the unmistakable beginnings of a tradition of speculation on culture and society that would gain in force and sophistication over the next two hundred years. As in the work of Galileo, mathematics was promoted from a propaedeutical role in liberal education and made the center of physical science, so in that of Vico rhetoric was advanced from its traditional adjunct status as part of the trivium and made to give structure and credibility to a burgeoning science of culture. Often crude in its statement and underdeveloped in its parts, Vico's work was nonetheless right in its essential assumptions, a monument to his age if not a legend in its time. That language has primacy in human life; that poetry is prior to prose, and image to concept; that society takes form as a growth of human senses; that human actions and arrangements are the first statements of ideas, and that mind and society, with language as a means, share a common history—these and other lead ideas of Vico's science, startling in his own day, have lost none of their luster in ours. From Isocrates and Aristotle, over Horace and Lucretius, Cicero and Varro, Quintilian and Augustine, through Valla and Bruni, Machiavelli and Bodin, down to Bacon, Grotius, Hobbes, and Spinoza, the ideas had come, and in Vico's hand they achieved a form that led on to the giants of social theory—to Tönnies,

Durkheim, and Weber, and to their manifold followers in our own bright times. That society is a structure of sentiment and thought as well as a cluster of rites and forms, and that its gods and heroes, its customs and laws, its words and its sciences depend for their plausibility as much on the common and collective sense of the people as on the refined ideas of intellectuals is as golden a principle today as when Vico urged it in the eighteenth century.

What is the strength of an infant culture and what is the process by which it matures? Why is one image formed and another rejected? How is a society of rational means and liberal ways so easily led to ruin and decay? These are large questions, all, ones that belong with the perennial issues debated and redebated in the cycle of moods and attitudes to which social theorists, like all things human, seem endlessly bound. From what we can tell, they are issues that turned over constantly in Vico's mind, occupying him even in the last weeks of his life when the third and final version of his *New Science* was being given to press. Had he had more time, he might have expressed himself on these as on many matters with greater clarity and thoroughness than he in fact achieved. But it was not to be. During the night of 22-23 January 1744, Vico died, leaving his body and his thought to be disposed of with whatever grace history could manage.

VICO'S WRITINGS

Though Vico wished, we are told in the Autobiography (*Opere* 5.70–71), for the *New Science* alone to remain known to history, and thus denied the request of two Neapolitan entrepreneurs for the gift of all his published and unpublished writings, history has succeeded in salvaging the bulk of his works, principally through the efforts of three Italian archivists: Carlantonio de Rosa, marchese di Villarosa (1762–1847), Giuseppe Ferrari (1811–1876), and Fausto Nicolini (1879–1965).

PRINCIPAL EDITIONS

Following years of intense searching in the libraries and private collections in Italy for the lost manuscripts and letters, Villarosa published four volumes of Vico's "minor works," three under the Italian title, *Opusculi di Giambattista Vico* (Naples: Porcelli, 1818–1819), and the last with a Latin title, *Jo. Baptistae Vici Opuscula* (Naples: Fernandes, 1823). These published volumes, together with the still unpublished materials in Villarosa's possession, were incorporated by Giuseppe Ferrari in his edition of the works some ten years later, *Opere di Giambattista Vico, ordinate ed illustrate coll'analisi storica della mente di Vico in relazione alla scienza della civiltà*, 6 vols. (Milan: Società tipografica de' classici italiani, 1835–1837; 2d ed., 1852–1854). Containing both the major and minor works, and embellished with notes, indexes, and a lengthy introduction, this was the first true corpus of Vico's writings.

Shortly thereafter, a lawyer named Francesco Saverio Pomodoro, in association with the publishing firm of Domenico and Antonio Morano, undertook a new edition of the works, with Italian translations of those written in Latin. The first six volumes appeared between 1858 and 1861, and they "slavishly imitated," in Nicolini's judgment, Ferrari's second edition. But two supplementary volumes, published in 1865 and 1869, included materials not found in Ferrari: that of 1865 reissued, together with Luigi Parchetti's Italian version, Carlo Tipa's 1845 edition of the *Institutiones oratoriae* of 1711, as well as the *Ragionamenti* previously published by Giuseppe Del Giudice; and that of 1869 published for the first time, from a manuscript edited by Antonio Galasso, five of the so-called Inaugural Orations. Together with the six volumes previously published, these formed the Pomodoro, or Morano, edition, *Opere di Giambattista Vico, versione italiana col testo latino a piè di pagina da Francesco Sa. Pomodoro*, 8 vols. (Naples: Morano, 1858–1869).

The edition of the works prepared for Laterza by Nicolini, which is described in detail in the Note on References above, not only expanded the offerings of previous editions, but was generally superior editorially. The texts were more accurate and better arranged, and the volumes were generously laced with textual and historical notes. Its principal defect was the omission of Vico's course manual of 1711, *Institutiones oratoriae*, printed in full in the seventh volume of the Morano edition. Citing the high cost of paper and printing at that time (1941), Nicolini chose to omit from the *Institutiones* "the relatively long passages of Cicero, Caesar, Sallust, and other Latin writers adduced as examples, as well as a considerable number of pages devoted to nothing but very familiar definitions and distinctions, endlessly repeated—often in Vico's very words—in innumerable other scholastic manuals, printed or in manuscript, of the seventeenth and eighteenth centuries" (*Opere* 8.229). These very passages, however, are ones that recent scholars are finding useful to recall.

Despite its general excellence, the Laterza edition has been criticized, both for the accuracy and the mode of its presentation, and partly for this reason a number of Italian presses have published partial editions of the works in recent years. Nicola Abbagnano prepared an anthology for the "Classici italiani" series of Unione tipografico-editrice torinese; Paolo

Rossi edited a volume for "I Classici Rizzoli"; and Francesco Flora began an edition for "I Classici Mondadori." Nicolini himself prepared an excellent anthology, with Italian translations of the Latin selections, as part of the Ricciardi series, "La letteratura italiana: Storia e testi." And most recently, Paolo Cristofolini has edited for Sansoni's "Le Voci del Mondo" two volumes of the works, *Opere filosofiche* and *Opere giuridiche*, with fresh translations of the Latin writings. An *Edizione nazionale* has been proposed (*Bollettino del Centro di Studi vichiani* 2 [1972]: 5–12), and discussed (ibid., 3 [1973]: 5–66, and 8 [1978]: 28–81), but to date only the first two Inaugural Orations (ibid., 5 [1975]: 4–39, and 6 [1976]: 5–40), the panegyric to Philip V of Spain (ibid., 11 [1981]: 112–145), and the *Vici vindiciae* (ibid., 12–13 [1982–1983]: 237–315) have appeared in critical form.

These, then, are the most frequently cited editions in contemporary Vico scholarship, that of Laterza being the standard:

Opere di Giambattista Vico. Arranged and elucidated by Giuseppe FERRARI, with a historical analysis of the mind of Vico concerning the science of civilization. 2d ed. 6 vols. Milan: Società tipografica de' classici italiani, 1852–1854.

Opere di Giambattista Vico. An Italian version prepared by Francesco Sa. POMODORO, with the Latin text at the bottom of the page. 8 vols. Naples: Morano (previously Tipografia de' classici latini), 1858–1869. Reprint (8 vols. in 4). Leipzig: Zentralantiquariat der Deutschen Demokratischen Republik, 1970.

Opere di G. B. Vico. Edited, with textual and historical notes, by Fausto NICOLINI, in collaboration with Giovanni Gentile (Volume 1) and Benedetto Croce (Volume 5). 8 vols. in 11. Bari: Laterza, 1911–1941.

La Scienza nuova e opere scelte di G. B. Vico. Edited, with an introduction, by Nicola ABBAGNANO. Turin: Unione tipografico-editrice torinese, 1952.

Opere di Giambattista Vico. Edited, with an introduction and notes, by Fausto NICOLINI. Milan and Naples: Ricciardi, 1953.

Tutte le opere di Giambattista Vico. Edited by Francesco FLORA. 1 vol. to date. Milan: Mondadori, 1957–.

Opere di Giambattista Vico. Edited, with an introduction, by Paolo Rossi. Milan: Rizzoli, 1959.

Vico, Giambattista. *Opere filosofiche*. Texts, translations, and notes by Paolo Cristofolini, with an introduction by Nicola Badaloni. Florence: Sansoni, 1971.

Vico, Giambattista. *Opere giuridiche*. Edited by Paolo Cristofolini, with an introduction by Nicola Badaloni. Florence: Sansoni, 1974.

CHRONOLOGY OF THE WORKS

Following is a chronological listing of Vico's writings, with page or paragraph references to the Laterza edition. It has been prepared from the editorial notes in the Laterza edition and from the essay, "Gli scritti di Giambattista Vico: Storia esterna," which Nicolini inserted as the first section of his revised version of Benedetto Croce's *Bibliografia vichiana*, 2 vols. (Naples: Ricciardi, 1947–1948), 1.7–162.

Omitted from the list are several book dedications of little importance and a number of perfunctory opinions that Vico prepared as a civil censor. Also omitted is a rather large body of commemorations and allocutions, panegyrics and elegies, memorial and burial inscriptions—in short, the commissioned products of Vico's pen deriving from his abilities as a professional rhetorician. Though indicative of Vico's culture and demonstrative of his humanist heritage, none of the excluded material contributes directly to an understanding of his thought. The interested reader can find it collected in Volume 6 and especially Volume 7 of the Laterza edition.

Included in the list, however, are certain of Vico's manuscripts, finished wholly or in part, but subsequently lost, as well as titles of other works for which Vico prepared sketches or which he indicated an intention to write. These are included because they are referred to regularly by Vico scholars, as indeed by Vico himself, and also because their appearance in the chronology serves to indicate the development of Vico's thought. The page references for such entries are to Nicolini's comments on the circumstances of these writings and their probable content. Of Vico's verse, three works of special importance are listed by name; the rest are indicated collectively at the end of the list. Similarly, several of Vico's more significant letters appear separately in the chronology, while the collected correspondence is noted at the end.

All italicized titles in the list derive from Vico; while most are titles of published works, others, as indicated, are later coinages for published writings, or projected titles for works written but never published, or conceived but never written. All nonitalicized titles, whether in English or Italian, and whether enclosed in quotations marks or not, were supplied over the years by Vico's several editors, usually to designate untitled works or manuscripts.

Affetti di un disperato (1692), verse	5.313–17
The unpublished trial lecture on a chapter in Quintilian (*Institutio oratoria* 3.6) given in competition for the chair in rhetoric (1698), lost	8.269
"Delle cene sontuose de' romani" (1698 or 1699), paper read in accepting an academic chair in the Accademia Palatina di Napoli	6.389–400
Principum neapolitanorum conjurationis anni MDCCI historia (1703)	6.301–362
Six University Inaugural Orations (text of 1709), delivered 1699–1707	1.1–67
De nostri temporis studiorum ratione (1709), Inaugural Oration of 1708	1.69–121
De antiquissima Italorum sapientia ex linguae latinae originibus eruenda (1710):	
"*Proemium*" (1710)	1.123–126
Liber metaphysicus (1710)	1.127–194
Appendix on logic, sketched (1711?); lost	8.270–271
Liber physicus, sketched (1709?); lost	8.272–275
Appendix: *De aequilibrio corporis animantis*, drafted (1713?); lost	8.276-280
Liber moralis, projected only	
Institutiones oratoriae (edition of 1711)	8.159–196
Polemic exchanges in the *Giornale de' letterati*	

ENGLISH TRANSLATIONS

Three major works of Vico have thus far appeared in their entirety in English. *The Autobiography of Giambattista Vico* and *The New Science of Giambattista Vico*, both translated by Thomas Goddard Bergin and Max Harold Fisch, were published in 1944 and 1948, respectively; and *On the Study Methods of Our Time*, a translation by Elio Gianturco of *De nostri temporis studiorum ratione*, appeared in 1965. A translation of *The Most Ancient Wisdom of the Italians* and of the polemic exchanges that followed it is now being prepared by Lucia Palmer. The Bergin and Fisch translation of the *New Science* is based on Nicolini's text in the Laterza edition and maintains his paragraph enumerations. Thus, with the exception of the variants, which appear only in the Laterza edition, the numbered paragraphs of the *New Science* and the *Scienza nuova seconda* are correlative.

Following is a complete list of English translations of Vico, arranged sequentially by date of original publication:

"The Third Book of Vico's *Scienza nuova* [1744]: On the Discovery of the True Homer." Translated [from the French of Michelet?] by Henry Nelson Coleridge. In *Introductions to the Study of the Greek Classic Poets: Designed Principally for the Use of Young Persons at School and College*, by Henry Nelson Coleridge, pp. 73–98. 2d ed. London: Murray, 1834. 3d. ed., 1846, pp. 63–84.

"[Selections from] The *Scienza nuova* [1744]." Translated from the Italian by E[dgar] F[rederick] Carritt. In *Philosophies of Beauty from Socrates to Robert Bridges: Being the Sources of Aesthetic Theory*, selected and edited by E. F. Carritt, pp. 73–74. Oxford: At the Clarendon Press, 1931.

"Affetti di un disperato." Translated from the Italian by H. P. Adams. In *The Life and Writings of Giambattista Vico*, by H. P. Adams, pp. 223–226. London: Allen and Unwin, 1935.

The Autobiography of Giambattista Vico. Translated from the Italian, with an introduction and notes, by Max Harold Fisch and Thomas Goddard Bergin. Ithaca, N.Y.: Cornell University Press, 1944. Reprinted, with corrections and supplementary notes, Cornell University Press, Great Seal Books, 1963.

"Letter of 25 October 1725 to Fr. Bernardo Maria Giacco." Translated from the Italian by Max Harold Fisch. In the introduction to *The Autobiography of Giambattista Vico*, pp. 14–16. Ithaca, N.Y.: Cornell University Press, 1944.

The New Science of Giambattista Vico. Translated from the third edition (1744) by Thomas Goddard Bergin and Max Harold Fisch. Ithaca, N.Y.: Cornell University Press, 1948. 2d rev. ed., with an introduction by Max Harold Fisch, 1968. Abridged version of the revised edition, Garden City, N.Y.: Doubleday, Anchor Books, 1961, reprinted by Cornell University Press, Cornell Paperbacks, 1970.

"Discovery of the True Dante." Translated from the Italian by Irma Brandeis. In *Discussions of the Divine Comedy*, edited, with an introduction, by Irma Brandeis, pp. 11–12. Boston: Heath, 1961.

On the Study Methods of Our Time. Translated from the Latin, with an introduction and notes, by Elio Gianturco. Indianapolis, Ind.: Bobbs-Merrill, Library of the Liberal Arts, 1965.

"Gli affetti di un disperato." Translated from the Italian by Thomas G. Bergin. *Forum Italicum* 2 (1968): 305–309.

"A Factual Digression on Human Genius, Sharp, Witty Remarks, and Laughter" [From the *Vici vindiciae*]. Translated from the Latin by A. Illiano, J. D. Tedder, and P. Treves. *Forum Italicum* 2 (1968): 310–314.

"Practic of the *New Science*" [from the unpublished 1731 version of the conclusion of the *Scienza nuova*]. Translated from the Italian by Thomas G. Bergin and Max H. Fisch. In *Giambattista Vico's Science of Humanity*, edited by Giorgio Tagliacozzo and Donald P. Verene, pp. 451–454. Baltimore: Johns Hopkins University Press, 1976.

"On the Heroic Mind." Translated from the Italian by Elizabeth Sewell and Anthony C. Sirignano. In *Social Research* 43 (1976): 886–903. Reprinted in *Vico and Contemporary Thought*, edited by Giorgio Tagliacozzo, Michael Mooney, and Donald P. Verene (Atlantic Highlands, N.J.: Humanities Press, 1979), pp. 228–245.

Selected Writings [from the *De studiorum ratione*, the *De Italorum sapientia*, the *Scienza nuova prima*, and the *Scienza nuova seconda*]. Edited and translated by Leon Pompa. Cambridge: At the University Press, 1982.

BIBLIOGRAPHY

A considerable body of Vico criticism is now available, and vaster still is the literature on which one might draw to understand the many contexts of Vico's ideas. What I have used of the latter is largely recorded in the notes to my work and will not be repeated here, and of the former I have selected and put down below only those writings which bear on my subject directly or seem generally important to the study of Vico. Before this listing I give two others, with entries ranged chronologically: the major Vico bibliographies and bibliographical essays to which one may turn for further materials; and some recent anthologies and series in which is represented much of contemporary Vico criticism.

BIBLIOGRAPHICAL SOURCES

Croce, Benedetto. *Bibliografia vichiana*. 1911. Revised and enlarged by Fausto Nicolini. 2 vols. Naples: Ricciardi, 1947–1948.
———. "The Later History of Vico's Thought" and "Bibliographical Notes." In *The Philosophy of Giambattista Vico*, translated by R. G. Collingwood, pp. 268–278, 302–310. New York: Russell and Russell, 1964.
Falzon, Paul L. "Some Additions to Croce's Bibliography of Vico." *Melita Theologica* 1 (1921): 488–495, 526–533.
Fisch, Max Harold, and Bergin, Thomas Goddard. "Vico's Reputation and Influence." In *The Autobiography of Giambattista Vico*, translated by Fisch and Bergin, pp. 61–107. 1944. Revised edition. Ithaca, N.Y.: Cornell University Press, 1963.
Rossi, Pietro. "Nota bibliografia." In *La Scienza nuova e opere scelte di Giambattista Vico*, edited by Nicola Abbagnano, pp. 27–41. Turin: Unione tipografico-editrice torinese, 1952.
Nicolini, Fausto. "Storia della fortuna: Cenni." In *Opere di Giambattista Vico*, edited by Fausto Nicolini, pp. xx–xlvi. Milan and Naples: Ricciardi, 1953.
Parenti, Marino. *Notizia bibliografica sulle edizioni originali della "Scienza nuova" di Giambattista Vico*. Florence: Sansoni Antiquariato, 1953.

Cione, Edmondo. "Cinquant'anni di studi vichiani." *Rassegna di scienze filosofiche* 14 (1961): 285–304.

Rossi, Paolo. "Lineamenti di storia della critica vichiana." In *I classici italiani nella storia della critica*, edited by Walter Binni, 2. 1–41. 2d ed. 2 vols. Florence: Editrice "La Nuova Italia," 1961.

Ronchini, F. F. "Interpretazioni vichiane." Dissertation, Università Cattolica di Milano, 1967.

Hora, Eginhard, "Die Vico-Forschung in Grundzügen." In G. B. Vico, *Die neue Wissenschaft*, translated by Erich Auerbach, pp. 243–248. Rowohlts Klassiker, 1966.

Gianturco, Elio. *A Selective Bibliography of Vico Scholarship (1948–1968)*. Florence: Grafica Toscana, 1968.

Calabrò, Gaetano. "Studi su G. B. Vico nel terzo centenario della nascita." *De Homine*, no. 27–28 (1968), pp. 195–218.

Chaix-Ruy, Jules. "La fortune de Vico." In *Campanella e Vico*, pp. 123–152. Padua: CEDAM, 1969.

Piovani, Pietro. "Per gli studi vichiani." In *Campanella e Vico*, pp. 69–96. Padua: CEDAM, 1969.

Donzelli, Maria. *Contributo alla bibliografia vichiana (1948–1970)*. Naples: Guida, 1973.

Crease, Robert. *Vico in English: A Bibliography of Writings by and about Vico*. Atlantic Highlands, N.J.: Humanities Press, 1978.

Supplement to *Vico in English*. Altantic Highlands, N.J.; Humanities Press, 1981.

Battistini, Andrea. "Le tendenze attuali degli studi vichiani." In *Vico oggi*, edited by Andrea Battistini, pp. 9–67. Rome: Armando Armandi, 1979. Translated as "Contemporary Trends in Vichian Studies." In *Vico: Past and Present*, edited by Giorgio Tagliacozzo, 1:1–42. Atlantic Highlands, N.J.: Humanities Press, 1981.

———. *Nuovo contributo alla bibliografia vichiana (1971–1980)*. Naples: Guida, 1983.

ANTHOLOGIES AND SERIES

Per il secondo centenario della "Scienza Nuova" di G. B. Vico (1725–1925), which is *Rivista internazionale di filosofia del diritto 5*, no. 3 (1925). Hereafter cited as *Per il secondo centenario*.

G. B. Vico, volume commemorativo nel secondo centenario della pubblicazione della "Scienza nuova" (1725–1925). Edited by

Agostino Gemelli. Publication of Università cattolica del Sacro Cuore. Milan: Società editrice "Vita e pensiero," 1926.

Vico y Herder: Ensayos conmemorativos del segundo centenario de la muerte de Vico y del nacimiento de Herder. Publication of the Universidad de Buenos Aires, Facultad de Filosofía y Letras, Instituto de Filosofía. Buenos Aires: López Perú, 1948.

Giambattista Vico (1668–1744): Une philosophie non-cartésienne, which is *Les études philosophiques* 23, nos. 3–4 (1968): 271–432.

Campanella e Vico. Publication of the Archivio di filosofia. Padua: CEDAM, 1969. Hereafter cited as *Campanella e Vico.*

Campanella e Vico, which is *Quaderni dell'Accademia Nazionale dei Lincei,* no. 126 (1969).

Giambattista Vico nel terzo centenario della nascita, which is *Quaderni contemporanei,* a publication of the Istituto Universitario di Magistero di Salerno, no. 2 (1968).

A Homage to G. B. Vico in the Tercentenary of His Birth, which is *Forum Italicum* 2, no. 4 (1968). Edited by M. Ricciardelli.

Omaggio a Vico. Naples: Morano, 1968.

Polivalente umanità di Giambattista Vico e nuovi itinerari della critica vichiana nel terzo centenario della nascita, which is *De Homine* 6, nos. 27–28 (1968), pp. 1–221.

Giambattista Vico: An International Symposium. Edited by Giorgio Tagliacozzo and Hayden V. White. Baltimore: Johns Hopkins University Press, 1969. Hereafter cited as *International Symposium.*

Studi vichiani. 14 vols. to date. Naples: Guida, 1969–.

Bollettino del Centro di Studi vichiani. 13 vols. to date. Naples, 1971–.

Giambattista Vico nel terzo centenario della nascita. Naples: Edizioni scientifiche italiane, 1971. Hereafter cited as *Vico nel terzo centenario.*

Giambattista Vico's Science of Humanity. Edited by Giorgio Tagliacozzo and Donald P. Verene. Baltimore: Johns Hopkins University Press, 1976. Hereafter cited as *Vico's Science of Humanity.*

Études sur Vico, which is *Archives de philosophie* 40 (1977), no. 1, pp. 3–137, and no. 2, pp. 177–281.

Vico and Contemporary Thought, which is *Social Research* 43, nos. 3–4 (1976): 389–914. Edited by Giorgio Tagliacozzo, Michael

Mooney, and Donald P. Verene. Reprint. 2 vols. in 1. Atlantic Highlands, N.J.: Humanities Press, 1979.

Vico: Past and Present. 2 vols in 1. Edited by Giorgio Tagliacozzo. Alantic Highlands, N.J.: Humanities Press, 1981.

Vico and Marx: Affinities and Contrasts. Edited by Giorgio Tagliacozzo. Atlantic Highlands, N.J.: Humanities Press, 1983.

New Vico Studies. Edited by Giorgio Tagliacozzo and Donald P. Verene. 1 vol. to date. Atlantic Highlands, N.J.: Humanities Press, 1983–.

WORKS OF CRITICISM

Abbagnano, Nicola. Introduction to *La Scienza nuova e opere scelte di Giambattista Vico,* edited by Nicola Abbagnano, pp. 9–23. Turin: Unione tipografico-editrice torinese, 1952.

———. *Storia della filosofia* 2.263–276. 2 vols. in 3. Turin: Unione tipografico-editrice torinese, 1946–1950.

———. "Vico e l' illuminismo: Risposta a Fausto Nicolini." *Rivista di Filosofia* 14 (1953): 338–343.

Adams, Henry P. *The Life and Writings of Giambattista Vico.* London: G. Allen and Unwin, 1935.

Agrimi, Mario. "La *aequitas* nella formazione del pensiero vichiano." *Itinerari* 17 (1978): 163–181.

Ajello, Raffaele. "Dal *facere* al *factum*: Sui rapporti tra Vico e il suo tempo, con una replica a G. Giarrizzo e F. Bologna." *Bollettino del Centro di Studi vichiani* 12–13 (1982–1983): 343–359.

———. *Il preilluminismo giuridico,* vol. 2, *Il problema della riforma giudiziaria e legislativa nel Regno di Napoli durante la prima metà del secolo XVIII.* Naples: Jovene, 1965.

Amerio, Franco. *Introduzione allo studio di G. B. Vico.* Turin: Società editrice internazionale, 1947.

———. "Sulla vichiana dialettica della storia." In *Omaggio a Vico,* pp. 113–140. Naples: Morano, 1968.

———. "Vico." In *Enciclopedia filosofica* 6.903–920. Florence: Sansoni, 1967.

———. "Vico e il barocco." *Giornale di metafisica* 3 (1948): 157–163.

Antoni, Carlo. *Dallo storicismo alla sociologia.* 2d ed. Florence: Sansoni, 1951.

Apel, Karl O. *Die Idee der Sprache in der Tradition des Humanismus:*

Von Dante bis Vico. Archiv für Begriffsgeschichte, vol. 8. Bonn: Bouvier, 1963.

Ascoli, Max. *Saggi vichiani.* Rome: Gozzani, 1928.

Auerbach, Erich. "Giambattista Vico und die Idee der Philologie." In *Homenatge a Antoni Rubió i Lluch.* 3 vols. 1.293–304. Barcelona, 1936. Reprinted in *Gesammelte Aufsätze zur romanischen Philologie,* pp. 233–241. Bern and Munich: Francke, 1967.

————. "Vico and Aesthetic Historicism." *Journal of Aesthetics and Art Criticism* 8 (1948): 110–118. Reprinted in *Scenes from the Drama of European Literature,* pp. 183–200. New York: Meridian, 1959. Reprinted in *Gesammelte Aufsätze zur romanischen Philologie,* pp. 266–274.

————. "Sprachliche Beiträge zur Erklärung der *Scienza nuova* von G. B. Vico." *Archivum romanicum* 21 (1937): 173–184. Reprinted in *Gesammelte Aufsätze zur romanischen Philologie,* pp. 251–258.

Badaloni, Nicola. Introduction to *Opere filosofiche,* edited by Paolo Cristofolini, pp. xi–lvii. Florence: Sansoni, 1971.

————. *Introduzione a G. B. Vico.* Milan: Feltrinelli, 1961.

————. Introduction to *Opere giuridiche: Il Diritto universale di Giambattista Vico,* edited by Paolo Cristofolini, pp. xiii–xli. Florence: Sansoni, 1974.

————. "La scienza vichiana e l'illuminismo." In *Vico nel terzo centenario,* pp. 101–125.

————. "Umanesimo e neoplatonismo nelle orazioni vichiane." *Società* 2 (1946): 202–215.

————. "Vico nell'ambito della filosofia europea." In *Omaggio a Vico,* pp. 233–266. Naples: Morano, 1968.

————. "Vico prima della *Scienza nuova.*" *Rivista di filosofia* 59 (1968): 127–148. Appearing also in *Campanella e Vico,* which is *Quaderni della Accademia Nazionale dei Lincei,* no. 126 (1969), pp. 339–355.

Banchetti, Silvestro. *Il significato morale dell'estetica vichiana.* Milan: Marzorati, 1957.

Barnouw, Jeffrey. "The Relation between the Certain and the True in Vico's Pragmatist Construction of Human History." *Comparative Literature Studies* 15 (1978): 242–264.

———. "Vico and the Continuity of Science." *Isis* 71 (1980), pp. 609–620.

Battistini, Andrea. "Antonomasia e universale fantastico." In *Retorica e critica letteraria*, edited by Lea Ritter Santini and Ezio Raimondi, pp. 105–121. Bologna: Mulino, 1978.

———. *La degnità della retorica: Studi su G. B. Vico*. Pisa: Pacini editore, 1975.

———. "Gli studi di Antonino Pagliaro." *Bollettino del Centro di Studi vichiani* 7 (1977): 81–112.

———. "Tradizione e innovazione nella tassonomia tropologica vichiana." *Bollettino del Centro di Studi vichiani* 3 (1973): 67–81.

———. "Vico e l'etimologia mitopoietica," *Lingua e Stile* 9 (1974): 31–66.

Baviera, Giovanni. *Giambattista Vico e la storia del diritto romano*. Palermo: Gaipa, 1912.

Belaval, Yvon. "Vico and Anti-Cartesianism." In *International Symposium*, pp. 77–91.

Bellofiore, Luigi. *La dottrina del diritto naturale in G. B. Vico*. Milan: Giuffrè, 1954.

———. *La dottrina della provvidenza in Vico*. Padua: CEDAM, 1962.

Berlin, Isaiah. "The Divorce between the Sciences and the Humanities." *Salmagundi*, no. 27 (1974), pp. 9–39.

———. "Giambattista Vico and Cultural History." In *How Many Questions? Essays in Honor of Sidney Morgenbesser*, edited by Leigh S. Cauman, Isaac Levi, Charles D. Parsons, and Robert Schwartz, pp. 474–498. Indianapolis, Ind.: Hackett, 1983.

———. "The Philosophical Ideas of G. B. Vico." In *Art and Ideas in Eighteenth-Century Italy*. Rome: Storia e letteratura, 1960.

———. *Vico and Herder: Two Studies in the History of Ideas*. New York: Viking, 1976.

———. "Vico and the Ideal of the Enlightenment." *Social Research* 43 (1976): 640–653.

Berry, Thomas M. *The Historical Theory of Giambattista Vico*. Washington, D.C.: Catholic University of America Press, 1949.

Bianca, Giovanni A. *Il concetto di poesia in Giambattista Vico*. Messina and Florence: D'Anna, 1967.

Bidney, David. "Vico's New Science of Myth." In *International Symposium*, pp. 259–277.

Bronzini, Giovanni B. "Ritorno al Vico nella poesia popolare e nel folklore fra idealismo e strutturalismo." In *Studi in onore di Antonio Corsano*, pp. 103–123. Bari: Lacaita, 1970.

Bruers, Antonio. "La tradizione italica nell'opera di Vico." In *Per il secondo centenario*, pp. 1–11.

Bustamante, Norberto Rodríguez. "Las ideas pedagógicas de Juan Bautista Vico." In *Vico y Herder*, pp. 227–245.

Cairns, Grace E. "Giambattista Vico: The 'Science' of the Culture Cycle." In *Philosophies of History*, pp. 337–352. London: Peter Owen, 1963.

Candela, Mercurio. *Diritto e umanità in G. B. Vico*. Empoli: Garibaldi, 1968.

Cantelli, Gianfranco. *Vico e Bayle: Premesse per un confronto*. Studi vichiani, no. 4. Naples: Guida, 1971.

Cantone, Carlo. *Il concetto filosofico di diritto in Giambattista Vico*. Mazara: Società editrice siciliana, 1952.

Cantoni, Carlo. *G. B. Vico*. Turin: Civelli, 1867.

Caponigri, A. Robert. "Philosophy and Philology: The 'New Art of Criticism' of Giam Battista Vico." *Modern Schoolman* 59 (1982): 81–116.

———. *Philosophy from the Renaissance to the Romantic Age*. Notre Dame, Ind.: University of Notre Dame Press, 1963.

———. *Time and Idea: The Theory of History of Giambattista Vico*. London: Routledge and Kegan Paul, 1953.

———. "Umanità and civiltà: Civil Education in Vico." *Review of Politics* 31 (1969): 477–494.

———. "Vico and the Theory of History." *Giornale di metafisica* 9 (1954): 183–197.

Caporali, Riccardo. "Ragione e natura nella filosofia di Vico: La lettura di N. Badaloni." *Bollettino del Centro di Studi vichiani* 12–13 (1982–1983): 151–197.

Cappello, Carlo G. *La dottrina della religione in G. B. Vico*. 2d ed. Chieri: Martano, 1952.

———. *La visione della storia in G. B. Vico*. Turin: Società editrice internazionale, 1946.

Caramella, Santino. "L'estetica di G. B. Vico." In *Momenti e problemi di storia dell'estetica*. 2 vols., continuously paginated. Milan: Marzorati, 1959, 2.785–874.

Carbonara, Cleto. "G. B. Vico tra neoplatonismo e storicismo." In *Vico nel terzo centenario*, pp. 75–99.

Cattaneo, Carlo. *Su la Scienza nuova di Vico.* In *Opere* 6.73–114. Florence, 1892.

Cerasuolo, Salvatore. "Le fonti classiche della dottrina del riso e del comico nelle *Vici vindiciae.*" *Bollettino del Centro di Studi vichiani* 12–13 (1982–1983): 319–332.

————. "L'inedito vichiano sull'Arte Poetica di Orazio." *Bollettino del Centro di Studi vichiani* 4 (1974): 36–50.

Chaix-Ruy, Jules. "Il 'buon senso' di Descartes e il 'senso comune' di Vico." *Humanitas* 5 (1950): 571–588.

————. *La formation de la pensée philosophique de G.-B. Vico.* Gap: L. Jean, 1943.

————. *J.-B. Vico et l'illuminisme athée.* Paris: Del Duca, 1968.

Child, Arthur. *Making and Knowing in Hobbes, Vico, and Dewey.* Berkeley and Los Angeles: University of California Press, 1953.

Chiocchetti, Emilio. *La filosofia di G. B. Vico.* Milan: "Vita e Pensiero," 1935.

Ciardo, Manlio. *Le quattro epoche dello storicismo: Vico, Kant, Hegel, Croce.* Bari: Laterza, 1947.

Corsano, Antonio. "Cicerone tra Cartesio e Vico." *Filosofia* 26 (1975): 67–70.

————. *Giambattista Vico.* Bari: Laterza, 1956.

————. "G. B. Vico e la semantica." *Rivista di filosofia* 45 (1954): 399–403.

————. Introduction to *Il metodo degli studi del nostro tempo.* Translated by Antonio Corsano. Florence: Vallecchi, 1957.

————. "Il pensiero politico di G. B. Vico." *Rivista di filosofia* 14 (1923): 163–174.

————. *Il pensiero religioso italiano dall'umanesimo al giurisdizionalismo.* Bari: Laterza, 1937.

————. "Per una rilettura del vichiano *De ratione.*" *Giornale critico della filosofia italiana* 57 (1978): 151–171.

————. 'Il Vico tra umanesimo e illuminismo." *Annali del Corso di Lingue e Letterature Straniere dell' Università di Bari* 1 (1950): 363–368.

————. *Umanesimo e religione in G. B. Vico.* Bari: Laterza, 1935.

Costa, Gustavo. *Le antichità germaniche nella cultura italiana da Machiavelli a Vico.* Naples: Bibliopolis, 1977.

————. "G. B. Vico e la 'natura simpatetica.' " *Giornale critico della filosofia italiana* 47 (1968): 401–418.

Costa, Gustavo. *La leggenda dei secoli d'oro nella letteratura italiana.* Bari: Laterza, 1972.

————. "Vico and Ancient Rhetoric." *Eighteenth Century Studies* 11 (1978): 247–262. Reprinted in *Classical Influences on Western Thought, A.D. 1650–1870*, edited by R. R. Bolgar. Cambridge: At the University Press, 1978.

Cotroneo, Girolamo. "A Renaissance Source of the *Scienza nuova:* Jean Bodin's *Methodus.*" In *International Symposium*, pp. 51–59.

Cotugno, Raffaele. *La sorte di Giovan Battista Vico e le polemiche scientifiche e letterarie dalla fine del XVII alla metà del XVIII secolo.* Bari: Laterza, 1914.

Croce, Benedetto. *Estetica come scienza dell'espressione e linguistica generale: Teoria e storia.* Milan and Palermo: Sandron, 1902. 9th ed., 1950. Translated by Douglas Ainslie as *Aesthetic as Science of Expression and General Linguistic.* London: Macmillan, 1909. 2d rev. ed., 1922. Reprint. London: Peter Owen, Vision Press, 1953, 1967.

————. "La dottrina del riso e dell'ironia in Giambattista Vico." *Saggi filosofici*, vol. 3, *Saggio sullo Hegel e altri scritti di storia della filosofia*, pp. 277–283. 3d ed. Bari: Laterza, 1927.

————. *La filosofia di Giambattista Vico.* Bari: Laterza, 1911. 6th ed., 1962. Translated by R. G. Collingwood as *The Philosophy of Giambattista Vico.* London, 1913. Reprint. New York: Russell and Russell, 1964.

————. *Le fonti della gnoseologia vichiana: Memoria all'Accademia Pontaniana nella tornata del 10 marzo 1912.* Naples: Giannini, 1912. Appears in translation as appendix to *The Philosophy of Giambattista Vico.*

————. "Poesia popolare e poesia d'arte." *Critica* 27 (1929): 321–339, 401–428. Reprinted in *Studi sulla poesia italiana dal Tre al Cinquecento.* Bari: Laterza, 1933.

————. "Studi sulla vita religiosa a Napoli nel Settecento." *Critica* 24 (1926): 1–33, 65–82.

Cuoco, Vincenzo. *Scritti vari.* Edited by Nino Cortese and Fausto Nicolini. Bari: Laterza, 1924.

De Falco, Enrico. *La biografia di G. B. Vico.* Rome: Ciranna, 1968.

————. Introduction to *L'ideale educativo secondo le "Orationes," il "De nostri temporis studiorum ratione," l' "Autobiografia," e il "Carteggio."* Translated by Enrico De Falco. Naples: S. Viti, 1954.

DeGennaro, Angelo, "Croce and Vico." *Journal of Aesthetics and Art Criticism* 22 (1963): 43–46.

De Giovanni, Biagio. *Filosofia e diritto in Francesco d'Andrea: Contributo alla storia del previchismo.* Milan: Giuffrè, 1958.

———. "G. B. Vico nella cultura meridionale." In *Storia di Napoli,* vol. 8: *La vita intellettuale a Napoli fra la metà del '600 e la restaurazione del Regno,* pp. 422–436. Naples: Edizioni scientifiche italiane, 1980.

———. "Il *De nostri temporis studiorum ratione* nella cultura napoletana del primo Settecento." In *Omaggio a Vico,* pp. 141–191.

De Mas, Enrico, "Bacone e Vico." In *Filosofia* 10 (1959): 505–559.

———. "On the New Method of a New Science: A Study of Giambattista Vico." *Journal of the History of Ideas* 32 (1971): 85–94.

———. "Vico and Italian Thought." In *International Symposium,* pp. 147–164.

———. "Vico's Four Authors." In *International Symposium,* pp. 3–14.

De Mauro, Tullio. "Giambattista Vico: From Rhetoric to Linguistic Historicism." In *International Symposium,* pp. 279–295.

De Ruggiero, Guido. *Storia della filosofia,* 4 vols. in 13 (1943–1948). Vol. 4, *La filosofia moderna,* pt. 3, *Da Vico a Kant.* 2d ed. Bari: Laterza, 1943.

De Sanctis, Francesco. *Storia della letteratura italiana,* 2.285–302. Bari: Laterza, 1912.

DeSantillana, Giorgio. "Vico and Descartes." *Osiris* 21 (1950): 565–580.

Donati, Benvenuto. "La definizione di Ulpiano di 'juris prudentia' e l'interpretazione del Vico." *Archivio giuridico "Filippo Serafini"* 98 (1927): 51–74.

———. "L'etica della *Scienza nuova* nel sistema della filosofia della storia." In *Per il secondo centenario,* pp. 217–245.

———. *Nuovi studi sulla filosofia civile di G. B. Vico.* Florence: Le Monnier, 1936.

Donzelli, Maria. *Natura e humanitas nel giovane Vico.* Naples: Istituto italiano per gli studi storici, 1970.

Dorfles, Gillo. *L'estetica del mito: Da Vico a Wittgenstein.* Milan: Mursia, 1968.

Droetto, Antonio. "Ugo Grozio nell'interpretazione italiana di G. B. Vico." *Studi groziani,* pp. 153–161. Turin: Giappichelli, 1968.

Fáj, Attila. "Vico: Philosopher of Metabasis." In *Vico's Science of Humanity,* pp. 87–109.

Fassò, Guido. "Genesi storica e genesi logica della filosofia della *Scienza nuova.*" *Rivista internazionale di filosofia del diritto* 25 (1948), pp. 319–336.

———. *I "quattro autori" del Vico: Saggio sulla genesi della 'Scienza nuova.'* Milan: Giuffrè, 1949.

———. "The Problem of Law and the Historical Origin of the *New Science.*" In *Vico's Science of Humanity,* pp. 3–14.

———. *La storia come esperienza giuridica.* Milan: Giuffrè, 1953.

———. *Vico e Grozio.* Studi vichiani, no. 7. Naples: Guida, 1971.

Faucci, Dario. "Vico e Grozio: giureconsulti del genere umano." *Filosofia* 19 (1968): 501–550.

Fellmann, Ferdinand. *Das Vico-Axiom: Der Mensch macht die Geschichte.* Freiburg and Munich: Verlag Karl Alber, 1976.

———. "Vicos Theorem der Gleichursprünglichkeit von Theorie und Praxis und die dogmatische Denkform." *Philosophisches Jahrbuch* 84 (1978): 259–273.

Ferrari, Giuseppe. *La mente del Vico.* Florence, 1837.

Fiorentino, Francesco. *Scritti vari di letteratura, filosofia e critica.* Naples: Domenico Morano, 1876.

Fisch, Max H. "The Academy of the Investigators." In *Science, Medicine, and History: Essays in Honor of Charles Singer,* edited by Edgar A. Underwood. 2 vols. 1.521–563. London: Oxford University Press, 1953. Translated as "L'Accademia degli investiganti." *De Homine* 6 (1968): 17–78.

———. Introduction to *The Autobiography of Giambattista Vico,* translated by Fisch and Bergin, pp. 1–107. Ithaca, N.Y.: Cornell University Press, 1944.

———. Introduction to *The New Science of Giambattista Vico,* translated by Bergin and Fisch, pp. xix–xlv. Ithaca, N.Y.: Cornell University Press, 1968.

———. "Vico and Pragmatism." In *International Symposium,* pp. 401–424.

———. "Vico on Roman Law." In *Essays on Political Theory: Presented to George H. Sabine,* edited by Milton R. Konvitz and

Arthur E. Murphy, pp. 62–88. Ithaca, N.Y.: Cornell University Press, 1948.

———. "Vico's *Pratica*." In *Vico's Science of Humanity*, pp. 423–430.

Flint, Robert. *Vico*. Edinburgh and London: W. Blackwood and Sons, 1884.

Flora, Francesco. "Vico." In *Storia della letteratura italiana*, vol. 4, *Il Settecento e il primo Ottocento*. 14th ed. Verona: Mondadori, 1964.

Folchieri, Giuseppe. "Bene comune e legislazione nella dottrina del Vico." In *Per il secondo centenario*, pp. 194–216.

Fornaca, Remo. *Il pensiero educativo di Giambattista Vico*. Turin: G. Giappichelli, 1957.

Frankel, Margherita. "The 'Dipintura' and the Structure of Vico's *New Science* as a Mirror of the World." In *Vico: Past and Present*, 1.43–51.

Fubini, Mario. *Stile e umanità di Giambattista Vico*. 2d ed. Naples: Ricciardi, 1965.

Funkenstein, Amos. "Natural Science and Social Theory: Hobbes, Spinoza, and Vico." In *Vico's Science of Humanity*, pp. 187–212.

Gadamer, Hans-Georg. *Wahrheit und Methode*, esp. pp. 1–39. 2d ed. Tübingen: J.C.B. Mohr, 1960.

Galasso, Giuseppe. "Napoli ai tempi del Vico." In *Vico nel terzo centenario*, pp. 13–36.

———. "Il Vico di Giarrizzo e un itinerario alternativo." *Bollettino del Centro di Studi vichiani* 12–13 (1982–1983): 199–235.

Gardiner-Janik, Linda. "G. B. Vico and the *Artes Historicae* of the Italian Renaissance." In *Vico: Past and Present*, 1.89–98.

———. "A Renaissance Quarrel: The Origin of Vico's Anti-Cartesianism." *New Vico Studies* 1 (1983): 39–50.

Garin, Eugenio. "Cartesio e l'Italia." *Giornale critico della filosofia italiana* 4 (1950): 385–405.

———. "Dell'interesse che gli scrittori del 600 e 700 ebbero per l'umanesimo." *Giornale critico della filosofia italiana* 25 (1956): 446–47.

———. *Storia della filosofia italiana*. 3 vols. Turin: Einaudi, 1966.

———. "Vico e l'eredità del pensiero del Rinascimento." In *Vico oggi*, edited by Andrea Battistini, pp. 69–93. Rome: Armando

Armandi, 1979. Translated as "Vico and the Heritage of Renaissance Thought." In *Vico: Past and Present*, 1.99–116.

Gentile, Giovanni. *Studi vichiani*. 2d ed. Florence: Le Monnier, 1927; 3d ed., enl. as Vol. 16 of the *Opere*. Florence: Sansoni, 1968.

Ghersi, Guido. "Vico e Croce." *Teoresi* 8 (1953): 22–44.

Giannone, Pietro. *Istoria civile del regno di Napoli*. 9 vols. Milan: Bettoni, 1821–1822.

Gianturco, Elio. "Bodin and Vico." *Revue de littérature comparée* 22 (1948): 272–290.

———. "Character, Essence, Origin and Content of the *Jus Gentium* according to Vico and Suárez." *Revue de littérature comparée* 10 (1936): 167–172.

———. Introduction to *On the Study Methods of Our Time*, translated by Elio Gianturco, pp. ix–xxxiii. Indianapolis, Ind.: Bobbs-Merrill, Library of Liberal Arts, 1965.

———. *Joseph de Maistre and Giambattista Vico*. Washington, D.C.: Murray and Heister, 1937.

———. "Vico's Significance in the History of Legal Thought." In *International Symposium*, pp. 327–347.

Giarrizzo, Giuseppe. "*Aequitas* e *prudentia*: Storia di un topos vichiano." *Bollettino del Centro di Studi vichiani* 7 (1977): 5–30.

———. "Del 'senso comune' in G. B. Vico: Note vichiane." *De Homine* 6 (1968): 89–104.

———. "La politica di Vico." *Quaderni contemporanei*, no. 2 (1968), pp. 63–133.

Gigante, Marcello. "Le Orazioni inaugurali di Vico: Lingua e contenuti." *Filosofia* 29 (1978): 399–410.

Giuliani, Alessandro. "Vico's Rhetorical Philosophy and the New Rhetoric." In *Vico's Science of Humanity*, pp. 31–46.

Giusso, Lorenzo. *La filosofia di G. B. Vico e l'età barocca*. Rome: Perrella, 1943.

———. "La *Scienza nuova* sistema d'armonia prestabilita." *Fiera letteraria* 6 (1951): 6.

Goretti, Maria. Introduction to *G. B. Vico: La difesa dell'umanesimo: il "De nostri temporis studiorum ratione,"* pp. 1–21. Florence: Le Monnier, 1958.

Grassi, Ernesto. "Can Rhetoric Provide a New Basis for Philosophizing? The Humanist Tradition." *Philosophy and Rhetoric* 11 (1978): 1–18, 75–97.

———. "Critical Philosophy or Topical Philosophy? Meditations on the *De nostri temporis studiorum ratione.*" In *International Symposium*, pp. 39–50.

———. "Marxism, Humanism, and the Problem of Fantasy in G. B. Vico's Works." In *Vico's Science of Humanity*, pp. 275–294.

———. "The Priority of Common Sense and Imagination: Vico's Philosophical Relevance Today." *Social Research* 43 (1976): 553–580.

———. *Rhetoric as Philosophy*. University Park: Pennsylvania State University Press, 1980.

———. *Verteidigung des individuellen Lebens: Studia humanitatis als philosophische Überlieferung*. Bern: Francke, 1946.

———. "Vom Wahren und Wahrscheinlichen bei Vico." *Kantstudien* 42 (1942–1943): 48–63.

Grimaldi, Alfonsina A. *The Universal Humanity of Giambattista Vico*. New York: Vanni, 1958.

Haddock, Bruce A. "Vico and the Methodology of the History of Ideas." In *Vico: Past and Present*, 1.277–239.

———. "Vico on Political Wisdom." *European Studies Review* 8 (1978): 165–191.

———. "Vico's Discovery of the True Homer: A Case Study in Historical Reconstruction." *Journal of the History of Ideas* 40 (1979): 583–602.

Hall, Robert A. "G. B. Vico and Linguistic Theory." *Italica* 18 (1941): 145–154.

Hampshire, Stuart. "Vico and Contemporary Philosophy of Language." In *International Symposium*, pp. 475–481.

t' Hart, August C. "La metodologia giuridica vichiana." *Bollettino del Centro di Studi vichiani* 12–13 (1982–1983): 5–28.

———. *Recht en Staat in het denken van Giambattista Vico*. Alphen aan den Rijn: H. D. Tjeenk Willink, 1979.

Hazard, Paul. "La pensée de Vico." *Revue des cours et conférences* 32 (1931): 707–718; 33 (1931): 42–55, 127–143.

Hughes, H. Stuart. "Vico and Contemporary Social Theory and Social History." In *International Symposium*, pp. 319–326.

Hutton, Patrick H. "The New Science of Giambattista Vico: Historicism in Its Relation to Poetics." *Journal of Aesthetics and Art Criticism* 30 (1972): 359–367.

Jacobelli-Isoldi, Angela Maria. *G. B. Vico: La vita e le opere*. Bologna: Cappelli, 1960.

Jacobelli-Isoldi, Angela Maria. "Il mito nel pensiero di Vico." In *Omaggio a Vico*, pp. 37–71.

———. "Il pensiero di Vico nell'interpretazione di Croce." *Giornale critico della filosofia italiana* 29 (1950): 30–55, 162–182.

Kelley, Donald R. "In Vico Veritas: The True Philosophy and the New Science." *Social Research* 43 (1976): 601–611.

———. "Louis Le Caron Philosophe." In *Philosophy and Humanism: Renaissance Essays in Honor of Paul Oskar Kristeller*, edited by Edward P. Mahoney, pp. 30–49. New York: Columbia University Press, 1976.

———. "The Prehistory of Sociology: Montesquieu, Vico and the Legal Tradition." *Journal of the History of the Behavioral Sciences* 16 (1980): 133–144.

———. "Vera Philosophia: The Philosophical Significance of Renaissance Jurisprudence." *Journal of the History of Philosophy* 14 (1976): 267–279.

———. "Vico and Gaianism: Perspective on a Paradigm." In *Vico: Past and Present*, 1.66–72.

———. "Vico's Road: From Philology to Jurisprudence—and Back." In *Vico's Science of Humanity*, pp. 15–29.

Kessler, Eckhard. "Vico's Attempt towards a Humanistic Foundation of Science." In *Vico: Past and Present*, 1.73–88.

Klemm, Otto. *G. B. Vico als Geschichtsphilosoph und Völkerpsycholog*. Leipzig: Engelmann, 1906.

Krzemien-Ojak, Slaw. "De la découverte du vrai Homère: Contribution aux études sur l'esthétique de Vico." *Organon* 6 (1969): 159–165.

———. "La vision de la science chez G. B. Vico." *Organon* 3 (1966): 185–200.

Levi, Alessandro. "Vico e Cattaneo." In *Per il secondo centenario*, pp. 101–111.

Löhde, Herman. *Giambattista Vico und das Problem der Bildung*. Erlangen: Krahl, 1932.

Löwith, Karl. *Meaning in History: The Theological Implications of the Philosophy of History*. Chicago: University of Chicago Press, 1949. 2d ed. *Weltgeschichte und Heilsgeschehen: Die theologischen Voraussetzungen der Geschichtsphilosophie*. Stuttgart: Kohlhammer, 1953.

———. *Vicos Grundsatz: Verum et factum convertuntur: Seine theologische Prämisse und deren säkulare Konsequenzen*. Heidelberg: C. Winter, 1968. Translated as "Verum et factum convertuntur: Le premesse teologiche del principio e loro conseguenze secolari." In *Omaggio a Vico*, pp. 73–112.

Manno, Ambrogio G. *Lo storicismo di Giambattista Vico*. Naples: Istituto editoriale del Mezzogiorno, 1965.

Manson, Richard. *The Theory of Knowledge of Giambattista Vico: On the Method of the New Science concerning the Common Nature of the Nations*. Hamden, Conn.: Archon Books, 1969.

Manuel, Frank E. "Vico: The 'giganti' and Their Joves." *The Eighteenth Century Confronts the Gods*. Cambridge, Mass.: Harvard University Press, 1959.

Mario, Fulvio. "L'interpretazione dei 'monstra' nella legislazione decemvirale secondo G. B. Vico." In *Per il secondo centenario*, pp. 153–165.

Martano, Giuseppe. "Estetica antica ed estetica vichiana." In *Vico nel terzo centenario*, pp. 53–74.

Mastellone, Salvo. *Pensiero politico e vita culturale a Napoli nella seconda metà del Seicento*. Messina and Florence: D'Anna, 1965.

Mathieu, Vittorio. "Vico e Leibniz." In *Omaggio a Vico*, pp. 267–301.

———. "Vico neoplatonico." *Campanella e Vico*, pp. 97–108.

Mazlisch, Bruce. *The Riddle of History: The Great Speculators from Vico to Freud*. New York: Harper and Row, 1966.

Meinecke, Friedrich. *Die Entstehung des Historismus*, pp. 53–69. 4th ed. Munich: Oldenbourg, 1959.

Michel, Alain. "Die römische Tradition in der Geschichte der Philosophie bis heute." In *Latein und Europa: Traditionen und Renaissancen*, edited by Karl Büchner, pp. 197–242. Stuttgart: Philipp Reclam, 1978.

Michelet, Jules. *Discours sur le système et la vie de Vico*. Paris, 1827.

Momigliano, Arnaldo. 'Vico's *Scienza nuova*: Roman 'bestioni' and Roman 'eroi.' " *History and Theory* 5 (1966): 3–23.

Mondolfo, Rodolfo. *Il "verum-factum" prima di Vico*. Studi vichiani, no. 1. Naples: Guida, 1969.

Monti, Salvatore. *Sulla tradizione e sul testo delle orazioni inaugurali di Vico*. Studi vichiani, no. 10. Naples: Guida, 1977.

Mooney, Michael. "The Primacy of Language in Vico." *Social Research* 43 (1976): 581–600.

Moravia, Sergio. "Vichismo e 'idéologie' nella cultura italiana del primo Ottocento." In *Omaggio a Vico*, pp. 417–482.

Morrison, James C. "Vico and Spinoza." *Journal of the History of Ideas* 41 (1980): 49–68.

———. "Vico's Doctrine of the Natural Law of the Gentes." *Journal of the History of Philosophy* 16 (1978): 47–60.

Nicolini, Fausto. *Commento storico alla seconda Scienza nuova.* 2 vols. Rome: Storia e letteratura, 1949–1950. Reprint. Rome: Storia e letteratura, 1978.

———. *La giovinezza di Giambattista Vico.* 2d ed. Bari: Laterza, 1932.

———. *La religiosità di Giambattista Vico: Quattro saggi.* Bari: Laterza, 1949.

———. *Saggi vichiani.* Naples: Giannini, 1955.

———. *Uomini di spada, di chiesa, di toga, di studio ai tempi di G. B. Vico.* Milan: Hoepli, 1942.

Nisbet, Robert. "Vico and the Idea of Progress." *Social Research* 43 (1976): 625–637.

Nuzzo, Enrico. "Vico e la tipologia del linguaggio storico." *Bollettino del Centro di Studi vichiani* 5 (1975): 148–153.

O'Neill, John. "On the History of the Human Senses in Vico." *Social Research* 43 (1976): 837–844.

———. "Time's Body: Vico on the Love of Language and Institution." In *Vico's Science of Humanity*, pp. 333–339.

———. "Vico on the Natural Workings of the Mind." In *Phenomenology and the Human Sciences*, pp. 117–125 (supplement to *Philosophical Topics* 12 [1981]).

Paci, Enzo. *Ingens Sylva: Saggio sulla filosofia di G. B. Vico.* Milan: Mondadori, 1949.

———. "Vico, Structuralism, and the Phenomenological Encyclopedia of the Sciences." In *International Symposium*, pp. 497–515.

Pagliaro, Antonino. "La dottrina linguistica di G. B. Vico." *Atti dell'Accademia Nazionale dei Lincei, Memorie*, ser. 8, 8 (1959): 379–486. Reprinted as "Lingua e poesia secondo G. B. Vico." In *Altri saggi di critica semantica*, pp. 299–444. Messina and Florence: D'Anna, 1961.

———. "G. Vico tra linguistica e retorica." In *Vico nel terzo centenario*, pp. 133–160.

———. "Omero e la poesia popolare in G. B. Vico." In *Altri saggi di critica semantica*, pp. 447–474. Messina and Florence: D'Anna, 1961.

————. "Le origini del linguaggio secondo Vico." In *Campanella e Vico*, which is *Quaderni dell'Accademia Nazionale dei Lincei*, no. 126 (1969): 269–288.

Pareyson, Luigi. "La dottrina vichiana dell'ingegno." *Atti della Accademia delle scienze di Torino* 83, no. 2 (1949): 82–115. Reprinted in his *L'estetica e i suoi problemi*, pp. 351–377. Milan: Marzorati, 1961.

Pasini, Dino. *Diritto, società e stato in Vico*. Naples: Jovene, 1970.

————. "Società e stato in Vico." In *Studi in onore di Antonio Corsano*, pp. 567–604. Bari: Lacaita, 1970.

Pattaro, Enrico. "Gli studi vichiani di Guido Fassò." *Bollettino del Centro di Studi vichiani* 5 (1975): 87–121.

Pecilli, Diego. "Diritto e religione nel pensiero di G. B. Vico." *Rivista internazionale di filosofia del diritto* 40 (1963): 715–736.

Pergolesi, Ferruccio. "G. B. Vico e la dottrina dello stato di diritto." In *Per il secondo centenario*, pp. 166–72.

Peters, Richard. *Der Aufbau der Weltgeschichte bei Giambattista Vico*. Stuttgart: Cotta, 1929.

————. *Aurelius Augustinus und G. B. Vico: Geist und Gesellschaft*. Breslau: Marcus, 1928.

Petruzzellis, Nicola. "*Vis veri e societas veri* nel pensiero di G. B. Vico." In *Vico nel terzo centenario*, pp. 37–49.

Piccoli, Valentino. "G. B. Vico e le fonti del diritto." In *Per il secondo centenario*, pp 123–127.

Piovani, Pietro. "*Ex legislatione philosophia*: Sopra un tema di Vico." *Filosofia* 11 (1960): 228–260.

————. "Pensiero e società in Vico." In *Vico nel terzo centenario*, pp. 127–132.

————. "Il pensiero filosofico meridionale tra la nuova scienza e la *Scienza nuova*." In *Atti dell'Accademia nazionale di scienze morali e politiche* 70 (1959): 77–109.

————. "Vico senza Hegel." In *Omaggio a Vico*, pp. 551–586.

Pompa, Leon. "Human Nature and the Concept of a Human Science." *Social Research* 43 (1976): 434–449.

————. "Imagination in Vico." In *Vico: Past and Present*, 1.162–170.

————. Introduction to Giambattista Vico, *Selected Writings*, pp. 1–29. Cambridge: At the University Press, 1982.

————. *Vico: A Study of the "New Science."* Cambridge: At the University Press, 1975.

Pompa, Leon. "Vico and the Presuppositions of Historical Knowledge." In *Vico's Science of Humanity*, pp. 125–140.

————. "Vico's Science." *History and Theory* 10 (1971): 49–83.

Pons, Alain. Introductions to Giambattista Vico, *Vie de Giambattista Vico écrite par lui-même; Lettres; La méthode des études de notre temps*, pp. 25–47, 149–154, 187–214. Paris: Grasset, 1981.

Prestipino, Giuseppe. "La teoria del mito e la modernità di G. B. Vico." *Annali della Facoltà di Magistero di Palermo* 3 (1961–1962): 13–68.

Ravagnan, Luis M. "Religión y poesía en Juan Bautista Vico." In *Vico y Herder*, pp. 217–225.

Read, Herbert. "Vico and the Genetic Theory of Poetry." In *International Symposium*, pp. 591–597.

Riverso, Emanuele. "Vico and the Humanistic Concept of *Prisca Theologia*." In *Vico: Past and Present*, 1.52–65.

Rossi, Paolo. *Le sterminate antichità: Studi vichiani*. Pisa: Nistri-Lischi, 1969.

Said, Edward W. *Beginnings: Intention and Method*. New York: Basic Books, 1975.

————. "Vico: Autodidact and Humanist." *Centennial Review* 11 (1967): 336–352.

————. "Vico on the Discipline of Bodies and Texts." *Modern Language Notes* 91 (1976): 817–826.

Salomone, William. "Pluralism and Universality in Vico's *Scienza nuova*." In *International Symposium*, pp. 517–541.

Salvatorelli, Luigi. *Il pensiero politico italiano dal 1700 al 1870*. 2d ed. Turin: Einaudi, 1941.

Semerari, Giuseppe. "Intorno all'anticartesianesimo di Vico." In *Omaggio a Vico*, pp. 193–232.

Severgnini, Dante. "Per una interpretazione del Vico." *Humanitas* 6 (1951): 719–722.

Sina, Mario. *Vico e Le Clerc: Tra filosofia e filologia*. Studi vichiani, no. 12. Naples: Guida, 1978.

Sorrentino, Andrea. *L'estetica di G. B. Vico attraverso la "Scienza nuova" e gli scritti minori*. Naples: Rondinella and Loffredo, 1926.

————. *La retorica e la poetica di Vico; ossia, La prima concezione estetica del linguaggio*. Turin: Fratelli Bocca, 1927.

Stark, Werner. "Giambattista Vico's Sociology of Knowledge." In *International Symposium*, pp. 297–307.

Struever, Nancy S. "Vico, Valla and the Logic of Historical Discovery." In *Vico's Science of Humanity*, pp. 173–185.

Tagliacozzo, Giorgio. "Epilogue: Unity of Knowledge and General Education." In *International Symposium*, pp. 599–613.

Tommaseo, Niccolò. *G. B. Vico*. Turin: Unione tipografico-editrice torinese, 1930.

Toulmin, Stephen, and Goodfield, June. "Vico: The Mendel of History." In *The Discovery of Time*, pp. 125–129. New York: Harper and Row, 1965.

Tristram, Robert J. "Explanation in the *New Science*: On Vico's Contribution to Scientific Sociohistorical Thought." *History and Theory* 22 (1983): 146–177.

Vasoli, Cesare. "Bodin, Vico e la topica." *Bollettino del Centro di Studi vichiani* 9 (1979): 123–129.

———. "Topica, retorica e argomentazione nella *prima filosofia* del Vico." *Revue internationale de philosophie* 33 (1979): 188–201.

Vaughan, Frederick. *The Political Philosophy of Giambattista Vico: An Introduction to "La Scienza Nuova."* The Hauge: Martinus Nijhoff, 1972.

Verene, Donald P. "Vico's Philosophical Originality." In *Vico: Past and Present*, 1.127–143.

———. "Vico's Philosophy of Imagination." *Social Research* 43 (1976): 410–433.

———. *Vico's Science of Imagination*. Ithaca, N.Y.: Cornell University Press, 1981.

———. "Vico's Science of Imaginative Universals and the Philosophy of Symbolic Forms." In *Vico's Science of Humanity*, pp. 295–317.

Verra, Valerio. "Linguaggio, storia e umanità in Vico e in Herder." In *Omaggio a Vico*, pp. 333–362.

Verri, Antonio. "Vico e Rousseau filosofi del linguaggio." *Bollettino del Centro di Studi vichiani* 4 (1974): 83–104.

Viechtbauer, Helmut. *Transzendentale Einsicht und Theorie der Geschichte: Überlegungen zu G. Vico's "Liber metaphysicus."* Die Geistesgeschichte und ihre Methode, vol. 1, edited by Stephan Otto. Munich: Fink, 1977.

Viehweg, Theodor. *Topik und Jurisprudenz.* 4th ed. Munich: Beck, 1969.

Villa, Giovanni. *La filosofia del mito in Vico.* Milan: Bocca, 1949.

Visconti, G. Galeazzo. "Il Vico e due grammatici latini del Cinque-cento." *Bollettino del Centro di Studi vichiani* 4 (1974): 51–82.

Vittorini, D. "Giambattista Vico and Reality: An Evaluation of the 'De nostri temporis studiorum ratione' (1708)." *Modern Language Quarterly* 13 (1952): 90–98.

Werner, Karl. *Giambattista Vico als Philosoph und gelehrter Forscher.* 1879. Reprint. New York: Burt Franklin, 1962.

White, Hayden V. *Tropics of Discourse: Essays in Cultural Criticism.* Baltimore: Johns Hopkins University Press, 1978.

———. "The Tropics of History: The Deep Structure of the *New Science*." In *Vico's Science of Humanity*, pp. 65–85.

———. "What Is Living and What Is Dead in Croce's Criticism of Vico." In *International Symposium*, pp. 379–389.

Whittaker, Thomas. *Reason: A Philosophical Essay, with Historical Illustrations—Comte, Mill, Schopenhauer, Vico, Spinoza.* Cambridge: At the University Press, 1934.

Wilson, Edmund. *To the Finland Station: A Study in the Writing and Acting of History.* 1940. Reissue. New York: Farrar, Straus and Giroux, 1972.

Wisser, Richard. "Giambattista Vico's *Neue Wissenschaft* als frühes Modell integrativen Denkens." In *Akten des XIV. Internationalen Kongresses für Philosophie.* 6 vols. 6.572–584. Vienna: Herder, 1971.

———. "Vico, Giambattista." In *Die Religion in Geschichte und Gegenwart*, 3d ed. 7 vols. 6 (1962): 1391–1394. Tübingen: Mohr, 1957–1965.

———. "Vico und Leibniz." Dissertation, University of Mainz, 1954.

Wohlfart, Günther. "Vico e il carattere poetico del linguaggio." *Bollettino del Centro di Studi vichiani* 11 (1981): 58–95.

INDEX

Aall, Anathon, 230n
Abelard, Peter, 88
Abrams, Meyer Howard, 27
Academy: Athenian, 35, 121n;
New, 121, 132, 193n; Florentine, 88
Accademia: degli Investiganti, 123,
194; degli Oziosi, 128n, 171;
dell'Arcadia, 147–148
Accolti, Benedetto, 96n
Accursius, 17, 177, 181; followers
of, 21n. See also *mos Italicus*
Achilles, 201–202, 228
Acta eruditorum Lipsiensia, 158n
action, 71, 83, 255; and contemplation, 86–94, 162
acuity (*acutezza*), keenness, sharp-
wittedness, 4, 67–68, 99, 105,
126–129, 136, 139, 142, 144,
154–158, 211, 250; and maxims,
139, 144, 147. *See also* conceit
(*concetto*); *dicta acuta*; maxims
(*gnomai*)
Adams, Henry P., 108n
Aesop, 228
aesthetics: Romantic, 27; of seven-
teenth century, 64
Africa, 94
Agamemnon, 201
Agricola, Rudolf, 47, 49, 91; *De
inventione dialectica*, 47
Alberti, Leon Battista, 90, 96, 98
Alciato, Andrea, 177, 180–181;
followers of, 180, 182. See also
mos Gallicus
Alcibiades, 204
Alcinous, 201
Alonso, Dámaso, 143n
Ambrose, Saint, 88
America, 61; native Indians of, 256
Amerio, Franco, 151n
Amphion, 172–173; 174n
Amphitrite (sea goddess), 174n
amplification, rhetorical, 63–64; in
Vico, 70

anachronism, 175
analysis, Cartesian, 100, 102–103,
115, 126–129, 162
ancients and moderns: distinction
of, 132, 260; on educational
process, 114; on human origins,
174–176; on jurisprudence, 163–
167; *querelle* of, 3–4, 94–100,
168
anima mundi, 213
antiquity, study of, 54, 63n
Apel, Karl O., 69n
Aphthonius, 64
Apollo, 223, 228
aptness (*quid deceat, prēpon*), 12–
13, 33, 37n, 76, 152
Aquinas, Thomas, 88
Arabic numerals, 98
Arcadians, 147–148
Aristophanes, 172
Aristotle, 5, 8, 21, 27n, 30–31, 34,
42, 44, 47–49, 53, 70–71, 74,
79, 87–88, 93, 99, 132n, 133,
137n, 138, 146, 148, 155, 158,
197, 208n, 225, 240, 262; *De
anima*, 226n; *De sophisticis elenchis*, 79, 133, 207; *Nicomachaen
Ethics*, 58n, 77n, 86; *Poetics*,
27n, 31–32, 73, 75n, 80n, 137–
139, 141, 148, 157, 207; *Politics*, 86n, 92, 183; *Posterior Analytics*, 6, 133–134; *Prior Analytics*, 130, 133–134, 210;
Rhetoric, 5, 27n, 31–32, 70n,
71n, 72–73, 130, 133–134, 138–
139, 146, 157, 207, 210, 217;
Topics, 31, 130, 133–134, 210,
217
Arkesilaos, 121
Arnauld, Antoine, 3, 55, 102–103,
126, 128n, 130, 133, 225, 254;
L'art de penser, 8, 52–53, 130n.
See also Port Royal Logic
arrangement, rhetorical. See *dispositio*